GARBO: THE SPY WHO SAVED D-DAY

GARBO

THE SPY WHO SAVED

D-DAY

Introduction by Mark Seaman

PUBLIC RECORD OFFICE

Public Record Office
Richmond
Surrey
TW9 4DU

ISBN 1 873162 81 2

A catalogue card for this book
is available from the British Library

Front cover: Juan Pujol, codenamed GARBO (PRO KV 2/71)
World War II illustration of amphibious craft landing, by C E Turner (PRO INF 3/1651)

Printed by Bath Press Ltd, Bath

Contents

Note: This publication brings you in full the 'Summary of the Garbo Case 1941–1945' by Tomás Harris. The original files may be consulted under supervision at the Public Record Office, Kew. Our intention is to reproduce the material as faithfully as possible without compromising the integrity of the original. This means that the occasional inconsistency or typing error survives from Harris's text. The symbol [...] is used where material from the original document has been retained under section 3(4) of the Public Records Act 1958.

The introduction and index are modern additions.

Introduction

The 'Summary of the Garbo Case 1941–1945' is a remarkable document. It is the chronicle of the operational activities of Juan Pujol, codenamed GARBO, who has been described as the greatest double agent of the Second World War. However, this is no simple narrative by a detached historian or journalist, but rather the official report of Pujol's MI5 case officer, Tomás Harris, a man who directed, channelled, encouraged and sustained the agent's remarkable talents. Together the two men, ably supported by various agencies of British intelligence, wove a web of deception that ensnared their German opposite numbers and misled the German High Command for years. Harris's summary offers a unique insight into the workings of British intelligence and the techniques of running an agent. Interestingly, it conflicts on several points with Pujol's own memoirs that were written decades later when the agent emerged from obscurity.[1] Neither account could claim to be impartial but Harris's clearly benefits from being based solidly upon the MI5 case files (many of which have not been released into the public domain) together with his own intimate knowledge of events. In his introduction Harris states an understandable pride in the success of the GARBO case:

> In 1941 when the Germans were all powerful in Spain, the British Embassy in Madrid was being stoned, France had collapsed and the German invasion of England was imminent, little were the Germans to know that the small meek young Spaniard who then approached them and volunteered to go to London to engage in espionage on their behalf would turn out to be an important British agent. Still less were they to discover that the network which they instructed him to build up in the United Kingdom was to be composed of 27 characters who were nothing more than a figment of the imagination.
>
> The summary of the story of this espionage network of imaginary characters, the GARBO NETWORK, the subject of this report is, if unorthodox, a record of the extent to which it is possible to deceive one's opponent, through what is probably the oldest weapon of deception in war, the double-cross agent.[2]

Harris's report was written for internal distribution within MI5 and was not originally intended for a general public. It has all the pace of a thriller and contains a mass of intricate operational detail. However, readers must keep their wits about them if the miasma of falsehood, deception and deceit that surrounded the GARBO case are not to confuse them as profoundly as it did German intelligence. The story begins with Pujol in Madrid, moves with him to Lisbon, and is then centred in the United Kingdom. But the impact of his activities also embraces the campaigns in North Africa, the Normandy landings and the V-weapon offensive. Its pages are full of references to invasions, armies, fleets and bombing offensives, but it remains primarily the story of two men weaving one of the most incredible deception stratagems in history.

Historical background

The British intelligence community originated in 1909 with the formation of the Secret Service Bureau. It was a response to growing fears of Imperial Germany that warranted increased vigilance against spies in Britain and greater knowledge of the Kaiser's military and political intentions. The Bureau consisted of two sections. The Home Section under Captain Vernon Kell was given the responsibility for countering hostile (and particularly German) espionage activity in Britain. It later acquired the titles MI5 and the Security Service, both of which it has retained. The Secret Service Bureau's Foreign Section, headed by Captain Mansfield Smith Cumming, was tasked with seeking information abroad on Britain's potential foes. This later meta- morphosed into MI6 or the Secret Intelligence Service (SIS).

Both organizations served their country well in the First World War. In the years before the outbreak of hostilities, Kell's Section had managed to penetrate all of the German espionage rings in Great Britain. Some spies were arrested but the majority were kept under close observation until the declaration of war. Then the trap was quickly shut and 21 of the 22 still remaining at liberty were taken into custody.[3]

> It was reported during the war and confirmed after the Armistice that the capture of these spies completely broke up the German intelligence organisation which was not able to act effectively again until some time in 1915.[4]

The effectiveness of the German espionage effort against Britain even after 1915 is open to question. The Germans did attempt to infiltrate a variety of agents, mostly of indifferent quality, but it proved extremely difficult to enter the United Kingdom, with strict travel regulations bolstered by a highly effective MI5 port watching branch. Those who did manage to enter the country rarely remained undetected due to a sophisticated postal censorship department that kept a watch for letters containing secret writing and correspondence sent to suspect addresses on the continent. The spies rarely remained at liberty for long. Their fate varied: deportation, internment, imprisonment and the death penalty. The arrest, trial and sentencing of the captured agents was not always made public and on at least one occasion MI5 exploited this state of affairs to their advantage. After a trial held in camera, Carl Frederick Muller was found guilty of espionage and executed by firing squad in the Tower of London on 23 June 1915. However, it soon became clear that his German controllers remained unaware of his fate for they continued to send money and requests for him to maintain his espionage activities. MI5 therefore decided to try and deceive the Germans into believing that Muller was still at large, and sent several fake messages from him containing misleading information to a *poste restante* address in Rotterdam. One source states that the subventions paid by the Germans to their agent were sufficient for MI5 to purchase a car that, with black humour, was nicknamed the 'Muller'.[5] But the ruse could not be maintained indefinitely and the Germans eventually realized the deception that had been played upon them. The affair was hardly a great intelligence coup but nevertheless served as a precursor of later events.

Although their success in the First World War helped to ensure their continued existence after the end of hostilities, MI5 and SIS both suffered in the post-war reductions of staffing and funding. Moreover, the areas of specific responsibility were far from clear-cut and each pursued operations that led them into territory considered the domain of their sister service.

The primary department of MI5 handling counter-espionage investigation during the inter-war period was B Branch. From 1929 this was headed by O A Harker and, by the end of 1938, it

> was divided into a number of sections dealing with internal security in the Forces, Communism and Soviet espionage, German espionage, the Nazi Party, the Italian and British Fascist Parties and Italian and Japanese espionage.[6]

Harker's deputy during this period was Guy Liddell, who succeeded him in 1940, and who headed the Branch (later Division) until the end of the war. Amongst many distinguished officers was T A Robertson, who was to head B1A section, which specialized in the handling of double agents.

In the late 1930s both MI5 and SIS changed the main focus of their operations from the menace represented by international communism to the threat from Nazi Germany. The presence of fascist sympathizers in British society who felt an allegiance to Nazi Germany gave cause for concern, as it was already known that Soviet intelligence was exploiting members of the Communist Party of Great Britain. But MI5's vigilance paid off and, using a variety of methods including informers, penetration agents, censorship and signals intelligence, the threat of a Fifth Column within Britain was neutralized.

While the proactive steps they took were commendable, MI5 was fortunate that Britain did not constitute a major target for German intelligence in the years leading up to war. The Abwehr, the primary German intelligence service under Admiral Wilhelm Canaris, devoted most of its attention to the Balkans, the Iberian peninsula and Germany's immediate neighbours. Another organization, the Sicherheitsdienst (SD), also conducted intelligence gathering operations under the aegis of the Nazi Party and SS. Although there was mutual mistrust and territorial disputes between the two services, the Abwehr and SD were frequently able to work in concert, not least because of the effective working relationship between Canaris and Reinhard Heydrich, the head of the SD.

Although not a major focus for German intelligence, some attempts were made to recruit agents to operate in the United Kingdom. Ironically, it was to emerge that far from securing secret information on a potential foe, the Abwehr's efforts helped to create opportunities for the acquisition of double agents by Robertson's B1A section. One of the most important German recruits was Arthur Owens, an electrical engineer with business contacts on the Continent that led to his services being secured by the Germans and SIS in the mid-1930s. When his British controllers became aware of his connections with the Abwehr they ran him as a double agent. In September 1938 he reported that the Germans had appointed him their chief agent in the United Kingdom, and subsequently received a short wave transceiver from them that he handed over to MI5. But there was rarely anything simple about Owens, codenamed SNOW by his British controllers in Robertson's B1A. As war loomed, in August 1939 he went to Hamburg for a meeting with his Abwehr contacts. In his absence, his family denounced him to the police as a German agent. On his eventual return to the United Kingdom, his arrival was missed by the port authorities and he remained undetected for a fortnight until, the day after Britain declared war on Germany, he telephoned Special Branch and once again offered his services. These were accepted in spite of understandable doubts concerning his loyalty, and he made several trips to neutral Belgium for meetings with his Abwehr controllers. On one occasion he was accompanied by an MI5 nominee, Gwilym Williams (GW), who posed as a Welsh Nationalist. Williams was promptly recruited by the Germans and trained to undertake sabotage in Britain on their behalf.

The Owens saga continued to have more than its share of problems and on more than one occasion teetered on the brink of disaster. In April a rendezvous at sea with the Germans was aborted when another MI5 agent whom Owens was to introduce suspected that Owens's true loyalties lay with the Germans. When both men returned to the United Kingdom they each accused the other of leading them into a trap. But all was not lost. In July the undercover MI5 agent, codenamed BISCUIT, met Owens's contact in Lisbon and made excuses for the abortive meeting. The Germans accepted the explanation and expressed their keenness to acquire British identity papers. This indicated to MI5 that the Abwehr was intending to infiltrate agents into the United Kingdom, an assumption later confirmed by test wireless transmissions from Northern France in preparation for the clandestine use of sets in Britain.

During the autumn of 1940 the Germans launched an intelligence offensive against Britain in preparation for Operation SEALION, the invasion of the United Kingdom. Germany had not anticipated a scenario that would see it needing extensive military and political intelligence from within the United Kingdom. As has been seen, it had little in the way of an existing intelligence apparatus upon which to build, and its pool of agents was of indifferent quality. Poorly motivated and trained, this new crop of spies were soon arrested after arrival and, in the main, proved susceptible to the sophisticated interrogation techniques of MI5. The stark choice between the death penalty and clemency in return for co-operation provided MI5 with the means of 'turning' the agents and having them play back information to their German controllers. This was the crux of what became known as the Double Cross System – an elaborate secret campaign that resulted in the arrest of every German agent sent to the United Kingdom, the acquisition of vital German codes and ciphers and the opportunity of planting false information on German intelligence and the High Command.

Between the beginning of September and 12 November 1940, fourteen enemy agents landed in Britain (ten by sea and four by parachute). Another nine surrendered themselves to the authorities on arrival. Five were tried and executed, twelve were interned, one committed suicide and three became double agents working for MI5. Of the latter three, Wulf Schmidt (codenamed

SUMMER by the British) sent a message under MI5 control to Germany that resulted in Owens being instructed to find him safe lodgings. This was by no means the last time the Germans sought to have their newly arrived agents call upon the services of spies already in place. In one respect it made excellent sense, permitting established agents to assist vulnerable newcomers, but at the same time it increased the risk of penetration of their networks by British security.

By the autumn of 1940 it was clear to MI5 that the exploitation of existing double agents and the recently captured spies required more than the existing ad hoc arrangements. Thus, at a meeting in October 1940 attended by the leading members of British intelligence, it was decided to establish a new body, the W Committee:

(i)   To keep our agents sufficiently well fed with accurate information so as not to lose the confidence of the enemy;
(ii) To control as many of the agents in this country as we can, in order to make [the enemy] feel that the ground is covered and they need not send any more of whose arrival we might not be aware;
(iii) By careful manoeuvring of these agents and a careful study of the questionnaires [submitted to them from Germany], to mislead the enemy on a big scale at the appropriate moment.[7]

It was clear that this undertaking also needed day-to-day oversight and consequently the Twenty (XX) Committee was formed, comprising representatives of SIS, the Services Intelligence Directorates, GHQ Home Forces, the Home Defence Executive and MI5. MI5's primacy on this new body, also known as the Double-Cross Committee, was reflected in the appointment of two of its members, J C Masterman and J A Marriott, to act as Chairman and Secretary respectively. There still remained problems over what genuine low-grade material to disclose to the Germans to establish the reputation of the double agents, and what false information to feed to them. Similarly, there remained the fundamental question of whether the double agents were best used in counter-espionage or in deception. At least these matters were now being addressed and the decision to create an interlocking system of checks and balances had been taken.

As layer upon layer of real and notional information began to be fed into the schemes, the task facing MI5 officers and their colleagues in the other government agencies was awesome. However, they did possess a trump card of incalculable importance – the ability to read German wireless traffic.

Deception was usually an imprecise practice, but the opportunity to read enciphered messages sent between German intelligence officers proved a godsend. SIS's Government Code and Cypher School (GC&CS) at Bletchley Park broke the Abwehr's first-hand cipher at the end of 1940 and a year later broke the Enigma used between Berlin and the various Abwehr outstations throughout Europe. Thus many of the innermost secrets of German intelligence, including their appreciation of the reliability of their agents, fell into British hands. Moreover, the codes and ciphers of the captured German agents provided a tremendous assistance to the Bletchley Park codebreakers. The decrypted Abwehr wireless traffic, codenamed ISOS material (an abbreviation of 'Intelligence Service, Oliver Strachey' after the GC&CS officer responsible for handling German intelligence material), proved a barometer of impeccable reliability in gauging enemy thinking. As a result, imperfections in the Double Cross system could be quickly identified and potential doubts in German minds were allayed even before they had been expressed.

In addition to the security work carried out by MI5 backed up by Signals Intelligence, the Secret Intelligence Service had its own interest in enemy agents acting against Britain. The department concerned with this activity was Section V. The distinction between MI5 and SIS's responsibilities has been described thus:

> Broadly speaking, MI5 was responsible for counter-espionage within the United Kingdom and the Empire, including Palestine and Egypt, whereas MI6 was responsible for the collection of all counter-espionage intelligence in foreign countries. It was to Section V that the head of MI6 delegated responsibility for the security of ISOS, and its officials considered it their duty to make available to MI5 only such intercepted Abwehr and other traffic as seemed strictly relevant to the exercise of their responsibilities within the Empire and the United Kingdom.[8]

These demarcation lines only hint at the territorial wrangles acted out by MI5 and SIS. It was usually possible to find some form of compromise solution but for a while it seemed as if this rivalry was going to deny British intelligence the services of a man who was to become one of its greatest assets.

The GARBO case

Over the years many of the most influential secret agents have been 'walk-ins' – individuals who have not been targeted or suborned by intelligence officers but who appear unexpectedly to volunteer their services. There is always the risk that however promising appearances might be, the walk-in might be a provocation – an attempt to entrap intelligence officers, penetrate an enemy's secret agencies under a cloak of co-operation or, if the 'courtship' takes place in a foreign country, to create an embarrassing diplomatic incident. Intelligence services tend to respond to such overtures with suspicion and, consequently, the history of espionage is full of cases in which genuine defectors have found themselves spurned by the countries they most wish to assist. Such was the situation in January 1941 when Juan Pujol, using his wife as an intermediary, made approaches to the British Embassy in Madrid. He was rebuffed, a fate that was repeated with monotonous regularity during the following months. It was a bizarre beginning to a remarkable career that was to see Pujol emerge as one of the most important secret agents of the 20th century.

Juan Pujol was, to say the least, an unlikely spy. He was born on 14 February 1912 in Barcelona to a family described by Harris as of 'moderate means' and liberal political beliefs. After a private education, he engaged in a variety of businesses, with a break in the early 1930s to complete his

Juan Pujol as he appeared in his wartime MI5 file. He was codenamed GARBO by MI5 and ARABEL/ARABAL by the Abwehr
(PRO, KV 2/70)

national service in the 7th Regiment of Light Artillery. Along with many of his fellow countrymen, he was a reluctant participant in the Spanish Civil War, being persecuted by the Republicans in his native Catalonia and feeling little sympathy with the fascist ideology of the Nationalists. Living in a Republican held region of Spain left him little option but to join their forces but he did so with the express intent of deserting to the Nationalists at the first opportunity. This he achieved in September 1938 on the River Ebro front, but not without difficulty and at considerable personal risk. Obliged to enlist in the army of his erstwhile enemy, he was nevertheless able to reflect that at the war's end 'I had managed not to fire a single bullet for either side'.[9] Before demobilization from the Army he was posted to Burgos where he met Aracelli Gonzalez, whom he married in Madrid in April 1940.

Motive is very important in the understanding of espionage. On the face of it, Pujol's motivation is crystal clear – he despised totalitarian regimes with a strong conviction bred during his liberal upbringing. Harris's report helps provide a further understanding of his motivation with a description of Pujol's beliefs at the time of the Spanish Civil War:

> The disorder and general confusion of the first few months of war in Spain and the prevailing Communist influence in the industrial areas intensified GARBO's already conservative sentiments and strengthened his dislike for extremist politics.[10]

However his experiences had taught him that 'Spain, under Fascism, was as intolerable as it would have been under Communism'.[11]

At first, it is not easy to reconcile these strong moral convictions with his activities during the Civil War, but his memoirs record that he considered the Second World War to be a truly momentous event:

> I yearned for justice. From the medley of tangled ideas and fantasies going round and round in my head, a plan slowly began to take shape. I must do something, something practical; I must make my contribution to the good of humanity.[12]

As Pujol observed the course of the war from neutral Spain, he saw British fortunes turning from bad to worse. His detestation of Nazi Germany increased in tandem with his admiration for its only remaining adversary. Whereas some might simply have expressed their feelings by enlisting in an Anglo-Spanish friendship society, instead,

It occurred to him that with his background, having deserted from the Republicans to Franco, it would not be difficult to get a job in either Germany or Italy. Once there he would be able to serve British interests.[13]

It appears that from the outset Pujol involved his wife in his decision to enter the world of espionage. Harris's report (presumably drawn in large measure on Pujol's own contemporary version of events made during MI5 interviews) states that not only did he consult her but that she made the first approach to the British Consulate in January 1941. She secured an interview with a consular official and offered her husband's services as a spy in either Germany or Italy. Hardly surprisingly, she found it a less than productive encounter. Unfortunately we do not have her version of events and Pujol omits her participation from his memoirs (perhaps as a result of the couple's later estrangement), stating that he made the first approach himself.

Following this rebuff, Pujol determined that if the British were reluctant to accept his offer to act as their agent against the Germans, he would initiate the contact on his own. There was no shortage of opportunity, for Spain under Franco was firmly in the Nazi camp.

> Spanish Police records and officers of the Seguridad were instructed to facilitate the Germans in all they required, passports to Spanish nationals were issued on German recommendation, or refused on their instructions. The Spanish press and radio services were under German control. The Spanish General Staff was collaborating to the maximum. The use of Spanish diplomatic bags was theirs for the asking.[14]

Pujol therefore sought an interview at the German Embassy, where he proposed to Gustav Leissner, Honorary Attaché at the Madrid Embassy, that he spy for the Reich in Lisbon or even the United Kingdom.[15] The response was not much more encouraging than he had received from the British diplomatic corps and, over the next few weeks, Pujol regularly telephoned the Germans to ask them for their decision. But even a further interview with a Spanish representative of the Germans failed to extract a decision. Eventually, after further pressing, he was granted another meeting with Leissner, who informed him that they were not interested in using him in Portugal but *might* be interested if he was able to get himself to Britain. How he accomplished this was left to him to arrange.

Thus far the level of Pujol's dissimulation had been minimal: he had masked his true motivation from the Germans and used the alias *Señor* LOPEZ. But he now embarked on what was to be a miasma of lies and deception. He told the Germans that he had the opportunity of exploiting a currency deal that involved a British national and the Spanish Security Police (*Seguridad*). His participation in the case would enable him to go to Britain as a Spanish government official. The Germans were not interested in this over-complex scenario and Pujol and his Abwehr contact George Helmut Lang (codename EMILIO) settled on his going to Lisbon where he was to gain press accreditation and hope to be granted an entry visa for the United Kingdom. On 26 April 1941 Pujol left Madrid with 1,000 pesetas towards his expenses provided by the still less than enthusiastic Germans.

In Lisbon Pujol continued to reveal his outstanding talent for the fabrication of stories and managed to have a forged diplomatic passport printed. He then returned to Madrid where he met two fresh faces from the Nazi intelligence community: Friedrich (Fritz) Knappe-Ratey (codename FEDERICO), and his superior Sonderfuehrer Karl Erich Kuehlanthal (codenames CARLOS and FELIPE). During the Civil War Kuehlanthal had been secretary to Joachim Rohleder, the chief of the Intelligence Department of the Condor Legion, the German expeditionary force fighting alongside the Nationalists. Kuehlanthal's career was unusual in as much as he was of part Jewish extraction and consequently was treated with suspicion by his superiors and the Sicherheitsdienst. However, the difficulties surrounding his parentage were overcome by the granting of Aryan status when his Abwehr station was established in Madrid in 1941. Through deft use of lies supplemented by half truths, Pujol managed to convince Kuehlanthal and Knappe-Ratey that he was well connected with the Spanish Security Police and Foreign Office, and duped the Germans with ambiguous and misleading telegrams from his contacts in Lisbon. At last the Germans were convinced of his bona fides:

> Any doubts which the Germans might have had in GARBO had now been for ever dispelled and their sole anxiety was to give Garbo some sort of rapid training so as to be able to take advantage of his visit to England under diplomatic cover.[16]

Pujol was furnished with questionnaires and given a crash course in secret writing – hardly the most comprehensive induction for a great spy. His secret messages were to be written in invisible ink and then camouflaged by an innocuous letter written over the top of them. Pujol told his controller that he

Letter sent by Pujol to Jose dias de Silva, who operated as a cover address for correspondence in Lisbon. The hidden message was written in secret ink beneath a typed letter. The Preston postmark corroborated Pujol's story that he visited one of his sub agents in Glasgow (see pp. 139–40, p. 152, this volume) (PRO, KV 2/66)

demanded absolute discretion regarding his recruitment, stating 'that any leakage through him would ruin his cover in England'.[17] In contrast the Germans were only too happy to reveal that Luis Calvo, the London correspondent of a Spanish newspaper, was a German agent. Moreover, they informed him that once in Britain, correspondence could be forwarded to them via the diplomatic bag of the Spanish Embassy in London courtesy of one of the military attachés. Kuehlanthal gave Pujol the final farewell address, passing him cover addresses and cash. He urged Pujol to set up networks of sub-agents that could remain in place even when Pujol was absent, and presciently warned him not to underestimate the British. Plans were laid for the Germans to take care of Pujol's wife, but he decided to risk taking her with him to Lisbon.

These major developments still did not significantly improve Pujol's reception when he presented himself at the British Embassy in Lisbon. In response to yet another rebuff he elected to develop his work as a German agent and secure even more proof of his position within the intelligence apparatus. On 19 July 1941 he sent a letter from Lisbon informing his German controllers of his safe arrival in England. He explained that he had secured a courier working for a civilian air line who was willing to carry his mail for $1 a letter and who would post it in Lisbon without it having to pass through the hands of the British censor. He also gave them a forwarding address in Lisbon (in reality Pujol had asked a friend if he could use his name and address as a *poste restante* to receive love letters from a mistress). A fortnight later a reply arrived, providing him with incontrovertible evidence of his connection with the Germans. This he took to the British Embassy. This time he was granted an audience, but the official was still not particularly interested and failed to attend a follow-up rendezvous at Estoril. Pujol recognized that if he were to stand any chance of convincing the British he would have to corroborate his story with a portfolio of letters, and began a series of bogus eyewitness reports to the Germans 'sent from England'.

Pujol's reports to the Germans were a concoction of material acquired from open sources and pure fiction. Even at this early stage he developed a verbose style 'the purpose of which was to fill his sheet with the minimum possible information'.[18] He made good use of the Lisbon Library, consulting its reference books and magazines for the names and addresses of bona fide British firms in order that he could weave them into his correspondence and thereby lend it a spurious note of authenticity. He even used newsreels and newspapers to provide him with the visual references he needed to make it appear as if his eyewitness accounts were true. Inevitably some errors did

Letter from the Abwehr to Pujol sent via his cover address in Lisbon. Accompanying it was a tube of anti-congestion cream in which was concealed seventeen miniature photographs of a new wireless transmission plan and ciphers (see p. 132, this volume) (PRO, KV 2/66)

creep into the texts, notably his lack of comprehension of the correct nomenclature of British Army units and an ignorance of British drinking habits revealed in the assertion that 'There are men here [in Glasgow] who would do anything for a litre of wine'.[19] But on the whole his reports carried such an aura of authenticity that not only did they convince the Germans but also gave cause for concern within British intelligence when versions of Pujol's reports transmitted by the Abwehr in Madrid to Berlin were intercepted. The deciphered wireless messages were believed to be 'substantial and plausible'.[20] Pujol's deception did not merely stop with his reports of what he personally had observed. He now introduced the first of what would become a small army of fictional sub-agents into his messages. By 17 August 1941 he was reporting to the Germans that he had begun to develop connections with individuals sympathetic to the Axis and in consequence had recruited two sub-agents, CARVALHO and GERBERS.[21]

The attempt to secure acceptance by the British authorities continued but showed no signs of success. In the autumn of 1941 Pujol visited Madrid but elicited the same cautiously suspicious response even when he produced the evidence of the Abwehr questionnaires. By now Pujol was too far into his deception of the Germans to simply await British acceptance of his story. He was growing concerned that they would instigate enquiries that would risk blowing his cover. With typical resourcefulness he came to the conclusion that if Britain would not accept his assistance, then the United States, although at this time still neutral, might find him of use.

Once again Harris's account and Pujol's own later memoirs part company here regarding the role of *Señora* Pujol in the course of events. Harris states that once back in Lisbon, Pujol's wife called on the US Embassy without notifying her husband and informed a member of the Naval Attaché's staff, Edward Rousseau, that she was in contact with a Spaniard working as a German agent. Although marginally more encouraging than his approaches to the British, the links with the Americans were slow to develop and by the end of November 1941 Pujol was reaching the point of despair. He applied for visas to emigrate to Brazil with his wife and child. But there was still time for *Señora* Pujol to reopen negotiations with Rousseau. In order to have him treat her seriously she asked for $200,000 in return for information on German spies in the USA, and to substantiate her claim she produced a letter written in secret ink purporting to come from a German agent: 'Agent 172 of Chicago reports that both he and his Detroit agents are awaiting your orders as they now have everything ready to commence sabotage in all the agreed factories at a moments [sic] notice'.[22]

A meeting was held between *Señora* Pujol, Rousseau and a British officer. In spite of *Señora* Pujol's collection of espionage paraphernalia, which included a microphoto of one of the German questionnaires, secret ink, developer and a letter (in secret ink) from Knappe-Ratey, the mysterious Englishman revealed himself as at best sceptical and at worst hostile to *Señora* Pujol. Once his companion had gone, Rousseau rebuilt the bridges with her and she was moved to reveal that the spy in question was her husband. On 15 January 1942 Rousseau and Pujol met and with Britain and the United States now firm allies, the American undertook to represent the Spaniard with the British authorities.

Establishing the precise chronology of Pujol's long and frustrating attempts to make meaningful contact with British intelligence is difficult. He must have left traces in the official paperwork of the various diplomats, military attachés and intelligence personnel in Lisbon and Madrid, but if these have survived they have not yet been released to the Public Record Office. We must therefore rely heavily upon Harris who states categorically that:

> GARBO's case first came to the notice of this Office [MI5] on the 22.2.42 when P.C.O. Lisbon, who happened to be on a visit to London, asked, in the course of conversation, whether Apartado 1099, Madrid, was a genuine German cover address since he was interested in a case in Lisbon in which this address had occurred. It happened that this same address was currently in use by a double-agent run by this Office. Thus the story of GARBO began to emerge.[23]

Harris further states that the inertia in Lisbon 'dragged on until the middle of March when he [Pujol] was finally introduced to a member of S.I.S. in Lisbon to whom he repeated his long story'.[24]

While the courtship in Lisbon was still stuttering along, in London things were hotting up. Understandably Harris does not dwell on the background in Whitehall surrounding Pujol's arrival and recruitment. In contrast the official historians of British intelligence in the Second World War convey a very interesting picture of rivalry between the services, one of whom commented that SIS's control over ISOS seemed 'arbitrary and unco-operative'.[25] The acquisition of Pujol as a British agent appears far from trouble-free. Whereas SIS knew of Pujol's approaches in Madrid and Lisbon and was in possession of the German wireless traffic, 'At this time B Division was puzzling about the source of reports "of superb accuracy", allegedly from

German agents in England controlled by the Abwehr station in Madrid', and consequently 'B Division was annoyed at not having been told of his existence earlier'.[26] On 3 March Guy Liddell, the head of B Division, wrote to SIS asking for a full report on Pujol and warned that 'unless his case was co-ordinated with other double-cross operations he might be inadvertently blown'.[27] Such was Pujol's potential that he became the subject of a struggle between SIS and MI5, both of which wanted control of him. The former wished to employ him in Lisbon, while the latter sought to exploit him from the United Kingdom. A succession of accusations and counter-accusations ensued, with each in turn affirming that their sister organization was failing to deal honestly and share information. Neither agency trusted the other not to exploit even a temporary advantage to their long term interests. Even Sir David Petrie, the Director-General of MI5, was moved to comment that the situation exemplified the need to amalgamate SIS's counter-espionage section with MI5's B Division.

Meanwhile, as Harris records, there was an urgent need to exfiltrate Pujol from Lisbon:

> We pressed that GARBO should be brought to England at the earliest opportunity as it was clear that he could not hope to continue his present career indefinitely without discovery unless he were given every assistance. It seemed a miracle that he had survived so long.[28]

Perhaps because of the wrangling in London, events still did not proceed with anything approaching rapidity. On 20 March 1942 it was proposed to Pujol that he be smuggled out of Lisbon to Gibraltar and thence to Britain by air. He agreed in spite of the need to leave his family behind, but it was still three more weeks before he embarked on a British merchant ship for Gibraltar. He arrived in Britain two weeks later by Sunderland flying boat on 24 April 1942. At Plymouth he was met by Cyril Mills and Tomás Harris of B1 Division of MI5. They escorted him to London where he was taken to the Royal Victoria Patriotic School, a processing centre for new arrivals from the continent, and then to a safehouse at 35 Crespigny Road, Hendon.

From the very outset Pujol proved highly co-operative. An important early visitor was Desmond Bristow of the Iberian Section of SIS's Section V, who translated copies of the messages Pujol had thus far sent to the Germans. He then spent several days debriefing him. At long last fully accepted by the British, Pujol soon dropped his earlier stipulation that he be permitted to rejoin his wife and family within a month. He stated his willingness to engage in deception stratagems with the proviso that his family be brought out of

Spain to join him.²⁹ At the beginning of May Mills (who spoke no Spanish) was relieved as Pujol's case officer, and Harris replaced him.

Tomás Harris was an ideal choice to handle the star agent. He was born on 10 April 1908 to a Spanish mother and a British father, Lionel Harris, a successful Mayfair art dealer who ran a gallery in London specializing in the works of El Greco, Velasquez and Goya. Prodigiously gifted, and commended for his work as an artist, sculptor, engraver and ceramicist, Tomás Harris had been awarded a scholarship to the Slade School of Art at the age of fifteen, and later studied in Rome. He followed his father into art dealership and travelled extensively in Spain securing works for the gallery. Back in London he became a member of a group of Cambridge graduates that included Guy Burgess, Anthony Blunt and Kim Philby. It was Burgess who effected Harris's introduction into the shadowy world of British intelligence when, in 1940, he recommended him for a position on the staff of a secret training establishment at Brickendonbury Hall. There is some uncertainty about how Harris switched from his rather menial position (he and his wife, Hilda, appear to have acted as a rather elevated form of housekeeper partnership) to joining the ranks of MI5. It has been suggested that he owed his move to his friendship with Blunt, whom he knew through the art world, and who had joined MI5 in 1940 and served with Guy Liddell in B1 Branch. Harris's

Tomás Harris, Juan Pujol's case officer and author of 'Summary of the Garbo Case 1941–1945'

sociability, wealth, generosity and gourmet tastes made his London home an unofficial club-cum-mess for intelligence officers. As Kim Philby later recorded:

> Tommy was an amazingly generous fellow. He'd already made a lot of money buying cheap from English country houses and selling dear and he liked to entertain a lot. So we had a little drinking circle at his place ... You'd drop in to see who was around. Tommy, as the host, was there most of the time. The others came and went. The regulars were me, Burgess, Blunt and perhaps Aneurin Bevan. Victor Rothschild dropped in from time to time but he wasn't one of the regulars. [30]

Countless connections and introductions were made there, including one by Harris that secured Kim Philby's acceptance into SIS:

> It must have been sometime in July [1941] that he [Harris] asked me if I would be interested in a job that called for my special knowledge of Franco Spain. He explained that it would not be with MI5, but with SIS.[31]

It is not surprising for a man of so many talents and interests that Harris did not stay in MI5 after the war's end. He returned to the art world, increasingly concentrating on producing his own works rather than buying and selling. He spent much of his time in Spain, and was living in Majorca when he was killed in a car crash on 27 January 1964. His wartime service, close connections with the Soviet 'moles' Blunt, Philby and Burgess, and the unusual circumstances of the accident have led to speculation concerning his death.[32]

Harris's working relationship with Pujol got off to a good start. The Spaniard came to Britain bearing copies of most of his correspondence with the Germans. This comprised 38 outgoing letters written between July 1941 and March 1942 and 15 incoming letters and questionnaires, all giving ample evidence of his work to date. But the document that clinched the trust of MI5 was a copy of a letter sent by him describing a British convoy. Reference to this had appeared on 2 April 1942 in an intercepted and deciphered Abwehr wireless message from Madrid to Berlin. Sent by Kuehlanthal, it referred to a source designated V-Mann 372 who reported from Liverpool on a Malta-bound convoy.[33] Examination of Pujol's letter no. 39 (after it turned up via the SIS Lisbon representative to whom it had been entrusted) identified him as V-372 and a trusted agent of the Abwehr. It was obvious to those handling Pujol's fledgling career that he was an ideal candidate as a double agent. Unfortunately, at that time only the SIS and Admiralty members of the XX Committee were members of the very limited circle of personnel initiated into the existence of the deciphered enemy wireless traffic, described as MSS (Most Secret Sources). With this insight denied to the whole committee, some of its members were understandably sceptical of Pujol. It was therefore decided that, because the Pujol case was of such potential, the Committee should be trusted with the secret of MSS in order to secure their support:

> It is somewhat doubtful whether we would have believed the already incredible story with which GARBO presented us on his first making contact had it not been that M.S.S. provided us with conclusive evidence that the essential of his story was true, and furthermore that the Germans believed him to be operating in England on their behalf.[34]

Harris's assignment as Pujol's case officer had signified the victory of MI5 in the wrangle over the control of the agent. He was an intelligent, versatile officer with a deep understanding of the Spanish mentality and adept at running double agents: 'We endeavoured to maintain the initiative throughout the running of the case, keeping one step ahead of the opposition in order to be able to direct the course of the case on the lines best suited to our plans'.[35] He did not have a very high regard for his opposite number in Madrid. 'His characteristic German lack of sense of humour, in such serious circumstances as these, blinded him to the absurdities of the story we were unfolding.'[36]

Harris was able to reflect that not only had the Abwehr accepted Pujol but their work processes had also became contaminated by him:

> Gradually they were persuaded to accept GARBO's verbose style until they, themselves, became longer, more explicit and more frequent. From their first telegraphic message in secret writing consisting of a few lines, they were worked up to the climax of sending no less than 24 foolscap pages of secret text in one letter.[37]

Pujol sent his first letter from London on 27 April 1942 (although it was dated 12 April) thereby beginning his long and effective career as one of British intelligence's greatest double agents. Harris and Pujol fused into an extraordinary partnership. Layer upon layer of deception began to be laid. The first of a new set of bogus sub-agents were 'recruited', including an RAF non-commissioned officer based in Scotland (No. 3) and a Gibraltarian waiter (No. 4). Together Harris and Pujol over the months expanded the network, building legends around the sub-agents, explaining how Pujol met them, how he won their confidence, where they worked, what was their character and how they could provide useful intelligence. Harris's report gives the fullest possible account of the GARBO network and how difficult it was to keep the various elements in place. The expansion of Pujol's network saw him rise in the Germans' esteem but it was essential that his success was incremental and no hint be given in his reports of his only recently having arrived in the United Kingdom. As the Germans accepted a steady stream of information, their supplementary questions revealed their own priorities and indicated areas of special interest where they wished the new agents to operate.

Soon Pujol and his MI5 controllers were sending two or three letters a week to Lisbon. In order to explain Pujol's entrées into areas where he could acquire useful intelligence, the legend was formed that he was doing freelance propaganda work for the BBC.[38] This also provided the justification for the claim that Pujol had acquired an unconscious source in the Spanish Department of the Ministry of Information, designated J(3), who was able to provide information from Whitehall. While Pujol's output increased, it was also vitally important to monitor the likelihood of questions that could not be answered. For example, MI5 appreciated that the build-up of invasion shipping for the invasion of North Africa, Operation TORCH, would not have escaped the spy in Liverpool. This placed GERBERS, Pujol's notional agent on Merseyside, in a difficult position. Consequently it was necessary to remove the fictitious agent from this sensitive area before the Germans asked Pujol to deploy him. It was therefore reported to the Abwehr that the sub-agent's reports had dried up, and that a trip by Pujol to Liverpool had revealed him to be seriously ill in hospital. Pujol later informed Madrid that GERBERS had succumbed to his illness and died on 19 November. An obituary notice was placed in the Liverpool Daily Post and sent to the Abwehr as corroboration of his demise.

Another TORCH scheme involved the sending of reports of Allied convoys *after* the landings had taken place. Their delivery to Spain was delayed so that they created no risk to the operations but nevertheless maintained Pujol's reputation as a first-rate source. While disappointed that the information had arrived too late to be of any use in interdicting the Allied assault, in a message dated 26 November 1942 the Germans nevertheless applauded Pujol's efforts: 'your last reports are all magnificent but we are sorry they arrived late, especially those relating to the Anglo-Yankee disembarkation in Africa'.[39]

The Germans came to regard Juan Pujol as their principal agent in the United Kingdom. They trusted and relied upon him and were so satisfied with the intelligence that he provided that they felt it unnecessary to develop further Spanish networks:

> We had the satisfaction of knowing through M.S.S. that all GARBO material was being given priority and that every military report which reached Madrid from the GARBO network was immediately re-transmitted to Berlin.[40]

The experience of the delay with the TORCH reports and the burgeoning of Pujol's network that eventually rose to 27 (notional) sub-agents meant that the courier system from London to Lisbon had to be improved. Pujol had already informed Madrid that he could procure the use of a wireless and operator in the United Kingdom and that all he needed was a signal plan and codes. These were eventually forthcoming and on 7 March 1943 he (or rather MI5) sent his first wireless report. By the end of August virtually all his messages were being sent by this medium.

The invasion of Europe

But however useful these schemes were in misleading the Germans regarding important Allied enterprises, the greatest test awaited them: the invasion of Europe. It was essential to the success of the operation that the Germans be confused over the time, the place and the magnitude of the attack. Even the Germans' limited intelligence resources indicated that an invasion of France was being planned. While they set about building an Atlantic Wall of coastal defences to meet the Allied threat, it became ever more important to discover details of the Allies' intentions. The sheer scale of the build-up of British and American resources in the United Kingdom was massive, rising to more than three million men, an immense fleet of warships, merchantmen and landing craft and 13,000 aircraft gathered together to carry out the invasion. Consequently Plan BODYGUARD, an intricate strategic deception scheme, was drawn up to mislead the Germans in their reading of Allied intentions and influence the disposition of their forces to meet the assault. BODYGUARD was divided into two main components: FORTITUDE NORTH and FORTITUDE SOUTH. The first of these deception plans was to convince the Germans that the Allies intended a landing in Norway and that substantial

Landing craft assembled at Southampton in preparation for D-Day, June 1944. The scale of the invasion preparations was immense, with over 4,000 British and American landing ships and craft taking part (photograph courtesy of the Imperial War Museum, London)

forces were being built up in Scotland and Northern Ireland to implement the attack. The second was to have the Germans draw the conclusion that the main cross-Channel assault was to be in the Pas de Calais area of northern France. An entirely bogus force, the First United States Army Group (FUSAG), was invented for FORTITUDE SOUTH, while the real forces assigned to the OVERLORD assault on Normandy were to be represented as being assigned to a diversionary attack on that coast. A massive range of deception methods was employed, ranging from dummy aircraft and landing craft to simulated wireless traffic for FUSAG. The full panoply of the Double Cross agents was deployed to support BODYGUARD. But even the best of team efforts can benefit from a star player and Harris's appreciation leaves the reader in no doubt that Pujol was just that.

Just as we were beginning to concentrate on the reporting of the FORTITUDE Order of Battle we received a most appropriate questionnaire which read:-

'It is to be assumed that the forces which will be engaged in the invasion operation will be divided into several independent armies,

Troops of the US 29th Infantry Division in England in preparation for the invasion. The Allied deception stratagems were so effective that less than a month before D-Day, the German High Command overestimated the number of divisions present in the United Kingdom by 50% (photograph courtesy of the Imperial War Museum, London)

British and U.S. It would be of the greatest interest to know how many armies there will be and how many have already been formed. Headquarters and names of the commanders of each Army as well as their composition, i.e., corps and divisions under command, the objectives assigned to each army.'

They explained that this work could only be accomplished by piecing together, little by little, the information which he was able to collect until the mosaic had been completed. Thus, they asked us for precisely the information which we had already planned to pass to them.[41]

As the great day approached Pujol's output increased:

During the entire year of 1944 nearly all GARBO reports were transmitted by wireless. Between January, 1944 and D Day of OVERLORD well over 500 wireless messages were exchanged between London and Madrid.[42]

British troops land on D-Day. Pujol convinced the Abwehr that he had tried to warn them of the invasion and that the Normandy landings were simply a diversion from the main assault in the Pas de Calais (photograph courtesy of the Imperial War Museum, London)

The importance of the work meant that both MI5 and their German counterparts had to cut out much of the customary verbosity in their communications. Pujol's usual flowery style was pruned in order to send the volume of material that the deception planners at the Supreme Headquarters Allied Expeditionary Force (SHAEF) requested. Five or six wireless messages were being sent every day with nine principal full time agents submitting reports. The notional and real burden this placed upon Pujol was immense and even Harris conceded with hindsight 'It is doubtful whether, in reality, one man could possibly have done all the work which was in this way attributed to GARBO'.[43]

Even though there was concern that the deception was at risk of being compromised, Harris felt that 'German satisfaction and confidence in GARBO was to some degree apparent in the fact that they failed to make any last minute efforts to penetrate our Security screen prior to the OVERLORD OPERATION'.[44]

Pujol's role in the success of Operation OVERLORD was crucial. In the weeks leading up to 6 June 1944 he fed the Germans regular reports supposedly based upon information from his informants supplemented by his own interpretations of Allied strategy. He sought to disguise the advanced state of invasion preparations and maintained the impression that FUSAG was at the centre of Allied planning. Clearly Pujol's reputation demanded that he give

Troops in Normandy following the D-Day landings (photograph courtesy of the Imperial War Museum, London)

some form of warning of the assault but in this he was fortuitously assisted by the negligence of the Abwehr's Madrid station. In the early hours of D-Day a wireless message was to be sent from London intimating that the invasion was imminent. It was calculated that this would arrive with the German High Command too late for any effective warning signals to be sent to the Normandy defenders. However the German wireless operator in Madrid was not standing by and a second message (altered to exploit the delay in transmission) had to be sent, arriving in Madrid as the first Allied troops were coming ashore.

But Pujol's contribution to the success of the invasion did not end on D-Day. Far from it, his most important contribution was still to come and on 8 June 1944 'Garbo sent over the most important report of his career'.[45] He claimed to have called together a conference of his agents and the report was a fusion of the information that they had imparted. It was an attempt to maintain FORTITUDE even when the evidence of the Normandy landings was there for all to see. In the days and weeks that followed Pujol's reports maintained the spectre of another attack on the Pas de Calais that demanded the Germans maintain their vigilance and strength in this area. Once again interception and deciphering of German wireless messages revealed that Pujol's estimates were reaching the German High Command and influencing

9.6.44.
2780.
1915-19 GMT

Madrid I - Berlin. 290. To ERIZO I. Other Stellen not informed.
V ALARIC reports on 9/6 from ENGLAND via FELIPE. I learn from V AMBROS
that in competent political circles there is a considerable difference
of opinion in re continuance of the restrictions imposed on foreign
diplomats. On both sides the opinion prevails that the restrictions
are only being accepted by diplomats in consideration of the requirements
necessary to the commencement of the big offensive operations, while a
continuation of the regulations after the big offensive has begun would
not be tolerable. On the other hand continuance of the restrictions
is regarded as necessary in view of the military situation, though in
this connection there is doubt as to how this is to be put to the
diplomats, as under no circumstances is it desired to let anything at all
be known about further landing manoeuvres. The questions has not yet
been decided. KOSP 5883.

9.6.44.
2771
1044 GMT.

Madrid I - Berlin. 266. To HEROLD. Ref your message 8898 of 7th
June. With respect to 28th USA Division you are referred to todays'
report of V DORICK KOSP 5878. KOSP 5889.

9.6.44.
2772.

Madrid I - Berlin. 267. To HEROLD. Please inform LUDWIG MARTIN at
your end. Other stellen not informed. V ALARIC ARABAL reports on 9th
June from ENGLAND via FELIPE; after personal discussion on 8th June in
LONDON with my agents DONNY DICK and DORRICK, whose reports were passed
over today, I am of the opinion, by reasons of the large troop
assemblage in South-West and East ENGLAND which are not taking part in
the present operations, that these operations are diversionary manoeuvres
aiming to draw on themselves enemy reserved in order subsequently to make
a decisive blow at another place. Having regard to the air-raids carried
out there and the situation strategically favourable for this purpose, of
the above mentioned assembly area, this (blow) might well be made in the
PAS DE CALAIS area, especially as, if there were such an attacke the near
air-bases would facilitate a continuous and very strong support by the
air force for such an undertaking. According to what I heard yesterday
from the connection V AMY (letter KO SP Most Secret No. 934 of 4/44)
there were 75 divisions in ENGLAND before the start of the operation in
FRANCE. KOSP 5879.

9.6.44.
2773.

Madrid I - Berlin. 268. To HEROLD. Please inform MARTIN, LUDWIG at
your end. Other Stellen not informed. ENGLAND, ARABAL, 9th of June 4
hours via FELIPE, V DORICK, network DAGOBERT reports on 8th of June. Stron
increase in military movement in the IPSWICH HARWICH area. Following
troops and insignia observed in the area named, without so far any
noticeable indications of imminent embarkation. 6th U.S.Division, 2
U.S. Division 80th U.S.Division, insignia 2 Romen x's intertwined, insigni
of Third U.S. Army, insignia First U.S. Army Group, insignia of SOS, USA
insignia outer blue circle cut in 4 places, inner blue disc similarly
divided 4 times, Dutch and Belgian troops, insignia EASTERN COMMAND, pand
Armoured Div., 61st English Div.,47th LONDON Div., insignia windmill
sails U.S.A Rangers, Royal Marine Commandos, members of the 8th and 9th
U.S.A.A.F. In addition the following troops newly observed in the area:
4th U.S.Armoured Div.m 5th U.S. Armoured Div. lion insignia of the
SCOTTISH COMMAND, insignia with word AIRBORNE, U.S. insignia black wild
on walnut tree, coloured gorund. Observed columns of vehicles in last
few days. Column of the 28th U.S.A. Division travelling in a southerly
direction. Large columns of the 49th English Division travelling in a
southerly direction. Column, travelling northwards, of 2 Division
with insignia sailing ships. Same V Mann learned from well informed
source that there are over 100 A.F.V. transport landing craft to transpor
about 500 A.F.V's in the harbours of YARMOUTH and LOWESTOFT, as well as in
the rivers DEBEN and ORWELL, where they have concentrated gradually. It
is not possible for V-Mann to check up personally as there are very
severe measures closing the areas. Addendum. V ALARIC. Please
report urgently whether this assemblage of landing craft is confirmed
by air recce so that we can assess the value of V DORICK's new contact.
KOSP 5878.

9.6.44.
101493.
12.14.GMT.

Paris - Madrid. 10. Urgent. To KO SPAIN. Ref. your no.5848
(Isk 100790). 1) 3rd English Inf.Div. in landing area correct. 2)
Bringing-up of Garde(5 corrupt) described by OB WEST as expecially
important. OB WEST requests further reports of a similar nature. 3)
So far the following enemy forces identified in the landing: with the V
and XXX English A.C.'s the 50th English, 90th English, 3rd English Inf.
Div., doubtful, 9th English Inf.Div. Further, 2nd and 3rd Canadian Inf.
(Cont. voer......

Transcripts of wireless messages sent by the Abwehr station in Madrid to Berlin.
Intercepted and deciphered by British Intelligence, they revealed that Pujol's
reports were being treated as accurate (PRO, KV 2/39)

their decisions in keeping divisions in the north and not deploying them against the Normandy bridgehead.

Inevitably a point was reached at which the deception threatened to unravel. At the end of June 1944 Madrid asked for more details of FUSAG and requested that Pujol report on the efficacy of the new V1 flying bomb offensive launched against London. Harris recognized it was neither possible to lie nor tell the truth and came up with the idea of avoiding these difficult commissions by having Pujol 'arrested' and thereby having his channel of communications shut down for a period. On 5 July one of the sub-agents reported that his leader had vanished. Discreet investigations were ordered by the Germans and it was revealed that the police had seen Pujol acting suspiciously while examining bomb damage in the East End of London, and had taken him into custody. Less than a week later news was sent to the Germans informing them of Pujol's release, followed shortly by his own description of events. This was received with great relief by the Germans, who instructed him to curtail his activities for his own safety. There was a pleasant surprise to mark the end of this crisis when on 29 July 1944 Madrid advised Pujol that he had been awarded the Iron Cross. It says much for Pujol's reputation that, in spite of the invasion and German intelligence's failure to offer adequate information to assist the commanders, he was still held in such high regard. Moreover, his controllers had had to fight a major battle with Berlin bureaucrats to overcome Pujol's ineligibility as a civilian for the decoration. No such problems appear to have been encountered with the award of an MBE in December 1944, which was presented to Pujol by Petrie, the Director-General of MI5.

In September 1944 following a scare that Pujol was about to be exposed by an Abwehr defector, it was decided that he should go to ground. His network would continue to provide misleading information for transmission to the Germans under the leadership of agent No. 3, but the chief was to go into hiding in South Wales. Some communication between Pujol and his controllers was maintained but this grew ever more morose and depressing as each speculated on the parlous state of the Third Reich. Pujol described his living conditions as far from comfortable, while the Abwehr station in Madrid was coming to the reluctant conclusion that the end of the Third Reich was nigh.

Even as the war was drawing to a close, MI5 assiduously protected the deceptions they had played on the Germans. Their motivation appears to have been centred upon protecting the 'concept' of the double agent, which, although not a novel idea, had arguably never been used with such efficacy. In the particular case of Pujol they sought to protect him from any likelihood of

Nazi retribution while also hoping that his favoured position and immaculate credentials would enable him to penetrate any post-war Nazi activity.

> Our main object was to get GARBO quickly to Madrid to make contact with his German masters as it was thought that he alone would be able to ascertain whether or not the Germans were proposing to carry on any form of underground organization in the post war.[46]

To this end Pujol went to Spain at the end of hostilities and met his erstwhile German controllers. He found both in distinctly reduced circumstances and neither Kuehlanthal nor Knappe-Ratey gave any indication of their being members of a threatening residual Nazi movement.

In his memoirs Pujol seems more than satisfied with MI5's treatment of him. He states that his British friends wished to have him stay in the United Kingdom and offered him employment with an insurance company. But he favoured starting a new life in South America and MI5 gave him a gratuity of £15,000 to start him on his way. He decided upon Venezuela, where he lived in anonymity. With the passage of time and an increased interest in the impact of intelligence upon the conduct of the Second World War, the Double Cross System was revealed in a variety of books of varying accuracy. Perhaps the most authoritative was that of the XX Committee's chairman, J C Masterman, who was able to describe the work of Pujol under his *nom de guerre*, GARBO. Tracking down a man of such stature became a mission for several journalists that was finally ended when the writer Rupert Allason located him living in Caracas. He was persuaded to make a sentimental return to London to meet some of his former comrades in MI5 and to receive formal recognition of the nation's debt to him in the form of an audience at Buckingham Palace with the Duke of Edinburgh. An account of his life subsequently appeared and then, as further books featured his exploits, he receded into relative obscurity. He died in Caracas in 1988.

Notes

1 Juan Pujol with Nigel West, *Garbo* (Weidenfeld & Nicolson, London, 1985).
2 Tomás Harris, 'The Summary of the Garbo Case', this volume, pp. 39–40. Public Record Office file KV2/41. Various other documents relating to the GARBO case are to be found in KV 2/39, KV 2/40, KV 2/42, KV 2/63, KV 2/64, KV 2/66 and KV 2/69.
3 The 'one who got away' was Otto Weigals who managed to make his escape from Hull. Leonard Sellers, *Shot in the Tower* (Leo Cooper, London, 1997), p. 6.

4 *The Security Service 1908–1945* (Public Record Office, London, 1999), p. 74.
5 *Picture Post*, 26 November 1938, pp. 61–71 and Bernard Newman, *Secrets of German Espionage* (The Right Book Club, London, 1940), p. 253.
6 *The Security Service 1908–1945*, p. 142
7 F H Hinsley & C A G Simkins, *British Intelligence in the Second World War Volume 4* (HMSO, London, 1990), p. 98.
8 Michael Howard, *British Intelligence in the Second World War, Volume 5* (HMSO, London, 1990), p. 16
9 Pujol, p. 56
10 Harris, p. 42.
11 Ibid, p. 43.
12 Pujol, pp. 64–5.
13 Harris, p. 43.
14 Ibid, p. 38.
15 MI5 and SIS reports seem uncertain whether Leissner's real name was Lenz, while Harris states that he also used the alias HEIDELBURG.
16 Harris, p. 49.
17 Ibid, p. 49. This was to protect him from the Germans discussing his recruitment with the Spanish authorities and thereby risk exposure of his connections with the Security Police as a sham.
18 Ibid, p. 54.
19 Ibid, p. 58.
20 Ibid, p. 41.
21 Ibid, p. 53.
22 Ibid, p. 64.
23 Ibid, p. 66.
24 According to published sources this was Gene Risso Gill.
25 Howard, p. 16.
26 Hinsley and Simkins, p. 113
27 Ibid, p. 113. There is a footnote that the anonymous reports passing through the Madrid Abwehr office were of such concern to MI5 that it was preparing a scheme to use another double-agent to discredit them.
28 Harris, p. 66.
29 The arrival of Pujol's family was not without problems. Harris described *Señora* Pujol as 'hysterical, spoilt and selfish' while conceding 'She was, nevertheless, intelligent and astute and probably entered into her husband's work because it was dangerous and exciting', p. 327. A crisis that arose in June 1943 necessitated an elaborate ruse to prevent her confessing her husband's work to the Spanish Embassy. Harris describes it as 'characteristic of many tense moments which existed from time to time in the GARBO household', ibid, p. 328.
30 Phillip Knightley, *Philby – KGB Masterspy* (Pan, London), pp. 83–4.
31 Kim Philby, *My Silent War* (Panther, London, 1979), p. 47.
32 There have been suggestions that he had been recruited by Soviet intelligence in Spain before the war and that he was under suspicion at the time of his death. These allegations have not been substantiated.
33 Harris, p. 41.
34 Ibid, p. 72.
35 Ibid, p. 70.
36 Ibid, p. 70.
37 Ibid, p. 71.
38 Ibid, p. 95.
39 Ibid, p. 104.
40 Ibid, pp. 177–8.
41 Ibid, p. 178.
42 Ibid, p. 177.
43 Ibid, p. 179.
44 Ibid, p. 70.
45 Ibid, p. 205.
46 Ibid, p. 274.

SUMMARY
OF
THE GARBO CASE
1941 - 1945

TABLE OF CONTENTS.

PREFACE

Until the extraordinary events of World War No. 2 had eclipsed
World War No. 1, vague stories were still being told about German
espionage activities in Spain during the first of these two wars.
Invariably they were stories which tended to show that the Spaniards
were helping the Germans either to refuel submarines or to spy
against our activities in Gibraltar and the Mediterranean. We do not
know the truth about these stories because, unfortunately, there
are no records. It is perhaps significant that, whereas nearly all
novelists have always represented the British Secret Service as
actively engaged in offensive espionage abroad, and in particular
in neutral countries, the stories which emerge from wars are always
of the advantages which the enemy gained through their espionage
activities in these same neutral countries. Had records existed
about the Secret Services engaged in World War No. 1 we would
perhaps have discovered that secrets, as closely guarded as the
subject of the present case, were responsible for placing the enemy
in this favourable light and it must be hoped that we will be allowed
to continue to deceive the world, and in particular the enemy, in
the belief that the Germans derived incalculable advantages from
their very preferential treatment in Franco-Spain during World War
No. 2, which we were denied.

   There are few, if any foreigners, who have penetrated deeply
into Spain who have not been completely captivated by her great
culture and the profound qualities of her people. The Spaniards,
in spite of this, have only reciprocated their admiration for two
races, the British and the German, whose difference both racially
and culturally is as fundamental as is the similarity between
themselves and the French and the Italians, whom they detest.

   If we know little about the life of the German community in
Spain, our knowledge of them is perhaps greater than that of the
larger and more prosperous British Colony there. We are told that
German residents in Spain rallied to the appeal of their Fatherland
during the 1914 - 18 war and it is probable that they then served
with the German Intelligence Service in Spain rather than with their
armies in France. With the approach of the Spanish Civil War there
can be little doubt that nearly all Germans resident in Spain were
ordered by their Government to support, if not serve, the Falangist
insurgent, Franco.

   Germany sent to Spain the famous Condor Legion to assist
Franco in his fight to overthrow the Spanish Republican Government.
Germany, when accused of having sent armed forces to fight with
Franco, denied the charge and insisted that the Condor Legion was

a small body of technicians or specialists. Although the exact composition of the Condor Legion is still obscure there can be little doubt that the German statement was to some extent truthful. The Legion was certainly composed of Intelligence officers of various descriptions and there can be little doubt that nearly all departments of the large machinery which eventually came under the control of Himmler during this war were there represented.

Neither did they all leave Spain after Franco's victory, and it is not therefore surprising that the large Abwehr network which continued to operate in Spain during the world war, which followed only a few months on the termination of the Spanish Civil War, should have been composed to some extent of those officers who had gained experience of Spain and its nationals during their three years of service in Spain during her civil war.

Franco now in full control, his opponents either exterminated or in concentration camps and prisons, awaiting their inevitable fate at his hands, promised to reward the Germans for their assistance with his co-operation. The records and facilities of the Spanish Foreign Office under Serrano Suner were made available to them. Spanish Police records and officers of the Seguridad were instructed to facilitate the Germans in all they required, passports to Spanish nationals were issued on German recommendation, or refused on their instructions. The Spanish press and radio services were under German control. The Spanish General Staff was collaborating to the maximum. The use of Spanish diplomatic bags was theirs for the asking. The Spanish Blue Division was fighting side by side with their German ally and Franco had made a public declaration that he would, if necessary, send a million men to defend Berlin. Yet Spain remained neutral. It should not have been difficult for a strong and numerous Intelligence Service to have exploited such a uniquely favourable position with great success; in fact it is difficult to understand how they could have failed to do so.

If there were thousands of young Spaniards who, still impassioned by the Civil War, were prepared to take up arms to fight side by side with their German spiritual leaders, surely there must have been plenty of openings to recruit amongst these fanatics, men whose loyalty need have been the last factor for consideration.

Their selection, therefore, was strange for, apart from a few low grade agents, they succeeded in recruiting the following Spaniards to operate on their behalf in this country:-

PIERNAVIEJA DEL POZO.   A Spanish athlete. A Falangist of long standing. A playboy whose behaviour here was so irresponsible that he was summoned back to Spain and temporarily imprisoned in 1941.

ALCAZAR DE VELASCO.   A high ranking Falangist official, fanatically pro-German, who was both dishonest and illiterate. He paid his last visit to this country in 1941. He found it easier to invent his reports than to trouble to seek genuine information.

MENDEZ DOMINGUEZ.   A Falangist journalist, who although recruited decided on arrival here in 1941 to abandon his mission.

LUIS CALVO.   A Falangist journalist who, intimidated by ALCAZAR DE VELASCO accepted an espionage mission which he carried out half-heartedly prior to his arrest by this Department in 1942.

JOSE BRUGADA.   Spanish Press Attache at the London Embassy. An ex-Intelligence officer in the services of Franco during the Civil War who likewise was intimidated by ALCAZAR DE VELASCO into accepting an espionage mission. He, however, preferred to operate until in 1943 his case collapsed due to the incompetence of ALCAZAR DE VELASCO

JAIME RIBAS.   A Catalan, who provoked the Germans to recruit him so that he might get to this country to assist the Catalan underground movement.

    Through counter-Intelligence investigations it has now become abundantly clear that all their efforts produced only one great Spanish source of information in this country which operated from 1941 until the cessation of hostilities. This source comprised a very large network of agents, the leader of which was a Spaniard, who reported to the German Intelligence Service in Madrid by wireless and by secret letters sent by courier via Lisbon. The network had out stations in North Africa, Canada and Ceylon and was composed of no less than 28 members, of which several were in direct communication with the Germans in secret writing. So important did this source become that it unquestionably influenced the strategy of the German High Command at the time of the Allied landing in the Cherbourg peninsula. A strategy which Jodl, since the German collapse, has himself described as fatal, though he is still unsuspecting of the planning and organization which inspired it and thus hastened the destruction of Hitlerite Germany.

    In 1941 when the Germans were all powerful in Spain, the British Embassy in Madrid was being stoned, France had collapsed and the German invasion of England was imminent, little were the Germans to know that the small meek young Spaniard who then approached them and volunteered to go to London to engage in espionage on their behalf would turn out to be an important British agent. Still less were they to discover that the network which they instructed him to build up in the United Kingdom was to be composed of 27 characters who were nothing more than a figment of the imagination.

The summary of the story of this espionage network of imaginary characters, the GARBO NETWORK, the subject of this report is, if unorthodox, a record of the extent to which it is possible to deceive one's opponent, through what is probably the oldest weapon of deception in war, the double-cross agent.

INTRODUCTION

On the 2.4.42 the following message appeared on Most Secret Sources[(i)] from Madrid to Berlin:-

> Agent (V-Mann) 372 of Stelle FELIPE reports from Liverpool on 26/3 the sailing from Liverpool of a convoy of 15 ships including 9 freighters, course BASTA (Gibraltar) and probably going on to Malta, possible intermediate port LISA (Lisbon). Composition: 1 collier 2,000 tons, 1 tanker 2,000 tons, 5 freighters 5,000 tons with following cargo: 2 freighter tanker 2,000 tons, 5 freighters 5,000 to 10,000 tons with following cargo: 2 freighter with A.A. ammunition and war material, 3 freighters with food; 1 further freighter 5,000 tons with Air Force technical personnel bound for Malta, 1 freighter 1,500 tons with hospital supplies and ambulances, other freighters with cargo of war material. Route of voyage Liverpool, possible LISA, BASTA, Malta according to statement of master of Greek freighter New Hellas now sailing for England. K.O.S.P.

This was the first indication of the existence of FELIPE's V-Mann 372, apparently a German agent operating from Liverpool. The fact that the information was being retransmitted to Berlin seven days after the date of the report in Liverpool indicated that the Liverpool agent had some special means of communication. The time lapse was too short for the information to have been passed by ordinary Air Mail and yet too slow for W/T. The information was checked by this Office and though a great number of convoys had sailed from Liverpool around this date none could be found which fitted exactly with this description.

The report was sufficiently substantial and plausible to leave the impression that it had been the work of an inaccurate reporter. The message seemed plausible enough to Berlin who immediately flashed out the signal of alert to Mediterranean outposts. We were soon to discover that the originator of this report was a character then domiciled in Lisbon, the subject of this case.

(i)   See Appendix No. XXXVII.

CHAPTER I.

EARLY HISTORY.

GARBO, the son of a Spanish industrialist, received a Catholic education in Spain up to the age of fifteen. His father, a man of moderate means, died in 1933 when GARBO was twenty-one years of age, leaving his family well provided for. GARBO ventured into the manufacturing business with his elder brother. He was a cinema proprietor and later owned a road transport business. Shortly before the Spanish Civil War he sold out his interest in his business to his elder brother. A few months later the factory on which GARBO's family depended for their livelihood was commandeered by the workers and with the outbreak of war GARBO was called up for service in the Republican Army.

The disorder and general confusion of the first few months of war in Spain and the prevailing Communist influence in the industrialist areas intensified GARBO's already conservative sentiments and strengthened his dislike for extremist politics. He decided that he would not fight on the side of a Government which was unable to maintain order and permitted the injustices which were being perpetrated against the Roman Catholic church and the Spanish constitution. In August, 1936 he went into hiding in the house of some friends and did not leave the house or venture into the streets for nearly two years. On seventeen occasions the house received a routine search by the Police. On the eighteenth occasion, in April 1938, he was discovered and arrested together with other male members of the household. For nineteen days he was held incommunicado in a prison cell. A woman prisoner, who was having an affair with one of the warders, managed to arrange for a party to escape. GARBO was one of forty-nine who got away. He again went into hiding until he managed to acquire some false identity papers. In possession of these documents he enlisted voluntarily in the services of the Republican Army with intent to desert to the Franco side. After a short training he was put into a Communications Company and sent to the Front at the time of the Franco counter-attack following the Ebro offensive.

In September, 1938, at the risk of his life he crossed to the Franco side. After a period in a concentration camp and following interrogations by the Franco authorities, he was enlisted in the Franco Army. After two months leave in Burgos he was posted to the Teruel Front in January, 1939. On the 13th February Tarragona fell. There were great celebrations. An incident then occurred which, it appears, convinced GARBO that the Falange was endeavouring to

dominate Franco Spain, with the same despotic intolerance, as the
Communists had tried to dominate Republican Spain. For expressing
his sympathy with the Monarchy he was struck in the face by his
Colonel and imprisoned, though after a few days he engineered his
release through intervention, but he was permanently left with the
knowledge that Spain, under Fascism, was as intolerable as it would
have been under Communism.

The Spanish Civil War had ended, he returned to Burgos where
he met his future wife.[(i)] In October, after his demobilization, he
went to live at her home town and in April, 1940, they were married
in Madrid. He soon discovered that unless one was in sympathy with
the Party there was little opening for a young man in Spain. He went
to Lisbon where he found conditions little better and in November
planned to go to the United States with his wife, or at least to
explore the possibilities of getting there. He had taken the
decision that he wanted to leave Spain until the Franco regime had
been overthrown. He returned to Madrid with the realization that the
prospects of a change of Government in Spain were dependent on a
British victory. It occurred to him that with his background, having
deserted from the Republicans to Franco, it would not be difficult
for him to get a job in either Germany or Italy. Once there he would
be able to serve British interests. He discussed with his wife, the
idea of offering his services for espionage to the British. She
approved. After making their plans she called in January, 1941, at
the British Consulate in Madrid. She obtained an interview and told
the story that she knew of a man who was willing to work for the
British and was prepared to go either to Germany or to Italy to do
espionage. The Consular official replied that he was not interested
in this sort of proposition. When GARBO was told the result of her
visit to the Consulate he decided that he would at least show us that
if we were not willing to engage in espionage against the Germans,
the Germans did not feel the same way about us. He decided to
endeavour to obtain evidence in proof of this belief and so prepared
a plan of approach to the Germans.

(i)   See appendix No. 29.

CHAPTER II.

GARBO'S INTRODUCTION TO THE GERMANS
FEBRUARY, 1941 - APRIL, 1941.

Shortly after the visit by his wife to our Consulate GARBO called on the German Embassy. He asked to be put in touch with the department dealing with secret affairs. He was interviewed by the Chancellor, Herr HEIDELBURG (probably identical with LEISSNER @ LENZ) to whom he explained the purpose of his visit. He declared that he was prepared to work for Germany in any type of work in which they considered he could be useful. He volunteered to go to Lisbon to operate as an informant for them there. If they could suggest the method of reaching England he would willingly go for them. He gave his alias as Senor LOPEZ and a telephone number where he could be reached after his offer of service had been considered. In the absence of news he telephoned the Embassy ten days later and was given the message that somebody would be calling on Senor LOPEZ in due course. Three days later he again telephoned the Embassy for news. He was told that someone would call on him that afternoon. The visitor was a Spaniard serving as a contact man for the Germans. He took note of GARBO'S origin, his service during the Spanish Civil War, past occupations, etc., and promised to make contact again in the near future. Two weeks past without news. GARBO again telephoned the Embassy and pressed for an interview with Herr HEIDELBURG which was granted the same afternoon. At the meeting he was told that his proposition to go to Lisbon had been rejected as uninteresting. He was told, however, that providing he could put up a project for going to England they would be interested. The difficulties were pointed out to GARBO. The Germans offered no suggestions and made it clear that it was up to GARBO, not only to work out a plan, but furthermore he would have to find suitable cover and make arrangements to travel. The interview ended.

Ten days later GARBO once again telephoned the Embassy to say that he had something important to communicate. He was told that he would receive a visit from someone that evening. The visitor was LANG @ EMILIO to whom GARBO told the following story.

He said that he had recently been in contact with a friend of his, a secret police agent employed on the investigation of contraband currency transactions. GARBO said that when he was last in Lisbon he had happened to meet a British subject called DALAMAL. DALAMAL, he stated, was trying to negotiate the exchange of some 5 million pesetas into sterling. He had returned to England without accomplishing his mission. In matters of this sort the Spanish secret police agents operate on a basis of commission. If the transaction were intercepted and the 5 million pesetas confiscated the police officer responsible for the case would receive a substantial commission on this sum. The police officer, GARBO said, had offered to split his commission with GARBO if he would be willing to go to England to continue the investigations and provoke DALAMAL's confidence. GARBO had accepted the proposition providing he could be sent there officially by the Spanish Security Police as a Government official. GARBO tested EMILIO with this story and asked whether the Germans would be prepared to help him to get a visa should he be sent to England as an agent of the Spanish Seguridad. EMILIO replied that he thought the proposition complicated and absurd. He said that it would be much better and simpler if GARBO could get himself a job as a correspondent of a Spanish newspaper and went to England under cover of that sort. He left his telephone number and told GARBO to ring him if he could arrange this.

GARBO's next move was to go to the British Consulate where he applied for a visa and was told that it was not likely to be forthcoming. A few days later he rang EMILIO and when they met he told him of his visit to the Consulate and the difficulties he anticipated. EMILIO replied that he was already aware of GARBO's visit to the Consulate since his movements were being watched. A further attempt was made to press EMILIO for his approval to carry out GARBO's plan to go to England in search of DALAMAL. EMILIO was adamant that he should go as a newspaper correspondent and recommended GARBO to go to Lisbon where he would find the possibilities were greater both for getting Press work and for getting a visa. GARBO accepted this proposal. After an examination of his passport by EMILIO he was told to try to obtain a Spanish Exit Permit and a Portuguese Entry visa. He was given 1,000 pesetas for his expenses and on the 26.4.41 GARBO left Madrid for Lisbon.

CHAPTER III.

GARBO'S DIPLOMATIC PASSPORT AND HIS RECRUITMENT BY THE GERMANS. MAY, 1941 - JULY, 1941.

Immediately on his arrival in Lisbon GARBO called at the British Consulate where he put in a formal application for a visa for England. This he did as cover in case he was watched by the Germans. He then set about obtaining a false Spanish Diplomatic passport. He called on a firm of engravers in Lisbon and asked them to make him a die. With this in his possession he called on a small printer to whom he told the following story.

GARBO said that he was an employee of the Spanish Embassy in Lisbon and offered to bring him the Embassy's printing. He would, of course, expect a commission. As a trial he wished the printer to set up some proofs for a Spanish Diplomatic passport on which the Embassy would judge the quality of his work. GARBO had made a sketch of the layout of the document and produced what purported to be the Embassy seal. After choosing with great care the types to be used and the quality of the paper, he arranged to call back in a few days to collect the proofs. With the document in his possession, his photograph affixed, and his name inserted as the bearer, he returned to Madrid and called at the German Embassy.

EMILIO was away and for the first time he met Fritz KNAPPE-RATEY @ FEDERICO, who was shortly joined by KUEHLANTHAL @ CARLOS. He was given a cold reception at first. He was told that they were extremely busy and that his visit was inconvenient and that in no circumstances should he call at the Embassy in future. Before leaving GARBO managed to whet their appetite by saying that he had ascertained from the British Consulate in Lisbon that he would be granted a visa to go to England. He also took this opportunity of handing FEDERICO his telephone number should further contact be desired. The following day FEDERICO telephoned. They met and GARBO was asked to go over his story and proposition for going to England on behalf of the Spanish Seguridad.

Realizing that he could no longer keep the identity of the notional police agent obscure he decided to substitute him for a genuine agent of the Seguridad, attached to the Spanish Embassy in Lisbon, a certain VARELA, whom he had met by chance on several occasions. This man VARELA, was working closely in contact with the Portuguese International Police, his job was that of Security Officer at the Spanish Embassy in Lisbon. FEDERICO asked GARBO whether he knew DALAMAL well and where he was at present. He replied

that he did, and that he was in England. He proposed to follow him
there. The 5 million pesetas which he claimed were owned by DALAMAL
were supposed to exist in Tangiers. GARBO said he was convinced that
he could persuade DALAMAL to handle the transaction on his behalf
and that he was anxious, therefore, to undertake the mission for the
Spanish Seguridad since he would profit to the extent of 25% of this
amount if he could provoke DALAMAL into allowing him to handle the
transaction with the result that the funds would be confiscated by
the Seguridad. VARELA would receive a similar percentage of the sum
confiscated which was the reason for his inducing the Seguridad to
facilitate GARBO in going to England on their behalf. The urgency of
the matter was impressed lest DALAMAL might negotiate through some
other channel over which GARBO would have no control.

Continuing his story he told FEDERICO that VARELA was trying
to get him a Diplomatic Passport for England and to arrange for him
to be sent to the Spanish Embassy in London as an Honorary Attache
there. VARELA, he pointed out, was a member of the Plantilla, or
professional police and therefore paid by salary, and as such he was
not entitled to any form of commission. In introducing GARBO as an
outside agent for the DALAMAL affair he had done so because he knew
that GARBO would give him half of his commission. If this were
discovered VARELA would be dismissed and thus GARBO's chances of
going to England terminated. It was essential, therefore, in their
mutual interest that FEDERICO should treat this confidence with the
greatest secrecy. FEDERICO seemed to fall for the story.

Three days later they met again, this time at FEDERICO's
instigation, to know whether GARBO had received any news from
VARELA. It appears that up till then the Germans had not been
convinced by GARBO's story. FEDERICO said that if it were genuine
they would be very much interested. He explained that they naturally
had to be extremely careful. He confided to GARBO that there had
been the case of an agent whom they had taken on, and after paying
him monies, they discovered that his project was a myth. He did not,
therefore, wish to be caught a second time.

GARBO, on his return home, thought out the following trick
to convince FEDERICO that he was genuine. On his first journey to
Lisbon he had met in the hotel there, a Spaniard, with whom he had
become friendly, named Dionicio FERNANDEZ. He decided that FERNANDEZ
should unwittingly be made to play a role in his set up. He forthwith
telephoned to FERNANDEZ in Lisbon and asked his assistance in a purely
personal matter. He said he was anxious to get back to Lisbon but
that he was prevented from doing so by his wife who suspected that he
had a girl friend there. He said it would be a very great favour if
FERNANDEZ would send him the following telegram for him to show to his
wife. He dictated the telegram as follows:-

"You must come here urgently. The affair has been arranged.
Signed: VARELA"

As soon as the telegram arrived with the Lisbon post mark he
contacted FEDERICO who read the telegram and put it in his pocket.
The next afternoon they met again. FEDERICO said he had been
instructed to tell GARBO to leave immediately for Lisbon to see
VARELA in connection with his telegram. He gave him 500 pesetas and
told him how he could get more money in Lisbon should he run short of
funds. He went to Lisbon as cover. He did not call on VARELA but made
contact with FEDERICO's people there, from whom he got additional
funds, at the same time proving that he had in fact been in Lisbon.

He returned to Madrid to tell FEDERICO that he had seen
VARELA who had given him instructions for making contact in the
Seguridad where his final arrangements would be made. He said that
VARELA had already laid on all the preliminary arrangements through
the Diplomatic Bag to the Seguridad in Madrid. The Seguridad had
agreed that GARBO should work directly under VARELA on the DALAMAL
case. His passport and final instructions, GARBO said, would be
issued to him personally by the Seguridad. GARBO said he was going,
that day, for his instructions and they arranged to meet the
following afternoon when FEDERICO was told everything had gone
according to plan and the whole affair now settled, GARBO was to
return the following day to collect his passport.

Early the next morning GARBO telephoned FEDERICO in an excited
state insisting on an urgent meeting which could not wait. FEDERICO,
alarmed and furious, agreed to meet him five minutes later at the cafe
opposite the offices of the Seguridad. For some time GARBO had been
holding the forged Diplomatic passport which he had obtained in
Lisbon, awaiting this opportunity. He had affixed his photograph, the
only thing now missing was the stamp of the Spanish Foreign Office
which could not be forged. Having worked FEDERICO into a state of
excitement he decided to give him a glimpse of the passport.

When they met at the Cafe he explained that he had only two
minutes to spare. He said that he had called him in order to be able
to satisfy him that he now had the passport and was about to leave.
He said there was a messenger and car waiting outside the Seguridad
doors opposite where they were sitting, to accompany him with
the passport to the Foreign Office where it had to be stamped.
From there it would be sent to the Spanish Embassy in Lisbon by
Diplomatic Bag. He was to pick it up on his arrival in Lisbon, where
he would travel on his ordinary passport. This, he explained, was
the only moment he would actually have the document in his
possession to show him. He was therefore anxious for FEDERICO to
take the opportunity of seeing it with his own eyes so that any

remaining doubts as to his genuineness should be dispelled. With this little speech he produced the document and, looking round to see that no one was watching, he opened it under the table, giving FEDERICO a chance to inspect it without too good an opportunity to examine it. He immediately folded it up again and put it back in his pocket. FEDERICO was greatly impressed, called him a good fellow, and patted him on the back.

Prior to the meeting GARBO had taken the precaution of getting the son of the owner of the Pension where he was staying to wait for him at the door of the office of the Seguridad where he also had a taxi waiting. Having shown FEDERICO the document he said that it was safer that they should not leave together, volunteering that he should go first. He got up, walked over to the doors of the Seguridad where he was picked up by the young man who was supposed to be his escort. They got into the waiting taxi and asked in a loud voice to be driven to the Foreign Office.

That night GARBO reported to FEDERICO that everything had gone well at the Foreign Office. FEDERICO said that GARBO should delay his departure for a few days, pending the arrival of instructions from Germany. GARBO replied that in that case he would have to telegraph VARELA at the Spanish Embassy in Lisbon to make some excuse for the delay. He drafted out a telegram saying:-

"In a few days I will leave for Lisbon. Signed: JUAN."

Pretending he was in a hurry he handed the draft telegram to FEDERICO asking if he would be good enough to send it off for him. Thus, FEDERICO, had not only seen and confiscated GARBO's telegram which purported to come from VARELA, but he had also despatched GARBO's reply to him. Any doubts which the Germans might have had in GARBO had now been for ever dispelled and their sole anxiety was to give GARBO some sort of rapid training so as to be able to take advantage of his visit to England under diplomatic cover. When they next met GARBO impressed on FEDERICO the necessity, in their mutual interest, of keeping the secret about VARELA and his contact with the Seguridad. He warned FEDERICO that any leakage through him would ruin his cover in England. FEDERICO promised that so far as the Germans were concerned what GARBO had told them would for ever remain a dead secret. He left GARBO four questionnaires which he was instructed to study. Within a few days GARBO had been trained in secret writing[i] and the questionnaires had been substituted by miniature reproductions which he could study at his leisure and conceal on his person when he left Spain.

(i)   See Appendix No. XXXIV.

FEDERICO boasted that he envied GARBO going on this mission because it was not dangerous and was only a job of collecting information as an observer and did not entail the theft of documents or dangerous exploits. To comfort GARBO FEDERICO told him that Luis CALVO, correspondent of the ABC in London was working for them. He also suggested that in case of need GARBO could use the Spanish Diplomatic Bag, as they could arrange for him to be given facilities in this way through one of the Service Attaches. At this GARBO took the offensive, and said he did not wish to know the names or particulars of anyone they were using. He did not expect them to disclose his name to others. He said he preferred to operate alone and the results would prove which of their agents were the best.

At the final farewell KUEHLANTHAL put in an appearance and gave GARBO his last instructions. In England he was to get as much information as possible and try to recruit sub-agents whom he could leave behind when he had to return. He was given cover addresses[i] and money and a warning that he should be careful not to underestimate the British as they were a formidable enemy. He warned GARBO that he should not anticipate a quick German victory as he was personally of the opinion that it would be a very long war. He said that the questionnaires were only to serve him as a guide since all information was of interest. Arrangements were made to make his wife and child an allowance whilst he was in England. GARBO then left Madrid to join his wife and, after making arrangements with his mother-in-law to cover the absence of his wife from Lugo should FEDERICO make enquiries there the GARBO family set out for Lisbon.

(i) See Appendix No. XXXV.

CHAPTER IV.

GARBO IN LISBON AND HIS EXCURSIONS TO MADRID JULY, 1941 - OCTOBER, 1941.

At the time of leaving for Lisbon GARBO had no idea of the adventures and experiences which were to envelop him. His first thought was that on arrival there he would immediately make contact with the British authorities and report on his penetration of the G.I.S. On the other hand he knew from past experiences that it was very difficult to get anyone in the British Embassy or Consulate to take seriously, matters appertaining to espionage. He nevertheless realized that it was essential for him to proceed as far as Lisbon if he were not to be discovered as an imposter by the Germans. In the event of his failing to make successful contact with the British he planned to write to the Germans explaining that he had come up against certain difficulties in Lisbon which had temporarily prevented him from proceeding to England.

GARBO endeavoured to get an interview at the British Embassy and, as he had anticipated, he failed to get a hearing. He promptly realized he would have to play for time and evolved a new plan through which he hoped to get further evidence of German espionage activities against the British.

In Lisbon he contacted his Spanish friend, Dionicio FERNANDEZ, and told him that he was embroiled in a love affair with someone in Madrid with whom he wished to be able to carry on correspondence without the knowledge of his wife. He asked whether, in order to make this possible, he would mind his using FERNANDEZ' name at the Poste Restante in Lisbon for the purpose of receiving letters from the woman in Madrid. FERNANDEZ agreed.

With this facility provided GARBO wrote his first secret ink letter to the Germans which he mailed in Lisbon on the 19.7.41, dating the letter the 15.7.41. In this he said:-

"I left on the 12th byplane and I am staying here with a Spaniard who was recommended to me in Lisbon. This gentleman has put me in touch with an official of the Air Line Company which runs the service England - Portugal. I put forward urgent reasons for sending letters to my wife which he has promised to post in Lisbon without their passing through British Censorship. He charges a dollar per letter. I am assured by the Spaniard, who also sends correspondence to Spain by this method that delivery will be safe and quick. When you receive this, write immediately so that I will have a check on the security and rapidity of this route to guide me for future correspondence. Reply to the name of Dionicio FERNANDEZ (For J.P.) Poste Restante, Lisbon. This gentleman will hand your letter to the English Air Line official. I trust you will not forget my wife."

GARBO did not write again until he received a reply to this letter which reached him some two weeks later, under date of the 29.7.41, signed by Federico KNAPPE, in which he said:-

"I received your letter of the 24th. The method of communication is good and the letter developed well. We await with interest further news. Do not forget to number your letters. Your wife is well and cared for. Kindest regards and good luck."

It will be recalled that his wife was in fact with him in Lisbon. As soon as this letter was in GARBO's possession, believing that he now had more than sufficient evidence to interest the British, he called again at the Embassy in Lisbon, and after difficulty he was interviewed by someone in the office of the Military Attache to whom he explained the purpose of his visit. He volunteered to produce, not only the secret inks used by the Germans for espionage communications, but also the questionnaires which they distributed to their agents. He explained the personal danger to which he had exposed himself in making contact and that after handing over the material which he had promised he would never be able to return to Spain. It would likewise be dangerous for him to remain in Portugal. He therefore proposed that in exchange for the information which he was prepared to supply he should be assisted to get to the U. S.A. The British official said that he would have to take advice in this matter and suggested that GARBO should return some other time. GARBO pointed out that it was extremely dangerous for him to keep visiting the Embassy. It was eventually arranged that the Embassy official should meet GARBO at the English Bar at Estoril at 7p.m. the following evening with another Englishman who would accompany him to discuss the matter with GARBO.

GARBO waited at the appointed time and place but no one appeared. He was extremely annoyed but nevertheless returned the following day to the Embassy to make a final appeal. He was again interviewed by the same official who explained his failure to appear at the appointment by saying that he had been unable to get hold of the other man whom he had hoped to bring along. Eventually, after a lengthy discussion, GARBO left the Embassy in disgust, convinced that there was no one there at all interested in Intelligence matters and decided that if he were ever to make a successful approach to us he would have to venture to Madrid.

GARBO next decided that he would have to cover up the story which he had told FEDERICO about DALAMAL and the illegal currency transactions which he was supposed to be investigating in London. There was always a risk that the Germans might check up on this. He therefore called on VARELA who immediately asked for an explanation of the curious telegram which GARBO had sent him some weeks previously to announce his arrival. GARBO replied by telling him the story of the imaginary DALAMAL and his illegal trafficking in pesetas and stated that he had come to Lisbon specially to discuss this with him. To GARBO's disappointment VARELA replied that there was nothing to be done about this unless DALAMAL one day set foot in Spain. The interview had at least served its purpose since if ever FEDERICO should confront VARELA he would get confirmation that VARELA knew about DALAMAL and had discussed him with GARBO. Any variation in the stories would be accounted for as subterfuge on the part of VARELA.

Towards the middle of August GARBO realized that if he were to get out of the very compromising situation in which he now found himself, and was to make contact with the British it might take a considerable time, and in order to safeguard himself and the successes which he had already achieved he would have to continue to send secret letters. He was confronted with the difficulty that he did not speak a word of English, he had never been to England and whatever information he passed to the Germans would, therefore, have to be imaginary with the result that he would soon be discovered. He therefore decided to comply with the instructions which he had received in Madrid to collect a network of agents. Having recruited his network the information which he would pass over he could always attribute to one or other of his imaginary agents. If an item were one day found to be false he could blame the agent responsible and liquidate him, and thus he hoped to safeguard his channel of communication for a longer period than might otherwise be possible.

By the 17.8.41 GARBO was able to report that, by cultivating friendships with people in sympathy with the Axis, he had recruited a Portuguese named CARVALHO, [i] a resident of Newport, Monmouthshire, whom he had instructed to watch, and report on, the Bristol Channel area, and take note of the shipping and the import and export of war materials. Furthermore, he stated, he had recruited a Swiss subject named GERBBERS, [ii] a resident of Bootle,

(i)   See Appendix No. VII.
(ii) See Appendix No. VIII.

Liverpool, whom he had instructed to cover that important district.
In the same letter he asked for a special ink for intercommunication
between agents. The purpose of this request was that the ink should
provide added Intelligence material to pass over to the British if,
and when, he succeeded in making contact.

In his third letter GARBO gave information about the arrival
of convoys in the Clyde. To safeguard against any possible damage
which his very obscure information might have caused us he stated
that on arrival off the coast of Scotland the convoys dispersed all
over England, that smaller ships, mostly of 2,000 tons or less were
used in these convoys, firstly so that the smaller British ports
could be used for disembarkation after the convoys had dispersed,
and, secondly, because they provided a smaller target against
submarine attack and smaller losses when hits were scored by the
enemy. It is not uninteresting to note that some two years later the
Admiralty directed this same policy for use by double agents when
reporting on the arrival of convoys.

GARBO had already adopted a very verbose style in his secret
letter writing, the purpose of which was to fill his sheet with the
minimum possible information. Up to this time GARBO had been
limiting his letters to approximately one letter a month, and having
filled his letter with this piece of information about the arrival
of convoys and having further information to impart he decided to
write another secret letter under the same date which he planned to
pass to the Germans through his wife, addressing the second letter
to her home in Lugo. He therefore added a postscript to his letter
about the arrival of convoys, stating that the continuation of this
letter was being sent to his wife in Lugo.

The purpose of this was twofold. In the first place he had
decided to go to Madrid to contact the British Embassy there with
the forlorn hope that they might receive him more sympathetically
than he had been received by the British in Lisbon, and secondly he
planned to allow his wife to make contact with FEDERICO in Madrid in
order that she should be able to discover from him whether or not
GARBO had so far successfully deceived the enemy about his mission
as a secret agent in England.

GARBO and his wife proceeded to Madrid. This time he was
armed with the name of a Secretary to the British Embassy in Madrid
which had been given to him by a friend. He called again at the
Embassy and asked to see Mr. THOMPSON. He was told that Mr. THOMPSON
was about to leave on a journey and that he should come back some
days later. This he was unable to do because he realized that it
would be far too dangerous to hang about in Madrid. He therefore
decided to implement the second object for his going to Madrid which
he did in the following way. He wrote the secret letter which he had

already told the Germans they would be receiving through his wife and adapted the cover text to read as a normal letter from husband to wife, adding a postscript that as soon as she received the letter she was to carry out the following instructions. She should proceed from Lugo to Madrid without delay and there telephone a number which he gave her and ask to speak to Don FEDERICO and arrange to meet him at a certain Cafe in Madrid where she should simply hand over the letter to him.

Having rehearsed their plan the wife telephoned FEDERICO who accepted the invitation to meet her. Before handing over the letter she read FEDERICO the postscript saying that she considered it very strange that her husband should make such a peculiar request as to pass on to an unknown friend of his a personal letter which could be of no interest whatever to anyone but herself. FEDERICO, anxious to get possession of the letter, stated that he was a very close personal friend of GARBO and that he had not heard from him since he had left for England and made the unconvincing excuse that he thought GARBO was anxious to let him know in this way that he was well and safe in England. This gave Mrs. Garbo the opening she had wanted. She told FEDERICO that his remark considerably increased her suspicions about her husband since he had told her when he left that he was proceeding to Ireland. FEDERICO now informed her that he had gone to England whilst the letter, she noted, had been mailed in Lisbon. She became highly excited and said that she was convinced that her husband had run off with a woman and that FEDERICO was an accomplice in his escapade. The unfortunate man was at a loss to know how to answer, but he succeeded in extracting the letter from her, promising to meet her again that afternoon when he hoped to be in a position to dispel her suspicions.

FEDERICO returned to the meeting in the afternoon with the secret text of the letter developed. No doubt, having been given approval by his chiefs, he showed her the letter and said that he had to confess that her husband had gone to England on a secret mission for the German Government.

At this she pretended to throw a fit and expressed her fears that he would be caught by the British police and executed. FEDERICO tried to convince her that he was immune from danger. He had gone there with Diplomatic cover and had already started to engage in most valuable work which she should not interrupt. She said that she could not understand how he could be of use to them when he did not even speak any English, to which FEDERICO replied that to have produced results without knowledge of the language of the country in which he was operating was an added proof of GARBO's ability. To pacify Mrs. GARBO FEDERICO offered her a job in the German Embassy in Madrid, or money to live at a luxury hotel, but she refused these

offers, insisting that she wanted to return to her family in Lugo.
She gave FEDERICO a photograph of her child, making him promise to
forward it to her husband whom she feared would never see his child
again, and on this sentimental note they parted.

After reporting the success of her meeting with FEDERICO to
her husband Mrs. GARBO proceeded to join her family in Lugo. GARBO
returned to Lisbon.

On his return to Lisbon GARBO received a letter from FEDERICO
in which he reported on his meeting with Mrs. GARBO and acknowledged
the letter which she had delivered, saying that everything was all
right but he should not send any further letters via Lugo.

By this time FEDERICO had already written to GARBO to say
that his stay in England would have to be a prolonged one and that
under no circumstances was he to return without their permission.
With the realization that he would have to continue until he had
succeeded in making contact with the British GARBO settled down to
invent more reports to forward to his masters. This imaginary
espionage material he constructed with the aid of the following
reference documents which he purchased in Lisbon:-

A map of Great Britain.
A Blue Guide to England.
A Portuguese publication entitled "The British Fleet."
An English/French Vocabulary of Military terms.

He also made use of a certain number of reference books and
magazines in the Lisbon library in which he found advertisements
which supplied the names and addresses of shipbuilding firms,
factories, etc., which he would frequently introduce into his
secret communications and produce remarkably good effects. The
following is one of many such reports which he sent:-

"The firm of SMITH & COVENTRY LTED., of Glasgow who before
the war made machinery have recently enlarged their factory
and are now producing munitions, aerial bombs of heavy
calibre etc.," "The same agent informs me that on the 2nd
instant part of a convoy amounting to five ships of about
2,000 tons each unloaded large cases in the port of Glasgow
addressed to HERBERT ALFREND LTD., of Birmingham which had
arrived from New York."

He would use the Blue Guide for allocating the position of
camps, training centres etc., which he would usually situate within
woods with plenty of camouflage. This sort of information gave an
opening for further expansion:-

"R.A.F. Pilot School situated near Sandwich, the camp is
camouflaged and also used as a landing ground for coastal
defence planes. It is on the right bank of the river Stour at
the mouth of the river just by the cross roads of the main
roads leading to Ramsgate and Sandwich. The aviation camp is
situated directly south of the Monastry of Minster west of
the railroad which goes to Sandwich. The School is situated
near the cross roads at Coopers Street, approximately two
kilometres north of the road which goes west out of Sandwich.
The School is for the instruction of pilots and classes are
given by R.A.F. officers who also maintain a defence service
over the coast and the Channel. I am trying to ascertain
certain details such as the types of planes used and other
materials supplied."

The reports would often be accompanied by drawn plans.
He made use of the book on the British Fleet in the following
way:-

"On the 5th a convoy of 22 merchant ships of medium tonnage,
3 -5,000 tons escorted by destroyers of a modern type,
possibly the JUPITER and the NORMAN passed along the coast
south of Newport in the direction of Bristol. I indicate the
name of these two destroyers because on the 6th I saw sailors
from these ships in Bristol."

His reservation in affirming the names of these destroyers was in
case they should have been known by the Germans to have been sunk.
He made use of the British News Reels and the press to
construct reports, an example of which is following:-

"The agent installed himself near Avonmouth, the merchandise
unloaded was primarily foodstuffs which he gathered from a
remark made by a workman who said 'Fortunately the winter of
hunger is over for us.' The goods came from North America. It
seems that this must be the convoy referred to by Churchill,
or part of it, since the Premier referred to the most
important convoy that had crossed the Atlantic. On my arrival
at Cardiff on the 7th they were still unloading supplies,
Army lorries were transporting the contents from warehouses
in the floating dock to the interior of the country. There is
still a large quantity of goods stored in the docks of
Avonmouth. The goods are camouflaged round the warehouses by
means of painted awnings. Amongst the war equipment unloaded
there were tanks which were uncovered and others in cases

with the markings "TOLEDO" and they were numbered from
T27,508 - T37,558. These numbers were stamped on top of the
turret of the tank. They were all American type tanks and
there were numerous quantities of Army lorries marked GMC/
FEDERAL."

Sometimes GARBO would resort entirely to his own
imagination:-

"All along the Windermere - Barness road and along the road
which follows the shores of the lake to where it crosses the
Windermere - Ambleside road (at a point called the Wood where
there is a small chapel of Santa Catalina) there are camps
full of troops. These forces are excellently equipped and
have modern weapons. They carry out intensive training
exercises daily. They practice landings on Lake Windermere.
They are equipped with numerous amphibious tanks
manufactured in North America. They are similar to land
tanks, they carry 20 men and equipment and have a speed of 25
- 30 kilometres on land and 20 - 25 kilometres in the water.
They have other strange equipment which is a form of ship
which is amour-plated. It has no crew since it is only
constructed for the transport of troops and it is towed by
assault craft. It has a narrow keel and is unsteady until
loaded. They can transport between 50 - 100 men. When loaded
it partly submerges. There is a sort of hatch at the front
and at the back from which the men emerge when making an
assault. The landing is protected by the crew of 12 in the
towing assault craft which is armed with machine guns and
takes up position to facilitate the disembarkation."

It is not so strange, however, that the Germans should have
believed these purely imaginary reports since it was not until we
had had an opportunity to thoroughly investigate GARBO in this
country that we were able to induce the British Services Departments
to believe that GARBO had never before been in the U.K. and that he
had created his reports only through his fertile imagination and
astuteness. On the other hand on careful examination of his letters
composed alone one saw clear indications that he was not conversant
with the habits of this country. A passage from one of his letters
which is worthy of quotation is the following:-

"There are men here (in Glasgow) who would do anything for a
litre of wine."

It was not, in fact, until he came here that he realized that it was not the custom of English labourers to drink their bottle of wine as they do in Spain.

His expense account rendered in November, 1941, is another example. A copy of the form in which it was rendered to the Germans is set out below:-

Railway expenses:-		£	s	d
1.	Journey Southampton - London	0.	17.	04.
2.	" London - Cardiff	0.	66.	06.
3.	" Cardiff - London	0.	66.	06.
4.	" London - Liverpool	0.	43.	04.
5.	" Liverpool - Glasgow	0.	42.	11.
6.	" Glasgow - London	0.	87.	10.
7.	" London - Liverpool	0.	43.	04.
8.	" Liverpool - London	0.	43.	04.

He obtained the fares from a railway guide in Wagons-Lits but he did not risk totalling these strange sums as he was not certain how to convert pence into shillings or shillings into pounds, therefore, he said in his letter that he would send a statement of the balance of his account in his next letter. From then on he rendered his accounts in dollars, the currency in which he was paid and which he understood.

The second letter received from the Germans gave GARBO encouragement to continue with his investigations. In this letter the enemy asked him for certain publications by the Institute of Statistics of Oxford. With the object of providing additional evidence that he was in England GARBO planned to obtain these. He called at the British Propaganda Department in Lisbon, and claiming that he was a "student of statistics" he asked if they would write over to England on his behalf and obtain pamphlets for him. The British Propaganda Department was most obliging, and within a short time handed them to him gratis! In possession of them he was confronted with the problem of sending them to Spain. He considered that the Germans would suspect him if he pretended that he had sent them to Lisbon by the Airways official. He therefore wrote to say:-

"I am forwarding the pamphlets you asked for which I have received after great delay. As anyhow these papers could not have been sent by air mail as they might have aroused the suspicions of the courier I have handed them to a Swiss friend of GERBBERS, my agent at Bootle, who is returning to his country by sea via Portugal."

The rest of the scheme which he had worked out was an elaborate one and he dealt with it over a series of letters. GARBO first wrote to the Germans instructing them to send a representative, whose connection with the German Secret Service should not be known, to collect the books from the Swiss against a letter of authorization for delivery which he enclosed. GARBO next went to a detective agency in Lisbon and hired a man to put up at a hotel in Lisbon in the assumed name of Mr. MAYER, to impersonate the notional Swiss traveller. This name, and the address of the hotel, he had already given to the Germans as the name and address in Lisbon of the good man who was facilitating the delivery of the books. After some delay the books were finally collected by the Germans, though contact between the German messenger and the Portuguese detective, alias MAYER, was never made. The Germans were, however, in a position to be able to check that the character featured by GARBO did appear to exist and had resided at the address given by him.

The balance of GARBO's letters over this period was filled with military reports which attempted to show the strength of the British anti-invasion defence forces all along the South coast of England. He, furthermore, endeavoured to draw the Germans to give him a sabotage mission in England, pretending that he had available a number of suitable characters for carrying out this mission. He hoped that such a mission, if given, would have been additional Intelligence information for us, but to his disappointment they turned down his proposals quite flatly, telling him to recruit his would-be saboteurs for espionage. This, GARBO protested, was impossible since they were nothing better than "thugs " of the lowest type of humanity.

GARBO did, however, recruit his third agent, [i] this time a Venezuelan, a character of some financial standing whom he claimed had been educated at the University of Glasgow, and who was to operate in Scotland. The motive behind this recruitment became apparent when, soon afterwards, this new agent produced a brother [ii] who was about to return to his native land where GARBO envisaged he would be able to assist the Germans by setting up a refuelling base for German submarines operating in the Caribbean near his property at Camana. Unfortunately for GARBO the Germans did not fall for this.

With his growing network and the increasing risk when travelling to contact his agents to collect their reports (GARBO said that all passengers at Kings Cross were controlled and their documentation examined by the police one day when he was returning

(i)   See Appendix No. X.
(ii) See Appendix No. XVIII.

from a meeting with an agent) GARBO managed to get the Germans to
supply him with some secret ink for inter-communication with his
network. This he hoped would be valuable additional Intelligence
material to hand over to us when he finally made contact.

Towards the end of October Mrs. GARBO wrote to her husband
to ask if he would go to fetch her as she wanted to rejoin him in
Portugal. En route he stopped in Madrid where he succeeded in making
contact with a Mr. THOMPSON at the British Embassy. He took with him
the miniature photographic questionnaires which he had been given
by the Germans and offered to produce evidence of the method used
by the G.I.S. when communicating with their agents in the U.K.
Although GARBO produced the miniature photographic questionnaires
he failed to convince THOMPSON that he was genuine. Unfortunately
he told THOMPSON that he was using an alias at the interview and
refused to disclose his real identity until THOMPSON gave him his
assurance that he was interested in the information and would
undertake to protect him for having double-crossed the Germans by
passing this information to him. GARBO was always suspicious that
the Germans had an agent in our Embassy. It is indeed a pity that
note of the questionnaires was not taken at that time. Had they been
examined and exploited it is possible that valuable Intelligence
might have been gained, in particular with regard to the forthcoming
Japanese war. The questions were certainly significant. This can be
realized from the following examples taken from the four pages of
questions which were then in his possession.

> "Does England expect aggression from Japan against British
> or Dutch possessions in the Far East during the course of
> 1941?"
> "What is to be the final objective of such aggression,
> Hong Kong, Singapore, India, the Dutch East Indies or
> Australia?"
> "What possibilities are considered to exist to defend Hong
> Kong?"
> "In what direction is an attack expected in the case of war
> with Japan? Against Singapore, Siam, or the Dutch East
> Indies?"
> "How does England expect to resist Japanese aggression? What
> help is expected from the U.S.A. in case of war with Japan?"
> "Is England in a condition to dispose of, and make available,
> Naval Forces and arms for use in the Far East?"

Even after showing these questionnaires GARBO felt that he
was not trusted and he reached the conclusion that if he persisted
further it would only result in the Embassy staff starting a check

up on him which, if inadequately handled, would have resulted in blowing him. He gained the impression that the person with whom he was dealing was not accustomed to handling matters of this delicate nature and reluctantly decided to abandon hope and collect his wife to return with her to Lisbon.

His wife, realizing GARBO's bitter disappointment decided, without his knowledge, to enter into negotiations with the Americans. She called at the American Embassy in Lisbon where she made contact with the Assistant Naval Attache, ROUSSEAU. She said that she knew a man whom she had reason to believe was a German spy who had a room at the Pension where she was staying. She said she had seen him in possession of what appeared to be unusual documents relating to military affairs, and she pretended she was trying to get further information about his activities which she would eventually pass to the Americans. The meetings with ROUSSEAU, which had started well, broke down due to his having to go to Madrid on a visit.

Meanwhile a further complication arose since GARBO's friend, Dionicio FERNANDEZ, had to leave Lisbon for Spain for family reasons, and thus he robbed GARBO of his only cover address.

To provide a new one GARBO went to a Bank in Lisbon and there rented a Safe Deposit Box in the name of Mr. Joseph SMITH JONES and forthwith wrote to the Germans giving them the brief instructions that they should, in future, send all letters and monies to Mr. Joseph SMITH JONES - J.P. and he furnished them with the box number and the name and address of the Bank. He added that this gentleman would receive the letters addressed for him and that the initials "J.P." which followed the name of SMITH JONES should not be omitted since they indicated that the letters were for GARBO.

This cover address operated from September, 1941, until the end of hostilities with Germany. It was undoubtedly the weakest link in the whole of the GARBO case through which it could have been blown at any moment had the Germans taken the trouble to investigate. Fortunately they never did so. That they did not do so is not so strange as it as first appears, for they had to realize, that from their point of view, an investigation of this nature might easily have led to the blowing of their agent GARBO.

During the development of the case it will be noted that numerous complications arose and great trouble was expended to try to get free from the embarrassment and risks which the continued use of this address entailed. The Germans, however, appeared to have had implicit confidence in the security of this address and the notional courier[i] who was responsible for smuggling the letters by air from England to Lisbon, and we were unable, even to the end, to persuade

(i) See Appendix No. II.

them to allow us to discontinue this channel for correspondence.

At this period the sum of $1,700, with which GARBO had been furnished by the Germans to cover his expenses for the first few months of his work for them was coming to an end and they were not forthcoming in sending him further monies. After repeated requests, small amounts usually of $50 or $100 were periodically enclosed with letters.

The practice which was started by GARBO during the early days, when he was working alone, of sending a statement of his expense account[i] on the first of every month, was maintained during the whole history of the case. An indication of the growth of the case can be observed by comparing the expense account for the four months from July - October, 1941, inclusive, which together with payments to agents amounted to $1,081 with that of the four months, January - April, 1945, which amounted to $22,644.

(i)   See Appendix No. XXXI.

CHAPTER V.

GARBO'S OFFER OF SERVICE IS FINALLY BROUGHT TO THE NOTICE OF M.I.5. NOVEMBER, 1941 - FEBRUARY, 1942.

Towards November, 1941, GARBO's patience and endurance reached its limits and in despair he made application to the Brazilian authorities in Lisbon to immigrate with his wife and child to Brazil. His wife, realizing that to have been forced to abandon his project would have had a very harmful and lasting effect on GARBO who is a man of great pride and character, tried to force the issue with the Americans. She again made contact with ROUSSEAU, who had now returned from Madrid, and promised to bring him evidence to expose the spy about whom she had previously told him. The methods she employed give some idea of her ingenuity.

The Americans had not yet entered into the war and therefore she decided her spy should be engaged in activities against the U.S.A. if she were to make them take notice of her. She opened her negotiations by offering to sell the information for $200,000. The high price was hoped to induce greater interest. She eventually produced the information without any financial consideration. In the first place she produced a secret ink letter written in French, a language which she did not know. She brought with her a bottle of developer which she claimed she had seen used by the spy and proceeded to develop the secret text which read on the following lines:-

> "Agent 172 of Chicago reports that both he and his Detroit agents are awaiting your orders as they now have everything ready to commence sabotage in all the agreed factories at a moments notice."

The letter had in fact been written by Mrs. GARBO in the ink which had shortly before been supplied by the Germans for inter-communication between the GARBO agents. She had chosen to write in French since she realized that ROUSSEAU knew she was unable to speak this language and thus it would tend to convince him of the genuineness of the letter. In order to get the French text she called on a French friend of hers and asked if she would be good enough to draft a telegram for her, pretending that she was sending a telegram on behalf of her husband who was a writer and who was temporarily away from Lisbon.

The telegram read:-

"LECLERC FILS of Paris reports that both he and his Madrid agents are awaiting your orders as they now have everything ready to commence publication in all the agreed journals at a moments notice."

By changing the words LECLERC, PARIS, MADRID, PUBLICATION and JOURNALS she was able to produce the above spy report threatening sabotage. This proved to be the first successful step towards making that contact for which GARBO had laboured so long without success.

Promising to endeavour to obtain further evidence of the spy's guilt a meeting between Mrs. GARBO, ROUSSEAU and a third party was arranged. ROUSSEAU's companion at this meeting was a rather cynical Englishman who was introduced to Mrs. GARBO as a member of the British Intelligence Service.

Mrs. GARBO brought with her one of the miniature photographic questionnaires, a bottle of secret ink and a secret ink letter from FEDERICO as well as the developer. The Englishman unfortunately adopted the attitude from the beginning of the interview that he regarded Mrs. GARBO as an adventuress and that being a man of considerable experience he did not propose to allow himself to be taken in. He spoke perfect Spanish and proceeded to be offensive to Mrs. GARBO to the extent that she left the interview without showing the material she had brought with her. To crown the Englishman's offensive attitude, on her getting up to leave, he brought from his pocket 20 escudos which he put on the table, saying: "Here you are. Take this for your trouble and your fare."

Mrs. GARBO's interviews had so far taken place unknown to her husband and there is no doubt that had he learnt about this incident at the time the case would have been irrevocably lost. The harm created was repaired by ROUSSEAU who apologised for the incident, and eventually Mrs. GARBO confided that the so-called spy was in fact her husband.

It was not, however, until the 15th January, 1942, that GARBO had an opportunity of explaining his whole situation to ROUSSEAU whom he at last convinced that he was genuine. Having once made contact it was only natural that GARBO did not like to take the responsibility of replying to the letters and questions which he was beginning to receive with greater regularity from FEDERICO unless with official guidance, and this was not forthcoming.

Still events failed to move quickly and GARBO was forced to continue to write unaided in the hope that his story would, in accordance with ROUSSEAU's promise, be passed to the British. This unsatisfactory state of affairs dragged on until the middle of March when he was finally introduced to a member of S.I.S. in Lisbon to whom he repeated his long story.

GARBO's case first came to the notice of this Office on the
22.2.42 when P.C.O. Lisbon, who happened to be on a visit to London,
asked, in the course of conversation, whether Apartado 1099,
Madrid, was a genuine German cover address since he was interested
in a case in Lisbon in which this address had occurred. It happened
that this same address was currently in use by a double-agent run by
this Office. Thus the story of GARBO began to emerge. We pressed
that GARBO should be brought to England at the earliest opportunity
as it was clear that he could not hope to continue his present career
indefinitely without discovery unless he were given every
assistance. It seemed a miracle that he had survived so long.

CHAPTER VI.

GARBO'S ARRIVAL IN ENGLAND
MARCH, 1942 - APRIL, 1942.

On the 20th March, 1942, it was proposed to GARBO that he should be
smuggled out of Portugal by ship to Gibraltar and thence proceed to
England by air where his case would be fully investigate. At the
sacrifice of leaving in Lisbon his infant son, and his wife who was
expecting a second child, he accepted this proposition, and after
handing over all his materials to S.I.S. representative in Lisbon,
he was finally smuggled out of Portugal on the 10.4.42, arriving in
the U.K. on the 24.4.42.

At this time GARBO had no idea that CALVO, the German agent
named by FEDERICO in Madrid before his departure, had already been
detained in connection with his espionage activities, and he had
assumed that on arrival here we intended to use him to make contact
with CALVO and discover his activities also that he would be asked
to operate for us on other C.E. work connected with Spaniards and
the Embassy here. He had left Lisbon on the understanding that he
would be allowed to return to his wife within a month, but he
immediately volunteered to carry out any order we gave him on the
condition that if we requested him to continue to double-cross the
Germans under our guidance we should arrange for his wife and child
to be brought over here as soon as possible.

During the course of the preliminary examination, in which he
was most co-operative, copies of 38 letters which he had written to
the Germans between July, 1941 and March, 1942, were examined in
detail and the context explained by GARBO. The copies of the 15
incoming letters and questionnaires were passed to the appropriate
authorities.

By this time we had already begun to suspect that GARBO was
identical with the unidentified V-Mann 372 who had appeared on M.S.S.
as the author of the famous Malta convoy report. On the other hand
there was no reference to this in any of GARBO's letters, but the copy
of one letter No. 39, appeared to be missing. After some reflection
GARBO was able to re-construct the contents of the missing letter and,
as had been suspected, the next turned out to be almost identical with
the unidentified M.S.S. message about the Malta convoy. Some days
later the copy of the missing letter, which GARBO had handed with the
others to S.I.S. representative in Lisbon, was discovered and
forwarded to London, and on examination it was conclusively proved
that GARBO was identical with the unidentified V-Mann, in whom, we had
evidence to prove, the Germans completely believed.

The advisability of using GARBO as a double-agent was put up
to the XX Committee who, at that time, with the exception of the
Admiralty and S.I.S. representatives, did not have access to M.S.S.
material. The majority of the members of the XX Committee, through
not having access to this material, and the GARBO story to date
being so incredible, were not at all satisfied as to his
authenticity or of the advisability of using him. It was over this
issue that it was finally decided that the members of this Committee
should be given access to this material.

CHAPTER VII.

GARBO'S CONTROL. (GERMAN.)

Before proceeding with the story it is perhaps appropriate to devote a few lines to his German control. The GARBO case has been handled on behalf of the Germans by Karl Erich KUEHLANTHAL, former Military Attache in Paris. He has worked under the direction of LEISSNER @ Gustav LENZ @ ELCANO, Honorary Attache at the German Embassy, Madrid, LEITER K.O. Spain, responsible for all Abwehr activities in Spain and Spanish dependencies.

During the Spanish Civil War, KUEHLANTHAL was employed as secretary to ROHLEDER, then chief of the Intelligence Department of the Condor Legion. He is of partly Jewish origin and in consequence was for a while regarded with suspicion by the S.D. and the Abwehr. His partly non-Aryan origin is said to have prevented him from entering the Army but being well connected in Spain and a protege of Admiral CANARIS, his role as Abwehr representative in Madrid was assured. He was created an Aryan at the instigation of his Stelle in Madrid in 1941. He has been described as a very efficient, ambitious and dangerous man with an enormous capacity for work. His efficiency and capacity for work have been proved.

We know that by 1941 KUEHLANTHAL @ FELIPE @ CARLOS assisted by his lieutenants Fritz KNAPPE-RATERY @ FEDERICO and George Helmut LANG @ EMILIO were busily recruiting agents to operate in North Africa, Gibraltar, the United Kingdom and the United States. Of the agents who have come to the U.K., VAN WIJK, the SNARK, CARELESS, PIERNAVIEJA DEL POZA, ALCAZAR DE VELASCO, DEL CAMPO, CALVO and PEPPERMINT have all operated under his orders. Their activities came to an end by the early part of 1942.

By summer 1942 we had, through GARBO, begun to swamp the Germans with information, mis-information and problems. Whether our ever increasing activities were beginning to satisfy KUEHLANTHAL's enormous appetite for work or not is hard to say but it appears that from that time KUEHLANTHAL made no further attempt to send more agents to the United Kingdom.

In the absence of a deception policy we endeavoured to report as much confusing bulk as possible and, in the absence of another objective, to increase our network of notional agents.

We asked for his collaboration and we were given it. As a keen and efficient officer he did everything in his power to supply GARBO with cyphers, secret inks and addresses of the highest grade to ensure his greater security. He was always forthcoming with considerable funds to cover GARBO's expenses in England.

We meanwhile strived to gain KUEHLANTHAL's ever increasing confidence in GARBO. We played up to what we believed to be the German understanding of Spanish psychology as they appear to have conceived it through their association with Falangist Spain. We endeavoured to maintain the initiative throughout the running of the case, keeping one step ahead of the opposition in order to be able to direct the course of the case on the lines best suited to our plans. KUEHLANTHAL was encouraged to regard GARBO as a quixotic, temperamental genius, whom he learned to be cautious not to offend. He came to regard GARBO as a fanatic, prepared to risk his life for the Fascist cause. His characteristic German lack of sense of humour, in such serious circumstances as these, blinded him to the absurdities of the story we were unfolding. Instead he was patient and confident in the ultimate success of his protege.

It was not, however, sufficient to make GARBO a hero in the eyes of KUEHLANTHAL. Until the time of OVERLORD there was little evidence, if any, to show that the German High Command was taking any action on the recommendation of the Abwehr.

It was not until the summer of 1943 that GARBO embarked on his first attempt to pass over operational deception.

Paradoxical as it may seem, the Abwehr immediately showed a noticeable increase in their interest in GARBO and his Madrid control. For the first time we saw evidence that the OKW was beginning to show some regard for Abwehr reports. This confidence chain grew in strength as more organized deception was practiced through this channel. German satisfaction and confidence in GARBO was to some degree apparent in the fact that they failed to make any last minute efforts to penetrate our Security screen prior to the OVERLORD OPERATION.

CHAPTER VIII.

GARBO'S CONTROL. (BRITISH)

The case officer controlling GARBO in London (the opposite number to KUEHLANTHAL in Madrid) had one great advantage over KUEHLANTHAL. Through Most Secret Sources it was possible to confirm German reactions to our work.

It was indeed fortunate that the team of KUEHLANTHAL, GARBO and the case officer in M.I.5. was maintained over the entire period of the case. It permitted a consistency in style and planning. It allowed us gradually to build up the character of GARBO in KUEHLANTHAL's eyes. From our point of view it gave us an opportunity to discover the strength and weaknesses of our opponent.

Just as KUEHLANTHAL found the pressure of the GARBO work increasing and becoming a full time job, we too, in forcing the pace, began to find our hands full.

From the time of Operation STARKEY, in the summer of 1943, the GARBO case became more than a full time job for three members of this Office to manage the routine running and planning of the case. In addition, GARBO himself worked regular office hours. The Germans in Madrid, not only had the work of maintaining their contact with us, which entailed an almost equal amount of work to that which was being done here, but in addition they had the duplication work of operating as intermediaries between GARBO and Berlin. Thus, everything which passed between GARBO and Berlin in both directions, involved Madrid in two processes of encyphering and transmitting to our one. If there was any advantage in pinning down manpower of the Abwehr personnel well placed in the field in exchange for equal manpower employed in our London headquarters it was only considered by us as an incidental one. More important was the consideration that the greater the work we caused them to put into the GARBO case the more they would become conscious of his importance to them.

Gradually they were persuaded to accept GARBO's verbose style until they, themselves, became infected by it. Their communications became longer, more explicit and more frequent. From their first telegraphic message in secret writing consisting of a few lines, they were worked up to the climax of sending us no less than 24 foolscap pages of secret text in one letter. It is true to say that whenever they have been encouraged by us to exert themselves in this way the contents of their longer letters, which occasionally arrived, were always of very considerable counter-espionage value.

CHAPTER IX.

MOST SECRET SOURCES.

Had if not been for the fact that we were able to judge the German
reactions to GARBO through Most Secret Sources there is little doubt
that the case would not have been exploited so extravagantly. In
fact it is somewhat doubtful whether we would have believed the
already incredible story with which GARBO presented us on his
first making contact had it not been that M.S.S. provided us with
conclusive evidence that the essential of his story was true, and
furthermore that the Germans believed him to be operating in England
on their behalf.

The Germans had, in addition to their wireless communications
from Madrid to Berlin, a courier service and it is therefore natural
that during the period of build up and until GARBO was himself
installed with a wireless set, the majority of the information which
was forwarded through GARBO, by letter to Madrid, was not given the
priority treatment of being sent on to Berlin by wireless. However,
during this period, there were enough checks through M.S.S. for us to
be able to judge that all was going well. As the traffic became more
interesting, and from the time GARBO had established wireless
communications between London and Madrid in the early part of 1943, a
great proportion of the traffic was retransmitted on to Berlin by W/T,
even if its nature did not appear to us to be urgent.

Not only, therefore, did M.S.S. provide us with conclusive
evidence as to the degree of success with which GARBO was meeting in
Madrid but it also allowed us to control the accuracy with which his
reports were being forwarded to Berlin and the degree of importance
which Headquarters in Berlin attached to them. Thus it became
apparent that the Madrid control had implicit trust in GARBO's
reports and that Berlin was beginning to recognize the important
work which was being accomplished by the FELIPE Stelle in Madrid. In
fact FELIPE had become our mouthpiece and the problem was no longer
one of building up GARBO in the eyes of FELIPE but of building up
FELIPE in the eyes of the Abwehr, Berlin. If we were to enhance the
Abwehr in the eyes of the OKW it was essential to maintain a high
standard of reports. If the OKW could be made to trust and rely on
Abwehr reports, then it was inevitable that the GARBO network would
provide an invaluable channel through which he would be able to
deceive the enemy.

Whilst it is true that the material provided by M.S.S.
was vital to the success of the GARBO case, the case in turn,
facilitated G.C. & C.S. to provide that very material.

The first code[(i)] which GARBO was given by the Germans for his wireless communications turned out to be the identical code which was currently in use on the German circuits, Tetuan - Melilla, Tetuan - Ceuta, Tetuan - Spartel. As well as by Bordeaux in its communications with three unidentified out stations.

It later became known to us that the Germans were concerned about the security of their cyphers and simultaneously they instructed GARBO to double encypher all his messages for greater security. These were indications of the high esteem in which they held GARBO. Soon they changed their cyphers on the Peninsula circuits with the result that we were unable to read their traffic. The Germans' confidence in GARBO was such that, regarding him as if he were one of their out stations, they supplied him within a few months with the identical type of cypher tables to which they had themselves changed over.[(ii)] Though it cannot be said that the GARBO cypher enabled G.C. & C.S. to read the lost traffic immediately, it gave them the nature of the cypher, without which knowledge, it might have been extremely difficult, if not impossible, to do.

Ironically enough, the Germans, on sending this new cypher to GARBO, sent him special instructions to guard it conscientiously and ensure that under no circumstances should it be allowed to fall into the hands of the British.

M.S.S. revealed that in addition to the great volume of traffic which was being passed through the GARBO channel a still greater volume of entirely imaginary reports was being passed from Peninsula to Berlin attributed to some unidentified V-men of FELIPE (which fortunately came to an end before D Day of OVERLORD) likewise an enormous volume of traffic which was being sold to the Germans by OSTRO, a bogus German agent in Lisbon, all of which, though very ingenious, was entire invention.

Whilst all the GARBO traffic, whenever inaccurate or passed on with intent to mislead, was carefully vetted by the various Service Departments to ensure that the inaccuracies would not be discovered by the enemy, OSTRO did not have these facilities. Thus we were constantly threatened that OSTRO, who was not intent on deceiving the enemy but solely on making money, might, by a stroke of luck, have contradicted GARBO in an issue in which he would eventually prove himself to be right and GARBO wrong. This was not our major preoccupation, and fortunately it never happened. A more real fear was that OSTRO, whose reports were deserving of being discredited, should have in turn discredited the Abwehr to the degree that the OKW would be bound to disregard all Abwehr reports.

(i) See Appendix No. XXXIII.
(ii) "   "   "   "

As the GARBO network grew, the volume and quality of the GARBO information far outweighed the OSTRO reports. We were soon able to discover that in spite of the fact that Berlin questionnaires were distributed simultaneously to both OSTRO and GARBO, the OKW was attaching an importance to the information received through the GARBO channel which they did not attach to the OSTRO information. Through M.S.S. we learnt that RUNDSTEDT himself had appraised a GARBO piece of information as being "especially important" and HIMMLER, shortly after becoming chief of the German Intelligence Services, sent a personal message of appreciation to Felipe in Madrid for the work achieved by his network in England.

Five days after the landing of the Allied Forces in Normandy when, had it not been for Most Secret Sources, we would have felt bound to suspect that GARBO was in danger of discovery for the deception material which he had already passed over in which he assured the Germans that there would be a further attack in the Pas de Calais area, we had the good fortune to read an appreciation of our work which was sent from Berlin to Madrid as follows:-

"Appreciation: The report is credible. The reports received in the last week from the ARABEL (GARBO) undertaking have been confirmed without exception and are to be described as especially valuable. The main line of investigation in future is to be the enemy group of forces south-eastern and eastern England. It would also be especially valuable to learn in good time when the formations which are at present assembled in Western Scottish ports put to sea and what their destination is."

Thus is was possible to continue to utilize GARBO for further deception with a confidence which would otherwise not have been permissible. Not infrequently the questionnaires transmitted from Berlin to Madrid for retransmission to GARBO would reach us through M.S.S. channels before they had been received by GARBO. This enabled us to devote more time to the replies.

Within the GARBO network was a woman agent who was operating from Ceylon, [(i)] passing on her information by secret letters via GARBO in London. With the aid of M.S.S. the course of her traffic from Ceylon to Tokio could be followed. For example, two of her letters dated 1.10.44 and 17.10.44 were notionally received by GARBO in the U.K. early in November and were forwarded by him via his courier on the 12.11.44 to a German cover address in Lisbon. There they were collected by the Germans and forwarded to Madrid by Bag

(i)   See Appendix No. XXIV.

where they arrived in time to be transmitted by wireless to Berlin on the 1.12.44. There, the information appears to have taken some three weeks to go through the machinery of the Intelligence Services before it was handed to Japanese Naval Attache in Berlin who retransmitted it to Tokio under the title "K. INTELLIGENCE (Secret Agent's report.)" on the 23.12.44.

We were able to follow the course of the reports sent by the GARBO sub-organization operating in Canada until they reached their final destination, and likewise those of his agent in North Africa. [i]

We were similarly able to trace GARBO information being passed from Madrid to Berlin, and later from the Japanese Military Attache in Stockholm to Tokio. Other reports of GARBO origin were seen to pass from the Japanese M.A. Berlin, and later from the Japanese Military Attache in Istanbul, Sofia, Madrid and Lisbon.

We learnt that GARBO was awarded the Iron Cross for his services long before GARBO was given news of this himself by Madrid. We also discovered through the same sources that the question of this award became the subject of a dispute as late as December, 1944. A message from Madrid to Berlin at this time relating to this subject is quoted in full as it gives a picture of GARBO in German eyes. (For the purpose of clarity German code words used have been substituted in this transcription by the English equivalent.)

"Re award of Iron Cross II to GARBO and Dr. SCHOENE's discussion in this connection in Berlin. In our message Most Secret 957 of 17/6 we applied for award of Iron Cross II to GARBO emphasizing that he was a Spanish National, but giving as justification the fact that activity of GARBO in England constantly at the price of his life was just as important as the service at the front of the Spanish members of the Blue Division. We were informed in your message from Chief in Berlin of 24/6 that award was agreed to and that the submission of the prescribed proposal had been put forward. On the basis of this information we at this end were under the impression that no difficulties were to be expected in obtaining the eventual award, and this was reported to GARBO, who was at that time, as a result of very great difficulties, in a state of mental depression for psychological reasons. The communication of this news about the award had the expected result and evoked from GARBO a written expression of his special pride at this distinction. Difficulties in maintaining and extending the GARBO network have been

(i)   See Appendix No. XX.

constantly increasing recently, but were mastered by GARBO
with an utter disregard for all personal interests and by
giving all he was capable of. GARBO has himself been in
hiding for weeks, separated from wife and children. The
extraordinary successes of GARBO have been made possible by
his constant, complete and express confidence in the Fuehrer
and our cause. It seems psychologically impossible now to
inform him that the award will not be made without exercising
the most adverse effect on him and his organization. For the
reasons stated please support the award from your end with
all possible means. Would it not be possible to classify
GARBO retrospectively as a member of the Blue Division?
Please report to us by W/T the results of your efforts as
GARBO has already asked for the decoration in question to be
sent to his next of kin to be kept for him.
Ob. KIECKBUSCH I/H SPAIN."

CHAPTER X.

GARBO'S PERSONAL CONTRIBUTION TO THE WORK OF THE ORGANIZATION.

Whereas GARBO had been his own master and entirely responsible for his own decisions during the period that he had operated as an uncontrolled double agent in Lisbon his status was bound to change fundamentally the moment he arrived in England and commenced to operate under the control of this Office. Previously he had been responsible for the entire production and execution of his work. Now he was only to be responsible for the delivery of the finished product, thus the greatest burden of the work was removed from his shoulders. This did not mean that he was to be any less busy or less fully occupied. The volume of his work in fact increased.

In all he wrote no less than 315 letters in secret writing out of the total of 423 letters written by the organization. None were documents of less than some 500 words and some of his letters were compositions of as many as some 8,000 words, estimating the average length of a letter at between 1,500 - 2,000 words. He was responsible for composing the cover text for all these letters which in itself was a considerable task which he fulfilled with the greatest ability. In addition, he produced the final version of some 1,200 wireless messages of an average length of 70 five-letter groups, out of the total of the 1,339 messages transmitted by the organization.

It is not our intention to give the impression that he acted purely as a scribe and that under our control his initiative and skill were suppressed. On the contrary, his entire existence remained wrapped up in the successful continuation of the work which he had so skilfully initiated, and he was allowed to supervise and help develop the unique and fanciful espionage organization which had been the creation of his imagination. He jealously examined the development of the work lest we should chose to pass material to the enemy through his medium which should result in discreditting the channel with which he had supplied us.

We could not have desired a more able or more clear-sighted critic.

In many ways GARBO's personal contribution to the case was handicapped by the fact that he was not in possession of all the material which was available to us. In spite of the great confidence which we gained in him as time went on he was never a member of this Office and thus he was never allowed to share the knowledge of the most secret material which was available here. He was not allowed to know that there were other agents engaged in work similar to his own, or that at times we were implementing, through his channel, plans in which not only other double-agents took part, but in which wireless and other deception weapons were being used. He was, after all, a foreigner who had been in touch with the enemy and although this Office never at any time had reason to doubt his absolute loyalty we were under an obligation to maintain certain Security measures general to the handling of all double-agents. This, in spite of the fact that in 1943 his contribution to our war effort was brought to the notice of the Prime Minister and in December, 1944, his services were brought to the notice of the King, who, in recognition awarded him the M.B.E.

The work to be undertaken was in the main divided into four categories. Firstly, we were concerned with the notional organization. Domestic matters relating to the agents had to be discussed in correspondence with the Germans. The character of each individual had to be built up. One would be represented as capable of investigating a Naval questionnaire, whereas another would have greater aptitude for handling a questionnaire on aviation. The Germans had to be given a clear idea of the virtues or limitations of each member of the organization. It was necessary to explain how they were able to collect their information. Expense accounts had to be kept and submitted monthly to the Germans. The movement of each agent had to be planned. The consistency in style of each of them had to be maintained. Thus we had to portray a character study of twenty-seven individuals, realistic enough to create a clear picture in the minds of the recipients, whilst omitting those details which might control our freedom of action to further model the characters to the form which best suited our interests as the case developed. In particular the fanatical loyalty, the Quixotic temperament and the untiring energy of the chief of the organization had to be impressed.

Together, GARBO and the case officer were made responsible for all these developments of the work, and in the main they were given complete freedom of action.

The second undertaking with which the organization was concerned was that of the counter-espionage Intelligence which could be obtained through the case. The technique here was mostly one of indirect provocation. We were supplied with no less than 26 cover addresses in the Peninsula. They furnished us with four different types of secret ink which they were currently using, we obtained specimens of their miniature photographs and of their micro-photographs. They confided their highest grade cyphers in us and disclosed hitherto unknown procedures for operating clandestine wireless stations. Their questionnaires not only provided

Intelligence for the Service Departments, but acted as cross-checks in our investigations of other cases. This aspect of the work was directed exclusively by M.I.5.

The third category of the work was the passing of information which would help to build up the reliability of the agents in German eyes. Here we were dependent on the Service approving authorities who co-operated in releasing to the organization as much true information as could safely be passed to the enemy without endangering the security of the Services or of operations.

The fourth concern of the organization was to serve as a channel for implementing deception plans. This did not materialize substantially until the last eighteen months of the war against Germany. At this stage, however, it became more than ever essential to maintain the characteristics of the GARBO organization whilst implementing the high grade material which was submitted to us by the Planners.

It is therefore true to say that GARBO personally played a very material part throughout. No matter which category of information we were passing GARBO was responsible for the final text, whenever in Spanish, which had to be an accurate translation of the draft drawn up in this Office on the material passed by the approving authorities, whilst at the same time maintaining the most personal style which GARBO had already created during the period of his uncontrolled work in Lisbon.

In the following summary of the activities of the GARBO network from the time of GARBO's arrival in England it has thus been found necessary to refer to "We" and/or "GARBO" as the operative party at this end, just as reference is made to "The Germans" as the operative party at the other end. "We" and/or "GARBO" should therefore be interpreted as meaning M.I.5, the Service Departments and/or SHAEF, according to the context in which it occurs, just as it will frequently refer to GARBO himself and/or his case officer.

CHAPTER XI.

GARBO'S FIRST LETTERS FROM LONDON AND THE ARRIVAL OF MRS. GARBO IN THE UNITED KINGDOM.

During the last months of GARBO's activities in Lisbon he had been writing with far greater frequency and regularity. That he was unable to write during the period he was in transit from Lisbon to England via Gibraltar was cause for immediate concern on his arrival here lest the Germans should come to suspect his period of silence and fear that he had been caught.

It was therefore essential that, on his resuming contact, now that he was under our control, there should be no change in his style or procedure to arouse the attention of the Germans.

Fortunately he had brought with him stationery which he had been accustomed to use in Lisbon and subject, therefore, to our allowing him to retain his characteristics, there were only two points for concern. Firstly that he would have to write his cover text on a typewriter which he had not previously used, and secondly, we had to ensure that the procedure of mailing letters in Lisbon should not differ from the procedure which GARBO had been accustomed to use.

It had been GARBO's general practice to mail his letters in Lisbon approximately five days after the date-line of his letter. We now had to rely on the regularity of the S.I.S. Bags to Lisbon which were to carry the GARBO secret letters in place of the notional airman courier, and this, as we were to find later, was to present enormous difficulties.

Whilst still in Lisbon, and preparing for the forthcoming breakdown in his communications during the period of his journey to England, GARBO wrote on the 21.3.42 to say that he had been in bed having had a relapse after influenza which had caused pneumonia. He asked the Germans not to mention this to his wife lest she should worry but to tell her that he was away travelling. In his letter No. 39, reporting the sailing of the Malta convoy, which he mailed a few days later he stated that he was still in bed but hoped soon to be about again. (He then left for England.)

The first letter which GARBO wrote after his arrival here was despatched on the 27.4.42 but dated the 12.4.42 and was sent together with another letter dated 21.4.42. In the later letter he said that when he went to hand over the previous letter to the courier he discovered that the airman had left the previous night for Lisbon, and having thus missed the mail they would receive the two letters at the same time. Thus he was able to cover up six days of his period of silence. The tone of the rest of the letters, which contained military reports, did not appear to show any signs of our influence or alteration in style from his uncontrolled letters, in spite of the fact that the information now passed was accurate "chicken food."

By the beginning of May it was decided that GARBO was to continue to operate from England and it was agreed that his wife and child should be brought over. To bring her here was extremely complicated since she and GARBO owned a joint passport which he had brought with him to England. It had unfortunately been stamped by the Immigration authorities at the port of entry in the United Kingdom and could not, therefore, be sent back to Lisbon for her use. Furthermore, it would have been dangerous for her to have travelled on this passport in case it came to the notice of the Germans who believed him to have required it, in addition to his "Diplomatic Passport" when he travelled to England nine months previously, as they thought. To have brought her over to England without notifying the Germans might have been dangerous lest they investigated and discovered that she had left the Peninsula. Therefore it was decided, firstly, to get approval from the Germans for her to come to England, and to smuggle her out of Portugal, leaving the Germans with the impression that she in fact came to this country in a regular way.

GARBO's request to be allowed to bring her here was approved by the Germans, particularly as he had pointed out that he would have better cover if he were living the life of a family man. He said that he had made application for her to get a visa to come to the U.K. with the assistance of a contact in the British Immigration Department and that it was therefore essential they should not attempt to make any enquiries about her in Spain prior to obtaining the visa since any suggestion that she was in contact with Germans would prove fatal to the plan.

GARBO told FEDERICO KNAPPE he would arrange for his wife to contact him before departure when he could give her any material that he thought safe for her to bring over for him. To make it appear as if she had in fact wanted to meet FEDERICO we arranged for her to write him a letter from Lisbon in which she said that as he would observe from the post mark she had already arrived in Lisbon where she had proceeded on the instructions of her husband, in order to pick up her travel papers which were all in order for her to proceed to England to join him. She went on to say that having ascertained she would probably have to wait a long time to get a passage she proposed to visit Madrid and would notify him in advance of the date of her arrival there.

The letter was written two days prior to the confirmed date of her departure and on the day of her actual departure she wrote a second letter to say that she had just received a communication from British Airways to say that a male passenger had cancelled his reservation and in view of the fact that she was accompanied by a young child his place had been offered to her. She proposed to accept this offer to avoid an indefinite delay, and she therefore regretted having to cancel her visit to Madrid. Though they had no time to comment on, or reply to, either letter, they were probably relieved to know she had departed so quietly without the suggested contact.

It appears that this correspondence completely satisfied the Germans and there is no evidence to indicate they ever checked up on her departure in Lisbon.

In due course they were notified by GARBO of her arrival in London.

CHAPTER XII.

THE EARLY PERIOD OF BUILD UP IN ENGLAND.
THE RECRUITMENT OF NEW AGENTS.
PLAN DREAM.
APRIL, 1942 - SEPTEMBER, 1942.

During the first period of GARBO's operations in London we were disquieted by the fact that for a long time we did not receive any letters from the Germans after their letter No. 15 dated 2.3.42 which GARBO received prior to his departure from Lisbon. When their letter No. 16 dated 14.5.42 reached us in due course it was most encouraging and gave us new cover addresses and promises of more money. It stated they had been very worried at the considerable period during which they had received no communications from GARBO and they had therefore not written to him for fear of attracting attention should anything unfortunate have happened to him. They told GARBO he could use the open air mail for corresponding in secret ink should anything happen to the courier system of communication previously used.

It happened, by chance, that a week before receiving this letter we had already, on our own initiative, decided to use the ordinary air mail for sending secret communications.

We pointed out that seventeen letters had been written to them during the period of their silence and since we had had no acknowledgment of these we feared that something might have gone wrong with the courier route and we had therefore decided to communicate by this method. This letter, the first to be mailed in London, on the 20.5.42, was the first concrete piece of evidence that the Germans had so far received to confirm that GARBO was in this country.

We continued to use the ordinary air mail with increasing regularity from this time onwards, keeping the courier alive meanwhile in order to be able to receive their letters and funds.

During the period we did not hear from the Germans GARBO had become increasingly worried that they might have suspected he had betrayed their agent CALVO and that he had been responsible for his arrest. To cover up this point we wrote to say that GARBO had learnt through a contact in the B.B.C. that several Spaniards had been detained on charges of espionage, which was in fact true and known to the Germans, and this had resulted in tightening up of surveyance of aliens in the United Kingdom.

During the early period of his work the standard of his military reporting, though more accurate than it had been, remained

low in category, but meanwhile new contacts were being developed who
might serve him usefully at a later date.

GARBO's Agent No. 3 was allowed to develop as a contact
an N.C.O. in the R.A.F. in Scotland. [i] GARBO likewise became
friendly with an officer in the R.A.F. [ii] with whom he maintained
friendship almost throughout the case. Air Ministry material passed
through GARBO was invariably attributed to one or other of these
sources.

From a C.E. point of view we tried to ascertain the regions
of England in which the Germans were most interested, hoping that
they might thus indicate to us those areas which were not covered by
their agents. We proposed sending the brother of Agent No. 3 to
Northern Ireland with commercial cover. This suggestion was
encouraged by the Germans though he did not make the journey.

We also took on a new agent, Agent No. 4. [iii] We presented
them with the "fait acompli" of having recruited a Gibraltarian
waiter whom GARBO stated he had been cultivating for some time and
had assured himself that he was 100% loyal to the German cause. The
Germans were asked whether they would approve that this agent should
be sent to Hull - Newcastle, Horsham - Maidstone, or Colchester -
Ipswich areas, pointing out that since the agent was a waiter and
there was a shortage of hotel staff, it would be possible to place
him almost anywhere they preferred. The Germans replied that he
should be situated in the Hull - Newcastle area.

We further explored the possibility of getting the Germans to
send money to GARBO through a Bank. We opened a banking account in
GARBO's name and informed the Germans of this fact and suggested
cover for their sending him money direct from Lisbon. We touched on
this point several times during the case and it appears that the
Germans firmly believed it to be impossible to send money through
Banking channels to pay agents without taking a very great risk
which they were not prepared to take in his case.

We had occasion to communicate by telegram in plain word code
but this procedure was promptly stopped by the Germans, who said
that it was extremely dangerous to use any form of telegraphic
communication, and we were instructed never to attempt it again. By
the above, and other indirect means we tried to discover whether the
Germans had agents working in this country unknown to this Office,
and whether they had means of communication which we had not yet
discovered. All the evidence seemed to show that this was not the
case.

(i)   See Appendix No. XI.
(ii)   See Appendix No. III.
(iii) See Appendix No. XIV.

During the days that GARBO was operating on his own he made one serious mistake which should have made the Germans suspect him had he not fought the issue and held his ground rather than retract.

In the original questionnaires which were handed to GARBO before he left Spain the Germans referred to Infantry Regiments and Machine Gun Regiments by numbers, for instance, they told him:-

"Between Bristol and London there are said to be 325 regiments, amongst them 43 motorized Divisions. 38 regiments of light and heavy artillery and 80 regiments of machine guns ...... It is said that the headquarters of the 207th Heavy Artillery Regiment of the 19th Division are to be found at Lewes ..... On the 17.1.41 the 32nd, 37th, 39th 41st, 44th and 45th Infantry Regiments were seen in the region of the north of London marching towards the south. Confirmation of this is required."

It is not therefore surprising that GARBO, knowing nothing at all about the formations in the British Army, when inventing his reports, should frequently have referred to regiments by numbers. There is nothing to indicate that the reference by the Germans to regiments by numbers was inserted in the questionnaire for the purpose of tricking the agent. The Naval, Air Force and other questionnaires supplied at the same time were undoubtedly serious. Some of them came to our notice through other agents. It is therefore probable that the Abwehr, without higher reference, constructed the military questionnaire on the basis of false information which they had received from other agents who were inventing their material. Possibly they had intended to refer to numbered Companies and had inserted the word "Regiment" in error. GARBO, to give verisimilitude to his reports, frequently referred to the 37th and 45th English Regiments, and others whose numbers had appeared in the questionnaire. He also reported (in his invented reports) that he saw the 2nd Armoured Brigade at Dorking.

Just prior to leaving Lisbon GARBO received a letter from the Germans in which they said:-

"You communicate the numbers of the Infantry Regiments seen on your journey to Guildford. Infantry Regiments do not have numbers but names. Therefore your communications are of no value. Please clarify. Likewise your reference to the 2nd Armoured Brigade. We are in possession of information that this is abroad. I await your clarification!"

GARBO, on his own initiative, in the penultimate letter
before coming over to England, replied with a counter-attack. He
said:-

"I am surprised at your announcement regarding the numbering
of Regiments and about the Armoured Brigades. Have you never
heard of the organizations which are known as the War Office
and the General Staff? Nearly a year ago these organizations,
in order to avoid espionage have referred to fighting units
by numbers. These numbers are not publicly known as are the
names. Since in your instructions on my departure from Spain
you referred to these numbers I imagined that you were aware
of them. Thus I and my agents have always endeavoured to
discover the numbers of units which has been no easy task. I
am in possession of proof of what I am now stating and of the
orders which have been issued, one of which I came by during
my travels. Please let me know which procedure you wish me to
follow."

Fortunately this occurred just prior to GARBO's arrival in
London and from then onwards regiments and other formations were
referred to accurately. The Germans did not reply to his statement
in defence of his action until the end of May by when they had
received some of his subsequent letters which seemed to prove his
point. They then replied as follows:-

"Regarding the names and markings of military units: It is
firstly of interest to know the English name of these units
and where possible also their number. If both are not
available give one or the other. It is unnecessary for you
to send us proof in evidence since we have absolute trust in
you. Your sojourn over there continues to be most important
and it is likewise important that you should extend your stay
for as long as possible. I repeat that we here are most
satisfied with your collaboration."

Perhaps this was the first clear indication that it was not
only essential to take the initiative with the Germans to hold one's
head above water, but it was also advisable to take a firm line and
show temperament if ever there were signs of their dissatisfaction.
It can be said that from this point onwards it became evident that
the Germans did not want to lose GARBO at any cost. The more we
dictated our terms the more they co-operated; the more arrogant and
temperamental GARBO became the more considerate they were in
return.

The frequency and length of GARBO's letters increased. We were continually faced with the complications which arose out of having to substitute what had been GARBO's notional courier for the use of the S.I.S. Bag. It was essential to keep the courier system going. Firstly the Germans had said that it was only possible for them to despatch funds by the present method, secondly, we wanted to maintain a channel for passing out documents and, thirdly, the GERMANS has asked GARBO to send them crystals from his gas mask for them to analyse and had we at this stage broken down the courier system they might have suspected.

The possibilities of establishing a new courier system were examined in great detail but never, at any time during the case, was it possible to work out a channel which, on examination, was found to be more secure than the one already in use.

To justify his being able to pay an increasingly large network of agents it was absolutely essential that we received regular payments from the Germans. Had it only been for this consideration it was evident that the courier system had to be maintained in spite of the increasing risk and suspicion which was being provoked by the irregularity of the service.

Our difficulties encountered in using the S.I.S. Bag arose in the following way:-

The essential was that the courier should never be represented as being both here and in Lisbon at the same time. The date on which GARBO's letters were mailed in Lisbon established the courier's presence there. Supposing the courier established himself as having been in Lisbon on the 20th of the month, and the Germans from their records knew that they had delivered money for GARBO at the courier's Lisbon cover address, on the 19th of the month, it was inevitable that he should have collected the incoming letter. In fact the incoming letter had to be forwarded by Bag. These were extremely irregular and frequently delays of more than two weeks occurred between the date of deliveries by the Germans in Lisbon to GARBO's cover address, and the receipt of the letters here. It was too dangerous to acknowledge receipt of these letters until they were in fact in our possession and had been examined. Meanwhile we were writing out at the rate of two and, sometimes three, letters a week, and it became almost impossible to co-ordinate the acknowledgment of incoming letters and the mailing of outgoing letters, which were sent both by ordinary mail and by courier, on account of the irregularity which were being experienced in the S.I.S. Bag service. The irregularities and change of procedure had to come to the notice of the Germans, with the consequent risk that they might decide to check up on the courier's sudden change of habits with fatal results.

We therefore decided to take the initiative by complaining about the courier's behaviour before they had an opportunity to do so, and to threaten to break down this means of communication which we already knew the Germans were most anxious to maintain. We complained about the erratic behaviour of the courier, stating that some letters had taken as long as three weeks to arrive, and we inferred the courier was no longer taking interest in this mission and that we would have to prepare to rely solely on the ordinary air mail.

By chance our letter crossed with one from the Germans to us in which they likewise complained of the irregular deliveries. It was not until the following year, however, that we broke down the courier service, but the break was only a temporary one because circumstances commanded his going back into service. By greatly reducing the frequency of sending courier letters and relying more on the ordinary mail, and later the wireless we were able to overcome many of the complications in co-ordinating the receipt and delivery of letters by courier.

The gas mask crystals, for which we had been asked, were specially prepared for the German analysts, and were concealed in a tin of Andrews Liver Salts, and forwarded by courier to an address in Lisbon which had been specially provided by the Germans for the receipt of parcels. Taking advantage of this consignment we enclosed our first long letter which was typewritten, and concealed in the same tin. This letter opened up a new chapter in the GARBO case, not only because it resulted in establishing wireless communications, but because it gave the Germans the first picture of GARBO's life in England and his unusual personality.

The following is the full text of the letter:-

"My dear friend F....
I am taking advantage of this opportunity to send you a long letter written on the typewriter which deals with my situation here. For a long time I have been wanting to communicate in detail with you, and if I have not done so it has been in order to avoid sacrificing more important information, and if it had not been for the present opportunity I would have had to have written in secret letters.

First I want to speak to you about your unnumbered letter of 5.8.42, the last to have reached me. In this you shift the blame for the irregularity in the sending of funds to the delay in the delivery of letters via Smith. You are to some extent right but I am not completely in agreement with this theory. What would you do if I had not organized this service? How would you have sent me money?

You must understand that if I have a courier it is more than anything else through great luck, as he has not only been the medium for the continued flow of correspondence between the two of us but through being able to use his services I have been able to organize secret service system which I can say with satisfaction is probably one of the best and safest which can be found and I do not believe that anyone in my place could have organized it better. Although I also admit the irregularities which have occurred I cannot terminate this service with him just for having received my money with some delay, as I consider it is more vital for my security in the question of receiving your letters than for the letters which I am able to send to you. As I am convinced that I do not expose myself to any risk in the letters which I write to you, even if I send them by ordinary mail as since I give a false name and address for the sender, and the letters are written by typewriter on common paper and envelopes, I am certain that the English police are not sufficiently able to discover the origin of the letters. I have also taken the precaution of changing, from time to time, my typewriter which is hired, and I am certain that even if the police should ever have some suspicion they would never be able to have sufficient proof to take any action against me. If I have made an error in all the work I have done it may be in that I have not sufficiently estimated the dangers of the Spanish censorship. Nevertheless, I think that the precautions which I have taken with regard to this are evident, since the proof exists that of 67 letters of which you have acknowledged receipt, only one, that is the letter No. 61, has been missing. Not enough time has elapsed to suspect that letter No. 66 is lost. The case of the loss of the letter No. 61 leaves itself open to much speculation. One of the possibilities is that the addressee has stuck to it.

Now as to the question of the letters which you sent me, this is a particularly difficult matter, as before leaving Madrid you assured me that the ink which I was to use was impossible to discover, but this is not the case with the ink which you write to me here with, as this is discovered with nothing more than the vapour of ammonia. Should the English censor test the correspondence from the Continent they would easily find the ink, the consequence of which to me would be that I would have to pay for it with my life, a very serious matter. Therefore, you can imagine the interest which I have to preserve this courier. In case Smith Jones should break down do not on any account write to me in your ink by ordinary mail. I think it advisable that you prepare for this emergency be sending me instructions as to how to develope another ink which you would use in this case, or that you find another means of sending me my letters, naturally advising me with the necessary advance notice.

With regard to the question of money, you know precisely from expenses in the extract of accounts which I have been sending you to date, the amounts I need. I do not therefore see why I have been made to suffer and take risks through lack of funds during the past months. You know how much my agents charge per day and approximately the expenses they incur in bonuses and incidental expenses, therefore it is extremely easy to calculate in advance what my requirements are for each fortnight. Therefore I feel that the responsibility for my not having received funds for at least a month ahead is only on your shoulders, as you must have thought of the possibility that one day the courier would be transferred, or that for some other reason he would not be able to continue. What would my situation have been then? All this has worried me a great deal and I want you to know that if it were not for the esteem which I feel personally for you, which I feel you reciprocate, as well as the interest which I have in helping our cause for which I have fought for three years during our war, and continue to fight for, though in a more responsible position in order to terminate this plague of Reds. I must tell you that in all sincerity, and as friend, that I would have returned to Spain some time ago.

Since my wife and child have been with me I am rather happier but at the same time I consider that now, less than ever must I expose myself to useless risks which are in our power to avoid if we study well our work with anticipation and caution.

You ask me to notify you in good time if some day Smith should definitely break down so that you will be able to negotiate with a Bank in Lisbon to be able to send me money. How, my dear friend, do you expect me to notify you in advance if the poor man should die on one of his flights, what would I do then? I think that I have already spoken to you a lot about this matter in various of my letters. I think that you should start to assume that the courier Smith no longer exists and arrange through a Bank to make the transfers. Already from this you can have complete confidence that I will maintain the courier as long as possible. I am also trying to establish another route, but for the present I do not see any possibility of success.

I am writing to you as a friend and therefore I ask you to forgive me if there are passages which you find unpleasant in this letter, but I have been passing through a long period of nervous strain which affects one's morale due to the responsibilities and delicacy of the work. You will certainly understand the reason why I always state that I am not to blame as I think that it is up to you to relieve me of this preoccupation and think out and arrange these things yourselves. You are the experts and have your organization worked out. I have often wondered whether you are satisfied your end with my class of work, as in spite of some comforting letter which you sent me once in a while, I begin to suspect that they are intended to pay me compliments. If this were so it would greatly disillusion me for my work as I am only here to fulfill a duty and not for pleasure. You do not know how homesick I sometimes feel for my own country. You cannot imagine how miserable life here is for me since I arrived. Since I arrived I have made a point of avoiding all contact with Spanish society or individuals, this in the interest of our work. My Catalan character does not adapt itself to casual friendship more so when it concerns Spaniards who talk through their arse and compromise one for less than nothing.

I have been thinking a great deal about the future, with the result that I propose to you the suggestion that Agent No. 3 should get in direct communication with you as a precaution against any possible unforeseen eventuality and (at the same time to help decentralise my work) the work that I have done would not be uselessly lost. This is precisely what you told me to do when you gave me instructions before I left Madrid. I think that I can now do so and I await your orders.

I don't know whether you are well informed on the situation here with regard to foreigners since they cannot remain here indefinitely unless they are political refugees. It has therefore not been without considerable difficulties that I have been able to overcome obstacles to remain here for some time past now. Still I do not know whether I will be able to prolong my stay and if it were not for the arrival of my family my difficulties would certainly have been more serious. My family being here helps me to some extent as my wife, is quite clever, she is liked for her vivacious character, and is better able to handle these matters than myself.

With regard to the question of the wireless about which you asked me for further explanation, I will take advantage of this long letter to give it to you.

A friend of the Gibraltarian who is an expert and amateur in wireless[i] knew that in Soho (an international district of London) there was for sale a transmitting apparatus which an amateur, who used to transmit without a permit before the outbreak of war, has sold. When the Government ordered that all transmitting apparatus belonging to amateurs were to be called in and licences taken away this man decided to sell his set clandestinely as he had no further use for it.

The present seller is a friend of the Gibraltarian, an individual who is mixed up in the Black Market, and he knew that it had been for sale for two years or more because it is a difficult thing to handle and cannot be offered to an unknown person for fear that the buyer might be an agent provocateur. They ask $350 for it.

The sellers, it happens, were wanting foreign currency and as the Gibraltarian knew that I possessed dollars he let me know about it.

The friend of the Gibraltarian says that it can easily be installed.

According to what they told me (I understand absolutely nothing about wireless) the man that used to use this apparatus got into contact easily with stations all over the world, since the apparatus has very powerful valves and transmits on 40 metres. He assured me that this wave is good. As I happened to notice that this wave is marked on the radio of the Pension I said that it seemed to me dangerous to use it, but according to the reply I was given, the wave cannot be got on an ordinary receiving apparatus. We would only have had to purchase a receiving apparatus for communications, which, according to him can be purchased second hand without difficulty, and costs approximately from $200 - $300. Then there would have existed a complete installation for receiving and transmitting. The organization was the following: I did not know either the seller or the friend, as I had everything arranged so that the friend of the Gibraltarian should transmit and I would pass coded messages to him through Agent No. 4. The friend was agreeable to doing the transmission secretly, thinking that he was working for the Spanish Reds. He was to charge £3 per transmission, guaranteeing him a minimum of £6 a week whether he transmitted or not. I, as I say, did not know anyone, because having a code with you which I had intended to ask you for,

(i)   See Appendix No. XV.

any urgent information there should have been would have been transmitted in cypher. In this way the man who transmitted would never have been able to discover the contents of the message. We would have been able to have had wireless communication on fixed days at fixed hours.

Against the possible danger of discovery through any misfortune, something which I do not think feasible, the man who transmitted would quite naturally be detained and would confess the truth (that is to say what he believed to be the truth) and would denounce his friend, Agent No. 4. Then if No. 4 were interrogated by the police instead of indicating me he would give the name of an actual person who, according to him, is an agent of Negrin who works in Soho doing propaganda and working as a watcher on behalf of Negrin against our people. As this person is known for what he is by the Police, and as the Agent No. 4 would confirm and indicate this individual as the author of the transmissions with the result that the truth (i.e. the lie) would be confirmed. Although, as is natural, Negrin's man would deny everything, I do not think the Police would do much about it as they would think that his denial was to escape from taking the responsibility. Anyway it is somewhat difficult to explain by letter so that you should understand the matter well, but I have already told you, and I now repeat, that everything had been arranged in such a way that it would have been impossible to discover the originator of the business. I must tell you that I would not have contacted the Agent No. 4 to give him the messages as all this I had arranged so that if the Police should have followed him they would not have discovered me.

In conclusion, as the matter would appear to be a clandestine business in favour of the Reds the Police would not make much fuss about it and all that would happen is that Negrin would be discredited. I can only tell you that I had this work as fully prepared and well studied as I have organized each one of my present agents. The only thing which I would have needed was a good and very safe code, this I had hoped you would have sent me.

Believing that at this time I would receive money from you in some quantity, I told the Agent that he should reserve it and that I would pay a deposit of $200 within eight days. As the money did not arrive I was put in an awkward position with them, and so as not to tell the true reason I said that I had studied the matter and that it did not interest me. Now, if you wish me to open up the question again I will only do so when I have available the funds here so that if it should materialize I would be able to pay cash.

In order to find out the present situation after receiving your letter, I asked Agent No. 4 quite casually if the apparatus was still for sale and he answered that he thought it was. In case you should decide that this method of communication should interest you, you will have to send me a code, explaining in detail how it works, for as I have told you, I don't understand much about it. You could send me the code in secret ink written in a book, or any other way well camouflaged, through Smith.

Please let me know if it is easy to acquire the medicine in which I send you the crystals and this letter. I told the courier that it is difficult to find this medicine in Portugal, and that I was sending it to a poor old woman who was ill with liver trouble. Now if this medicine should exist I will have to make some excuse, if not I shall take advantage of being able to send more packets of the same to the same sick party, if ever I should possess some documents or object which was impossible to send by mail.

So that the courier shall not suspect anything I will do up the packet and seal it in front of him, saying that as it is urgent to get it to her, and she is very ill and has asked for it by telegram, I would be grateful if he would send it personally as soon as he arrived by registered mail and therefore I had sealed it. Alternatively, I would prefer that he should have it delivered by a messenger giving him a good tip which I would refund to him when he returned.

I will take every precaution to ensure its safe arrival, at the same time, avoiding that he should take it personally as I do not know what sort of house it is nor who lives there.

Regarding what you told me about changing the paper and envelopes I am in complete agreement with your instructions. As proof that I have been worried about this is that some time ago I told the Gibraltarian that he should get his friends who are serving in hotels and restaurants to get me some sheets of paper from the room, if they could, as in the writing rooms they only supply very small sheets. This I did so as to be able to use the paper to write to you.

I hope you have received the first trials with this paper. Tell me if it came out well as I shall continue to use the same, as well as paper from other places. If I have not brought this matter up before it is because you told me in a recent letter that I should continue to use the same paper and this I have done, but I think that what we have both considered is the best course.

With regard to your notification that I should transfer Agent No. 4 to Hull - Newcastle, I must tell you that I have never received this in any of the letters which you have sent me, undoubtedly you intended to tell me to do this but overlooked doing so. I have taken note of this and will endeavour to find him work there.

With regard to addresses, you should send me more. If you give me more addresses in Portugal we can avoid loss of days through the Spanish Censorship, as from time to time when I have an interview with some agent he gives me more detailed information and naturally I am only able to transmit the more interesting passages in order to avoid having to send you a lot of sheets.

I do not wish to end this letter without sending a Viva Victorioso for our brave troops who fight in Russia, annihilating the Bolshevic beast.

I have complete confidence that my mission here cannot last very long now because victory must soon be ours. If, on the other hand, the English open a Second Front I am quite certain that you will receive them properly. I am proud to be able to contribute from here to your efforts by informing you on matters which may contribute to hasten the defeat of our enemy.

With many cordial greetings to all my friends, and in particular to you, from your friend and comrade who is always at your orders,

(Signed) J."

This letter undoubtedly made an excellent impression and after its receipt remittances were forthcoming with greater regularity and in larger quantities; their letters became more frequent and extensive, and in consequence their questionnaires became more interesting. They frequently conveyed their expressions of high satisfaction for the work we had accomplished, and went to pains to try to boost up GARBO's morale and to encourage him as much as possible.

As cover for his espionage activities we stated that GARBO had been doing free lance propaganda work for the B.B.C. and Ministry of Information. In this way his entre into British Government offices was provided, not only to build him up, but to serve as a valuable source for deception at a later stage.

By July, 1942, the Germans had already become apprehensive as to the possibilities of a landing based on Great Britain and GARBO was instructed to concentrate on obtaining any information in this connection which they classified as of "vital importance."

The plans for Operation TORCH (the landing in North Africa) were already being considered insofar as they would affect agents, and it was decided that sooner or later Agent No. 2, who was unfortunately situated in the Liverpool area from which the main task force would embark, should disappear from the picture. For him to remain there and fail to notice the preparations and the final embarkation would have blown, not only the agent, but GARBO's whole network; if he were transferred to another and obviously less important area during this period it would have looked suspicious. Pending the working out of a final plan for disposing of this agent he was made to cease sending in his reports to GARBO. Worried by the non-arrival of his reports GARBO went to visit the agent in Liverpool. He discovered that the agent had been taken seriously ill and was about to undergo an operation and would not be able to report for some time. GARBO accordingly informed the Germans of this and they replied authorizing GARBO to continue to pay him during his period of illness, on the basis that the agent would repay them in work on his recovery.

To compensate the loss of this agent three new characters were developed.

The first was a well placed British official in the Spanish Department of the Ministry of Information. This character, who was later given the symbol J(3) [i] was represented as being a perfectly loyal British subject who, believing GARBO to be a Spanish exiled Republican whose heart was as much in the British war effort as was his own, saw no reason why he should not discuss current, though confidential affairs with GARBO.

We told the Germans that GARBO had written a propaganda leaflet of some 24 pages on the morale and high spirit of the citizens of London, which material was supposed to have been used by the British Press service in the Peninsula. It was not, therefore, surprising that J(3) should have introduced GARBO to his friends in the Services who, on the strength of the introduction, spoke freely in GARBO's presence.

As time went on and J(3) grew more attached to GARBO, he gave him access to documents and material which were at first relatively innocuous by nature. But with the growing importance of the Ministry and the passing of time, the nature of the documents became more and more confidential. By the time of the preparations for invasion in 1944 it did not appear strange that GARBO should have been able to see documents of a "TOP SECRET" category.

(i) See Appendix No. IV.

Preparations were considered for the build up of SOLO I (a deceptive threat against Norway) which was the cover plan for Operation TORCH. It was in this connection that Agent No. 5, the brother of Agent No. 3, was recruited as a full time paid agent. It will be recalled that the Germans had been offered this man to operate in Northern Ireland, in which project they had shown a keen interest. It appeared from their reactions that they probably had no agent there and as we had no particular interest to give information about Ireland we created some difficulties in getting him adequate cover to make the journey at that time. Instead he was sent to join his brother in Glasgow with whom he was put to work for a period of training and, when more experienced, he was sent to the east coast of Scotland to report on activities there whilst Agent No. 3 continued to report on the Clyde area.

Thus we eliminated our agent in the Liverpool area from which the main task force for TORCH was to embark, and provided two agents to cover Scotland where the forces which were to threaten Norway were represented as going into training.

Within a few weeks we had recruited another agent to whom we had referred in vague terms in earlier traffic. He was the person who was represented as having introduced GARBO in the first place to the Ministry of Information. We represented him as a far higher grade agent than any we had previously recruited, he was a South African, a first class linguist who had contacts in other Government Departments, and above all he was violently anti-Russian. We did not know how long we could sustain this agent for fear that after TORCH the volume of our traffic would have to be considerably reduced owing to lack of any constructive plan for reporting. We therefore prepared the ground for him later to be able to disappear from the network by saying he was already looking for an opportunity to go abroad. This agent was given the designation of Agent No.6.

He was believed by the Germans to be working for them for ideological reasons. GARBO had promised him that after the German victory he would recommend him for a high post in the New World Order which was to follow, he did not, therefore, accept any remuneration for his work. During the period of build up, and prior to TORCH, Agent No. 6 did not play a very active role.

At the request of I.P.I. we attributed to Agent No. 6 a conversation held with the Secretary of the "Indian Congressmen in Great Britain" which was aimed at making the Germans suspicious of SUBHAS BOSE who was then in Germany, and was about to be sent by the Germans to the Far East to assist the Japanese to stir up trouble in India. We provided the Germans with a document to support our story that when once BOSE contacted the Japanese it was his real intention to try to stir up the Indians to eliminate all classes of European

influence in Asia, and thus it was his proposal to double-cross the
Germans in favour of the Japanese. It is known that this plan met
with no success though it did not appear to discredit the agent in
any way.

Agent No. 6 served a useful purpose in connection with an
operation known as, PLAN DREAM.

To pass from the notional to the factual, it was reported to
this Office by a C.E. agent, operating in Spanish circles in London,
that Leonardo MUNOZ, the Assistant Military Attache of the Spanish
Embassy was endeavouring to negotiate the illegal transfer of funds
from this country to Spain.

The Assistant Military Attache, who was shortly to return to
Spain as a Diplomatic courier (it was at that time the custom in the
Spanish Embassy to send a member of their staff each month to Spain
to take the Diplomatic Bag) had been approached by some Spanish
fruit merchants in London who represented a syndicate of merchants
which had available some £30,000 in cash in this country which they
wanted to transfer to Spain. The fruiterers told the Assistant
Military Attache that if, during his travels, he could find a buyer
for the funds already in the U.K. they would be prepared to sell
their sterling against payment in either pesetas or escudos in Spain
or Portugal. He was promised a commission for his services Due to
the delicate source of this information and the fact that it would
have been virtually impossible to control an illicit transaction of
this nature it was decided to exploit the situation in favour of the
GARBO case.

Our C.E. agent was introduced to a member of this Office,
whose identity and occupation were not disclosed even to the agent,
and claiming that he was the representative of a big British
Insurance Company which had frozen funds in Spain, he asked to be
put in touch with the Assistant Military Attache, stating he would
be interested in this business. The agent was given to understand
the Bank of England was going to close a blind eye to the transaction
which we had brought to their notice, provided it was conducted in
the interests of an important British firm. A meeting was arranged
between our Officer (the Insurance agent) and the Assistant
Military Attache. After complicated negotiations a price, which
was exaggeratedly in favour of the fruit merchants, was finally
agreed upon. Our Officer used the alias Douglas WILLS in all his
negotiations. Pending the completion of the transaction the
Assistant Military Attache, on behalf of the fruit merchants,
agreed to deposit the sterling in cash with CHARLES RUSSEL & CO.,
solicitors (a member of this firm was at that time also an officer in
this Department) who would act as stake holders pending completion
of the transaction. WILLS explained that in order to make available

the peseta equivalent in Madrid he would need some secret means of communicating with his office there. It was agreed that the Spanish Attache would carry a letter in the Spanish Diplomatic Bag which he would hand over to WILLS' nominee in Madrid as his authority to receive the payment.

Having completed these arrangements we put the proposition to the Germans in a GARBO letter which summarized the facts almost as they had actually taken place. He said:-

"The following possibility exists for you to have available sterling funds in Great Britain for my future payments or other expedients of the service. The matter has been dealt with by Agent No. 6 who has up to the present been changing my dollars since I cancelled the instructions to courier Smith who in the past used to change them for me in Lisbon. Arrangements have already been made and only your immediate approval is required to complete. A Spanish fruitmerchant in London is prepared to exchange money which he had deposited here against peseta payments in Madrid........I have succeeded in getting his price down to 100 pesetas to the £1. It concerns the sale of £5,000 in London. The transfer can be effected immediately in the following way....The seller has deposited this money in sterling notes with the lawyer CHARLES RUSSELL & CO., of London who is acting as stake holder. As soon as you approve the operation the sterling will be handed over to me after deducting the expenses of the lawyer. I will thennotify you by telegram the address of the fruit merchant's nominee in Spain to whom you are to pay the pesetas...and I will sign the telegram Douglas WILLS. Whereupon you must immediately pay the sum of 500,000 pesetas to the person at the address in the telegram. Agent No. 6 has started the business with the fruit merchant, representing himself as the intermediary of an Insurance Company which has branches in Spain and which possesses there a deposit of three million pesetas which they wanted to get out of that country......The transaction can be carried out without risk of any sort and I do not enter into the business directly......."

The transaction eventually took several months to materialize. In the end we were able to "plant" on the Attache a secret letter from GARBO to the Germans which, in the cover text, contained the password to authorize the handing over of the pesetas.

GARBO announced to the Germans that the password and secret ink letter would be carried by a Spanish Diplomat to Madrid and

warned them it was important that the person selected by them to
attend the meeting to hand over the money should not be compromised
as connected with them since the Spanish Diplomat had no idea that
he was carrying a secret ink letter, neither had he the remotest
suspicion that the transaction was in any way connected with the
Germans. Though we did not name the Spanish Military Attache we know
they ascertained this.

Thus they had, for the first time, an opportunity of
witnessing something tangible in the GARBO organization. They had
proof of GARBO's ingenuity and of his ability to be able to engineer
even a diplomat to work unwittingly on their behalf. It may well be
that this incident helped to convince them of the plausibility of so
many other fanciful aspects of the GARBO case which were to folow
and to accept the many incredible things we were later to ask them to
believe, even without such material support in evidence.

All subsequent PLAN DREAM transactions were based on this
procedure and were carried out without incident, though we were
later successful in cutting out the Assistant Military Attache and
were able to deal direct with the fruit merchants. When the officer
using the cover name of Mr. WILLS was eventually transferred
overseas we were able to substitute him for another member of this
Office who, in the role of a junior member of WILLS' staff,
continued to conduct the operations without arousing the suspicion
of the fruitmerchants in any way.

CHAPTER XIII.

ORGANIZATIONAL CHANGES.
IMPLEMENTATION OF SOLO I.
OPERATION TORCH.
THE LAUNCHING OF THE ANSON.
GARBO AND THE MINISTRY OF INFORMATION.
AGENT NO. 6 LEAVES FOR NORTH AFRICA.
GARBO'S RED DOCUMENTATION.
SEPTEMBER - DECEMBER, 1942.

In September 1942 other organizational changes were made. GARBO was authorized to give his agents supplies of [...] ink so that they could correspond direct to cover addresses in the Peninsula which would be supplied to each of them for their exclusive use. GARBO was to instruct them in the method of writing. Agent No. 3 wrote his first secret letter under GARBO's supervision on the 23.9.42, this was forwarded to the Germans together with a GARBO letter. The cover texts were typed in English. An officer was appointed to act as scribe for this agent and his style was allowed to develop in the cover text and in the method of adapting the material which was supplied for the secret text.

In the early days of the case, partly with a view to padding out the letters and also to protect himself in the event of a piece of information being proved inaccurate, GARBO had gone to great trouble to qualify the source of his information. For instance he would say: "Whilst Agent No. 3 was travelling in the area of Troon he stopped in at a pub where he got into conversation with a soldier who had been drinking rather heavily, through whom he was able to discover the following information......" This procedure involved a great deal of work and also limited the type of information which we were able to send. The Services Departments were by now supplying us with information which they were interested to pass over and in many cases it became extremely difficult to think out a plausible way in which the agents could have come by the information. At the same time the Germans' confidence in GARBO was steadily increasing and they were urging him to curtail the lengthy explanations which he had been accustomed to submit together with his reports.

We therefore decided to change our style of reporting and we notified the Germans that we would in future simply submit our information together with one of three classifying prefixes A, B or C. "A" would indicate that the information was the result of personal observation by an agent; "B" that the information was obtained through a third party, indiscretion or overheard in conversation; and "C" would indicate rumour or public opinion. Each piece of information would carry with it the symbol of the agent responsible for the report and the place of origin. Thus, a report commencing: "1(A) Avonmouth" would mean that the report was the outcome of a personal observation made by Agent No. 1 whilst in Avonmouth. Care was taken, however, throughout the running of the case to put into categories "B" and "C" a fair proportion of information which was wholly accurate and of a nature which would later be checkable by the opposition. Thus, it became dangerous for them to attach too little importance to reports in these categories. It should be pointed out that the great majority of the reports were category "A" reports.

At this time we started to develop the reporting of insignias seen on British and American troops and occasionally to identify them. In this manner the way was prepared to be able to report on the build up of the Order of Battle of Allied troops in the U.K., though this was allowed to develop very slowly and no clear picture of the Order of Battle was allowed to materialize until the early part of 1944.

In October, 1942, the main weight of the activities were devoted to implementing Operation SOLO I, thus the military reports mainly related to Scotland. Canadian and Scottish troops as well as Commandos were reported as training in the areas of Ayr and Troon and many indications were given to suggest that the training was such as might have been expected in the case of the target area being a mountainous country, leaving little doubt that the attack would come in Norway. Large supplies of anti-freeze for vehicles were observed, likewise snow chains, ski troops etc., etc.,

By the middle of October the Vichy and Paris radios were already speculating that preparations were being made for an attack against Dakar. Similar speculation was voiced in the British press. We suggested that from information received through the Ministry of Information it would appear that the rumours about Dakar were officially inspired and that in view of the concentration of troops in the south of England, and in particular the Canadian 1st Infantry and 5th Armoured Divisions, and the presence of the 52nd British Mountain Division in Scotland (which had by then been built up as the assault division for an attack against Norway, and was now reported as completing training) the possibility of a simultaneous attack against Norway and France should not be ignored.

There is little doubt that the deception information passed through the GARBO organization at this time could not have influenced the enemy to any extent and at the most it can be hoped that it might have helped to confuse them.

From the incoming questionnaires received at the end of

October it would appear that the enemy had no idea of our plans. They were, however, apprehensive that a Second Front was imminent and they stressed that it was of the utmost importance for GARBO to intensify all his efforts to discovering the location of troop concentrations and materials as well as the bases of departure in the south of England, and especially the Isle of Wight and Wales. He was asked to send agents to these areas.

On the 29.10.42 it was decided that, as a build up, GARBO should be allowed to report the sailing of one of the principal convoys of the North African landing which left the Clyde on the 26.10.42. The destination of this convoy was not hinted and it was remarked that none of the troops trained in mountain warfare had embarked, thus, after the landing in North Africa the threat to Norway could be maintained. The letter was forwarded to Lisbon with instructions that it should not be mailed until a signal was received from the Admiralty informing us that the convoy in question had been spotted by the enemy which would inevitably happen prior to its passing through Gibraltar.

On the 1.11.42 GARBO forwarded a further report received from Agent No. 3 to say that other troop transports had secretly left the Clyde and that the battleships were camouflaged in Mediterranean colours. In the same letter he reported that he had an opportunity of examining a file in the Ministry of Information during the absence of his friend for a few minutes from his office. The file, he said, was marked "Most Secret" and entitled "Policy - French North Africa." Inside he saw a document dated the 14.6.42 which contained a directive which would come into force in the event of Allied action against French Morocco and/or Algeria. Here followed instructions to the Press and to the B.B.C. Home and Overseas programmes for various European countries. It was pointed out that in the few minutes available it was not possible to read and memorize the text but GARBO voiced the opinion that this document was no doubt connected with the large convoys which had recently been leaving British ports and he reminded them that if the landing should take place in North Africa it would further confirm the information which he had recently given that the rumours which had circulated that the attack would be made against Dakar had been officially inspired.

This letter was released by G.P.O. on the 7.11.42 for immediate despatch to Lisbon by air mail, bearing the post mark of the 2.11.42. The landing took place on the 7.11.42. Thus, the Germans had evidence that GARBO's organization had, in the first place, reported the sailing of one of the main convoys in a letter dated eight days prior to the landing, and mailed by the courier in Lisbon three days before the attack was made; and, in the second

place, GARBO had discovered the target area six days prior to the
landing and had communicated it immediately by air mail as was borne
out by the post mark on the envelope. Though the information,
naturally enough, reached the Germans too late to be of any use to
them they could only blame themselves for not having taken quicker
action to make use of the wireless facilities which GARBO had
offered them as far back as August that year.

An indication of the extent to which the Germans were
impressed by the efficiency of GARBO's organization at this time is
proved by an M.S.S. message from Madrid to Berlin which was passed
some two years later when they reminded Berlin that ALARIC (the
M.S.S. code name for GARBO) was identical with V-Mann 319 (a
previous M.S.S. symbol for GARBO) who had been responsible for
advising them about the landing in North Africa in some reports
which had only arrived two days late.

In a letter which the Germans wrote to GARBO on the 26.11.42
they said:-

> "Your last reports are all magnificent but we are sorry they
> arrived late, especially those relating to the Anglo-Yankee
> disembarkation in Africa.....You must stay in London and
> continue investigations with your Ministry friends."

At this same time another piece of build up material came
to a head. The Admiralty were anxious earlier in the year (in
accordance with their policy of giving the impression that our
shipbuilding programme had advanced further than was in fact the
case) to inform the enemy that the battleship ANSON had been launched
before this had in fact occured. It was therefore decided that Agent
No. 2 should, in May that year, report that the ANSON had been
launched, and late in October, after it had really been put into
commission, the information was given out in the Press. GARBO was then
in a position to draw their attention to this important confirmation
of a very valuable piece of information, and he asked whether he might
be given authority to pay the agent a special bonus. They replied to
say that GARBO should pay him whatever amount he chose.

On the 2.11.42, that is to say immediately after GARBO's
discovery of the imminence of the landing in North Africa, he
reported that his Agent No. 6 who had recently been around offering
his services to various Ministries, hoping he would in this way
discover something about the impending operation, managed through
some influential friends to get himself recruited in secret work in
connection with which he was instructed to leave immediately for
Africa. Realizing the agent's mission must be directly connected
with the impending operation GARBO trained him forthwith in the use

of secret ink and provided him with a supply of ink and instructed him in the mission which he would be expected to fulfil on his arrival overseas. The agent was told to write to a cover address in London, and GARBO told the Germans he would forward the letters received, by courier to Lisbon since he was not in possession of the developer for the superior ink with which he had supplied the agent.

We asked for the developer for this ink so that when wireless communications had been established GARBO would be able to develop the agent's letters and transmit the contents by wireless. This, however, was not forthcoming and it in fact suited us that they did not supply it since the added delay in transmitting the reports allowed us to send important high grade information which, in view of the long delay in transit, inevitably arrived too late. Furthermore, the forwarding of the original letters gave verisimilitude to the agent. In fact the secret and cover texts were supplied to us by the Deception staff attached to Army Group in Algiers, writing paper and envelopes were likewise supplied as well as Field Post Office franking dies. The letters were in fact written in this Office by an officer who was appointed scribe for Agent No. 6 and the finished letter was forwarded in the original envelope to Lisbon, via the courier. The first letter from this agent was acknowledged by GARBO as having been received here by the 22.1.43. The letter contained very high grade and accurate, though out of date, information. The Germans were fascinated by this development in the case and expressed their hearty approval to GARBO.

Immediately after the North African landing we were somewhat apprehensive lest Spain should enter the war, we wanted to ensure that GARBO would not lose contact with his German masters in this event and furthermore that they should not become concerned that he, as a Spaniard, would be likely to be interned. We therefore wrote a letter to say that GARBO was proposing to take a job in the Latin-American Press Department of the Ministry of Information, and that since he had represented himself as a Republican escapee from Franco Spain it was essential that the Germans should supply him with a set of Spanish Republican documentation in his name so that he might be able to support this cover story if ever challenged. With this in his possession, he assured them that he would be able to continue to operate even in the event that Spain should enter the war. In the same letter it was suggested that the Germans should supply us with an address in Latin-America in case communications with Spain should break down. Though they failed to supply the new cover address the Germans did, after considerable delay, supply GARBO with a great quantity of magnificently forged documents which represented him as a well accredited Republican Spaniard who had been in Spain and France during the Civil War.

CHAPTER XIV.

POST TORCH PERIOD.
DEATH OF AGENT NO. 2.
THE SAILING OF THE INDEFATIGABLE TO THE INDIAN OCEAN.
CANCELLATION OF SPANISH COVER ADDRESSES.
GERMANS SUPPLY NEW INK, COVER ADDRESSES AND A CYPHER.
THE RECRUITMENT OF AGENT NO. 7.
DECEMBER, 1942 - JANUARY, 1943.

The North African operation having been successfully launched
there was little for this large network of agents to do. The
Service Departments had little information to offer us, no further
operational plans were pending, and yet we had no legitimate grounds
for cutting down the activities of the organization. For the next
several months, therefore, we dedicated ourselves mainly to
objective reporting based on observation reports which were
collected by special observers who were sent round the country to
the areas in which the various agents were supposed to be located.
The full observation reports were submitted to the various Approving
Authorities, and in the main they were allowed to go forward.

Agent No. 3 continued to send his reports direct. These were
all based on the Glasgow area.

Agent No. 5 was, in accordance with the requirements of the
Germans, sent to reconnoitre the south coast, the Isle of Wight and
south Wales. This provided ample scope for padding, since it was
well known at the time that it was practically impossible to enter
the Isle of Wight. Being an adventurous character, however, he
achieved the impossible and in so doing we were able to build him up
as a personality in whom the Germans came to have great confidence.

Agent No. 1 continued to send in rather steady, if dull,
reports on south west England which helped to tide us over.

We received numerous questionnaires from the Germans which
we endeavoured to answer to their liking as much as was possible.

At the beginning of December, 1942, GARBO, astonished at
having no news from Agent No. 2, or even an acknowledgement of the
money which he had sent him for the month of November, left for
Liverpool to see what had occurred. There, the agent's wife[(i)]
confronted GARBO with the sad news that the agent had died on the
19th November. She showed GARBO a cutting from The Liverpool Daily
Post of the 24.11.42 (which had been inserted at our request) which
was the agent's obituary notice and read as follows:-

(i) See Appendix No. IX.

"GERBERS. - November 19 at Bootle, after a long illness, aged
52, WILLIAM MAXIMILLIAN. Private funeral. (No flowers,
please.)"

The cutting was forwarded by GARBO to the Germans who replied with a
message of condolence for the unfortunate widow. On taking leave of
the widow, she handed GARBO an envelope with some notes which had
been made by her late husband, as well as his secret ink. The notes,
though somewhat cryptic, were examined by GARBO who decided that
they were certainly annotations made during the course of the
agent's espionage travels. Thinking that the Germans would be more
clever than he in decyphering them, he decided to send them on,
particularly in view of the fact that part of them were in German
which was reasonable since the agent was of German-Swiss origin. In
most cases it is true to say that the only virtue in passing on these
notes was that they were a satisfactory leg pull, for instance, they
read:-

"Grosse olbek zwischen Birkenhead e -"
"Speke Rd. L.M. - 2 neue Fabrk." etc., etc.,

Amongst the numerous messages of this character one was inserted for
purely deceptive purposes. It was known to the Germans that the KING
GEORGE V had come into the Clyde for repairs and steps had
previously been taken to suggest that she was probably being fitted
with torpedo tubes, in fact she had none at all. Therefore we
inserted, together with the other cryptic notes, the following:-

"Posit torpedorohre king G.V. 21 in. 26 in?"

The traffic was further padded out by enclosing rough diagrams of
what were obviously airfields, indicating the position of aircraft
on the field and hangars. They lacked, however, any indication of
the location of the aerodrome. The Germans, though they accepted
these reports in all seriousness, eventually decided that there was
no good purpose to be served by forwarding any more and that it would
be better for GARBO to confine his letters to the more valuable
information of his agents.

In December Agent No. 3 was instrumental in implementing an
Admiralty plan known as OPERATION BIJOU. The last aircraft carrier
still in the Indian Ocean was about to be withdrawn and sent to other
waters where she was urgently needed. The object of the plan was to
conceal the return of this aircraft carrier from Indian waters and
to lead the enemy to believe that she had instead been reinforced by
H.M.S. INDEFATIGABLE. The operation was supported by wireless

deception. As will be recalled, this agent had already prematurely launched the ANSON in accordance with Admiralty policy to make it appear as though we were in advance with our shipbuilding programme, and it was particularly suitable that Agent No. 3 should prematurely announce the launching of the INDEFATIGABLE since she was one of the capital ships whose name had appeared in the original Naval questionnaire handed to GARBO before he left Spain.

On the 19.12.42 the VICTORIOUS was due to sail from the Clyde for the Pacific. The ARGOS was also in the Clyde and thus there was the appropriate wireless traffic on the air which would easily be recognizable to the Germans and which would support his information. On the 17.12.42 GARBO's agent No. 3, reported that there were three aircraft carriers in the Clyde, one the VICTORIOUS, the second the INDEFATIGABLE, but the third he could not identify. The second, he said, was completely new and was sailing in commission for the first time. The first two were reported as being due to sail any day and the INDEFATIGABLE was, according to an officer of the crew, sailing for the Indian Ocean with specially equipped aircraft for tropical flights. The officer, in his indiscretion, disclosed that the INDEFATIGABLE would be stopping at Cape Town where certain high ranking Air Ministry officials would disembark.

The plan was further implemented through wireless deception by which the returning ILLUSTRIOUS, whilst in African waters, was made to appear as if she were the outgoing INDEFATIGABLE. The operation was entirely successful, as was proved by M.S.S. which revealed that both the Germans and the Japanese believed we had two aircraft carriers in the Indian Ocean over the material period. Their names appearing in some appreciations as the INDEFATIGABLE and the ILLUSTRIOUS. The notional INDEFATIGABLE carried out a year's "service" there before she was brought back to be linked up with the commissioning of her real self. The real INDEFATIGABLE, when launched, was sent to operate in the Indian Ocean.

In one of the long letters which GARBO wrote at this period he said he could not understand why it was they appeared to be taking no action whatever on the information which his organization was passing over. He explained that he was continually giving positions of aerodromes, etc., yet they had so far taken no steps to bomb any of the targets which he had given. The tone of his letter rather suggested that he was beginning to feel his work was futile and was not in any way serving the interests of the German war effort. Alternatively, he said, it was an indication that the Germans did not believe in the information which he was sending. They were prompt to reply to this provokation as follows:-

"We do not question the veracity of your information which is very useful to us. We beg you not to be impatient if the objectives indicated have not been bombed because this is outside our control here. There are reasons why this has not been done up to now and you can rest assured that everything will be done in time and you should therefore keep calm and continue to encourage your collaborators in their valuable work."

At the end of December the Germans cancelled all the cover addresses in Spain. They, furthermore, instructed GARBO to use a cypher for encoding the key words in the secret text of his letters. All name places and names of people etc., were to be encyphered, and the necessary cypher tables were promised in the near future. They stressed that this was only a precautionary measure for his security and was not motivated by any suspicion or fears that the enemy was on his track. They added:-

"The real reason is that your collaboration and activities are of so much value to us that we wish to take every precaution humanly possible."

They supplied him with three new addresses in Lisbon in substitution for those cancelled in Spain. It was not until some weeks later that we discovered what had motivated this change of procedure. It had always been our custom to notify S.I.S.' representative in Madrid or Lisbon of all cover addresses given to agents by the Germans in their countries. The information was not only useful to them for C.E. purposes but it enabled them to make discreet enquiries about the nationals who were facilitating the Germans in this connection. It later was brought to our notice that, in the case of the last Madrid address which had been supplied to GARBO, the S.I.S. agent responsible for making the enquiries in Madrid had been over zealous and had disclosed to the addressee that we were aware that he was receiving suspect correspondence from England. Fortunately, when the addressee reported his discovery to the Germans they did not suspect the reason which had inspired our investigations but instead imagined that we had made some discovery about GARBO's correspondence which we had clumsily endeavoured to investigate. Thus, to protect GARBO without alarming him, they took the above measures.

Simultaneously they substituted the […] ink, in which they had been accustomed to write to GARBO, for […] ink of rather higher grade. They sent GARBO the developer for this ink in the form of impregnated wads of cotton wool concealed in the packing of a parcel

and issued him with the necessary instructions for making up the
solution. At about the same time we learnt that the Germans had
issued this developer to another agent whom we detained in this
country. The ink, however, was not satisfactory and many of the
letters which we received from the Germans written in it were almost
illegible and some pages had to be repeated.

The problem and risks of maintaining the air courier service
were still a major preoccupation and it was therefore decided to
recruit a new agent, this time a seaman, whom we envisaged would
later be able to arrange the establishment of a courier service to
the Peninsula through some of his seamen friends. Furthermore, by
establishing a seaman courier system we would be permitted to send
out bulkier objects than would have been possible by air. Thus,
Agent No. 7[i] was created. He was introduced to the GARBO network by
Agent No. 4 who guaranteed his loyalty and from the beginning GARBO
prophesied that this agent would eventually facilitate the growth
of the network, though this did not materialize until about a year
later. Although the recruitment of this agent was advantageous on a
long-term basis it was somewhat embarrassing at the time since we
were already short of information for the existing network. In
order, therefore, that we should not have to provide much material
for this new recruit and to conform with the Admiralty who feared
that the Germans might ask this new seaman agent a number of
embarrassing questions about convoy routing and composition we made
it clear to the enemy that this agent, on account of his long
association with the Merchant Navy, would not provide any
information which might lead, even indirectly, to the death of his
fellow seamen.

When the first letter was received by GARBO from his Agent
No. 6 in North Africa it was the new agent, No. 7, who, through his
seamen colleagues in south Wales, arranged for it to be taken to
Lisbon for mailing, camouflaged in a parcel. The explanation for not
sending it in the normal way, through the airman courier, was that
in view of its place of origin it might have aroused the courier's
suspicions. We claimed that all the seamen couriers used were
unaware of the nature of their mission and thus we were able to
prevent the Germans from making any suggestions for contacting
them. In fact the letters and parcels subsequently sent as if by
seamen courier were in reality despatched to Lisbon by S.I.S. Bag,
where they were mailed to correspond with the arrival in Lisbon of a
ship proceeding from a British port.

In order that the airmail letters should not arrive with too
great a regularity it was decided to allow some of GARBO's letters

(i) See Appendix No. XXI.

to go astray. In fact since the time of CALVO's arrest all GARBO letters addressed to Calle Viriato 73, Madrid, the residence of Federico KNAPPE, failed to reach their destination. The Germans were bound to interpret from this that CALVO, who had visited this address whilst in Madrid immediately prior to his arrest, had disclosed that this was an address of a member of the German Secret Service and thus it would be natural that we should have put the address on our Censorship Watch List.

Assuming, therefore, that we had intercepted some of GARBO's letters it was a tribute to GARBO that the cover text of his letters was so good as to give us no clue of the identity of the writer. It will be recalled that GARBO invariably typed the cover text, he used a variety of paper, including the writing paper of all the leading London hotels; the sender's name was continually changed and from the post marks the Germans were able to observe that GARBO went to the trouble of mailing his letters from several different postal districts in London.

Although the Germans had always tried to make GARBO believe that the ink which he was using could not be developed by the British they must, in fact, have known that this was untrue. The fact that they should now have given GARBO a cypher so that he could partly encode his letters was an admission to this effect. Providing, therefore, there was nothing in the secret text which could lead to the identification of GARBO or any member of his network there was no cause for alarm even should an occasional letter fall into the hands of the censor and be developed. GARBO, in his letters, never hinted at the names or identity of any of his agents. He would instead, stress their reliability, characteristics and ability for the work, and since symbols were in any case used, one could say that as from the beginning of 1943 the Germans had every reason to be confident in the security of GARBO and his network. To further protect him they provided him with a great variety of cover addresses and instructed him to write to each of the addresses in rotation so that no addressee should receive a letter from him more frequently than once a fortnight. A further check on the safe arrival of his correspondence was provided in addition to the numbering of his letters, by their instructing GARBO to notify them at the end of each letter the address to which he would be mailing the subsequent one. This notification was naturally enough made in cypher.

If ever a letter went astray the Germans would notify GARBO of this fact and ask him for a repeat. In reply they were told that GARBO did not keep any records and in view of the immense volume of his correspondence it was obviously impossible for him to recall the contents of a lost letter by reminding him of its number. Thus, we were occasionally able to claim that we had given them a piece of information which they did not receive, from which they would have to draw the conclusion that it had been passed in one of the lost letters.

It should here be added that the cypher table which they sent GARBO for the purpose of encyphering groups in his letters was the identical cypher which was currently in use on the German circuits Tetuan - Mililla, Tetuan - Ceuta and others. This was perhaps the greatest proof at this time of their high regard and implicit confidence in GARBO.

CHAPTER XV.

GARBO IS ORDERED BY THE GERMANS
TO CORRESPOND ON THEIR BEHALF WITH CARELESS
JANUARY - FEBRUARY, 1943.

It had been our policy to take every precaution against getting
GARBO linked up with other agents in this country. Our principal
reason for this was that we already had good reason to believe that
through B.1.A. we controlled all German agents operating in this
country and therefore it was highly advisable that GARBO should
remain an isolated unit lest one or other of the agents should later
become compromised, and through his contact with GARBO, compromise
the latter.

Of the agents controlled by B.1.A. operating to the Peninsula
was a Pole, known in this Office as the double-agent, CARELESS, with
whom the Germans used to correspond under his alias, CLARK KORAB.

On the 7.1.43 we received a letter from the Germans in which,
without previous warning, they linked up GARBO with the CARELESS
case. They asked GARBO to write a letter to CARELESS in the secret
ink which he was accustomed to use for internal communications with
his agents, the text which they supplied was written in French. It
acknowledged CARELESS' recent letters, it gave him a new cover
address in Madrid and instructions in a new method of writing which
he was to use. GARBO was also furnished with a copy of the cover text
for the secret letter he was to write to CARELESS on their behalf. He
was also given the address which CARELESS was using in London. They
told GARBO that he should mail the letter from the outskirts of
London and that when he had completed this mission he should destroy
their instructions, forget the name and address of their agent and
notify them that he had fulfilled his mission. Though this was in a
sense a further mark of their confidence in GARBO it was a most
unfortunate occurrence. In the first place, CARELESS, who was a
member of the British Pioneer Corps, had been misbehaving himself
and had several months previously been detained on disciplinary
grounds, but in consideration of certain privileges he had
continued to operate from Camp 020, the place of his detention, by
writing occasional letters under our instructions. The case, run
this way, was very unsatisfactory, and at the time GARBO received
these unexpected instructions we had already planned to close it
down. In view of GARBO's enforced link up with him it was obviously
essential that CARELESS should continue to operate at least for a
time lest by ceasing to do so now he should draw suspicion on GARBO.
The letter was therefore written in accordance with instructions

received from the Germans, the envelope was franked and the finished letter was shown to CARELESS by his case officer who requested him to write to the new cover address contained in this letter with material which we provided.

CARELESS at first received the news with some enthusiasm. He denied any knowledge of the writer and not unnaturally assumed, as we had in fact intended him to, that the Germans had a spy-master over here whom we were anxious to catch. Suddenly he changed his mood and adamantly refused to continue to operate unless we put him at liberty. This for numerous reasons we could not do. On the other hand the situation was serious since we risked not only losing GARBO's confidence if we failed to get the man to write, but also in causing the Germans to lose their confidence in GARBO if he did not do so.

The matter dragged on for weeks, CARELESS stood his ground and was unfortunately permitted to blackmail us into complete submission with the consequent risk of jeopardizing the entire GARBO organization. Fortunately the incident did not appear to produce any adverse German reactions. They never brought up the subject again and neither did we. Our only mention was made on the 13.1.43 when GARBO said that although he had always told them that he did not, in any circumstances, want to be put in contact with any other of their agents over here he wished to let them know that their mission had been carried out and that he would be prepared, if necessary, to carry out any other orders from them providing he was not exposed to danger. What he wished to avoid was their ever giving his address to a third party, or that correspondence should reach him in this way.

To round off the incident a message was sent by another double agent, BRUTUS, who was also a Pole. He told his German control that he had received information through the Polish Intelligence Service in London that CARELESS, a Pole who had been enrolled in the British Army had been arrested for espionage by the British. He added that the British had refused the Polish authorities permission to see CARELESS whilst in detention and that he was being held by the British who had not yet brought a charge against him since they were trying to make him talk and give details about another organization in London with which, it was alleged, he had been in contact. BRUTUS, in warning the Germans of this, said that so far as he had been able to ascertain CARELESS had not yet been made to talk but that it would nevertheless be advisable for them to warn the other organization of what had occurred.

The Germans did not, in fact, warn GARBO about this since they must have realized that CARELESS was not in a position to disclose any details about the GARBO organization since he was not even aware of the source of origin of the letter which he had received.

CHAPTER XVI.

THE CHISLEHURST CAVES. (PLAN BODEGA) 1943.

Apart from the rather unimportant information which was being collected by Agent No. 3 in Scotland, Agent No. 1 in Devon and Cornwall, and Agent No. 5 who had by now arrived in south Wales on his extensive tour which had taken him to the Isle of Wight, the bulk of the traffic was padded out with lengthy letters from GARBO about the future planning of his organization.

The Germans had at that time been showing a great interest in underground factories, and it occurred to us that we might well create a notional underground depot and extensive workings which could provide a great bulk of information which would not be checkable. This plan was intended to provide the opposition with a great deal of apparently interesting information which would lead them nowhere. It was also envisaged at the time that if once the plan had been developed and accepted by the Germans the material might later have been turned to good purpose for deception.

Agent No. 4 was allotted the job of discovering these notional underground workings and to develop PLAN BODEGA. In view of the fact that we were shortly hoping to establish wireless communications in which this agent would be required as an intermediary for the wireless operator it was clear that he should not leave London, therefore GARBO decided to instruct him to go to the Ministry of Labour to try to get a job in one of the big London hotels where it was hoped he would have been able to have picked up a great deal of gossip. On applying at the Labour Exchange for work, and on giving his nationality as Gibraltarian he was told, to his great disappointment, that in spite of his past experience in hotel work he would be directed to take work in a quarry on the assumption that all Gibraltarians should have a natural aptitude for tunnelling. A few days later he received a notice to present himself for work with Highways Construction Ltd., one of the most important firms working on military contracts. He was told he would be given employment in connection with certain excavation work and on GARBO's recommendation he accepted his job, thinking it might lead him to the discovery of some underground factories. His first job was in connection with underground workings on the outskirts of London where he learnt that certain extensions were being made to the Metropolitan and Underground lines which had been brought to a stop at the outbreak of war.

The plan was allowed to develop in a most complex and

elaborate way which for several months constituted the great bulk of
the GARBO traffic. All the information passed over in this
connection was untrue, it being entirely imaginary.

As the story developed the focal point of interest became the
Chislehurst Caves which, we stated, were again being used by the War
Office, as they had been in World War 1, for the purpose of storing
explosives and small arms. (In fact the caves were a public air
raid shelter.) This discovery was well received by GARBO's Madrid
control who instructed him to carry on the investigations since
the matter was one of the utmost importance to them. The further
investigations disclosed that immense quantities of small arms and
munitions were being transported direct from factories in the
Midlands by rail to the principal London termini. These munitions
travelled from the factories in crates mounted on small guage trucks
which were carried on the main line goods trucks. On their arrival
at the London termini the small guage trucks were unloaded from the
main line carriers and transferred to a small guage electric railway
line on which they were carried to the storage depots in, and
around, the Chislehurst Caves. Here, it was claimed, vast reserves
were being built up for use at the time of the opening of the Second
Front. It was further discovered that secret tunnelling of a small
diameter had been progressing since the early days of the war for
the purpose of extending the present system of underground
communications based on the London Underground Railway system. This
work had originally been intended to serve the purpose of supplying
the defence aerodromes in the Outer London area and anti-aircraft
emplacements in London with ammunition fed from these underground
depots without risk of their having to come to ground level whilst
being transported during the time of the blitz. Now this network of
communications was being further extended so that it would be able
to serve a useful purpose in connection with offensive, rather than
defensive, operations.

Amongst the latest developments which were discovered
in this underground communications network were a number of new
lines, all terminating at Chislehurst. One of these connected the
Chislehurst Depots with the Woolwich dockyards via Eltham and
Charlton, another branched off from the main Underground line in the
Kennington area and was projected to terminate near Warlingham,
within easy reach of the aerodromes of Kenley, Croydon and Biggin
Hill. According to the workmen engaged it was estimated that the
last mentioned line would not be ready for operations until shortly
before the opening of the Second Front against Europe. Thus, from
the speed of progress of the work the timing of the Second Front
would be able to be estimated. Furthermore, there were a great
number of workings south of Chislehurst which were reported as

possibly being connected with this same underground network of communications, though insufficient concrete detail was ascertained to be able to ensure this. The whole system of transport was electric and controlled from a central point within the Chislehurst Caves which operated along similar lines to the existing London G.P.O. automatic inter-communication system. Thus, the munition trains would travel from the London termini to the depots at Chislehurst without personnel, controlled by the staff within the caves who operated the automatic control switchboard.

On arrival at their destination the munitions were unloaded and transported on belt conveyors to the depots. By the reverse process the arms and munitions were despatched to the operational aerodromes fed by the caves.

Numerous plans and drawings were sent over to the Germans to further explain the workings of these depots.

At the beginning of June, 1943, GARBO sent out a very lengthy report with several diagrams summarizing the entire discoveries about the Chislehurst Caves to date. In so far as these depots were connected with the opening of the Second Front, he pointed out that, within the depots were large supplies of small arms which would be distributed to Commandos and/or Paratroops and it was believed there also existed in the caves large supplies of uniforms and arms which would be drawn on to supply the "Fifth Column" in France, Holland and/or Belgium either just prior to, or immediately after, a landing. The Germans were reminded that GARBO had reported nearly a year previously that Fifth Column cells were then being organized by parachutists who were supplying the Patriots with explosives and other equipment.

It was at that time envisaged that when an appropriate cover plan for the landing in Europe had been approved we would have been able to have indicated to the Germans that the equipment was being brought out from the storage depots and from other indications it should have been possible for GARBO to have given the Germans the target (i.e. cover area) for the operation.

We knew from M.S.S the Germans in Madrid believed in these reports since they had been sending them on to Berlin without any hesitation. Since the objectives were all underground they were obviously unsuitable targets for attack by the G.A.F. Unless, therefore, the communication system could be disrupted by successful sabotage the flow of arms to the Patriots at the time of our opening a Second Front could not be checked. Therefore, GARBO, in his long letter, proposed that a plan to sabotage the depots should be studied. The possibility of entering the tunnel leading to the store by way of a siding near the approach to the caves was proposed and it was explained that by blowing up one of the trains

whilst in the main tunnel by means of a time bomb the tunnel itself
would collapse and thus the stores would be entombed at the vital
moment when they would be required.

Federico KNAPPE was invited to come to London to discuss
future plans with GARBO. To make this feasible FEDERICO was
told that GARBO had recently told his friend at the Ministry of
Information that his brother-in-law in Spain was anxious to come to
this country, and GARBO had been promised that steps would be taken
to facilitate his journey here. The brother-in-law, GARBO had told
his British friends, had come across some very important
information which he wished to bring to this country and, having
handed it over, to return without delay to Spain.

GARBO, therefore, suggested to FEDERICO that he should go to
Lisbon documented as GARBO's brother-in-law, bringing with him some
deception document prepared by the German High Command which he
should hand over on his arrival. During the few days he would remain
here GARBO promised that he would introduce him to his agents, show
him the caves, and together work out a plan for sabotaging them.
It was our intention at the time, had FEDERICO accepted, to allow
him to enter this country and, conducted by GARBO, to get a secret
view of some real underground depot which he would be told was the
Chislehurst depot. He would likewise have been allowed to return to
Spain from where he would undoubtedly have proceeded to Berlin to
report on his extraordinary adventure, full of praise for GARBO's
astuteness and ability, and conscious of the importance of the
underground depots.

Unfortunately the plan did not materialize for two reasons.
In the first place it is evident that the Abwehr in Madrid had
no desire to hand over their star agent to their competitors
responsible for sabotage. In the second place, it was equally
apparent that FEDERICO, confident as he may have been in GARBO,
did not welcome GARBO's invitation to penetrate the enemy's camp.
Furthermore, we know from M.S.S. that GARBO's long letter, which
was intentionally confusing hoping to draw FEDERICO here for
discussion, was sent to Berlin in its entirety for examination
by specialists. The appreciation which Berlin sent was not
particularly encouraging since they voiced the opinion that,
whereas the information was interesting in character, the report
would have been more valuable had the agent reported more fact and
less opinion.

GARBO, therefore, interpreted FEDERICO's somewhat
discouraging reply to his invitation as lack of appreciation for
the painstaking and valuable work which his organization had
carried out in this connection and, indicating that he was somewhat
hurt, if not offended, said he did not propose to give them any

further information in this connection unless something of vital importance should materialize, although he intended, for his own satisfaction, to continue his investigations.

Thus we were able to close down our reporting on the caves and yet keep open the channel for deception should it later be decided that it could advantageously be used. We only referred to the Chislehurst Caves on two later occasions. Once, at the time of STARKEY, when in spite of the apparently imminent threat of invasion, we pointed out that there were no indications that the stores were being moved from the Chislehurst Caves, and later, after the Germans had started to use their "V" weapons in August, 1944, Agent No. 3 reported that he had learnt from a quite independent source that the Chislehurst Caves had been one of the principal depots for weapons and material dropped to the Maquis in France and that the caves were now being prepared as shelters against the use of the V-2 rocket weapon.

In this way the chapter on the Chislehurst Caves was closed. The Planners of the deception cover plan for OVERLORD were unable usefully to incorporate PLAN BODEGA in the Operation FORTITUDE.

The long GARBO report referred to above which was sent to Madrid in June, 1943, amounted to some twelve foolscap pages of closely written secret text. The package was therefore bulky and to avoid having to send it by courier GARBO suggested to the Germans that he would send it to them by safe hand of his friend at the Ministry of Information who was then about to leave for Madrid. He said that he would therefore write a cover text to the letter as if he were a Republican refugee sending a general report on life and morale in England for the benefit of his Republican friends in Spain. He said that the man from the Ministry would be staying at the Palace Hotel, Madrid, between certain fixed dates and that he would leave the letter with the hotel concierge to be called for by a certain Martin DELGADO, therefore the Germans should send someone in that name and ask for the envelope.

It happened that at that time the head of the Peninsula Section of the Ministry of Information was due to go to Madrid to inspect the Press Office. We therefore contacted him and gave him a brief outline of the case. He volunteered to assist us in any way. We asked him to stay at the Palace Hotel during the period which we had indicated GARBO's friend would be there so that the Germans who would undoubtedly check up on the arrival there of an Englishman from the Ministry of Information, would be able to discover the identity of GARBO's Ministry friend, J(3) whose name we had always carefully withheld from them. We also disclosed GARBO's name and notional role in the Ministry of Information to the official who was proceeding to Madrid so that if he were challenged by anyone on behalf of the Germans he would be able to confirm that he knew GARBO, and that he had in fact worked for him.

Eventually the letter was not carried by him lest it should cause him embarrassment and the Germans were later informed that when GARBO took the letter to his friend at the Ministry he read the cover text which he found to be rather "Red" in tone, and became apprehensive lest, whilst it was deposited with the concierge pending collection, it should be opened and read by the Spanish authorities who might then accuse him of intriguing with Spanish Republican elements. GARBO said that he quickly relieved his friend of any embarrassment by saying that in those circumstances he would rather he did not take the letter which, after all, was not of any real consequence.

GARBO decided, therefore, to forward the letter to the Germans via the courier in spite of its rather bulky nature.

There can be little doubt, however, that this incident gave verisimilitude to GARBO's story of his intimacy with a prominent officer of the Ministry of Information who, from then onwards, we had to assume had been identified by the Germans.

CHAPTER XVII.

WIRELESS COMMUNICATIONS STARTED.
THE TRAIN TIMETABLE QUESTIONNAIRES.
AGENT NO. 5 PREPARES TO LEAVE THE U.K.
TROUBLE WITH THE COURIER.
GARBO SENDS AIRCRAFT RECOGNITION BOOK CONCEALED IN CAKE.
THE DEATH OF AGENT NO. 6.
GARBO IS GIVEN THE LATEST M.S.S. CYPHER.
THE CAMOUFLAGE MILITARY WIRELESS TRANSMITTING PLAN.
JANUARY - JUNE, 1943.

Towards the end of January, 1943 we prepared to be able to revive the
threat to Norway if, and when, it should be required. We claimed
that it was the general opinion amongst the public that the Second
Front would be opened in Europe against Norway or France.
We claimed that there were ten divisions concentrated in Scotland
receiving special training and that there were several formations
which had been issued with Arctic kit and had been trained in
mountain warfare. It was also stated that there were numerous
Norwegian troops in Scotland who had received special assault
training and others who would operate as guides in the event of
opening an offensive against Norway.
      GARBO learnt from J (3) that a plan to attack Norway was to have
come into operation several months ago (i.e. SOLO I) but as this was
to have been carried out in co-operation with the Russians who were
simultaneously to have started an offensive on their Front, and since
at that time they had suffered a series of reverses, the operation had
to be cancelled. Now, however, due to the Russian offensive, the
interest in Norway had revived. GARBO learnt that the attack would
come as soon as the Russians had been able to advance to a certain prearranged line. The valueless information which we thus passed
suggested that SOLO I had been real and furthermore it maintained the
threat to Norway on the basis that it would materialize when the
Russians had reached a certain undefined and elastic line.
      During the early months of 1943 we endeavoured to implement
the Admiralty's plan for writing up the efficiency of anti-
submarine nets and this was done in a series of messages, mostly
from Agents Nos. 3 and 7.
      By the beginning of February we were in possession of the
transmitting plan for the wireless station. We were given
alternative frequencies, call signs for each day of the month, and
code groups to indicate which of three times given would be selected
for transmissions.

A new cypher table was also provided and the first
transmission was made on the 7.3.43. Impressions of the results were
exchanged by letter between GARBO and Madrid, and within a few weeks
regular transmissions were established. According to our experts
here the times selected by the Germans were rather disadvantageous
for the particular time of the year and on the pretext that they did
not suit the operator due to his fixed working hours we asked them to
change the times, which they did.

In February, 1943, we were confronted with what was probably
the most embarrassing questionnaire as yet received. It asked GARBO
to copy from railway timetables the hours of departure of trains
from London for the south and south east of England, and in
particular the times of trains between Canterbury and Dover,
Canterbury - Ramsgate, Dover - Deal, Deal - Sandwich, Folkestone -
Canterbury, Canterbury - Ashford, Ashford - Folkestone, Folkestone
- Dover, Tunbridge - Ashford, Dungeness - Ashford. Other railway
networks in which they were specially interested were promised
to follow in future letters.

It will be recalled that at about this time the R.A.F.
had been busily engaged on "train busting" operations. The
questionnaires were therefore submitted to the Minister of Home
Security and the conclusion was drawn that the Germans, who had
already started to carry out "sneak raids" against the south east
coast of England, were anxious to try to time these raids to
coincide with the passing of a train along one of these routes so
that they could retaliate against our attacks on their French
railway communications by shooting up some of our passenger trains.

The German request for the times of trains was in itself
rather a strange one since it is almost certain that had they taken
the trouble to send an agent to Messrs. Thomas Cook in Lisbon they
could have had access to a reasonably up-to-date railway timetable.
Nevertheless it was against the policy to give the enemy any
information which could result in supplying them with direct
Intelligence on which they might have taken action, particularly
against the civilian population in this country. Against this,
it was argued, to deny the enemy this information which GARBO could
quite obviously obtain without any effort, would be tantamount to
exposing himself as a controlled agent. The possibility that this
questionnaire had been posed as a test was considered, and whilst it
was thought unlikely that this was the case, it was at the same time
realized that it would have been too dangerous to ignore it.

Had we, at that time, been passing over material which
appeared to be more important we would have had an excuse for
delaying our reply, but in fact the GARBO organization was
relatively quiet and unproductive of information at that period.

Whilst all these views were being considered we padded out the GARBO
network's reports until the end of February, by when we had been
given approval to reply accurately to this specific question,
though we were requested to give as little information as possible.
Thus, on 23.2.43 we replied to their question which they had marked
"urgent."

We started our reply with a long preamble in which we
informed the Germans that no edition of Bradshaw for the month of
February was available and we had therefore purchased the January
issue. We further pointed out that from experience of travelling
the published times could not be relied on since last minute
changes were continually being made in the timetable routine. We
furthermore explained that Bradshaw was a somewhat complicated
guide for a foreigner such as GARBO to use and that in order to avoid
dealing exclusively in his correspondence with the times of trains
he proposed to distribute the information over a series of letters,
giving priority to the routine enquires on which his organization
had been working for so long. We then pointed out that though we had
tried to set out the timetables in the same form in which they
appeared in Bradshaw this could not be done since after the name of
the town had been written the ink would immediately dry and become
invisible and thus it was impossible to set out the timetable in
tabulated form. It was therefore decided to adopt the following
method for re-adapting the published information:-

"Timetable Canterbury - Dover.
1. Canterbury East. Departure 5.28 (morning) stopping in the
following towns:- Adisham 5.39. - Snowdown and Nonington
Halt 5.45 - Shepherd's Well 5.50 - Kearnsey 5.58 arriving at
Dover Priory station 6.07.
2. Canterbury East. Departure 6.20 stopping in the following
towns:-
(a) Bekesbourne 6.25 (b) Adisham 6.31. (c) Aysham Halt 6.35.
(d) Snowdown and Nonington Halt 6.29. (e) Shepherd's Well
6.45. (f) Stonehall and Lydden Halt 6.50. (g) Kearnsey 6.54
(h) Dover Priory 7.00.
3. Canterbury East stopping at the same stations as in 2 with
the following timetable (the letters are added by me
representing the name of the town in the following timetable)
Departure 6.36

(a) 6.44	(b) 6.51	(c) 6.55	(d) 6.59
(e) 7.5	(f) 7.11	(g) 7.16	(h) 7.22

4. Canterbury East. Departure 7.53.

(a) 8.0	(b) 8.07	(c) 8.11	(d) 8.15
(e) 8.20	(f) 8.25	(g) 8.29	(h) 8.35

5. Canterbury East. Departure 8.30

| (a) 8.36 | (b) 8.42 | (c) 8.46 | (d) 8.50 |
| (e) 8.55 | (f) 9.00 | (g) 9.04 | (h) 9.10. |

6. Canterbury East. Departure 9.37

| (a) 9.43 | (b) 9.49 | (c) 9.52 | (d) 9.56 |
| (e) 10.00 | (f) 10.05 | (g) 10.10 | (h) 10.16. |

7. Canterbury East. Departure 10.30

| (a) 10.36 | (b) 10.42 | (c) 10.46 | (d) 10.50 |
| (e) 10.55 | (f) 11.00 | (g) 11.04 | (h) 11.10. |

8. Canterbury East. Departure 12.26

| (a) 12.32 | (b) 12.38 | (c) 12.42 | (d) 12.46 |
| (e) 12.52 | (f) 12.57 | (g) 1.01 | (h) 1.07 |

9. Canterbury East. Saturdays only. Departure 12.26

| (a) 12.32 | (b) 12.38 | (c) 12.42 | (d) 12.46 |
| (e) 12.52 | (f) 12.57 | (g) 1.01 | (h) 1.07. |

10. Canterbury East. Saturdays excepted. Departure 12.26

| (a) 12.32 | (b) 12.38 | (c) 12.42 | (d) 12.46 |
| (e) 12.57 | (f) 1.03 | (g) 1.07 | (h) 1.13. |

11. Canterbury East. Departure 12.58

| (a) 1.04 | (b) 1.10 | (c) 1.14 | (d) 1.18 |
| (e) 1.23 | (f) 1.28 | (g) 1.32 | (h) 1.38. |

12. Canterbury East. Departure 12.58

| (a) 1.04 | (b) 1.10 | (c) 1.14 | (d) 1.18 |
| (e) 1.27 | (f) 1.33 | (g) 1.39 | (h) 1.45. |

13. Canterbury East. Departure 1.46

| (a) 1.52 | (b) 1.58 | (c) 2.02 | (d) 2.06 |
| (e) 2.22 | (f) 2.28 | (g) 2.32 | (h) 2.38. |

The courier was continuing to function, mainly because all our attempts to break down this system were still being countered by the Germans who continued to express their feelings that he was rendering the organization a great service. We therefore thought that we should try other tactics. We wrote a letter solely on the question of the courier, in which GARBO expressed his opinion that, contrary to the views of the Germans, the procedure of using the courier should be dropped. He pointed out to them that they would already have noticed that he had avoided using this route for some time and that this was due to a discovery which he made and which he now felt it his duty to disclose to them. He said that he had learnt from the Spaniard who had originally introduced him to the courier that the latter was in fact working for a certain individual who earned his living by purchasing Bank of England notes which were the proceeds of frauds or robberies. These "hot" notes were sent to Lisbon by the courier where they were changed for others of equal value which were not traceable. GARBO therefore feared that the courier would one day get caught, with the consequent risk that he would be compromised. He pleaded that now he had the facilities for using seamen couriers who had been recruited by his Agent No. 7 it would be a good plan to give up the airman courier altogether.

The German reply was characteristic. They said that when we had safely established an alternative route for receiving their letters to GARBO we could start giving up the courier but first we must let them know how they were to continue to send their correspondence. This was the one problem we could not safely resolve and we had hoped that for once they might have assisted in the direction of the case but they did not rise to this. To try to excuse the courier they went as far as to say that certain irregularities which we had noticed in the arrival of letters which we had based on the dating of their letters was in no way due to the courier, but was due to the fact that, for cover purposes, they had used false dates. They ended up by saying:-

"We have no reason here to suspect him."

They followed this up in a later letter with a recommendation to GARBO that he should increase the courier's pay as an encouragement for him to work more enthusiastically, and finally with the instructions that all letters relating to organizational matters of the service should only be sent by the courier. In view of their attitude we decided to let the courier run for a while though we had every intention of coming back to the attack later.

In February, 1943, Agent No. 1 started to write direct to the Germans in secret ink, having been provided with a cover address in Lisbon for this purpose. Again a scribe in this Office was appointed. The agent was represented as being a Portuguese, but since there was no bi-lingual Portuguese speaking officer in this organization to do the writing it was decided that the letters should be written in French. The Germans were told that in view of the fact that the agent's French was fluent we had decided to transmit all his letters in that language for security reasons. It was pointed out that since there were a great number of Frenchmen and Belgians in south Wales and at Tenby suspicion would be thrown on them should one of the agent's letters be intercepted by Censorship, whereas if the letters were written in Portuguese the agent would inevitably come under suspicion in such circumstances since he was probably the only Portuguese subject who had access to the areas which he was accustomed to visit.

Agent No. 1, who was supposed to be a traveller for a commercial firm, announced that he would probably be sent to Ireland on business in the near future. GARBO welcomed this prospect enthusiastically in view of the interest which the Germans had previously shown in this country and particularly since Agent No. 5 had withdrawn his offer to go there for investigation work as had previously been proposed. It was some few months before Agent No.1 was represented as travelling to Northern Ireland and meanwhile we sent over an observer to obtain local background and information which later comprised the substance of the agent's reports.

Towards the end of February the Germans were showing a keen interest to discover the effects of their (then reduced) bombing activities. Not only did they want to have the result of targets hit but also to know the effect bombing was having on British morale. This information GARBO sought at the Ministry of Information. He was able to assure the Germans that the British newspaper accounts of the effects of German bombing were truthful and by provoking his contacts at the Ministry he was given access to the Home Security Intelligence Summaries on air raids. From these GARBO was able to memorize certain incidents which it was not against our interests to report, but since the net result was so unimportant GARBO decided that he would not continue his investigations in this connection. He asked them, instead, if they would let him know by radio should they at any time wish to know the result of an air attack against a specific important objective in which case he would send one of his agents specially to investigate. In this way we were able to avoid the compromise of having to report on air raid damage which, in principle, we were against, yet leave open the door for the Germans to notify us of any specific target raids which they might subsequently make, the results of which they were unable to obtain through aerial reconnaissance.

At the end of February, 1943, the Ministry of Home Security supplied us with a copy of a document compiled by the Service Departments and War Ministries for Mr. Stettinius setting out the statistics of Reverse Lend-Lease. The document was, at the time, still on the Secret List though it was no longer of any security interest and was to be released to the Press a month or two later. The contents of this document thus served as excellent build up material and was spread over a number of GARBO's letters at that time. He claimed that he was given access to the document in the course of his work at the Ministry of Information.

At the beginning of March GARBO was called to Liverpool by the widow of Agent No.2. Thinking she had some important information to pass to him he answered her call immediately. He found her in a desperate financial situation, her husband had left her penniless and she begged GARBO to assist her. She volunteered to work for GARBO as her husband had done but her offer was turned down since GARBO realized she was unsuited to the task. GARBO decided that it

would be a great pity to lose so loyal a collaborator and he offered
her employment in his home where she could help his wife with the
housework and the children. He had always been reluctant to have a
stranger to help in the house lest she might discover his activities
and therefore the future of his ex-agent's widow was resolved
to the satisfaction of both. She was soon transferred to London
and although at the beginning, to show her good intentions, she
endeavoured to collect some odd bits of information for GARBO, her
reports were of such low calibre that he dissuaded her from engaging
further in these activities. Eventually she became maid of all work.
During the busy spells she helped GARBO encypher wireless messages
and acted as cut out between the various agents. When Agent No.4
left London she acted as courier between GARBO and the wireless
operator; after GARBO went into hiding she acted as cut out between
Mrs. GARBO and the organization. In fact she was ready to turn her
hand to anything and remained active until the closing of the case.

During March GARBO's organization came by yet another
document. GARBO's Agent No.3, in Glasgow, had for some while
been friendly with an N.C.O. in the R.A.F., referred to in the
organization by the symbol 3(1), who had supplied the agent with a
certain amount of information about the R.A.F. 3(1) was a man of
rather weak character and although he had never accepted any money
for the information passed, since he was in fact an unconscious
informant, he was frequently hard up for a few pounds. He happened
one day to show Agent No.3 an R.A.F. aircraft recognition handbook
which was a loose-leaf book with illustrations and specifications
of most of the types of planes used by the R.A.F. 3(1) was hard up
at the time, and when Agent No.3 suggested that he would like to buy
it to keep as a souvenir, the former indicated that he might be
disposed to sell it at a price. Before negotiating, however, Agent
No.3 referred the matter to GARBO who, in turn, referred it to the
Germans suggesting that he would, subject to their approval,
authorize Agent No.3 to pay up to a maximum of £100 for it but that
he should try to acquire it for as little as possible. Agent No.3,
when he received permission to give up to £100 for it, decided to
handle the matter in his own way; he argued that if he were to offer
3(1) a high price for the book he might suspect his motive, whereas
if he offered him a pound or two, suggesting that it was nothing more
than a whim of his which prompted him to buy it, the worst that could
happen would be that 3(1) would refuse to sell it. It transpired
that his judgement was good since the book eventually changed hands
for the price of £3.

GARBO was most impressed by the integrity of his agent which
had been proved by this incident, and in expressing this view to the
Germans, and by charging them up with this very reduced sum he

incidentally proved his own integrity. The document, which was a perfectly genuine one, would have been most valuable to the Germans, had it not been for the fact that we removed all the up-to-date material and reduced it to a recognition book some months out of date so as to be identical with a copy which we had reason to believe had already fallen into the hands of the enemy in North Africa.

The question of camouflaging it in order to send it to the Germans was next considered. We eventually decided to seal it in grease proof paper and bake it within a cake. A large home made cake was baked by the Widow and inscribed by GARBO in chocolate icing: "With good wishes to Odette." Enclosed in the packing was a cover letter to make it appear as if it were a birthday cake from a British seaman to a girl friend of his, Miss Odette da CONCEICA, in Lisbon, the cover addressee to whom it was delivered by hand by one of the seamen friends of Agent No.7. In fact the parcel was sent by S.I.S. Bag to Lisbon and delivered to the addressee by an S.I.S. agent there. The secret text of the covering letter read as follows:-

> "Inside the cake you will find the book on aviation which was obtained by Three......The cake was made for me by the Widow and I did the lettering myself. I had to use several rationed products which I have given in a good cause......If it does not arrive too hard it can be eaten. I hope you appreciate the culinary art of the Widow. Good appetite!"

This rather comic incident was reported back to us more than a year later by a C.E. agent in the Peninsula. He stated that when the chief of the German Intelligence Service was on a tour of inspection in Spain a meeting was called of the principal Abwehr agents so that they might each give "The Chief" an account of their activities. KUHLENTHAL, we were told, was the star turn at this meeting. He told a great number of GARBO stories, among them the story of the cake. The story was spread around in Abwehr circles and came back to us in the form that KUHLENTHAL boasted he had an agent in England who was also a cook, who made cakes which were unpleasant in taste in spite of the fact that their contents were excellent.

In April GARBO received a letter from his brother-in-law, a Spanish lawyer, from which it appeared that he had no work and asked GARBO for his advice. We decided that to bring reality into the picture there would be no harm in asking the Germans whether they, through their influential contacts in Spain, would be prepared to help get him a job as lawyer to one of the large Spanish industrial companies. GARBO gave them his brother-in-law's name and address but warned them that any indiscretion on their part about the work which GARBO was doing for them might be very dangerous for him since

his brother-in-law had no knowledge about the mission which GARBO
was performing for the Germans in this country. They replied to say
that, whilst they could not help him in the way GARBO proposed they
would be prepared to give him money or employment in their own
organization. The possibility of using GARBO's brother-in-law to
penetrate the German organization in Madrid was considered but
GARBO was of the opinion that he was unsuited to this sort of work
and strongly advised against it. The suggestion that we should plant
an agent on them who should take on the personality of GARBO's
brother-in-law was also considered but it was decided that the
undertaking would be too difficult, and, if unsuccessful, would
lead to the exposure of the GARBO organization.

The brother-in-law did, however, unwittingly play a role in
the work. At the end of each year the Germans used to give GARBO a
bonus in pesetas. Furthermore, they used to credit him in Madrid with
the sum of 2,000 pesetas per month which money they held for him. They
had, on several occasions, asked GARBO for instructions to dispose of
the sum which had accumulated, but GARBO, to show his confidence in
them, had always replied that he preferred them to keep it for him.
When the Germans replied that they were willing to assist GARBO's
brother-in-law by giving him money GARBO replied that he would not
accept this kind of charity. He told them that they could instead send
his brother-in-law the monies which they were holding for him,
but they must make the payments appear as if they were from some
commercial concern which had owed GARBO money. After confirming with
his brother-in-law the story which he had told the Germans to use, the
monies were paid over periodically by banker's draft, as directed by
GARBO. The Germans never attempted to make contact with him and
maintained the secret of GARBO's relations with them.

Before Agent No.6 went to North Africa he introduced GARBO to
his "unmarried wife" named DOROTHY. When GARBO received letters from
this agent he would mention the fact to DOROTHY who, without knowing
the significance of the letters, would acknowledge them on GARBO's
behalf. It will be recalled that GARBO was not supposed to know the
contents of the secret text and since the Germans would not send him
the developer for the ink which Agent No.6 was using GARBO, as he
pointed out to the Germans, was forced to work at a great disadvantage
which fully justified his saying in one of his letters:-

"We don't seem to be running this agent very well."

The Germans, however, seemed to be perfectly satisfied with
the high grade, though out of date information, which they were
getting. GARBO only intervened inasmuch as he acted as post box for
the letters in London, and arranged for sending them on to Lisbon by

his seamen courier. The fact that he was forwarding letters to Lisbon which, from the cover text, had obviously come from a serving soldier in North Africa, was a very compromising business, particularly as they were invariably forwarded in their original envelopes to ensure the Germans' maximum confidence. To safeguard his own security and that of his agent GARBO went to the trouble of deleting with an ink eradicating solution his name and the cover address which appeared on the envelope, as well as the agent's signature in the letter, and that of the Field Censor in North Africa. In addition he went to the trouble of camouflaging the letters in packages. Invariably they were concealed in the binding of a book. The agent, however, was not very happy working at such a distance without any encouragement, he would ask in his secret text whether the information he was sending was the type which was required or whether there were any special points on which he should concentrate, but GARBO could not know he was asking these questions in his secret text unless informed by the Germans which caused long delays.

Gradually the agent was built up to pass deception material, in fact he was already implementing a deception plan prior to the Allied landing in Sicily. He speculated that on account of certain documents which had come to his notice whilst working in the Intelligence Section at Headquarters the landing would probably be made in Nice and Corsica. He managed to steal some documents relating to the impending operation which he announced in a secret letter would be forwarded in a parcel of fruit. The letter with this advice reached the Germans after the normal long delay. The documents were presumably of importance since in the agent's opinion they confirmed the target area which he had already indicated. On receipt of the letter, therefore, the Germans immediately signalled GARBO by wireless to say that Agent No. 6 had stated in his letter of the 24th April that he had sent some documents to GARBO hidden in a package of fruit. They asked him to let them know immediately whether the documents had arrived and confirm their safe arrival to Agent No. 6. Their warning arrived too late.

GARBO replied to say that he had received two presents of fruit from Agent No. 6 and that he had searched the first parcel very carefully in case there had been a hidden note but had found nothing, therefore when the second one arrived, the one to which they were referring, he had examined it less meticulously believing that it was a normal present which he had received and he had found nothing. On reflection, however, he recalled that two of the lemons were completely bad and he had thrown them away. Their present query made him suspect that the two lemons referred to might have concealed a document which would have accounted for their going bad en route.

Just as the case of this agent had become well established a real misfortune occurred. Our officer who had been acting as scribe for Agent No. 6 met with a fatal air accident whilst returning to London from leave in Scotland. To have continued to run the case would either have meant resorting to the trick of pretending that the agent had damaged his right and hand was therefore obliged to write with his left, or to attempt to forge his handwriting. Neither idea was thought advisable. On the other hand it was not easy to explain the agent's death without giving them cause to suspect that he might in fact have been discovered and we wished to avoid giving them any grounds, however slight, for imagining that GARBO might have been under surveillance, or through any incident have been discovered and turned around.

On the 5th July, 1943, it was decided that we would have to break the news to the Germans and, in the first place, GARBO reported that he had heard from a not very reliable source that Agent No. 6 had died. Against this he told them DOROTHY had not been notified of his death though she had been without news from him since 27th May. His last letter which had been forwarded to the Germans was dated 3rd June. We asked whether the agent had given any indication in the secret text of his last letter to suggest he was in any danger. They reacted as follows:-

"Last letter from Six dated 11th May, number nine. It only had military reports. The letter referred to in your message of the 23rd camouflaged in book has not yet arrived. Let us know the results of your check up about the packet of fruit. Bear in mind the possibility of Six having been arrested. Take precautionary measures also against the possibility of secret ink and other details relating to the service being found amongst Six's belongings. Take the greatest care when you visit or have dealings with Dorothy."

This message which was transmitted by wireless crossed with a letter from GARBO in which he likewise expressed his fear that the agent's death might in some way be connected with his espionage activities. Two weeks were allowed to pass before GARBO was able to confirm the death. He ascertained from DOROTHY, who as the agent's "unmarried wife" was eventually notified of his death by the War Office, that he was killed in an air crash. She had been told that the accident occurred at the time of his being moved to another station and so it was reasonable to assume he was carrying his kit with him and that any compromising evidence would have been destroyed. GARBO expressed his confidence that the agent's death had not compromised him in any way. He had set aside some £200 as payment for Agent No. 6 which amount he decided he would have to credit back to general funds since he considered it unwise to hand the money over to DOROTHY, who was not aware that the agent was engaged in espionage, or that his relations with GARBO were more than a normal friendship.

The wireless was by now, functioning with regularity. In May the Germans sent GARBO seventeen miniature photographs which contained a completely new transmitting plan, together with a new and far more elaborate and higher grade cypher table. This was the most important development in the case so far.

Some while prior to this development the Germans had warned GARBO that he should double encypher all his messages for greater security. At that time we knew the Germans had come to suspect we had broken the M.S.S. cypher which they were then using on the Peninsula circuit and they had changed to a new cypher which we were unable to break. Though the experts were not convinced that the new cypher was unbreakable they anticipated it might take a considerable time if they were eventually to be able to break it.

The new cypher which they had now sent GARBO turned out to be based on the same principle as the new cyphers which they had changed to on the M.S.S. Peninsula circuits. The material which we were now able to supply enabled G.C. & C.S. to read these lost circuits within a very short time.

There can be no doubt the Germans confided this extremely high grade cypher to GARBO (though it was so vital to their own security that it should never be discovered) because they considered the security of GARBO's work as vital as their own. There can be little doubt from later events Berlin was aware that GARBO had been given this cypher although this action must stand out as incredibly stupid on their part. They ended up their letter which contained this material with the following note marked "Important":-

"We trust that you will be able to guard all this material which we confide in you conscientiously and prevent it at any time from ever falling into the hands of the enemy."

The same batch of miniature photographs contained a new cover plan for the wireless service. The object of this transmitting cover plan was to make the GARBO station appear as if it were a British military station, so that it should avoid detection by our interception services. The most detailed instructions were given and GARBO was furnished with a number of rules for transmitting which he was instructed to pass on to his operator. The operator was also given instructions to use the military procedure signs and to drop the international "Q" Code which had previously been in use. As further cover the Germans would continue to use the international amateur procedure and thus the two stations would not in any way appear to be in contact.

As Military wireless activity in this country was, by this time, quite considerable and it was steadily increasing in volume, the cover plan which the Germans now proposed for GARBO's use caused considerable concern since, without changing military procedure, it was envisaged that it would be practically impossible to detect an uncontrolled agent, had any such agent been given similar instructions.

Up to the time of adopting this wireless cover plan the GARBO transmissions were being intercepted by the network of amateur interceptors working to R.S.S. and reports and intercepts on the GARBO station were being sent in from listeners as far afield as Scotland, Gibraltar and Canada. As soon as the new plan was put into operation the GARBO station was lost in the mass of military traffic which was constantly on the air.

In the original instructions GARBO's operator was told that whilst the Madrid station was transmitting it was essential that he should not break in and that if repeats were necessary they should be requested at the end of the transmission. It was in fact several months before this plan was actually put into operation, and had the original instructions been carried out to the letter, it is highly improbable that the GARBO station would ever have been detected. In fact when the plan was operating it was found quite impossible to carry on transmissions when conditions were unfavourable without breaking in. The Germans were the first to realize this and to act contrary to their own instructions. As a tribute to the efficiency of R.S.S the change over to the new plan was not disclosed to their intercepting staff but in spite of this they did, after a period of six weeks or so, detect the GARBO transmittor and report it as a suspect station.

In the same long letter a new system was adopted for the sending of secret letters. Three new cover addresses in Portugal were given and a new address in Madrid was provided. In all eight addresses were then operating. Each address was given a code number and four sender's names were provided for each cover address which GARBO was to use in rotation. GARBO was instructed to advise the Germans by wireless message whenever he despatched a letter, and to state the code number of the address to which it was being sent. This was to ensure that it would be promptly collected. The four sender's names for each cover address were to make it appear as if each addressee had four friends in England who wrote to them periodically.

CHAPTER XVIII.

GERMAN QUESTIONNAIRES.
CANADIAN 1ST DIVISION GOES OVERSEAS.
GARBO'S LETTER OF THE 2.8.43.
JUNE - JULY, 1943.

In June, 1943, it became apparent from the incoming questionnaires
that the Germans were becoming apprehensive that preparations were
in progress to carry out another surprise operation. The targets
which they appeared to suspect were widespread. They sent GARBO a
considerable number of questionnaires of which the following are
extracts:-

> "Try to find out if Greek troops are stationed close to the
> First Canadian Army or elsewhere in the south of England, and
> if so which Greek troops these are?"
> "It is of the greatest importance to discover the next
> operation."
> "Keep most careful watch for possible attacks against Spain
> and the Balearic Islands."
> "Very important to know the numbers of Divisions sent to
> North Africa and those which are still leaving for that
> destination."
> "Principal objective Northern Ireland. American and English
> activity and troop movements."
> "Various reports talk of Forces and ships in Iceland and in
> northern Scottish ports, especially Dundee and Aberdeen,
> ready to attack Norway. Large troop movements in the north of
> Scotland are reported. Check up on these reports."
> "Try to find out whether there are prohibited areas in the
> county of Yorkshire, the location of these zones and whether
> they are preparing to evacuate. Are there prohibited areas on
> the east coast of Scotland north of Aberdeen?"

Whilst these questionnaires were coming in the preparations
for the invasion of Sicily and Italy were advancing. Perhaps the
clearest indication that a further attack in the Mediterranean was
envisaged was the fact that the Canadian 1st Division, which had
already been identified and located and was well known to GARBO's
network, was shortly to embark from the Clyde and to land in Sicily.
In the normal course of events it would have been difficult for
the agents to have avoided discovering this but the German
questionnaires which reached us at that time gave us a perfect

opportunity to be put off the scent. We had received numerous important questionnaires which it was our first duty to investigate.

Preparations were already being made for Agent No. 5 to go to Canada. Before doing so he was instructed by GARBO to investigate the questionnaire about the presence of Greek troops in the vicinity of the 1st Canadian Army. He discovered none but learnt that the 3rd Canadian Infantry Division and 4th Canadian Armoured Division were stationed in the Brighton area, and that the 1st Canadian Infantry Division had left for the north where it had gone to undertake a training "and was expected to be away for a long time." Having terminated this investigation and before departing for Canada, he went up to Scotland to assist his brother, Agent No. 3, in the investigation of the questionnaire about the concentration of troops north of Aberdeen for an attack against Norway. Agents Nos. 3 and 5 sent GARBO an extensive joint report which permitted him to send a wireless message stating that his agents were able to confirm that no danger of an attack against Norway existed at the present, but there were considerable numbers of troops in training and the zone to the extreme north of Scotland was a prohibited area.

Agent No. 1 went off to Ireland to carry out enquires there. Agent No. 4 was still engaged in the Chislehurst Caves where he reported that no special activity had been noted to suggest an impending operation.

GARBO decided to investigate the Yorkshire questionnaire personally and was able, on his return, to report that there were no prohibited areas in Yorkshire though some farming areas on the coast had been prepared for evacuation to facilitate the exercising of armoured divisions already stationed in Yorkshire. In particular, he made reference in his letters to the 9th Armoured Division, which he commonly referred to as the "Panda Division" and the Guards Armoured Division.

It was during this period that the news of the death of Agent No. 6 was reported.

Thus, we were only left with the problem of occupying Agent No. 7 who was allowed to discover that numerous assault barges were preparing to assemble at Tenby and that troops were concentrating at Creselly and Marros in south Wales, and that notices had been put up signed by "Lieutenant-General Schreiber, Commander-in-Chief of Western Command" prohibiting the entry of non-residents in towns in the counties of Carmarthen and Pembroke between the 6th July and the 9th August. The opposition was invited to make aerial reconnaissance of the area in the hope that these activities, which were accurately reported, would be interpreted by the enemy as a rehearsal for an impending operation based on those shores. In fact the movement, reported were those of a genuine exercise, JANTZEN, which was allowed to be reported in order to encourage the enemy later to believe in PLAN WADHAM which was built up to threaten an attack with U.S. forces against the Brittany peninsula based on south Wales, the purpose of which was to contain German forces in Western France after our landing in Italy.

All these activities kept the GARBO organization busy without jeopardizing the security of forthcoming operations or of compromising his organization. At the end of July it was thought fit for GARBO to send a wireless message strongly deprecating the useless missions which the Germans had recently given his organization. He requested that he should be given some explanation as to how they obtained their false rumours and he complained that for about two months he had only received information from them suggesting that attacks would be made against Norway, France or the Balearics and that this information had been most misleading to him and constituted a dangerous procedure.

A few days later, on the 2.8.43, GARBO completed his second anniversary in England. He took this occasion to write one of his longer "Personal" letters to KUHLENTHAL. This letter perfectly illustrates their relationship and the eccentric mannerisms which GARBO had developed in his role as secret agent.

The following is an extract:-

"A few days ago I completed the second anniversary of my stay here, fulfilling from the start the sacred duty of defending the ideals which inspire me so profoundly against our common enemies, disturbers of justice and social order. I have accomplished a great deal since then, always without thought for the dangers through which I must pass, leaping all obstacles which they put in my way. I believe that I have accomplished my duty to the maximum of my power and ability, in spite of the bad training I had for this work, which, if it were not for the astuteness displayed and the daring of my temperament, it would certainly not have been possible now for me to be directing a service of such size and responsibility.......I am ensconced in an observation point situated in the opposite camp itself, and therefore can formulate with greater aptitude and more authority an opinion (which, from the behaviour of our high command) appears to be placed amongst the many which have to be temporarily pigeonholed.......Don't you realize that this is a sacrifice for me to write these long letters? My work weighs on me, God alive! But I know, although at times you smile at my humour, you appreciate the contents as more valuable than if you read a hundred English newspapers and heard a thousand Anglo-American radio transmissions, because through those you would only hear lies, and my writings only tell you concrete realities......My cool head and effrontery with which I defend the democratic-Jewish-Masonic ideology have opened many doors to me, and from there I have drawn opinions.......I am not therefore generally taken by surprise by all the moves of our enemy. He is cunning and has ambushes fit for bandits. The enemy's vitality gives cause for reflection...The time has come to take rather draconian decisions. I think the enemy laughs at his invulnerability, since he sees himself free from pitfalls and aerial attack, his factories continue to increase rhythmically, free from sabotage and paralysation. The Englishman has a belief in his potentiality and smiles with satisfaction at his progress in the military art......Why, I ask myself, do not our high command prepare for an attack against this island?.....Why do not they give them the enormous fright of having their arrogance brought low?.......I must discover the truth, even at the risk of you thinking me impertinent. My good will in advising you will cancel all the vice of indiscipline with which I do not fear that you will accuse me at this time.....England must be taken by arms, she must be fallen upon, destroyed and dominated, she must be sabotaged, destroying all her potentialities......We must take advantage of our boldness, our superiority, our integrity and strength, to anhialate them. If we suffer a reverse in Italy, I cannot admit that it is due to the weakness of German soldiers, a thousand times victorious. We are not lucky with our Italian ally....I love a struggle which is hard and cool, difficult and dangerous. I am not afraid of death, because I am a madman convinced by my ideals. I would prefer to die rather than see myself called democratic. Therefore I want to take action, and if for fear of losing the service, you order me and deprive me from moving along the lines I have suggested my co-operation shall still be the same......With a raised arm I end this letter with a pious remembrance for all our dead."

CHAPTER XIX.

DECEPTION
AUGUST - SEPTEMBER, 1943.

In August 1943, the GARBO organization was given its first task of
implementing deception plans.

OPERATION COCKADE had been planned with the object of
containing Axis forces on the Western seaboard of Europe to prevent
them from reinforcing either the Russian or the Mediterranean
theatres of war. It was designed to operate until the end of October,
1943, and was sub-divided into three operational deception plans:-

(i)   OPERATION WADHAM.
        Object:- To contain German forces in Western France by
        threatening an attack on the Brittany Peninsula based on
        south Wales ports.
        (Note: It will be recalled that GARBO's agent, No. 7, had
        already reported from south Wales the genuine Exercise
        JANTZEN the previous month which was the build up for
        WADHAM.)
(ii)   OPERATION TINDALL.
        Object:- To develop a deceptive threat aimed primarily at
        Stavenger to pin down German forces in Norway.
        Imaginary Order of Battle:- The British 4th Army (notional)
        incorporating the 52nd British Infantry Division, 3rd
        Canadian Inf. Division and the 3rd British Infantry
        Division.
        (Note: This operation was prolonged in phases up to June,
        1944, until after D Day of OVERLORD, when the notional 4th
        Army was transferred to southern England. Reduced threats
        to Norway were subsequently built up from time to time to
        suggest that in the event of a German withdrawal of their
        troops from Norway an operation would be mounted with two
        divisions under Scottish Command.)
(iii)   OPERATION STARKEY.
        Object:- To mount a major amphibious feint against the Pas de
        Calais area to convince the enemy that a large scale landing
        was imminent and to induce the German Air Force to engage
        their fighters in air battles at times, and in places, most
        suitable to ourselves.
        Imaginary Order of Battle:- 21 Army Group, with 1st Canadian
        Army, 2nd British Army and the 6th British Army (notional)
        under command.

(Note: In fact no mention of the 6th British Army was ever reported by our organization in this connection. The II British Corps, one of the two Corps which appeared in the imaginary Order of Battle as under its command was mentioned.)

Apart from the build up material passed by Agent No. 7 in support of OPERATION WADHAM the GARBO organization was unable to further implement this plan after the middle of August as it was decided to remove this agent from the south Wales region in order to situate him at Dover where he could combine with the rest of the GARBO organization to implement the most important of these operations, i.e. STARKEY.

OPERATION TINDALL was implemented by Agent No. 3 until the 25.8.43 when he too was sent to the south coast of England to combine in the implementation of STARKEY.

The plan was developed in the following way. On the 2.8.43 GARBO wrote to say that his Agent No. 7 had returned from south Wales and brought with him a detailed account of EXERCISE JANTZEN which, it was reported, he had witnessed, from which the conclusion could be drawn that the Exercise there had been a rehearsal for an operation to be undertaken against the coast of Brittany. Mention of this likely objective was included in the report. (In support of WADHAM.)

On the 4.8.43 Agent No. 1, who had returned from Northern Ireland, took a few days holiday at his home in south Wales before proceeding to Southampton at the request of his commercial employer. Whilst in south Wales the agent learnt about the Exercise which had recently been taking place and independently reported this to GARBO by stating that manoeuvres for the attack against the Continent had recently been carried out there. This, therefore, was independent confirmation of what Agent No. 7 had already reported. (In support of WADHAM.)

Henceforth until 9.9.45 the GARBO traffic was concentrated in support of OPERATION TINDALL.

On the 6.8.43 GARBO wrote to say that he had read in the Press that the Russians had attempted to attack the extreme north of Norway in assault barges but that the Germans had given them a hot reception. Recalling, however, his previous report that an Anglo-Russian offensive against Norway would be undertaken as soon as the Russians had advanced to a certain pre-arranged line, he became concerned lest the alleged Russian attack against northern Norway might not be the preliminary for the joint Anglo-Russian attack. The radio operator was at that time away on holiday and since GARBO had nothing to keep him in London he decided to go personally to

Scotland to consult with his Agent No. 3 and investigate this threat
to Norway. From Glasgow he mailed a letter in which he incorporated
numerous approved themes to indicate an increased threat to Norway,
i.e., Commandos had been training in mountain warfare prior to
joining the 52nd Division which was the already familiar mountain
trained Division reserved for the attack against Norway.

In the north of Scotland new camps were being constructed
near aerodromes for the accommodation of Airborne troops. Transport
planes had arrived for the use of Airborne troops; R.A.F. personnel
had been increased; new cranes and dock unloading equipment had been
observed. A considerable increase in the movement of troops and
material was noted as compared with the occasion when GARBO last
visited Scotland, etc.,

Leaving Agent No. 3 responsible to give the alert should the
threatened attack to Norway materialize, GARBO returned to London
on the 15.8.43 to find that on his arrival Agent No. 1, who had
already been in Southampton, was awaiting him in London with some
urgent reports. The agent was quite convinced that another
offensive would shortly be launched from the south coast and all the
suggestions indicated that the attack would be made against France.
Agent No. 1, who was by then in direct communication with the
Germans in secret writing, had already sent a more concrete report
by letter on the 11.8.43 giving credence to the state of alert by
saying he was under the impression that a military censorship had
been imposed on all communications from Southampton, therefore he
had decided to mail his letter from Winchester. In spite of this
precaution the Germans were to discover, on receipt of the letter,
that it had been tested for secret writing though the reagents which
had been used had failed to develop the agent's ink. Our faked
Censorship striping had the reaction of causing the Germans to warn
GARBO by wireless a few weeks later, that agents should no longer
send letters from regions where troops were concentrating for
future operations since they had evidence from various channels
that special Censorship measures were in force.

GARBO, preoccupied by the alert which he had received from
Agent No. 1 and recalling that whilst he was in Yorkshire he had been
told that the British 9th Armoured Division was proceeding to the
south coast, decided it would be a good plan to go personally to
Brighton to investigate the activities of the 1st Canadian Army.

On the 18.8.43 we received an incoming message stating that
Berlin was very interested to obtain confirmation whether the Panda
Division (9th Armoured Division) had in fact left Yorkshire.

On the 19.8.43 it was decided to implement the deception
plan by imposing a 100% overt Censorship test for secret writing on
all mail proceeding to the Iberian Peninsula. This entailed the

striping of all mail with a series of reagents. We had previously always withheld, from the Germans, the knowledge that we had a general reagent for testing bulk mail for […] the ink which GARBO and his agents were using. The Germans had, during the war, tested their own foreign mails with a reagent named […] which was especially applicable for the discovery of […] . Thus, we decided to use this same reagent, which is […] in colour, to stripe all the Peninsula mail. From this they had to assume that all future letters from the GARBO network must have been picked up in Censorship. Therefore, we continued notionally to write by air mail, intermitently sending them a letter through the courier which was allowed to reach them, from the numbering of which they were encouraged to gain the impression that a number of letters sent by air mail had been intercepted. From the fragmentary story contained in the courier letters they were given the impression that probably important and perhaps qualifying and more detailed information had been contained in the considerable number of letters which failed to reach them, than had been contained in the wireless messages on which they were, in the circumstances, now obliged to rely.

On his return from Brighton on the 23.8.43 GARBO sent a series of wireless messages which contained the following information about the south coast:-

The 1st Canadian Army and the 2nd British Army, as well as considerable Commando forces were concentrating along the south coast. Considerable armour was observed as well as large concentrations of fighter planes. From rumour GARBO learnt that nine first line divisions, including specially trained Canadian assault troops, were prepared to form the spearhead to establish a Second Front in the Pas de Calais area. New camps had been located at Bassett, Stoneham, Toothill, Chilworth, Broadlands, Hiltingbury and Hursley. Assault barges were moving along the coast, presumably to a concentration area. Anti-aircraft convoys were moving towards the south coast, GARBO concluded in a tone of apprehension by stating that he had urgently summoned Agents Nos. 7 and 3 to London and in view of the serious situation he requested daily transmissions.

Agent No. 4 had, for the last month, been transferred from the heavy labourer's work in the Chislehurst Caves to the canteen there. Before taking up his new job he was sent to a N.A.A.F.I. training school and from the headquarters he was sent out to various areas where there were troop camps so that he might gain experience. Thus, he was able to keep contact with the activities in the Chislehurst Caves whilst, at the same time, picking up a piece of information here and there. It was therefore convenient that at this time he should be sent by the N.A.A.F.I. to Dover for a few days, and on his return on the 26.8.43, he was able to increase the threat by

adding his report that large scale preparations for an attack were
coming to a head. He said that assault craft were concentrating
around Dover and Folkestone and that the large scale aerial attacks
by the Allied Air Forces which were then being carried out across
the Channel were designed to destroy German defences at the points
where the landing was anticipated.

On the 30.8.43 Agent No.1 reported the concentration of
assault craft in the Hamble river and that large convoys of Canadian
troops and armour were continually arriving in that area. The full
details, GARBO stated, were being forwarded in a letter which, due
to the recent Censorship measure in force never arrived.

By the 1.9.43 the first report from Agent No.7 from Dover was
transmitted, the agent having proceeded there after his meeting in
London with GARBO, to investigate the rather alarming reports which
Agent No. 4 had brought back after his brief visit. Agent No. 7
reported that all embarkation runways had been cleared of defence
obstacles, such as barbed wire and anti-tank blocks and that 45
motor torpedo boats had arrived in Dover harbour as well as a
minesweeping flotilla.

On the same day we received an incoming message in which
they pointed out that apart from the preparations at present being
controlled by GARBO's network the probability existed of other
preparations being made in Scapa Flow, the Humber river, Plymouth,
Lerwick and the Shetland Isles.

The following day Agent No. 3, who had proceeded to Shoreham at
the request of GARBO, sent in his first report from the south coast.
He stated that there were some hundred light naval craft there,
amongst them assault barges, torpedo boats and gun boats and that more
were expected. He added that they were daily embarking vehicles on the
embarkation slipways and that when loaded the boats departed for
camouflaged hideouts at dispersed points. The same day GARBO obtained
some information from an officer in the Merchant Navy, with whom he
had been in contact in London, to the effect that there was a large
concentration of shipping in various north west ports in England and
that all R.A.F. leave had been suspended since the 25.8.43.

Agent No. 7 contributed the information that a second
minesweeping flotilla had arrived at Dover and that both flotillas
had sailed for minesweeping in the Channel. GARBO urged them to
make aerial reconnaissances to ascertain whether the shipping
alleged to be in the north western ports of England was in fact
there, expressing the opinion that unless this was the case he did
not consider, after analysis of the agents' reports, that there was
sufficient tonnage on the south coast to justify a large scale
attack against the Continent. (This was an observation which the
enemy must have been bound to make, but it was thought highly

improbable that they could have succeeded in making a large scale
reconnaissance of the north west at that time against our superior
fighter opposition.) GARBO insisted that if they did not make this
reconnaissance he would be bound to move his Agent No. 3 from the
south coast to investigate in the north west. This brought a quick
reply that Agent No. 3 was to continue his mission in the south of
England, which was followed up by a further message which stated
that whilst it was quite probable that there were concentrations in
other parts of England it was not advisable to disperse the agents
at present engaged on the south and south east coasts. They told
GARBO that he should try to obtain information about the rest of
England through other channels, ending their message by stating
that they were very satisfied with his results to date.

It was at this period that GARBO first announced that he was
in contact with a new source, J(5)[(i)] an employee at the "Ministry of
War." Later it turned out that she was a secretary with whom GARBO
had developed a rather amorous association in order to extract
information from her. He gathered the impression through this
channel that either it was planned to attack with small forces to
probe, and then penetrate into enemy territory if opposition were
found to be weak, alternatively that there must be other large
unidentified forces elsewhere in preparation for an attack. (Though
this message slightly weakened the threat it was hoped that it would
safeguard GARBO when the operation failed to come off, whilst at the
same time showing his astuteness in observing the essential which
should have been apparent to any good military reporter.)

On the 5.9.43 Agent No. 1 reported that the 54th Division, as
well as two Canadian divisions, one armoured, were concentrating in
the Southampton area in addition to numerous other troops, and from
his report it became fairly obvious that Southampton was to be the
main concentration area. It was decided at this stage that there
would be little more that this agent could report from Southampton
which could usefully increase the threat. Therefore we made it
appear as if the letters which had been written by this agent from
the Southampton area and which had filed to reach their destination,
had been intercepted in Censorship, with the result that a search
had been made for the author who, in view of the fact that they had
been written in French, was suspected of being either a Frenchman or
a Belgian. Several of these nationals, the agent reported, had been
detained. The agent himself, was reported to have been subjected to
a search since he too was an alien, fortunately he had cleverly
concealed his working materials and he did not come under suspicion.
The authorities, therefore, unable to discover the spy, had decided

(i)   See Appendix No. VI.

to expel all non-resident foreigners from the area. The agent, very much shaken by this experience, was authorized by GARBO to return to his home to recover.

From GARBO's source, J(5), he learnt that General Anderson, C-in-C Second Army, was in Dover. This was intended to focus attention on the Dover area.

From Agent No. 3 he received a most important piece of information on the 7.9.43 which he transmitted at 2033 hours GMT that night. The agent had discovered from a very reliable source that the operation was to take place at dawn the following day subject to weather conditions being favourable, if not it was liable to be delayed a day or two. On the same day he learnt from Agent No. 7 that the General Headquarters of Commandos had been established at Dover and that Commandos 5 and 7 were concentrated there ready for operations.

Warned of the likelihood of an attack the Germans proceeded to sink block ships in the approaches to Calais. A warning was flashed from Berlin to the operational headquarters in France. They called their troops to the alert.

The operation did not come off at dawn on 8.9.43 so GARBO came up on the air at the scheduled time that night to report that troops were removing their insignias, small assault craft were concentrating at Dover and troops and craft had assembled at the embarkation hards at Hythe, Folkestone, Deal and Walmer. At the end of the transmission the operator gave the "wait" sign to make the impression that GARBO, having received a last moment communication had contacted the operator requesting him to keep on the air until GARBO had had time to encypher the additional information and get it to him. The message which followed, when contact was resumed, stated that Agent No. 3 had come up to London that night to report that iron rations for four days had been handed out that very evening at 6 o'clock to assault troops, and that all men had been confined to barracks and that it was expected the operation would take place that same night.

The following morning the operation was carried out. Troops were embarked at Southampton, they sailed into the Channel to within sight of Calais whilst protected by the enormous forces of Fighter Command which unfortunately failed to draw the German Air Force into battle. The main object of the operation having failed, the troops returned to the south coast where they disembarked and carried out landing exercises.

Later that day an announcement was made by the B.B.C. to the effect that large scale invasion exercises had been carried out in the Channel, that our troops had been within sight of the French coast, but that the enemy had failed to take any action.

There was, it will be recalled, a good deal of speculation amongst the British public at the time as to what had really taken place. Some members of the public speculated that a raid had been planned and called off at the last minute, others believed the announcement. The Germans, we hope, were even more confused.

Though it can be said that GARBO had reported accurately, and would have failed in his duty as a spy had he withheld the information, the announcement was likely, we feared, to discredit him to some extent.

On the 9.9.43 GARBO forwarded a report from his Agent No. 7 which stated that the troops had again disembarked and were returning to their bases, he added that the reasons were unknown, but it appeared that the operation had been suspended. The troops, he claimed, were both surprised and disappointed. GARBO, characteristically taking the initiative, added that he could definitely prove the lie of the ridiculous Press and radio official announcement that the operation had only been a practice. He added that he was in possession of some very interesting information which he would send by letter. The following day he had said that, whilst there was absolute reserve in official circles it was speculated that the failure to carry out the operation was connected with the Italian Armistice (which had just been announced) and he hinted that there were people who believed that Germany might react the same way. He concluded by saying there existed confusion, unchecked optimism, and extravagant rumours.

Throughout the operation we were able to observe German reactions On Most Secret Sources. GARBO's reports were retransmitted from Madrid to Berlin fully and accurately. There can be little doubt that KUHLENTHAL was greatly relieved to receive GARBO's let out at the end of the operation, maintaining that the British statement that it had been no more than an exercise was a lie, for he transmitted this on in full, and he was guilty of adding colour to our statement that the troops were both surprised and disappointed when they were made to disembark by retransmitting this as:-

"The measure caused disgust amongst the troops."

On the 13.9.43 any preoccupation which we had had as to whether we might not have played our hand a little too freely was allayed. We were provided with the following M.S.S. message from Berlin to Madrid, giving Berlin's appreication on two of the messages which had been transmitted and apparently checked by O.K.W:-

"Both reports are first class. Between 1 and 3/9 English minesweepers were observed in the Channel off Boulogne.

These boats are presumably connected with V-Mann's reports
about the sailing of 2 minesweepers flotillas on 1/9 from the
harbour of Dover. The loading of motorized vehicles on to
landing barges near Shoreham appears possible. The report
about the arrival of the Panda Division in the Brighton areas
is a confirmation of other reports. The report according to
which General Anderson is with his H.Q. in Dover as C-in-C
of the 2nd Army is creditable. Please get the V-Mann to keep
an eye on all troop movements and preparations, and also
any possible embarkations, especially in eastern and south
eastern England. Speedy reports on this subject are urgently
desired."

A comparative table was drawn up of all the GARBO network
messages implementing OPERATION STARKEY together with the Most
Secret Source retransmissions from which it was possible to judge
that the entire Special Means plan as drawn up by the Planners of
COSSAC was retransmitted to Berlin. It was also noted from the same
source that on the 6.9.43 Berlin had classified GARBO's reports as
"Particularly valuable." It was also stated that the close
investigations of troop movements etc., in the areas covered by the
GARBO network were: "Of extreme importance."
      M.S.S. also revealed that when, on the 7.9.43, GARBO
requested that his report should be passed to France, his
instructions were carried out and the message was retransmitted to
France, marked "Urgent."
      If the operation served a useful purpose as a practice for
the troops engaged, it can be said to have served us equally
valuably as a rehearsal for the implementation of a major deception
plan. Now we had evidence that GARBO's integrity had not been
jeopardized through the practicing of this operational deception it
became evident that, providing we did not arouse suspicion prior to
the carrying out of OVERLORD, we had established a channel for
deception which was capable of rendering a valuable service. It
taught us that the more sensational the reports the more certain
could we be of Madrid retransmitting them to headquarters. It served
as a lesson that wherever possible we should, in future, aim at
making our reports as specific as possible, rather than to take any
risk in transmitting more subtle messages, the point of which, were
more likely than not, to be missed. We were able to discover that in
some cases where messages appeared to be of extreme urgency they
were retransmitted to Berlin with approximately one hour's delay in
Madrid. Other valuable experiences were gained.
      Throughout the operation we were working to a plan which had
been drawn up by COSSAC (Chief of Staff, Supreme Allied Command,

later superseded by SHAEF, Supreme Headquarters, Allied
Expeditionary Forces.) They provided us with a Special Means
(double-agents) implementation plan. This was drawn up in the form
of a number of serials. Each serial contained a story which was to be
passed to the enemy, the target date by when the information should
be in the possession of the enemy and, the factual events with which
the deceptive story was to be connected, thus, we would be informed
that two minesweeping flotillas would sail from Dover harbour on the
1.9.43 and that it was desirable that the enemy's attention should
be drawn to the minesweeping operations which they would be carrying
out in the Pas de Calais area by the 2.9.43 and it should be implied
that these operations were connected with a forthcoming cross
channel assault.

In spite of careful planning on the part of COSSAC the
difficulties with which we were confronted were enormous. In the
first place, COSSAC was not a recognized approving authority. The
procedure adopted was the following: The case officer would draft
a message based on the serial for the day in accordance with the
network's style of reporting. This would be submitted to GARBO who
would inevitably make certain modifications in the final Spanish
version. After translating the message back into English it would be
submitted to COSSAC to ensure that it interpreted the meaning of the
serial. Further changes were invariably made by COSSAC and the
revised message was then submitted to the Service approving
authorities, and, if modified in any way re-submitted to COSSAC for
final approval. Lastly, the amended message would have to be re-
checked with GARBO before forwarding the final message in Spanish.
If, as frequently occurred, he took the view that the alterations
made were inconsistent with his style and urged that he should be
allowed to make further modifications then the whole process of
making fresh translations and submitting them to COSSAC and the
approving authorities would have to be repeated. This procedure was
altogether chaotic since we were transmitting every day and in
addition there were invariably last minute changes of plan. For
instance, the minesweeping flotilla which was due to arrive in Dover
on the 1.9.43 in accordance with the plan might, at the last moment,
be delayed and not reach there until the 2.9.43, thus, late in the
afternoon we might be confronted with having to cancel the messages
which we had worked on all that day and substitute some other
material in its place. Although the enormous difficulties which we
experienced during the period of implementing STARKEY were to some
extent remedied by the time we were to implement the cover plan for
OVERLORD they were by no means ever overcome, and they always
constituted by far the most strenuous and exasperating work in the
running of the case.

Another experience which we gained at this time was the vital necessity of controlling the Press and other sources of information lest they should contradict the work of our organization.

For instance, it came to our notice that on the 6.9.43 a decision had been reached, without consultation with us, for the B.B.C. to broadcast a message on its French service to warn the French Underground Movements that the activities which were taking place in England did not concern them and they were not to rise or show their hand. The message was drafted in such a way as to constitute a serious threat of compromising the GARBO network and the plan he was trying to implement. The point at issue was that if our deception achieved its aim it risked involving a rising amongst the French patriots, and, in consequence, the Underground organizations would be prematurely brought to light.

After bringing considerable pressure to bear we were able to induce the authorities concerned to accept the following draft message which we had drawn up to substitute the most compromising message which was about to be put out by the B.B.C.:-

"Be careful of German provocations. We have learnt that the Germans are circulating inspired rumours that we are concentrating armies on our coasts with intentions of invading the Continent. Take no notice as these provocations are intended to create among you manifestations and disorders which the Germans will use as an excuse for repressive measures against you. Be disciplined, use discretion, and maintain order; for when the time arrives for action you will be advised in advance."

To round off the incident GARBO wrote a long letter on the 13.9.43 which he forwarded by courier in which he summarized the events which had taken place. He enclosed with it numerous cuttings from the daily press which backed up his arguments to prove that the recent military manoeuvres had been the prelude to a large-scale raid which had been called off at the last moment and that the British official statement that it had been nothing more than a military practice was therefore officially inspired. He argued that he did not think the British High Command had sufficient sense of humour to take their troops for an outing on the high seas nor that they had such a surplus of petrol and bombs as to amuse themselves by using these against objectives which had no strategic value unless the aerial bombardments were followed up by the landing of troops. In addition, he suggested, it would have been far less dangerous to have carried out a practice in an area where the enemy was less able to disrupt their tactical plans.

GARBO took this opportunity to build up his new contact, the secretary in the Ministry of War, by attributing to her the statement that the operation had been studied and planned to take place about the middle of September; it was to have been a large scale raid intended to facilitate the disembarkation in Italy by obliging the Germans to engage in battle in Northern France.

He concluded by saying that the rapid developments in Italy had removed all interest in this operation which had resulted abortive after the enormous energy and expenditure entailed. The British public announcement had thus been put out as a last minute attempt to cover the sudden change of plan.

GARBO's letter, crossed with an incoming wireless message from the Germans of the same date, in which they notified him that Berlin was very satisfied with his reports over the past few weeks, they went on to say that the possibility of an assault from the south and south east coast of England still existed, since the British had everything prepared in readiness for an operation which could be carried at quick notice, without further lengthy preparations. GARBO was requested to keep a strict watch on the movements and concentrations of troops and he was told they would be listening daily at the agreed hours for any urgent news.

CHAPTER XX.

THE "BLOWING" OF THE GARBO COVER ADDRESSES IN LISBON.

To indicate to the enemy that special Security measures were being taken to prevent leakages of information prior to an important military operation and thus to implement OPERATION STARKEY a 100% Censorship was imposed on mails to the Iberian Peninsula and Switzerland.

The categories of letters previously tested by Censorship for secret writing were all letters which aroused the suspicion of Censorship examiners irrespective of their destination, and all letters addressed to Iberian, Swiss or Swedish towns where the enemy was known to be operating cover addresses.

Under normal conditions only 10% - 15% of the letters which passed through Censorship Testing Department were released bearing visible signs of testing, this represented approximately 5% of the total volume of mail to European countries.

By increasing the testing of mails to the Iberian Peninsula and Switzerland, excluding special categories, to 100% during the period of STARKEY, involved the marking of a total 22,000 items during the first week.

Apart from this overt testing of bulk mails drawing attention to OPERATION STARKEY, it was designed to assist Censorship, by letting it become known to the enemy that we were in possession of the reagent for [...] and thus discourage them from using this ink which, on account of its complex development, if tested other than in the overt way of using [...] created considerable difficulty if mails were to be secretly bulk tested for this ink.

Other double agents operating from this country were, with two exceptions, using various forms of [...] inks. So as not to interfere with their operations, the variety of reagents selected for special testing was so arranged as to exclude a reagent which would detect the [...] group of inks. This had the advantage of making the Germans believe that we had not captured any agent who had been sent to this country with a [...] ink and that we therefore had no grounds to assume that they were using it. The two exceptions, it was decided, should not write during this period of censorship.

It was taken into consideration that, since the secret writing in GARBO's letters was partly encyphered the interception of his letters in Censorship and their development should not give the Germans grounds to feat that we would be led to the discovery of his organization. Before applying the [...] test the plan was referred to G.C. & C.S to ensure that the Germans would have no reason to fear that the GARBO cypher had become compromised through the discovery of his secret letters. We were advised in reply, that this was not a risk to be considered, as the Germans would know that the interception of these letters would not enable us to discover the cypher.

A plan was considered and discussed with S.I.S. for producing the GARBO letters, notionally intercepted, as a pretext for a protest to the Portuguese Government against the use, by the Germans, of addresses in their capital for the reception of espionage material against this country. The plan was finally dropped, mainly on account of shortage of time to carry it out satisfactorily.

On the assumption that M.I.5, to whose notice the intercepted GARBO letters would be brought, would have to take drastic action, and because we wished to make the Germans believe that the intercepted letters had given no clue as to the identities of the writers, it was decided to carry out an interrogation of the addresses in Lisbon. It was hoped that these interrogations would bring to the notice of the German Intelligence organization the fact that the British authorities were trying to identify a network of agents operating in the United Kingdom. The manoeuvre had the further objective of harassing the enemy and forcing him to undertake the difficult task of providing further cover addresses in order to keep their agents' lines of communication open.

As will be recalled the operation was initiated by GARBO's Agent No. 1 in his first letter from the Southampton area. This letter reached its destination. The second and third were intercepted, leading to the expulsion of all aliens from the Southampton area.

Agent No. 3 was represented as having lost three letters during the period of censorship and GARBO himself as having lost 13 letters. Two of GARBO's letters were allowed to reach their destination. These were both written to his Madrid cover address. The purpose of this was to leave one address uncompromised. The first of these two letters, dated 21.8.43, had overt signs of testing with the general developer and was forwarded in the period immediately prior to using [...] developer. The second, dated 3.9.43, was allowed to go forward without any markings, in spite of the fact that this was mailed after [...] test had been introduced. It was therefore made to appear as if this letter had come into the category of letters exempted from testing. This special category comprised genuine trade letters between established banks, shipping companies etc., To make this plausible the letter was written on Claridges Hotel notepaper, the cover text dealt with the writer's appointments with various ambassadors and referred to a lunch which

he had had the previous day with the Duke of Alba. It was signed in
the name of a Spanish nobleman. Thus, it was presumed that the
Censor hesitated to leave evidence, by testing, to suggest that we
even suspected such a high personage of possibly engaging in
espionage. Our hope of saving this address in this manner was not
fulfilled since the Germans were prepared to take no risks and they
cancelled it for all further communications. The same applied to
GARBO's Agent No. 5, who was by then established in Montreal, and a
letter from him dated 18.8.43 was allowed to reach its destination
without incident, nevertheless, the Germans instructed this agent
to cease all correspondence with Portugal on the assumption that
since the addresses he was using were simultaneously being used by
Agents Nos. 1 and 3 from Great Britain they had become compromised.

In all, ten GARBO cover addresses were compromised through
this manoeuvre.

By sheer coincidence a certain Jose DIAS DE SILVA, who had at
one time acted as a German cover addressee in Lisbon for GARBO
correspondence, contacted the S.I.S. representative in Lisbon
immediately prior to the imposition of the special censorship
testing. He informed S.I.S. that some months previously he had been
approached by a certain Antonio de SOUZA LOPEZ (another GARBO
addressee) and had been persuaded to act as a German cover addressee
for correspondence from the United Kingdom. He maintained that,
whilst at the time he had not realized the significance of this
correspondence, its embarrassing nature had since come to his
notice, whereupon he decided to report the matter to the appropriate
British authorities in Lisbon. He brought with him a letter
addressed to Maria ESTRELA, a further GARBO addressee, whom he
maintained was his girl friend.

SILVA was given the impression that after investigations had
been made we had conclusive evidence that the correspondence which
he had submitted to us was from a German spy and we asked for his
collaboration to assist in the identification of the unknown
writer. These addresses were therefore technically compromised
through SILVA's action, though it is improbable that the Germans,
though we later brought this incident to their notice, were ever
convinced of this, and they were rather inclined to the belief that
we discovered the addresses through Censorship.

A list of all the notional letters supposed to have been
intercepted in Censorship from the GARBO organization was supplied
to S.I.S. Lisbon, together with the dates on which they were
supposed to have been written and the corresponding names which
would have appeared as sender of each of the letters.

On the assumption that these letters had been discovered in
Censorship and found to be suspect, and having failed to proceed

with our enquiries here due to the fact that the senders had used
fictitious names and addresses, S.I.S. Lisbon was asked to
interrogate the addressees and obtain information about the
senders. They were asked to make it appear as if we were genuinely
trying to identify unknown spies in this country. They could offer
bribes for information or for the subsequent handing over of letters
arriving from other parts of the world not controlled by our
Censorship.

The object of these enquiries was to ensure that the news
would leak back to the Germans to convince them we were really doing
everything in our power, if unsuccessfuly, to catch the authors of
the spy letters.

It was not until the 2.10.43 that the Germans seemed to
realize what had taken place when they sent GARBO the message that a
large number of letters had failed to arrive. This, they said, was
apparent from the numbering of the letters to Madrid which had
reached them. They recommended that GARBO should only use the
courier until the missing letters had arrived. It was evident,
however, that at that time our interrogations of the addressees had
not come to the notice of the Germans. Little was obtained from
these interrogations. Possibly the addressees were too afraid to
talk, at least they professed innocence and were evasive in replying
to our questions.

On the 8.10.43 we asked S.I.S. to interrogate Odette da
CONCEICAO, the addressee to whom the famous cake containing the
aircraft recognition book had been delivered. It was anticipated that
her interrogation would start the alarm since, it appeared from the
fact that the Germans had signalled her out on a previous occasion as
the one person with whom GARBO's courier could safely make contact,
it was likely that she was their most trusted cover address. Her
interrogation was non-productive, since she maintained that she had
never offered her address for accommodation purposes to anyone.

It would appear as if she notified her German masters
immediately of what had occurred for, on the night of the 12.10.43
we received a wireless message registering their first serious
reaction, which read as follows:-

"Nearly all Lisbon addresses have been interrogated with
regard to the origin of letters. This appears to be a
general measure all over the country. In accordance with
instructions addressees have replied satisfactorily.
Nevertheless no more letters have arrived. Our
representative has left for Lisbon. Cease all correspondence
also via the courier until further notice. Likewise agents'
correspondence. We will have to study a new procedure for

sending correspondence avoiding English mail, also
Portuguese, by making use of cut-outs. I will continue to
keep you informed as to the results of our representative's
journey. It is advisable that you should be on your guard."

From M.S.S. messages there can be little doubt that a special
envoy was sent to Lisbon, presumably to investigate these
occurrences and to arrange for new cover addresses.

After three days delay in making contact with Madrid by
wireless due to unfavourable weather conditions we sent the
following message on the 16.10.43:-

"I have some letters written which I had proposed to hand to
the courier in view of the addresses having been suspended I
suggest sending them by courier to Poste Restante in Lisbon.
Let me know if your representative can collect them there
and in what name I should address them. I have everything
prepared should the English police investigate........Let me
know to-morrow which is the last letter you have received by
air mail also whether the possibility exists that the British
censor has discovered the good ink."

In view of the fact that they had always pretended to GARBO
that the ink he was using was so high grade that it could never be
developed by the British we knew that they would resent having to
admit to him now that it could be discovered. Their reply the
following day showed that they were embarrassed:-

"There is no probability that your ink is discoverable, but
one must take into account incalculable factors, possibly
being worked out with the chemical means at the disposal of
the enemy."

Further messages of that day notified GARBO of those letters
which they had received. He was instructed not to send letters to
Poste Restante, Lisbon, but that he should await their
representative's return from Lisbon and that meanwhile they would
be listening every day in case he called them by wireless.

On the 1.10.43 we had prepared a great batch of
correspondence for forwarding by courier which instead of being
written in secret ink, part of it had been typed en clair on tissue
paper, and embedded in plaster of Paris inside a flask. On the
2.10.43 we sent a wireless message confirming that this package had
left by courier addressed to Senora OLIVEIRA in Lisbon. This was
forwarded prior to receiving their notification of alarm and we had

instructed S.I.S. to hold up the interrogation of OLIVEIRA until the letter had been mailed in Lisbon. Due to unforeseen circumstances caused by delays in the S.I.S. Bag to Lisbon the package was not mailed until the 14.10.43 by which date the Germans had already reacted to the interrogation of the other addressees. When, on the 19.10.43, we had still received no advice of receipt of the flask containing the correspondence, we sent a wireless message asking for its immediate acknowledgment, pointing out that part of the correspondence had been written en clair. The following day they replied to say that on account of the state of alarm created by the enemy service investigations Senora OLIVEIRA had refused to accept delivery of the package containing the flask and that although they were doing everything in their power to recover it they would have to count on its loss.

The loss of the flask was an unanticipated development in the manoeuvre. It was most unsatisfactory that we should have to remain in ignorance of the final destination of this compromising package. At this time we had to assume that it had reached the dead letter section of the Portuguese post office. The fact that the addressee had refused to accept delivery, and the discovery by the Portuguese authorities that the name and address of the sender was that of a fictitious Portuguese, would be bound to arouse their suspicion. If the postal authorities, therefore, brought the package to the notice of the Portuguese police there was a danger that it would be broken open and its contents discovered. If the Portuguese officer handling the investigations were friendly with the Germans he might have handed it to them. If he were friendly with us he might bring it to our notice. The worst situation would develop if the package should remain lost but the Germans suspect that it had been brought to our notice and that from the en clair contents we had obtained information which would have jeopardized GARBO's security. The uncertainty was very unsatisfactory and so on the 23.10.43 we sent the following wireless message:-

"There exists really grave danger. The flask is highly compromising, it contains a letter from Agent No. 5 on Canadian hotel notepaper. I think there was some reference made to the radio and to the increase of the service. You must get it at all costs, suborning the post man or the post office. I also sent a four page secret ink letter dated 6.10.43 to the same address. Do not permit OLIVEIRA to betray you. You must force her to comply even by threats, making her realize the danger should the flask and the letters fall into the hands of the Portuguese police. Should she absolutely refuse to co-operate you should get someone to contact the

postman who should tell him the story that he has been
courting the niece of OLIVEIRA and that the aunt had refused
to allow her to accept a valuable present from him being a
married man, in consequence of which he had put a false name
on the package as the sender. He should offer the postman a
large reward for the return of the package."

This message, in spite of its somewhat comic note, produced
the desired results. We know from Most Secret Source that the
package was recovered and that the Germans in Madrid had been most
anxious about it, even suspecting that during the period it had been
lost it might have been tampered with by the British. They confirmed
its receipt on the 28.10.43 in the following message:-

"Steps taken in Lisbon have resulted in the recovery of the
flask complete with contents. I am very happy."

Prior to its receipt their state of preoccupation was summed
up in a long message instructing us as follows:-

"You should all remain quiet in your normal occupations. No
paper or similar reference to the service should be left in
your houses. As to the radio we will continue to listen daily
but you must only make use of it for matters of the greatest
importance. It is preferable, should it be possible, that you
do not operate more than once every ten or fifteen days. The
other collaborators letters are also missing. All measures
have been taken to prevent enemy investigations from
obtaining any detail regarding the destination or origin of
the letters........From to-day on and for the next six or
eight weeks you must reduce your activity and that of your
agents, paying them their wages but avoiding all contact with
them unless in case of news of extreme urgency, for example,
preparations to attack the Continent. Taking into
consideration the situation in general there exists no
reason for you to alarm yourself too much assuming that the
contents of the lost letters would not give away a direct
clue to you according to the advice I have always given you.
Result of our delegate's investigation in Lisbon shows close
collaboration of English and Portuguese Censorship checking
up on the existence of the senders which appear on
intercepted letters which come from England in all cases when
they are not perfectly clear. Your station must be listening
on fixed days according to the plan in case of urgent matters
on our part. Maintain close contact with the courier and you

can offer him good payment since we will need him very much
later on. We will let you know in due course when the service
is to return to normal. In spite of these measures I beg you
not to lose touch with the south and south east and that
Three should attend to Scotland in regard to preparations for
such an attack."

There can be no doubt that our manoeuvre completely destroyed
the greater proportion, if not all, the German cover address network
in Lisbon. Together with the cover addresses which had been given to
GARBO and subsequently cancelled, the Germans had wasted twenty-
three cover addresses through him. We had deprived them of the
future use of some of their best secret inks. We made them realize
the necessity of keeping GARBO supplied with only the most reliable
cover addresses, cyphers and secret means of communication. We
increased their confidence in GARBO's ability to run his
organization and to evade detection by the British Security
Service. It furthermore gave verisimilitude to his notional network
and to the suggestion that the Security Service was exhausting
itself in vain in an attempt to discover this evasive German agent.
What was difficult to assess was whether they associated all this
with OPERATION STARKEY.

From subsequent evidence it appears that the Germans were
never able to re-establish, in Portugal, a new cover address network
on the scale of the one which they had previously been using. It was
not until the middle of December that they were able to furnish
GARBO with the first of a new series of "confidential addresses."
They permanently cancelled all air mail correspondence and obliged
him to use the courier exclusively. He was instructed to discontinue
the old numeration of his letters after having reached Letter No.
274, and to recommence numbering his letters at No. 1. From this
time they corresponded with GARBO exclusively in microphotography.

CHAPTER XXI.

TRANSFER OF AGENT NO. 5 TO CANADA.
THE NOTIONAL DEAD CUT-OUT.
AGENT NO. 1 RESIGNS.
GARBO'S DIARY.
RECRUITMENT OF 4(3).
IMPLEMENTATION OF PLAN JAEL.
RECRUITMENT OF AGENT NO. 3(3).
THE BROTHERHOOD OF THE ARYAN WORLD ORDER.

It was during STARKEY that Agent No. 5 was transferred to Canada. He left the country legally and it was his intention to establish himself in Canada, if possible, but if not to proceed to the U.S.A. Having been given good notification of this, the Germans were enabled to send GARBO questionnaires for these two countries to pass on to the agent.

GARBO supplied the agent with the [...] ink and a cover address in Lisbon. As was shown in the accounts of the organization GARBO still had in hand the sum of $1,052 which he handed over to Agent No. 5 to cover his expenses during his first months activities in the Western Hemisphere. He arranged that the Germans should never write to the agent direct but that all instructions and questionnaires should be sent to GARBO who would forward them on from London. This entailed minimum risk for the agent, since it was to be assumed that Canadian Censorship was less severe with correspondence coming from the U.K. than with that coming from the Iberian Peninsula. Furthermore, GARBO had the courier service operating between Portugal and London, and there was always the possibility of his being able to recruit a courier to carry communications from England to Canada should this ever become necessary. In addition, correspondence was to be maintained between the agent and GARBO in London, and GARBO undertook to give him adequate instructions both for his personal security and to ensure the maximum accomplishment in his undertaking. Agent No. 5 was given two cover addresses for communicating with GARBO in London. He could communicate through his brother, Agent No. 3 in Scotland, concealing his secret communication in the wrapping of a parcel. For this the agent was instructed in the wax method of writing, thus the wrapping of the parcel which would contain the secret messages, could be developed by applying graphite powder.

To ensure that he would be able to continue to communicate, even should Agent No. 3 ever meet with a misfortune, he was supplied with an additional cover address which was that of Agent No. 4 in London.

We told the Germans that Agent No. 4 had, some two months previously, moved to one of the hotels which had been taken over by Gibraltarian refugees. The room which Agent No. 4 was occupying had previously been occupied by a Gibraltarian refugee whose name had been identical with that of the agent. (It is not uncommon for two or more Gibraltarians to have identical names.) The previous occupier had, however, died shortly before the agent took over the room. The coincidence of the similarity of names gave GARBO an idea which he thought we should exploit. Agent No. 5 was therefore instructed to use this address when necessary but, as cover, to send a certain number of innocuous letters which would be recognizable on receipt by a prearranged code sign, the idea being that the innocent letters would be handed over to the porter in the building by Agent No. 4 who would state that the writer was unknown to him and that they must have been intended for the deceased Gibraltarian. The secret letters, which would be recognizable by a code sign, he would retain. Thus, he would be provided with an alibi should a secret letter ever be intercepted by Censorship, for it would then be assumed that this too had been intended for the dead man. This cover address did not operate indefinitely since the hotel in which Agent No. 4 was living was hit by one of the early V-1 bombs.

A brisk correspondence was, however, maintained between GARBO and his Agent No. 5 dealing with organizational matters and GARBO would frequently quote extracts from this notional correspondence in his letters to the Germans.

The task of running Agent No. 5 from Canada was a great deal more complicated than that of running the agent from North Africa where a deception staff was installed which was able to supply us with the traffic. In fact it would have been impossible to have run a notional agent from Canada had it not been for the fact that the M.I.5 representative in Montreal had previously served in London as a case officer of double agents who, at the same time, was conversant with the GARBO case. He was in fact the officer who had carried out the meetings with the Spanish Assistant Military Attache in connection with PLAN DREAM under the alias DOUGLAS WILLS. He, therefore, was able to assume the responsibility of finding adequate traffic, much of which, was based on information which had appeared in the local press and other traffic which he was able to get the Directors of Intelligence of the Service Departments to approve whenever necessary. He too acted as scribe for the secret letters which were forwarded to the Germans, he likewise wrote the cover texts, and maintained a close correspondence with GARBO's case officer here which formed the basis of the notional correspondence between GARBO and his Agent No. 5.

When, on the 12.10.43, the Germans instructed GARBO to tell

all his agents to cease writing to Lisbon following on our "blowing" the Lisbon cover addresses, GARBO was assumed to have taken steps to warn his Agent No. 5 in Canada. He was instructed to continue to write in the best ink to the British cover address so that his original letters could be forwarded by courier to the Germans. This procedure was hereafter adopted and continued until the end of the case, during which some 45 letters were written by Agent No. 5 to the Germans.

Various plans were considered for using this channel for deception. The possibility of his sailing notional convoys which would be received in Glasgow and acknowledged here by Agent No. 3, were examined by the Admiralty but for various reasons this and other proposals which we put forward were not used. The agent's reports, however, were highly appreciated in Madrid from where the entire contents of the letters were eventually transmitted verbatim by wireless to headquarters. This, in spite of the fact that the information was invariably considerably out of date by the time it reached Madrid. To justify this action it may be said that this was probably the only information which the Germans received from Canada and therefore it was not without academic interest to them.

Within a short period of Agent No. 5's arrival in Canada he set about building up a network. The first person to collaborate with him was his cousin from Buffalo who visited him in Montreal before the end of 1943, and was subsequently quoted with regularity under the symbol of 5(1) [(i)] alias CON, as a source of his information.

Since the danger of an attack from the south coast had been called off we again found ourselves short of traffic and GARBO had to resort to the old plan of padding out his letters, suggesting various organizational changes, he proposed training the various agents as wireless operators and having small portable transmitters built for them by the Operator. He suggested that he should be supplied with carrier pigeons. Neither of these proposals were adopted. The question of payments to agents was discussed. A special bonus for the work achieved during STARKEY was approved. The salaries of all agents were increased by 50%. GARBO was authorized to spend lavishly on his new contact, J(5). GARBO was told that he might carry out his plan of confiding all the secrets of the organization in Agent No. 3 who would, if necessity arose, deputize for GARBO, whilst, meanwhile he would act as GARBO's assistant. It was approved that each of the established agents, i.e., Agents Nos. 3,4 and 7 should endeavour to recruit and form their own networks which would operate to GARBO.

(i)   See Appendix No. XIX.

In this connection Agent No. 7 was pointed out as GARBO's greatest hope since he was a Welsh Nationalist and knew a number of individuals who would be glad of an opportunity to engage in hostile activities against the English. Agent No. 7, however, was planning to go back to sea, but was induced to stay on after the Germans had signalled GARBO that in view of his excellent collaboration GARBO was to endeavour to retain this agent for special purposes and to pay him an increased wage, if necessary, to persuade him not to return to the Merchant Navy.

Agent No. 4 was to try to pick up subversive Italians in Soho and recruit them into his sub-organization.

Agent No. 1, however, did not appreciate GARBO's generous offer of promotion. He was too shaken by the incident which he had experienced when interrogated whilst engaged on his espionage work in Southampton, and in spite of a holiday with pay which GARBO had ordered him to take, he still remained panicky until GARBO finally paid him off, pretending to him that the work of the organization had come to an end and that he was dividing up the cash in hand with those who had collaborated with him. He handed the agent the arbitrary sum of £114. According to his monthly statement of account as submitted to the Germans GARBO had a credit balance of German funds amounting to between £5,000 - £6,000 at the time.

The STARKEY operation and the excitement over the letters caught in Censorship resulted in GARBO having been on the air almost every evening for several months, and although both we and the Germans used to point out to one another the grave risks of this practice the transmissions were allowed to continue, with little, if any, reduction in their frequency and regularity. The Germans were perhaps more apprehensive of this danger since they had only just been given the shock of the discovery of the letter writing system, and to have compromised the wireless now would have been disastrous.

During the period that we were waiting for them to work out a new system of correspondence GARBO continued to write his secret letters with regularity in the form of a diary, pending receipt of a new address to which he could forward them. Preoccupied since the interception of so many of his letters, he decided to make greater use of his code and to encypher a substantial part of the text. Some letters contained no less than 250 encyphered groups. This procedure, apart from demonstrating his desire to safeguard himself, also accounted for a great deal of his time and thus it limited to some degree the quantity of his information.

Between the 6.10.43 and the 13.12.43, by when we received the first of the new cover addresses, we wrote no less than 49 pages of secret text which must have contained some 2,000 encoded groups. The letters were eventually concealed at the back of a glazed and framed engraving and forwarded by courier as a Christmas present for the new addressee. The letters in this package contained a great variety of information. There were replies to questionnaires, reports from Agent No. 3 who had made a reconnaissance of the Southampton area which covered an Exercise which had taken place there in October, 1943, and was reported by wireless. It told how Agent No. 3 had re-established himself in the Glasgow area during October and that Agent No. 7 had returned to south Wales the following month. Organizational questions were dealt with. GARBO reported numerous new security measures which he had adopted. He set out a list of the symbols which he would in future use for agents and their contacts. The proposal was advanced that when communications had been re-established GARBO would confine all important military reports to wireless messages and only transmit non-urgent and organizational matters by courier letter. Some of the letters were descriptive and chatty accounts of his life in England. For instance, when, on the 23.10.43 GARBO received the warning from the Germans that in view of the investigation he should keep no paper or similar reference to the service in his house, he wrote a long and characteristic letter to explain why this precaution was impossible and even unnecessary:-

> "....As you will understand if I were to destroy compromising documents I would also have to rid myself of the cyphers and if I were to do this I would be without means of communicating with you. For a long time past all these documents as well as the ink and the money have been, in my opinion, perfectly hidden and for your peace of mind I will tell you where I have concealed them.
>
> In the small garden of my house I have constructed a hen house so as to be able to have a couple of birds in order that they might furnish us with a few fresh eggs each week for my children. I then constructed within, two nest boxes adjoining one another, adding to them false bottoms, leaving a space between the two of about five centimetres which is completely invisible from outside. Inside this space I have all the things concerning the service and if I want to take them out all I have to do is to slide out a small panel which is very well faked on one side of it. It even has in it the head of a nail which makes it look as if it were solidly fixed down. When I had finished the task I had a bet with my wife that she could not discover where the documents were hidden, inciting her with odds. She spent several days turning the hen house inside out and finally gave up in evidence of her failure.

I therefore believe that if my wife, who knew that
something was hidden there, was unable to discover it that
the English Police would not be so good humoured as to start
searching for something either in the hen house or its
occupants with the risk of only discovering that they had
become covered in lice. You will note by my good humour in
this respect that I am completely convinced that they cannot
find us and therefore since I am a man incapable in present
times of being inactive, though I will diminish my contacts
with my collaborators I will not, on account of this, give up
writing my diary so that when the day comes when I am able to
send you all these letters you will see with satisfaction
the work which I have realized with the accumulation of
documents, reports and matters relating to the service which
I feel it incumbent on me to send you.

I am very grateful to you for the appreciation which
you show for my person in the interests of safeguarding me
against dangers even at the cost of being several weeks
without having any information about the enemy. I truly
appreciate it as a mark of courtesy and esteemed
friendship."

In this series of letters GARBO took the opportunity of
suggesting that certain modifications in times and frequencies of
wireless transmission should be made in order to improve wireless
contacts which, as winter approached, were becoming less good than
they had been during the summer and autumn months. We continued to
identify insignias seen on troops and to locate the areas in which
various military formations and units were located. Lastly we
created two new characters who were recruited into the
organization.

Agent No. 4 became very friendly with an American sergeant
working in S.O.S. (Service of Supply) in London. The American,
believing the Gibraltarian, Agent No. 4, to be a Spaniard, quickly
developed a close comradeship, for he too was of Spanish origin "as
his name suggested" (his name was never disclosed.) In the early
stages of this new friendship it became apparent that this American,
who was later to become very prominent in the GARBO case under the
symbol, 4(3)[i] was firstly extremely pro-Franco and secondly, very
anti-British.

Agent No. 4, who had by now virtually abandoned the
Chislehurst Caves, was meeting his new contact regularly whenever
the former came to London between the journeys he was making with

(i)   See Appendix No. XVII.

regularity in connection with his work for the N.A.A.F.I. Within a
very short time Agent No. 4 had, through this new contact, succeeded
in locating the 101st U.S. Airborne Division in the Reading area
(this information confirmed other reports which had already reached
the Germans) and within a week or two this same source was
instrumental in implementing an item of deception connected with
PLAN JAEL, the overall world wide deception policy drawn up by the
Controlling Officer, War Cabinet, for the Chiefs of Staff, which
directed that we should induce the enemy to believe that "landing
craft transferred from the Mediterranean will, after refitting, be
largely used for training purposes." Other directives issued were
that all endeavours should be made to prevent the enemy from
learning that forces and material were being brought back for the
OVERLORD operation.

In November an accurate observation report from the German
watching service opposite Gibraltar was seen on M.S.S. which
confirmed the return from the Mediterranean of certain assault
landing craft of various types. From this information alone it would
inevitably appear that the landing craft which had been used in the
Italian campaign, now no longer required, were returning to the U.K.
in preparation for the great offensive, as was in fact the case.

It was decided that GARBO should confirm the report seen on
M.S.S. at the same time interpreting the activity in accordance with
the policy directed. The M.S.S. material was confirmed back to the
Germans in the following way.

Agent No. 3 furnished a long report in which he described the
various types of assault landing craft currently in use, these
descriptions tallied with those which had appeared in the M.S.S.
message. Agent No. 4 completed the confirmation of the M.S.S.
message by reporting on a conversation which he had with his new
American contact. The latter was represented as having stated that
the British had failed to anticipate the damage which the landing
craft had suffered in maintaining the supplies over the beaches
during the Sicilian campaign and that due to lack of adequate
equipment for repairs, to be carried out on the spot, no less than
some hundred of these craft had recently been sent back to England
to be refitted and repaired. (The number corresponded with the
correct number as had been reported by the German observers.)
GARBO added a recommendation, when forwarding this report, that the
Germans should check up at Algeciras to ascertain whether, in fact,
this number of assault craft had passed Gibraltar en route for the
U.K. since on this check he would be able to assess the reliability
and value of this new contact.

It would be too much to hope that the Germans were in any way
influenced by our story. They were, however, impressed by the

accuracy of the concrete information which the story contained and
replied to say that the information obtained from the American
friend of Agent No. 4 about the withdrawal of landing craft from the
Mediterranean was accurate.

Agent No. 3 had also recruited a new collaborator. The full
particulars of whom were shortly to be provided. He was to turn out
to be a Greek seaman, subsequently referred to as Agent No. 3(3).[i]
whom our Glasgow agent had known for some time and had occasionally
helped with a loan of a pound or two. At this stage the young Greek
came to confess to our agent that he was in fact a deserter from
the Merchant Navy. He claimed that he had deserted, after nearly
drowning, following the sinking of the 3,000 ton s.s. BRISTOL CITY
by a German submarine attack in the Atlantic when she was hit by two
torpedoes on the 5th May that year. These and other details supplied
were undoubtedly checkable by the German Admiralty. The seaman,
now very hard up and fearing to take employment lest he should be
discovered as a deserter, asked Agent No. 3 for his assistance. The
agent was quick to sum up the situation. Knowing the Greek to be a
strong Communist sympathiser, he exchanged confidences with him,
pretending that he was a Russian secret agent, and in this role he
offered to employ the Greek. Pretending that the British were
withholding from the Russians the secret of the date of the Second
Front he recruited this new collaborator to help discover this
secret, so that it might be passed on to the Russians. After warning
him that he would pay for any indiscretion or betrayal with his life
at the hands of the Russians, he was sent off on his first mission.

In accordance with GARBO's instructions to each of his old
established agents that they should all endeavour to recruit new
agents and form their own sub-organizations, Agent No. 7, after
a few weeks in Swansea investigating possibilities in this
connection, reported back to GARBO. For some time past he had told
GARBO that there was in Swansea, a fellow Welshman and old school
mate, on whose collaboration he could almost certainly rely. The
news which he brought back from Wales is best summed up in the
following extract from GARBO's letter reporting the developments:-

> "When Agent No. 7 made his first approach to his old
> schoolmate he was a little nervous since from some remark
> that his friend made he thought for a moment that this man
> was already working for you in some other organization. When
> the matter was cleared up, however, it appears that his
> friend is not, and never has been, in contact with you but is
> a member of a small group that has worked enthusiastically

(i) See Appendix No. XIII.

for some years on political information, hoping one day to be able to have the opportunity to communicate it to you.

The friend of Agent Seven has been a member of the Welsh Nationalist Party but he had advanced ideas and he was not pleased with the liberal sentiment of the Party, maintaining that the emancipation of his country would depend entirely on the establishment of what he calls "Aryan World Order Movement" to collaborate with all the Aryans all over the world. The Welsh, however, are only interested in their nationalist aims, although there were some who were in favour of strikes and sabotage in order to directly prejudice the English war effort. On account of this he left the party more than two years ago together with a friend and joined an Indian, a friend of his, who has lived for many years in this country, forming a group which he calls "Brothers in the Aryan World Order." As its position, owing to it being clandestine, is very dangerous, they have had little success, as only about twelve revolutionary members are affiliated, but their activities are very limited and, as you will see further on, are rather ridiculous. (That is my opinion.)

Four of their members have already been called up and are now serving in the army against their will. The secretary (who looks after the organization and the files) is an English woman, and mistress of the above-mentioned Indian. She has been called up for the W.R.N.S. and considers she must abandon the organization immediately. Until now the activities of this organization consisted solely in making lists of names of Communists and Jews who must be eliminated when their aspirations are achieved, and they have also worked within the limited means at their disposal, in spreading terrorist rumours underground among Welsh workers.

They listen regularly to the German transmissions and based on what they hear they circulate those comments among the public.

The friend suggested presenting this group to the agent but he prudently refused, but he took advantage of the offer, hinting that he could get across to the Germans the documents that the organization possessed, being the fruit of their constant work. Believing that the information would reach the German police they confided some documents to Number Seven who has handed them to me at our interview. I have studied them judiciously but they are no use because they are absurd things which have nothing to do with military matters. The interesting point of this matter is that he

asked his friend whether he thinks that there would be
members of this group ready to undertake a more active
mission, and his friend answered in the affirmative. The
agent explained various reasons, among them, the one that in
order to be able to attain their aims it would be necessary
in the first place to win the war against the Imperialists,
then the Communist menace would also disappear and the
possibility would exist of an Aryan world control, but that
the most vital thing at the moment was to be able to obtain
all the military information that could help our friends who
struggle against the Anglo-Saxon oppression.

     Seven is convinced that we will be able to obtain
satisfactory results with the collaboration of these
individuals, and vouches for the loyalty of his friend, who
in turn vouches for that of his companions."

The German reactions to this letter were most curious. They
wirelessed GARBO the warning that whilst the proposition made by
Agent No. 7 was very interesting great care should be taken with
those groups whose aspirations and beliefs are known to the British
Government since they must be considered to be very carefully
watched. They went on to request that GARBO should furnish certain
particulars about the friend of Agent No. 7 in view of the remote
possibility that he was identical with a dangerous person with whom
they had been in contact several years previously. To check up they
requested his physical description, age, occupation for the past
seven years and his name, without mentioning the surname.

     We replied a few days later to say that Seven had been warned
to suspend all further contact pending instructions, and he had been
asked to furnish the full particulars required by the Germans.
Pending their arrival GARBO said he was able to furnish the
following particulars which were known to him. The Christian name
of Agent No. 7's friend was DAVID, he was aged about thirty and was
released from military service due to asthma. Also that he had left
the Merchant Navy six years ago due to the above-mentioned
infirmity. These particulars were sufficient for the Germans to be
able to signal back the message that GARBO could exclude the
possibility of this person being their suspect, and therefore he
might continue to develop the organization.

     The reason for their nervousness was immediately apparent.
The double agent "G.W." had personally been in contact with the
Germans before the war and had been trained by them in sabotage.
When later, the German agents PIERNAVIEJA DEL POZO, ALCAZAR DE
VELASCO and Luis CALVO were operating for KUHLENTHAL they were in
turn put in contact with G.W. in England. The arrest of Luis CALVO

undoubtedly compromised G.W. whose part as a provocateur became
apparent. It happened that G.W.'s background was also that a Welsh
Nationalist. The Germans, therefore, not unnaturally, suspected
that he was now endeavouring to provoke and penetrate the GARBO
network. The particulars which they had requested could easily have
identified the suspect as G.W. for he was a very tall and heavily
built man of advanced middle age at that time. His name was [...]
    Whilst the surname was one probably familiar to the Germans,
the Christian name, it seems, appeared to them as being most
unusual, which would explain their having asked GARBO only to let
them know the Christian name of his man. Having thus allayed their
fears we eventually recruited six new agents from this strange Welsh
brotherhood.
    Lest the reader should consider these recruitments too
fantastic he should be reminded that the truth is often stranger
than fiction. This was subsequently to be proved to us, for several
months later the activities of a Welsh seaman who had been arrested
were brought to the notice of M.I.5. It transpired that he had been
detained for spreading subversive propaganda among his fellow
seamen. He had been circulating subversive typewritten leaflets
and had spread anti-Semitic propaganda in the name of a small
organization which, from the material discovered amongst his
property, ornamented with swastikas and other Nazi emblems, was the
"ARYAN WORLD ORDER."

CHAPTER XXII.

GARBO BLACKMAILED BY THE COURIER.

From the beginning of February, 1944, our entire energies were
devoted to making our preparations so as to be in the strongest
possible position for implementing the OVERLORD deception
plan. After the numerous upheavals which we had provoked, the
organization had been put on a very strong footing and the Germans
were now satisfied that GARBO was very securely established. From
our point of view we had only one major security problem. This was
the possibility that the Germans would yet discover the GARBO hoax
through investigations at the courier's cover address in Lisbon
where S.I.S. were still regularly calling to collect the incoming
letters from the Germans.

Up to this time we had always been very evasive about the
courier; we had never made it clear whether he took GARBO's
consignments personally to Lisbon or arranged this through a third
party; we had given no clear picture of his personal relationship
with GARBO, why it was that he did not suspect these strange
missions which he was asked to fulfil and still less how it was that
he was willing to accept such paltry payments as GARBO had been used
to giving him when, through the Black Market transactions he was
said to be performing, he should be a reasonably wealthy man.

We decided, therefore, to stage a scene in which the courier
would blackmail GARBO for a large sum of money, and towards the end
of February GARBO wrote a very long letter explaining what had
occurred.

From this letter it was made to appear that the courier had
requested GARBO to call on him and in the seclusion of his room,
behind locked doors, the courier accused him of being a German spy.

Characteristic of all long GARBO letters it was extremely
confusing and in parts, very obscure, but the Germans were able to
gain the following impression from it.

It appeared that the courier had not, for a considerable
period, been personally to Lisbon, but that he had a partner over
there who used to carry out that end of his Black Market dealings.
Correspondence between them was carried by a number of airmen engaged
on the London - Lisbon run and the courier, who it appeared, was
engaged at the British airport, had facilities for collecting and
delivering the packages before the carriers passed through Customs.
The same facilities presumably existed the other end where his
colleague was operating. His colleague in Lisbon was either closely
in touch with British Embassy personnel or attached to the Embassy

himself. It would seem as though the courier used to enclose GARBO's letters in a package with various other correspondence addressed to his Lisbon colleague, who used to extract the GARBO letters and mail them in Lisbon. Nearly all the GARBO letters had been addressed to Senora OLIVEIRA, whom GARBO had claimed was his aunt, and the courier professed that he had hitherto arranged this correspondence for GARBO, more as a personal favour because he liked him, than for the monetary consideration. It transpired that his Lisbon colleague discovered through the Embassy that enquiries were being made at certain Lisbon addresses in order to discover the identity of a certain agent in England and, included in the list of suspect Lisbon addresses, he had been horrified to discover the name of Senora OLIVEIRA. He therefore warned GARBO's courier immediately, but whether he was responsible for the suggestion that GARBO could be blackmailed on this issue was not made clear. The facts were that the courier demanded £2,000 for his silence. After a good deal of fencing with words, and unsuccessful attempts by GARBO to bluff the courier into believing that the information he had received was untrue he finally agreed to write to the Germans for the necessary money to be furnished in order to satisfy the courier's blackmailing demands. The courier demanded something on account, and GARBO offered to pay him £100 which was, he maintained, all the money he had. To get the balance of the money, he explained to the courier that he would have to satisfactorily convince the Germans that he had committed himself to making this payment. Alternatively the Germans might have suspected that it was a ruse to extract money from them, and furthermore he would have to convince them that he had reached an amicable arrangement with the courier, lest they should suspect further blackmail or denunciation at a later date. The receipt for the £100 deposit was drafted by GARBO and read as follows:-

> "I have received £100 on account of the amount of £2,000 due to me for special services rendered to date in arranging for the delivery of special packages and letters in Lisbon. I further undertake on payment of the balance to continue with this work to the best of my ability for payments to be agreed upon."

GARBO explained that after the receipt had been signed he would return to his home and write the Germans a secret letter in which he would recommend in the strongest terms that they should forward him the balance of the money required with the minimum delay. To encourage the courier to sign the receipt, he said that he would forward it to the Germans in his letter as evidence of the understanding which had been reached between him and GARBO. To

GARBO's great astonishment the courier signed without hesitation, probably it was his intention when doing so, to extract it from the letter, the forwarding of which would be in his hands. On handing over the finished letter to the courier the following day GARBO disclosed to him that he had safely hidden the receipt which he had been stupid enough to sign, and warned him that should he make any attempt at any time to betray him (GARBO) the receipt would be forwarded to the British police who would not be slow to realize that in accepting the sum of £2,000 for carrying correspondence, the nature of which he must have been aware in view of the large remuneration paid, he was a fully conscious accomplice in espionage activities. Thus, GARBO countered the courier's threat to blackmail him and was in the position to recommend that they should mutually continue to assist one another, whilst GARBO promised to pay him the £2,000 for past services if, and when, it was received, and furthermore to give him a flat rate remuneration of £50 a month for future services. They parted good friends, each in admiration for the other's astuteness. The courier promised to continue with the service in the hope that he would get his money, GARBO having assured him that the request for it was contained in the letter which had just been handed to him for despatch.

GARBO terminated his long letter by saying that he was much shaken by this experience and though he had the money available to make the payment he would not do so without their authority, and had handled the matter in this way as he thought it a prohibitive sum, apart from the fact that in view of what had occurred it would be far too dangerous to continue to work at all with this man. He therefore suggested that he should leave England for South America, where he would engage in working out a new organization for them, leaving the British organization in the hands of Agent No. 3 who was quite unknown to the courier, and thus the work of the organization would be able to continue without incident.

Had the Germans accepted this last suggestion it was our intention to carry it out. Though the organization would have been far less colourful without GARBO's personality, opinions were expressed that so much colour was not necessarily an asset for the future.

To coincide with the despatch of the letter by courier GARBO sent a wireless message to announce its departure and to say that until it was safely in their possession they should send no further written correspondence but confine themselves entirely to wireless messages.

The letter was written in GARBO's most florid style and the transcription of the secret text amounted to no less than ten foolscap pages of single space typescript, and described every

detail of the interview, even to the changes of expression on the
courier's face at different moments of the conversation, as well
as all the thoughts which passed through GARBO's mind during the
moments he was listening to the courier's threats. It read like a
scene from a commonplace detective story in which the hero outwits
the less subtle, though cunning, crook. In spite of this it seemed
to strike a note of reality with the Germans, who replied by
wireless:-

"I have read your letter about the courier and we marvel at
your fantastic handling of the situation which is equivalent
to the supreme bravery of a soldier in the front line. We
send you herewith our profound recognition...... I agree
with your opinion that due to the influence which you have
exercised over the courier, and with the receipt which you
have in your possession, you have a hold over him and should
be able to use him as a collaborator. You must agree to his
request for money but you should make it appear as if it will
be a great sacrifice for us to have to find this foreign
currency. You should therefore pay him part now and I would
suggest you hand him three or four hundred pounds, but leave
the amount to your discretion. The balance should be paid in
instalments over a period of six or seven months, always
alleging difficulties in obtaining foreign currency. In
addition I would suggest it would be a good plan to arrange
with the courier to make him a payment for each individual
service rendered so as to encourage his interest and so that
he should be able to consider the agreed payment of £2,000 as
something which will not necessitate new efforts. After what
has happened in Lisbon, and the reference now made by the
courier regarding the origin of the discovery of the
cover addresses we have already started to make careful
investigations in Portugal. I will write to you in detail as
soon as the reorganization of the cover addresses has been
completed. We are dispensing with all the intermediaries who
have worked on our behalf up to the present. Let us know by
wireless as soon as you have made your arrangements with the
courier for us to be able to mail further letters to you. It
is necessary to explain to the courier how, without his
having brought you correspondence, you have received this
reply from us. You might suggest that you got a reply from us
by airmail so as to prevent him from suspecting the existence
of a wireless. If you make him the initial payment suggested
you will have to give him some explanation as to how you
received the money since you told him that you were low in

funds. You might tell him that you have borrowed the money.
On account of this development, and due to the increase in
the network and the possibility that Agent No. 5 will be
organizing his own network (in Canada) it is of primary
importance to consider the question of funds, and I should be
glad to hear from you that you are able to arrange a new
exchange deal for the amount of £7,500. If not let me know
whether we can send you several remittances in escudos via
the courier since dollars and pounds involve the risk that
the origin of the notes can possibly be checked. Also let me
know whether large denomination notes are usable......."

This wireless message was followed up by a long and detailed
letter in which they set out an analysis of GARBO's letter with
their comments. They went out of their way to try to make GARBO feel
that the courier was not such a bad fellow after all, and they
expressed their confidence that he would not now betray GARBO since
he was thoroughly committed. They told GARBO that, whilst he should
not let the courier gain any idea of the importance of the network,
they firmly believed the man should still be used and encouraged.

The situation hereafter was a great deal more secure, for
even had they ever decided to investigate the courier's cover
address in Lisbon the strange picture which they would have
discovered would no doubt have connected up in their mind as a
ramification of the courier set-up in Lisbon, rather than lead them
to the deduction that the owner of the deposit box at the Bank, which
served as a cover address, was in fact GARBO himself, now handled on
his behalf, by S.I.S. Some months later we were able to break down
this address altogether and substitute for it a new cover address
which was obtained for us and vouched for as safe by S.I.S. Lisbon.

We furthermore had the satisfaction of learning that the
Germans were prepared to accept with a smile the liability of a
£2,000 payment to the courier in these circumstances.

CHAPTER XXIII.

PLAN BODYGUARD.
PREPARATIONS FOR OVERLORD.
RECRUITMENT OF THE MEMBERS OF
THE BROTHERHOOD OF THE AYRIAN WORLD ORDER.
STRATEGIC DISPLACEMENT OF THE
AGENTS IN PREPARATION FOR OVERLORD.
AGENT NO. 7(3) TRANSFERRED TO CEYLON.

Towards the end of December, 1943, Plan BODYGUARD, the overall deception policy for the war against Germany was submitted by the Controlling Officer of the War Cabinet which directed the policy to be adopted up to D Day of OVERLORD. In brief it dictated that the enemy should be induced to believe:-

(a)   The bombing by Allied air forces would be continued and increased in the hope that it might bring about a total German collapse without necessity for an amphibious invasion.

(b)   The Allies were in readiness to occupy and maintain order in any western European countries from which the Germans might decide, through a serious weakening, to withdraw, utilizing the troops in the U.K. yet untrained for assault operation.

(c)   An attack on northern Norway, to be concerted with the Russians, would be launched in the spring.

(d)   No large scale cross channel operation would be possible until the late summer.

(e)   Owing to shortage of manpower it had been impossible to maintain all formations at full strength.

(f)   Some of the U.S. Divisions arriving in the U.K. had not yet completed their training.

(g)   Some personnel from Anglo-American formations in the Mediterranean were being returned to the U.K. for training inexperienced formations.

(h)   The supply of invasion craft was not up to schedule. etc., etc.,

These points were all intended to make the enemy believe that our state of preparedness for the cross-channel invasion was not far advanced and in consequence they would draw the conclusion that the attack was planned to take place considerably later than the real target date.

All these points were brought out in the messages transmitted by the GARBO network during the first months of 1944.

It shortly became impossible to support these directives to any substantial degree. In the first place, to draw the attention of the Germans to the forces which we were building up in support of FORTITUDE NORTH and FORTITUDE SOUTH it became necessary to write up the state of preparedness of those formations, either notional or real, which were to stay behind to maintain the threat to the Pas de Calais after the forces destined for the real Cherbourg operation had launched their initial assault; in the second place, it would have been unrealistic had we continued to write down the state of preparedness to a marked degree when all the Security measures which had been made public obviously pointed to the imminence of an important operation; and, thirdly, the vast concentration of shipping in the Channel ports which assembled shortly before D Day could, we had wrongly imagined, hardly have failed to be observed by the enemy. As D Day approached it was natural that we should endeavour to persuade the enemy that the imminence of an attack was not immediate, and there is ample evidence to prove conclusively that the Germans were taken completely by surprise on D Day.

From the beginning of January the Germans were apprehensive that the attack might come at any time and it was no doubt due to the long period of anticipation and the many false alarms that they were taken so much by surprise.

On the 5.1.44 the Germans communicated to GARBO that the information which they had received from various sources indicated that preparations were in full swing for an operation of great importance based on Great Britain which they considered might be expected to materialize at a very near date. Above all, they asked him to try to discover the date and place of any attack intended to be made against northern France, the Atlantic, Mediterranean or Adriatic coasts. To ascertain this, they said, he should discover the ground, sea and air forces available at the different embarkation points, their state of preparedness and the quantity of assault craft available in England as well as their distribution in ports. In addition, he was asked to ascertain the number of warships and defence craft available for the operation.

These instructions were followed by others of a similar nature at short intervals. A few days later they told GARBO that they were as interested to learn about the preparations which were being made in the north for an attack against Norway and Denmark as they were to know about the preparations which were being made in the south of England. On the 14.1.44 we received the following significant questionnaire:-

"For tactical reasons one must assume that the danger centres
for future operations are Devon, Cornwall and the south coast
between Weymouth and Southampton. I recommend you to try to
explore these regions."

In fact they were perfectly correct. Had an agent been
reporting accurately from the areas indicated there is little doubt
that he would have been covering far the most important area from
which he could have gained the greatest information about the
forthcoming operations. It will be recalled that this area had so
far been covered in the GARBO organization by the least spectacular
of his agents, Agent No. 1, who, after the terrible fright which he
was given whilst spying for GARBO in Southampton during the period
of STARKEY, had resigned from active service. What was GARBO to do?
He dare not now risk leaving this area uncovered. In any case it
would have been inadvisable to do so. To cover this important area
of the real preparations to a limited degree suited our plans which,
in brief outline, were to result in our passing the enemy a
percentage of deceptive material carefully woven into a pattern,
the balance of which would be made up of truth. The procedure at the
beginning was to ensure that the percentage of checkable truth
should be high, so that the falsehoods inserted into the reports
would, on the principle of all Intelligence appreciation, have to be
accepted. Gradually we were to increase the percentage of false in
our mixture until the entire substance of our reports would be based
on the false or notional.

The Germans had urged us to control the preparations and
activities in Scotland, the south west, south and south east
England. By this time the six new agents[i] from the "BROTHERHOOD IN
THE ARYAN WORLD ORDER" had been recruited.

The organization was now sufficiently large to cover all
these areas and GARBO dispersed them as follows:-

(a) Agent No. 3. Deputy Chief. In charge of investigations in
     Scotland. Responsible for the Clyde. To operate from
     Glasgow.
(b) Agent No. 3(3). Responsible for the east coast of Scotland.
(c) Agent No. 4. To report from marshalling area north of
     Southampton.
(d) Agent No. 7. To be free to move between south Wales and
     London as general contact man, to serve as "cut out" with the
     wireless operator.

[i] See Appendices XXIII - XXVIII.

(e)   Agent No. 7(2). Stationed at Dover to cover the county of
      Kent.
(f)   Agent No. 7(3). To transfer to India.
(g)   Agent No. 7(4). Stationed at Brighton to cover the counties
      of Sussex and Surrey.
(h)   Agent No. 7(5). To cover Cornwall, Devon and Exeter area.
(i)   Agent No. 7(6). Stationed at Swansea to cover south Wales.
(j)   Agent No. 7(7). Stationed in Harwich to cover the counties of
      Essex and Suffolk; and, later Norfolk.
(k)   J. GARBO. In charge of the organization in London.
(l)   J(3). Supplying political information through the Ministry
      of Information and Political Warfare Executive.
(m)   J(5). Supplying information obtained through the War Office.
(n)   4(3). Supplying U.S. Order of Battle.

     This strategic disposition of GARBO's forces was submitted
to the enemy. Experience had already taught them that it was not
good policy to move the agents about. In fact the coastal ban which
was soon to be imposed would make this almost impossible. It was
obviously better to have an agent established in a banned coastal
area than to move him out with the risk that he might not easily be
able to return there. Through working and establishing themselves
each in a fixed area, the agents were able to become familiar with
the insignias constantly observed, and by making friends locally,
discover the names and locations of headquarters and camps of all
the formations within a 20, 30 or 50 mile radius, as the
circumstances might demand.
     Since the Lisbon investigations into the cover addresses all
direct correspondence between agents and the Germans had been
brought to an end. Agents' reports were now submitted to GARBO for
retransmission Either they were written in an elementary secret ink
and mailed to GARBO's cover address in London, or in the case of the
head agents, they were handed in at personal interviews with GARBO.
     During the entire year of 1944 nearly all GARBO reports were
transmitted by wireless. Between January, 1944 and D Day of OVERLORD
well over 500 wireless messages were exchanged between London and
Madrid. GARBO would only write an occasional letter to accompany the
forwarding of letters which reached him from his agents in Canada
and later, Ceylon. So much was being sent over the air that GARBO
could not have been expected to have time to write during the few
months prior to, and following D Day of OVERLORD. In fact he did not
have the time to do so.
     From the time of STARKEY we had the satisfaction of knowing
through M.S.S. that all GARBO material was being given priority and
that every military report which reached Madrid from the GARBO

network was immediately retransmitted to Berlin. Whenever, GARBO
added his appreciation to a report this too would be forwarded.
Eventually they adopted the principle of forwarding the message
without transcription (or translation) leaving them in the first
person.

Thus, one would read the following type of message on M.S.S.
Madrid - Berlin:-

> "....V BENEDICT, UNDERTAKING ARABAL 10/5 from England via
> FELIPE: ....I estimate that up to 1100 hours more than a bde.
> of the div. had landed. Landing of troops was continued in a
> similar way. Apart from the transports which brought the
> landing craft I was able to see another 10 transports, which
> lay in the neighbourhood and were doubtless connected with
> the exercise. One of these transports flew the flag WHITESIGN
> (sic) had a remarkably large number of aerials on board and
> continually sent light signals with searchlights to the
> shore. The exercise lasted until the 11/5. General
> impression gained by the VM on the basis of what he
> ascertained during the exercises and former information
> about this division is that it is intended for action in
> Norway as the division is continually receiving training in
> mountain warfare and all its equipment points to the
> probability of its going into action in northern regions.
> Have taken all measures to continue to watch every movement
> of transport fleet and troops."

Just as we were beginning to concentrate on the reporting of
the FORTITUDE Order of Battle we received a most appropriate
questionnaire which read:-

> "It is to be assumed that the forces which will be engaged in
> the invasion operation will be divided into several
> independent armies, British and U.S. It would be of the
> greatest interest to know how many armies there will be and
> how many have already been formed. Headquarters and names
> of the commanders of each Army as well as their composition,
> i.e., corps and divisions under command, the objectives
> assigned to each army."

They explained that this work could only be accomplished by
piecing together little by little, the information which he was able
to collect until the mosaic had been completed. Thus, they asked us
for precisely the information which we had already planned to pass
to them.

At this stage it became necessary to eliminate the customary embroidering of the GARBO messages and to cut them down to the bare essentials if we were to be able to put over, in the limited time available, all the material which we were now being requested to put over by the deception planners of SHAEF, with whom we were by now working in the closest contact. A great deal of the information was extremely high grade and sometimes requests were made that it should be passed on at very short notice. We were transmitting an average of five or six messages daily; we now had nine principal full time agents sending in regular reports, in addition to the numerous part time informants who were frequently imparting information which had to be analysed, classified, extracted and redrafted by GARBO into messages, which he then had to encypher and transmit through his wireless channel which, in consequence, tended to become overloaded. It is doubtful whether, in reality, one man could possibly have done all the work which was in this way attributed to GARBO.

In addition, there was the purely organizational side of the work which could not be overlooked, neither were we to be allowed to proceed without interruptions by the Germans. A typical illustration of the sort of complications which were continuously arising is the following:-

Agent No. 4, after completing his training in the N.A.A.F.I. volunteered for Special Service in a sealed area where he envisaged he would be able to get access to vital information. Before he was accepted in this work he was obliged to sign a Security Certificate in which he undertook to conform with the regulations which would be imposed on all persons within the camp to which he was to proceed. He had to undertake to have no contact with any person outside the "sealed" area, and to submit all letters to military censorship.

After telling GARBO of this important development he departed for an unknown destination. In the circumstances we were obliged to explain to the Germans how it was he had managed to re establish contact with GARBO. We could hardly ask them to believe that he had risked communicating in secret ink; neither would this have suited our plans since we wished to restrict his communications to a minimum, for the agent was to be represented as situated in a camp just north of Southampton where, in reality, the main invasion troops were to assemble. He was represented as having arrived there at the end of April so as to be in time to report on a rehearsal exercise, then about to take place, as if it were the real operation. To do this we had to explain the means by which Agent No. 4 had managed to contact GARBO and so he inserted the following preamble to the series of messages attributed to this agent:-

"Yesterday Agent No. 4 telephoned me and made an appointment
for me to meet him this morning at Winchester......"

This was followed by some very high grade reports on the
outcome of the meeting. To our surprise the Germans replied:-

"Should service requirements necessitate telephonic
conversations with your collaborators in protected zones,
as occurred with Agent No. 4 last Sunday it is advisable
to arrange with the agents that they should discuss some
camouflage subject to avoid, on all occasions, speaking on
the telephone of appointments or similar matters since it is
almost certain that telephone calls are intercepted by
Censorship."

For obvious reasons it was undesirable that the Germans
should continue to challenge the methods we employed in the
organizational side of our work, and to discourage them from this,
and to induce them to accept the fact that whatever GARBO did was
well and thoroughly considered, we replied to say that whilst GARBO
wished to avoid telephone calls such as he had been forced to accept
in the recent case of extreme emergency, he had taken the necessary
measures to ensure security which he had not set out in his previous
messages to save unnecessary work. After this preamble he went on to
explain the measures taken. He said that, on leaving London, the
agent was himself unaware of his destination, therefore they had
arranged to get in touch in the following way. The agent was to
endeavour to telephone GARBO from a place some distance from his
station, and in the conversation which would ensue he would indicate
the place for rendez-vous, which would be the first place name
mentioned (i.e., George has just come back from Winchester; would
mean that GARBO should meet him at Winchester.) The town chosen for
the meeting was to be outside the protected coastal area. The time,
it was prearranged, would be the morning following the telephone
call to coincide with the arrival at the town of the first train
after 10 a.m. To give verisimilitude and to lengthen the explanation
GARBO confirmed the exact times of the trains which he alleged he
took, both on his journey down to Winchester, and on his return, and
he went into details of how the agent had managed to reach the
rendez-vous, on the pretext that he wished to attend Sunday morning
mass, since the day of their meeting had happened to be a Sunday.

Our messages must have given them at least four or five hours
work to decypher since the explanation was very long winded. They
produced the desired results, for in replying the Germans admitted
that it had not been their intention, when they warned him of

the dangers of long distance telephone calls, to provoke a full explanation, but purely to put at his disposal the advantages of their experience and advice to ensure his greater security. In spite of this they added, it was their conviction that his "behaviour and work were perfect, as they had proved to be in the case in question." Therefore, it was unnecessary for him to give any further explanation since they were in complete conformity with his omitting all explanatory details in future.

Hereafter we complied with this directive whenever it best suited our interests to observe it.

During the period of build up for OVERLORD Agent No. 7(3), who had been the secretary of the Aryan World Order prior to her joining the W.R.N.S., was moved to a special training school for Wrens near Newbury. It was at first envisaged that she would be required to assist the implementation of the FORTITUDE Naval deception plan. As this plan developed she seemed to fit less and less into the picture. Meanwhile, the deception staff of SEAC had asked whether we had an agent who was available to be sent out to them for their much-needed requirements. Since no attempt was made to utilize her services here we decided to send this notional character to Ceylon. She had been represented as the mistress of GARBO's Indian agent, No. 7(4), and this was fitting background for her to volunteer to go overseas to join Mountbatten's staff. Before she departed she was given the usual instructions in secret writing, provided with ink, questionnaires, and a cover address in London. As in the case of Agent No. 6, both the secret and cover texts were supplied to us by the deception staff in Ceylon. A scribe was provided by this Office where the letters were written. At first she was represented as sending her letters to GARBO by airmail, later, with GARBO's approval, they were forwarded in the Admiralty Bag to London, which facility was offered to personnel attached to SEAC. The traffic was extremely high grade, and in view of the long delays which the information was bound to suffer in transit from Ceylon to Berlin via London, Lisbon, and Madrid much of it could, with safety, be accurate. The information was passed by the Germans to the Japanese, but by the time it had passed through the machinery in the Abwehr in Berlin, and the various Intelligence Branches of the German Service Departments, a further delay of several weeks was experienced before the information was transmitted by wireless by the Japanese in Berlin to their headquarters in Tokio. The case of this agent appeared to be proceeding well, though it was to some extent unsatisfactory that we did not always have the background knowledge to appreciate the secret material transmitted through this channel.

Since we did not control the information passed we were unable to judge its significance or to know how compromising any part of it might be. Neither were we aware of the methods used in the Far East to co-ordinate the work of the various channels through which they were passing information. We were soon to have cause to become apprehensive that the method they were adopting was that of ensuring that the information reached and penetrated the enemy even at some degree of risk to the security of the agent concerned. We were somewhat astonished to read a message on M.S.S. after Agent No. 7(3) had been operating for a few months, which registered surprise on the part of Berlin at having discovered that the information contained in her reports was almost identical with other information which they had received through independent channels. Investigations disclosed that the deception staff in Ceylon had been accustomed to pass, what we here would have considered dangerously similar material, over a variety of their channels. Since the information thus put out through several channels was eventually to reach the same Department for which it had been intended, it was inevitable that the similarity would have been noticed, if not suspected. Whilst, from the point of view of the deception unit concerned this need not necessarily have been a preoccupation, providing they considered the method a means of impressing the reliability of a vital piece of information, it was a matter of considerable concern to us that Agent No. 7(3) might have thus become embroiled without our realization, since the security of the entire GARBO organization was dependent on each of its components.

Madrid was quick to reply to Berlin's query and to save the situation. Recalling the history of this agent as summarized in various GARBO letters they were fully aware of her connection with the Indian, Agent No. 7(4). They speculated in their reply that in view of this connection it was quite possible that her Indian friend had given her introductions to certain Indian Nationalists to whom she might easily have passed the information, which she had also included in her secret letters to the Germans, without the realization that they too were in contact with the Axis powers. It was fortunate that amongst the agents controlled by the Far East deception unit were Indian nationals, and therefore the explanation which Madrid had given was, in the light of all circumstances, a plausible one. Nevertheless, we considered the stakes were too great to allow a member of our network to continue to operate in these circumstances and we decided to put the agent, 7(3), out of action at least temporarily, if not permanently. GARBO reported that he had received news from her in an en clair text in which she said that she had met with a car accident in which the bottle of perfume which he had given her (presumably the secret ink) had been smashed. She asked whether he could send her some more from London.

She explained that although she had recovered from the accident she would have to go before a medical board before she would know whether or not she would be invalided out and sent back to England. She was making every effort, she said, to stay on if possible. Her fate was never decided, since the war against Germany came to a close before a decision was reached.

Before embarking on the story of the implementation of FORTITUDE, the cover plan for OVERLORD, it should be said that prior to D Day the unofficial estimate of our probable success in holding the enemy from reinforcing the Cherbourg battle front was, that if it could afterwards be proved that we had been instrumental in causing one Division to hesitate 48 hours before proceeding to oppose our landing in the Cherbourg peninsula, we would have been well repaid for the energies expended in organizing this deception. Opinions were divided as to whether our attempt to deceive the enemy would result in exposing the entire GARBO network. As the following chapter will show our success was infinitely greater than we had dared to hope. As a tribute to the Planners it should be added that the more we practiced deception the higher was the estimation of GARBO's organization in the eyes of the German Intelligence Service and the German Supreme Command.

The climax was reached when, with the use of entirely notional forces[i] we continued to maintain the threat to the Pas de Calais area until Allied Forces had by-passed it and annihilated the forces which we had been instrumental in persuading the Germans to retain there until after the Normandy battle had been won.

More than three months after the cessation of hostilities with Germany, GARBO was afforded the opportunity of a reunion with his German "masters" on Spanish soil, and to hear from their own lips their praise for his unselfish sacrifices for the cause for which they, and Germany, had fought and lost.

(i)   See Appendix No. XXXVIII.

CHAPTER XXIV.

FORTITUDE.
A COVER PLAN FOR OPERATION OVERLORD.

To consider the operation from the point of view of deceiving the enemy one must first examine its essential features.

The success of the operation depended on the speedier build up of Allied forces in the bridgehead, in the initial stages, than the enemy could anticipate or contain. It seemed likely that the enemy would be able to draw upon its superior and mobile reserves at a greater speed than we, in carrying out the most hazardous of all amphibious operations, could hope to land large formations and their supplies.

In a less magnificently conceived plan, the enemy would logically be expected to draw upon their reserves, and with great speed, supply the already well established defending forces with unlimited reinforcements, with the inevitable result, that the attacking forces would be thrown back into the sea before they had time to establish a substantial bridgehead.

From this picture two essentials emerged:-

(i)   The enemy would have to be taken by surprise as to the target area. (A fundamentally difficult problem in view of the gigantic preparations which could not be concealed from them.)

(ii) The nature of the undertaking must be concealed from the enemy. (This was dependent on the enemy being led to believe that the invasion would be launched in at least two stages.)

Both requirements were essentially a responsibility of M.I.5, operating, in the first case, in its more general role as the Security Service, and in the second, as the Department in control of double-cross agents.

Let us first examine the situation after the Security Service, in co-operation with the Fighting Services and other Departments, had enforced the most drastic Security measures which had ever been applied in this country to preserve the security of a military operation.

The British Isles became a military fortress. With the exception of the United States and Soviet Governments, all Allied Governments were prohibited from communicating abroad in cypher telegrams or by Diplomatic Bag. All neutral diplomats were subjected to similar drastic restrictions. All air mail correspondence between the United Kingdom and the Continent was suspended. Surface mail was so delayed as to make any secret information, were it to have evaded the test of 100% Censorship, so out of date as to be valueless. These and other measures of security were enforced It would have been safe to conclude that, apart from aerial reconnaissance, which was negligible owing to our air superiority, there remained open only the following possible channels for leakages:-

(i)   The sending of messages by carrier pigeons. (This firstly presupposes that the birds and agents could have entered this country, evading all controls, and, secondly, that the pigeons could, in their return flight, have evaded the careful vigilance kept by the M.I.5 Security section to safeguard against leakages by carrier pigeon. In addition a constant watch was always maintained by amateur falconers whose services had been recruited to safeguard against such a very remote danger.

(ii) The sending of messages through clandestine wireless channels. (Such leakages could only be possible if an agent had established himself in this country unobserved by the Security Service and he had discovered a method by which his apparatus would not be detected by the vigilance of R.S.S.)

(iii) Leakages through British Embassies abroad with whom the Foreign Office was still in cypher communication. (A danger which had not been seriously envisaged at the time.)

(iv) Wireless intercepts. (Leakage through interception of wireless traffic was of course dealt with (a) by Security measures, e.g., use of codes, and (b) by deception.)

(v)   Prisoners of War. (P/W leakage could only be overcome by instructions to troops. In any case danger in this connection was comparatively small and confined mainly to airmen shot down over enemy territory.)

The unprecedented Security precautions which had been applied, could thus be assumed to make it virtually impossible for the enemy to gain information about our intentions.

They had been forewarned by obvious indications as well as by the Press, and by the statement made by our Government that sooner or later, Allied forces, in great strength, would invade the European fortress.

To land, and build up, vast forces and equipment on enemy soil, would, in normal circumstances have entailed the seizure of major ports at an early stage in the operation, as was the requirement for the landing in North Africa, Sicily and Italy. Our

planners had also considered this problem and realizing the
gigantic, if not impossible, task which the seizure of a large
number of highly defended major ports would entail, they decided
that the operation would have to be effected against a large expanse
of beaches, landing forces and equipment by specially constructed
craft, facilitated by the new and secret weapon, the artificial
harbours. This was the secret which it was imperative, at all costs,
should be kept from the enemy.

The artificial port was to give us two distinct advantages:-

(a)   It gave us the benefit of surprise so as to be able to attack
       initially where the enemy was weakest.
(b)   It supplemented port capacities. Neither Cherbourg alone,
       nor for that matter, the combined Pas de Calais harbours,
       could have supported unaided an operation of the scale of
       OVERLORD.

There was only one suitable place in the Channel for the
assembly of a large artificial harbour. Once the Germans had been
allowed to discover that we were proposing to use an artificial
harbour they would have known at least one target area, and probably
the first target of our attack.

We had available three channels through which we could
deceive the enemy about our intentions. All were used. They were:-

(i)   Special Means. (Double-cross agents whose success depended
       on the confidence which they enjoyed with the Abwehr, and in
       turn, the Abwehr with the OKW.)
(ii)   Wireless deception. (Misleading wireless networks, the
       success of which depended on the efficiency of the enemy
       interception service.)
(iii) Physical. (Camouflage and dummies. The success of which
       depended on air reconnaissance.)

These three sources had to be co-ordinated. Source (i) was
capable of interpreting (ii) and (iii). (ii) and (iii) were capable
of confirming (i).

The Security measures enforced not only, therefore, robbed
the enemy of all genuine information, but in addition they forced
the enemy to rely exclusively on the information which they were
able to obtain through one or more of the above channels.

Prior to D Day of OVERLORD there were two independent plans
which had to be implemented: FORTITUDE (NORTH), a threatened attack
against Norway, to be carried out by the (notional Fourth British
Army,) and FORTITUDE (SOUTH) a threatened attack against the Pas de

Calais, to be carried out by the First U.S. Army Group, known as FUSAG, notionally regrouped.

FORTITUDE (NORTH) was principally concerned with Naval deception and was worked out in considerable detail on lines similar to OPERATION STARKEY. An implementation chart was provided and each serial represented a part of the story for one or other of the agents to be reported on a fixed day. Agents Nos. 3 and 3(3) were the GARBO agents responsible for covering this operation.

The following is a rough outline of the plan. A large transport fleet was to assemble off the east coast of Scotland. GARBO's agent discovered that these troop transports were being fitted with special davits to be able to launch small assault landing craft in place of the lifeboats normally carried. To coincide with the agents' reports a real fleet gradually assembled at the point disclosed, and air reconnaissance was invited until the build up had been completed. The Planners, believing that the German Naval staff would realize that port facilities in the east coast of Scotland were inadquate for the requirements of an operation of the scale of FORTITUDE (NORTH), decided to route the transport fleet north around Scotland to the Clyde. In fact it continued on its journey south, to the real invasion bases but it was reported as having put into the Clyde to join up with the (notional) battle fleet meanwhile reported by Agent No. 3 as exercising there. Formations under command of the (notional) Fourth British Army were then reported as assembling at camps in the Glasgow vicinity. The plan culminated on D - 1.

It now appears that we overestimated the intelligence of the enemy. We had assumed that they would have pieced together the eye witness reports transmitted, and together with the Intelligence obtained by their wireless intercepting units and through air reconnaissance have visualized the picture we had endeavoured to convey to them.

We now possess conclusive evidence to prove that the contrary was the case, and that although they continued to believe in the threat to Norway so long as our transport fleet was maintained off the east coast of Scotland, they considered the threat to Norway as called off the moment we reported that it had moved over to the west coast.

In the Freude Heere West Intelligence report for the German High Command of the 8th June, 1944 (D+2) under reference, "O.K.H. Situation Report West No. 1290" the following reference on the situation in Great Britain reflects their reaction to our information. It states:-

"According to a credible Abwehr message the II English Corps,
hitherto reported in the Stirling area (Scottish command)
and the 58th English Infantry Division, stationed west of
Edinburgh, were transferred at the beginning of the month to
the Dumfries area (Solway Firth). At the same time the VII
English Corps, hitherto assumed to be in Dundee, has been
reported on the west coast of Scotland."

NOTE:- All the formations mentioned were notional.

When, later, to increase the threat to Norway, we identified
both the 52nd and 58th Divisions in the Glasgow area, the conclusion
drawn by the O.K.H. was that the threat to Norway could definitely
be considered as "off" but that it was nevertheless possible that
these Divisions might embark to support an operation against
France.

Apparently they failed to make the assessment that the ports
on the east coast were inadequate for such an operation, and
therefore failed to understand why, if we were preparing to
undertake an operation against Norway, we should base it on the
Scottish ports which were furthest removed from the objective. It
is, however, reasonable to speculate that FORTITUDE (NORTH) if it
failed to achieve the threat to Norway succeeded in assisting the
Security of OVERLORD, and in causing the enemy to be taken by
surprise.

The conclusion which we wish to be drawn from this, is that
the enemy cannot be relied upon to reconstruct the plans of their
opponents from eye witness reports unless they are supported and
confirmed by circumstantial evidence, explanations and/or, in the
case of a high grade agent, his appreciation.

GARBO had, in the past, developed the practice of qualifying
his reports. He would invariably conclude an eye witness report with
his appreciation, for instance:-

".....from which I conclude that the Harwich - Ipswich area
had become an important operational base for future
operations....."
or
"....which indicates the possibility of an imminent attack
against Norway....."
or
".....from which I am able to state categorically that the
threat to Norway no longer exists for the present......"

Frequently he would quote in great detail, conversations
which had taken place with one or other of his well placed friends.

He would draw conclusions from the intonation of his friends' voices as well as from the meanings inferred during such chats.

These practices had developed into one of GARBO's principal characteristics, in spite of criticism by some of the Approving Authorities, who would frequently advocate that the practice should be dropped in favour of reporting concrete fact from which the enemy should be encouraged to draw their own conclusions. Against these views we argued that in order to maintain the character of the GARBO case it was essential to preserve the principle of annexing GARBO appreciations to the eye witness traffic of his agents.

GARBO could, at the most, be considered by the Germans as a self trained military reporter. He had personally been responsible for very few eye witness reports. He was first and foremost an organizer who, in addition, had highly placed contacts. It was obvious, therefore, that if through conversations with these contacts GARBO could be enabled to make a logical and plausible appreciation of a situation which, at the same time, supported his agents' eye witness reports, the ideal combination would be produced.

Against the suggestion that the German High Command would certainly pay no attention to GARBO's appreciations and might even consider them pretentious, we argued that this possibility could best be judged by considering the situation in the reverse. Had the German threat to invade England developed into a reality, there could be no doubt that the opinion of C.S.S. would have considerably influenced decisions taken by the British Chiefs of Staff in their counter-invasion measures, had he at the time been able to produce impressive reports about German intentions reaching him from a large organization of long standing and reliability operating from Berlin. In such a situation C.S.S would have been obliged to put forward, with strong recommendations, any conclusions reached by the chief of his trusted Berlin organization.

In the German case there was every reason to suppose that the situation would be similar. After the Normandy landing there would inevitably be certain divergences of opinion in the German High Command as to further Allied intentions. There would be some German leaders who, we anticipated, would draw the conclusions which we were trying to inspire through FORTITUDE. If, therefore, we could, through GARBO and the Abwehr, supply every form of ammunition, for the arguments of those Germans inclined to believe in our cover plan, then we would be assisting those elements to influence their colleagues to the same belief.

When, after the cessation of hostilities, we were fortunate enough to discover a great proportion of the O.K.W. files, together with their Intelligence reports and summaries, covering the period with which we are now dealing, we discovered ample and abundant evidence to prove that our judgment had not been at fault in the above respect.

Perhaps the most unusual document to come to light was a F.H.W. appreciation of enemy intentions report (the F.H.W. was the Intelligence Department in the German Supreme Command responsible for all Intelligence appreciations connected with the Allied armies in the west) in which a conversation between GARBO and his friend in the Ministry of Information is used as an Appendix to the report.

The Lagebericht West (Situation or Intelligence report) to which the GARBO material was appended was the highest form of appreciation made in the German Armed Forces on "enemy" ground forces. According to a SHAEF appreciation on this document, it is a unique case of an agent's report being quoted verbatim in an official report of so high a level. The report referred to above is the Lagerbericht West report No. 1230 dated 9.4.44 which contained information from GARBO Letter No. 18 of the 23.2.44.

Similarly we were to discover that all eye witness reports were incorporated in Daily Situation reports on the Allied Armies published by F.H.W. Thus, the movement and regrouping of all notional and misplaced formations, the subject of the reports of the GARBO network, became the subject of the Daily Intelligence reports of the German Supreme Command, to be widely circulated in German official circles, and on which all German appreciations were subsequently based.

As far as we are able to judge an exact copy of the GARBO reports was, after being retransmitted from Madrid to Berlin, teleprinted on to the German Supreme Command at Zossen where it was distributed to the appropriate Intelligence sections. Copies were invariably sent direct to the Commander-in-Chief of the German armies in the west. In addition, he would receive the substance of the same material in the form of the Daily Situation reports of the F.H.W. and fortnightly review of Allied intentions, as published by the O.K.H. (Army High Command.) Changes in the location of formation swould sometimes appear in print in F.H.W. reports within 24 hours of the information having been transmitted by GARBO.

We were naturally not to know all these remarkable facts at the time of our planning, though we were soon to know through M.S.S. that our information was being passed to RUNDSTEDT himself, and later we were to discover that it was being acted upon, presumably on the instructions of the German Supreme Command.

It is noticeable in the F.H.W. appreciation, that neither the interception of our wireless deception network nor physical deception, played any substantial part in implementing the work of the agents. The success of wireless deception was dependent on the efficiency of their interception services. It must be realized that prior to D Day the enormous volume of traffic on the air in a relatively concentrated space was so great, that the task for any interception service to analyse it all would have been an enormous one. After D Day it is highly probable, and there is some evidence in the F.H.W. reports to suggest, that all their energies were concentrated in covering the formations which had entered operations to which priority would necessarily have to be given.

If physical deception was not effective to any great extent, it could be accounted for by the risks which the Germans were bound to entail in making aerial reconnaissances against the formidable allied air forces. In fact we know that astonishingly few attempts were made to reconnoitre.

Fortunately, in the case of FORTITUDE (SOUTH), unlike STARKEY and FORTITUDE (NORTH), planning was far less rigid, and it was this flexibility that permitted the deception plan to be developed as reactions were perceived. From the point of view of managing the case it was a far more strenuous and exacting proposition in the first phases, than it would have been had we been implementing a plan worked out to the closest detail. This elasticity in planning, however, made possible the effective prolongation of the threat until after the Pas de Calais had been overrun by Allied troops, when threats to Denmark and later, Western Germany were created, as the German Armies retreated.

The plan, which embodied the passing of deceptive information to assist the three Services, cannot be dealt with in detail in this summary by nature of its exceedingly complex character. The following outline of the four phases of deception, it is hoped, will suffice to illustrate the essentials.

CHAPTER XXIV (A)

FORTITUDE (CONTINUED)
PHASE I.
PRIOR TO D DAY OF OVERLORD

GARBO's agents were allowed to identify and locate the following
formations under SHAEF:-

	21 Army Group	(Montgomery)
NOTIONAL	FUSAG (1st US Army Group)	(Patton)
	1st Canadian Army	(Crerar)
	1st U.S. Army	(Hodges)
	2nd British Army	(Dempsey)
	3rd U.S. Army	(Factually, Patton - the notional commander was not disclosed.)
NOTIONAL	4th British Army	(Thorn, and later, Morgan.

Detailed reports were also furnished about the formations
under 2nd British Army, 1st Canadian Army, 3rd U.S. Army and
(notional) 4th British Army. Comparatively little mention was made
of formations under the 1st U.S. Army since it had been conveniently
arranged that no agent should be allowed to succeed in situating
himself in the area in which it was exercising.

With few exceptions all divisions then in the United Kingdom
were identified by the organization prior to D Day. In addition the
(notional) 55th U.S. Division was identified in Iceland, and the
(notional) 58th British Division under (notional) 4th Army was
identified in the U.K.

The locations of formations were inaccurately reported to
give the false picture that the main weight of the Allied Forces in
the United Kingdom was concentrated in Scotland, the Eastern
Counties and the south west and south coasts. The true picture would
have shown the forces concentrating in the Liverpool area, the
Midlands, South Wales and the south of England.

Whereas the reporting on the location of formations was,
perhaps 75% inaccurate, the percentage of accuracy in the
identification of large and small Allied formations was extremely
high. The conclusions which the enemy were to draw from these
reports was, very far from the truth, for the notional 4th British
Army and independent formations in Scotland constituted a threat to
Norway (FORTITUDE NORTH) and the notional 1st U.S. Army Group under

Patton (composed at that period of genuine, but misplaced formations) implied a threat to the Pas de Calais area, (FORTITUDE SOUTH.)

It can therefore be said that prior to D Day (apart from the threat to Norway) no direct deception was practised, but that an imaginary Order of Battle had been built up and passed on to the enemy. This had prepared the ground for deception to be practised from that time.

In addition, it was the opinion of the British deception staffs that, on the culmination of PHASE I, the information already passed would be interpreted by the enemy Intelligence Services as follows:-

(a) Two American Armies, one Canadian Army and one British Army were training for an amphibious cross-channel operation which would probably be launched against some part, or parts, of the coastline between Denmark and Brest. (True.)

(b) An independent force incorporating the 4th British Army was in training in Scotland, possibly for the purpose of an attack against Norway which, if effected, would probably precede the main attack, and might be intended as a diversionary attack. (Untrue.)

(c) The main cross-channel assault was not imminent. (Untrue.)

(d) That in preparation for the main cross-channel attack two Army Groups each with two Armies under command had been formed under Supreme Command of SHAEF. (True.) One, an American Army Group under command of Patton, was concentrating in the south east. (Untrue.) The other, a British Army Group, under Montgomery, was concentrating in the south. (True.)

(e) Allied strategy would direct that the operation would be carried out in one of the following ways:-

(i)   By a simultaneous assault against several areas by all available forces. (Untrue.)

(ii) A major assault in one area to be launched by one Army Group to be followed by a second assault by the Second Army Group. (Untrue.)

(iii) A large scale diversionary attack to be launched against one area to draw German reinforcements to that area prior to launching the major assault against the more important strategical target area. (Untrue.)

(iv) The strategic disposition of the forces in the United Kingdom threatened that the main weight of the attack would come against the Pas de Calais area which not only offered the shortest road to Berlin, but also menaced

the German forces which might be cut off in the west and
the security of secret weapon sites concentrated in the
Pas de Calais area. (Untrue.)

This period was also to serve to prove to the enemy the
reliability of their sources. Embodied in the immense quantity of
material passed to the enemy at this stage was the following
accurate information:-

(a) 21st Army Group commanded by Montgomery was to carry out an
     operation under the Supreme Command of SHAEF.
(b) The 1st U.S. Army and the 2nd British Army were under Command
     of 21st Army Group.
(c) These two armies were concentrated in the south coast area.
(d) Accurate information was given regarding the identity and
     role of formations which were to take part in the initial
     phase of the operation.

After the start of operations the enemy could not fail to
observe the accuracy of this information with which they had long in
advance been furnished by their agents. It was hoped, therefore,
that they would draw from this the conclusion that the balance of
the reports received through these agents was likely to be equally
accurate. In fact this is precisely what transpired.

The following summaries from GARBO messages transmitted
between D - 23 and D Day of OVERLORD serve to illustrate the
implementation of the first phase of the deception plan as carried
out by the GARBO network.

Whilst the agents, strategically dispersed in coastal areas
throughout Great Britain, were sending in their eye witness reports
in support of the notional Order of Battle of Allied Forces in Great
Britain a more circumstantial and picturesque account of events was
being produced by GARBO.

On D - 23 GARBO met J(5) from whom he learnt that before the
main Second Front was opened attacks would be made by diversionary
forces to disperse concentrations of German reserves from vital
points of attack. She assured GARBO that the invasion would not take
place then since a great number of American troops were still due to
arrive. She believed that diversionary attacks would soon be made to
confuse the enemy and she affirmed that aerial bombardments would
increase. This was intended to persuade the enemy that the attack
was not imminent.

On D - 18 GARBO (having learnt on the 1.5.44 that J(3) was
abroad) had, in accordance with instructions received, kept in
contact with the Ministry of Information and now he discovered that

J(3) had returned from Spain. Having prepared a new propaganda leaflet for this Department GARBO used this as an excuse in order to get a prompt interview with him. It will be recalled that J(3) could, from the analysis of the traffic, be identified by the Germans as the Head of the Spanish Department of the Ministry of Information who had the previous year (at our request) stayed at the Palace Hotel in Madrid during the period that GARBO's friend, J(3), had been reported as staying there. Earlier in 1944, GARBO, with the approval of the Germans, had given up his work for the Ministry though he had maintained contact with J(3) whose departure for Spain at the end of April had been reported by GARBO to the Germans on the 1.5.44. The departure of J(3) from England was again made to coincide with the second journey to Spain made by the Head of the Spanish Section of the Ministry of Information. We, therefore, had to assume that the Germans would check on GARBO's message of the 1.5.44 and discover that the Head of the Spanish Section had arrived in Madrid. To implement our message of D - 18 we, therefore, had to ensure that the M.o.I. officer would return before that date. A request was made to the Director General of the M.o.I by this Office to arrange for his officer to be recalled immediately from Madrid and, in order to assist our plans, he agreed to take this action. It may be assumed that the sudden departure of this official from Madrid at that time came to the notice of the Germans there and gave verisimilitude to the GARBO messages which followed. The purpose of this message was to give GARBO a new entree to the Ministry of Information in order later, to be able to provide, circumstantial evidence in support of his agents' eye witness reports.

On D - 15 GARBO had a meeting with J(3) who asked him to contribute some ideas to assist in propaganda for consumption by Spain and Latin-American countries which was then being prepared in connection with the Second Front. He asked for two days to think it over, and meanwhile he signalled the Germans for their approval before accepting employment in the pay of the enemy, recommending that by so doing he might obtain valuable information. He added, that should he accept he would then recall Agent No. 3 from the Clyde to assist in the work in London, and would replace him with Agent No. 3(3) whose usefulness as an observer on the east coast of Scotland appeared to have come to an end. The recalling of Agent No. 3 to London was in order to create a deputy for GARBO. In the event that he, through illness or other circumstances, should have been unable to operate as scribe for the organization we would have established an efficient deputy (in the form of M.I.5.) who could continue to operate in GARBO's stead.

On D - 12 GARBO accepted J(3)'s proposition to work for the Ministry in his spare time. He was made to sign the Official Secrets

Act which, he commented, was a document only signed by persons who, through their work, were in a position to obtain information which, if divulged, could compromise secret plans. He was asked to study a memorandum on the propaganda plan in operation prior to, and after, the landing in North Africa, in order that he should be able to appreciate the systems and methods used. The main outlines of this plan, he said, were supplied by the military authorities. He remarked on the experience gained from this document which he estimated would be of value in his future work. Thus, we established that GARBO was henceforth to be in possession of secret material related to the Second Front.

On D - 10 GARBO reported that Agent No. 3 had taken over the management of the radio service though he, GARBO, was continuing to edit the agents' messages. He added that should he at any time be too busy to do so he had instructed Agent No. 3 to transmit them in English, as received from the agents, so as to avoid putting the responsibility of evaluating them, or re-wording them, on his Deputy. Agent No. 3, on his arrival in London from the Clyde reported that the Naval forces were still stationed there, and that he believed that they were there in preparation for an attack against Norway. He said that he had instructed Agent No. 3(3) to watch and report on the movement of these ships. This provided for all communications to be transmitted in English in the event that GARBO should become incapacitated. The second portion of the message maintained the FORTITUDE (NORTH) threat.

On D - 8 GARBO, having now taken part-time employment in the Ministry of Information to work with his friend, J(3), was given a file which described the propaganda methods used in connection with recent operations in Italy. GARBO explained that strategic military policy was reflected in propaganda policy and that since he would, in future, have access to P.W.E. directives issued to the Ministry he considered that these, together with the agents' reports on the Allied Order of Battle, would give a clear indication of the enemy's future intentions. A long report was forwarded by Madrid to Berlin in connection with the above in which they wrote up GARBO's story and pointed out that it was through the Ministry of Information that GARBO had obtained the information about the landing in North Africa "which had only arrived two days late." Berlin replied to Madrid to say that in view of the excellent work of the GARBO organization to date they did not want GARBO to be burdened with the additional work at the Ministry if it would mean a sacrifice of the quality of his military reports. Our message was intended to inspire them to read in the reverse all the directives which were in future to be issued to the Ministry of Information, which, we proposed, GARBO should retransmit to them.

From D - 7 to D - 4 GARBO concentrated mainly on a series of military reports from his agents in the east, south-east and south of England in which the Order of Battle of FUSAG was further built up.

On D - 3 GARBO reported that he was awaiting the arrival of his agent, No. 3(3), from Glasgow at any moment. This agent had been instructed to keep a watch on the notional fleet of 33 troop transports which had previously been built up as arriving there, and which was being covered by wireless and had engaged in several Naval exercises in which the 52nd Division and the (notional) 58th Division were supposed to have taken part. The renewed activity of this agent, at this stage, was intended to distract from the great activity then taking place on the south coast, and to implement FORTITUDE (NORTH.) A short while previously Berlin had asked Madrid to ascertain from GARBO how long it would take to get news from Glasgow should the 52nd Division embark. Before GARBO had, in fact, replied, Madrid impatiently anticipated GARBO's answer in their reply to Berlin, by stating that news could be got through to them in approximately 48 hours.

On D - 2 GARBO reported the messages which had been brought to him by 3(3) from Glasgow. The information was that the (notional) 55th British Division had arrived in Dumfries from Ireland and that a concentration of the (notional) British II Corps, and the (notional) 58th Division had been observed at Motherwell. It had previously been reported that the 52nd Division was in the Troon area and that the (notional) 4th Army was also concentrating in the west of Scotland. No indication was made as to whether the notional II Corps, 55th Division and 58th Division were concentrating to embark in the Clyde or to proceed south (these divisions were later to be reported as having come south when they were required to build up the strength of (notional) FUSAG, after the departure of certain of its real formations overseas, and thus maintain the FORTITUDE threat by the reinforcement of (notional) FUSAG with notional formations.) GARBO, angry with the agent, at his stupidity in having come to London to report instead of having proceeded to the Clyde where it was reasonable to anticipate these troops would by now be embarking, ordered the agent to return forthwith to Glasgow, and gave him a code word to report by telephone should he discover, on arrival, that the troops in question had started to embark in the Clyde. This was to provide the way to keep the Germans in Madrid on the alert on the eve of D Day so that we should be enabled to pass them a last moment pre-release that the invasion was about to commence.

On D - 1, still with intention to distract from the real preparations which were culminating on the south coast, GARBO's

Agent No. 7, was reported to have returned from Swansea where he had proceeded to investigate a previous report which had been received from Agent No. 7(6) stationed at Swansea. He brought back with him an unconfirmed report to the effect that an unidentified (notional) American assault division had recently disembarked at Liverpool and was awaiting re-embarkation, together with another (notional) American Division, at a date subsequent to the 8.6.44, by when their assault craft, which were under repair, would be ready. These assault divisions, he had learnt, were to form the spearhead of an attack in the Bordeaux area which was to be followed up by a shore to shore landing with large forces from the U.S.A. (This was in support of an independent operational deception plan known as OPERATION IRONSIDE.) GARBO concluded his message by saying that as he was anticipating a telephone call from his Glasgow agent at any time during the night, the Madrid station should be listening at the emergency schedule times of 0300 hours BST in case there should be news. The purpose of this was to have Madrid standing by at H - 3½ hours, since a plan had been prepared to let the enemy have prenotification, through GARBO, of the impending OVERLORD operation which would have reached German headquarters shortly after the first wave of the assault had been launched. The Germans in Madrid failed to listen at the early hour on D Day. The messages drafted for transmission at that hour were therefore rewritten and strengthened since the next scheduled time for transmission was not until approximately H Hour, by when better information could be released without endangering the operation, with the knowledge that it would later become apparent to the Germans that these facts would have been available to them before H Hour had they been less negligent and inefficient.

The information eventually passed was supplied by Agent No. 4 who had for some while been silent within his sealed camp at Hiltingbury. On D - 1 this agent decided to break camp together with two American deserters to bring GARBO the news that iron rations and vomit bags had been issued to the 3rd Canadian Division which had left Hiltingbury to embark, the camp having been taken over by American troops of the 1st U.S. Army. The first of this series of messages was eventually transmitted eight minutes after the 3rd Canadian Division had landed on French soil.

The following is evidence in support of the successful implementation by GARBO of PHASE I of FORTITUDE.

The fact that the Germans were in a receptive frame of mind to absorb our cover plan is indicated in B.J. No. 508 of the 28.5.44 in which the Japanese Ambassador in Berlin gave a resume of a conversation which he had had with Hitler the previous day:-

"Speaking of the Second Front, Hitler said that he, himself, though that sooner or later operations for the invasion of Europe would be undertaken. He thought that about eighty divisions had already been assembled in England (of these divisions about eight had had actual experience of fighting and were very good troops.) I accordingly asked the Fuehrer if he thought that these British and American troops had completed their preparations for landing operations and he replied in the affirmative. I then asked him in what form he thought the Second Front would materialize, and he told me that at the moment what he himself thought was most probable was that after having carried out diversionary operations in Norway, Denmark and the southern part of the west coast of France and the French Mediterranean coast, they would establish a bridgehead in Normandy or Brittany, and after seeing how things went would then embark upon the establishment of a real Second Front in the channel. Germany would like nothing better, he said, than to be given an opportunity of coming to blows with large forces of the enemy as soon as possible. But if the enemy adopted these methods his numerical strength would be dispersed and he (Hitler) intended to watch for this........"

That the invasion came as a surprise is evident from the following B.J. No. 73 dated 15.6.44:-

Extract from a despatch from the Japanese Ambassador, Berlin:
"Leaving for the moment the Anglo-American claim that the landing (in France) was a surprise, it is a fact that although the Germans had long been warning their people of the danger of enemy landings, there is a tendency to think that German military authorities were making preparations with July in their minds and that the present landing occurred rather too early to suit them......"

The following extracts from German Army High Command F.H.W. "Review of British Empire No. 27" dated 21.4.44 are relevant:-

"......News of the concentration and readiness of the strong group of forces in Scotland has continued.........The English Army Command believed to be in Scottish Command is, according to a credible Abwehr source, the Fourth."

The following is a quotation from the German source "Review of the British Empire No. 27" dated 15.5.44:-

"......The SCHWERPUNKT of the enemy concentrations has shown more and more clearly to be in the south and south east of the British Isles..."

and from the "Review of the British Empire No. 30" dated 31.5.44:-

"......Further transfer of formations to the south and south east of the British Isles again emphasises that the main point of enemy concentrations is in this area."

Map No. 29 of Great Britain and Ireland published by F.H.W. to show the location of Allied formations at 15.5.44 proves conclusively that agents' reports constituted a principal source of their information; i.e. (notional) formations are located in the areas identified by agents. The Germans were apparently under the impression at that time that Northern, Eastern and South Eastern Commands corresponded to British 3rd, 6th and 5th Armies respectively. Also they believed in the existence of County Divisions, known by the means of Counties, as well as in several non-existent Canadian divisions.

In all they calculated that there were in the U.K., 56 Infantry Divisions, 14 Armoured Divisions, 7 Airborne Divisions, 14 Armoured Brigades and 5 independent Infantry Brigades; a total of 77 Divisions, and 19 Brigades. Thus, overestimating our strength by more than 50%.

A comparison between the above-mentioned map and maps of FORTITUDE (SOUTH) and OVERLORD, both taken at D - 30 can be made by reference to Appendix No. XL.

Reactions from incoming messages as to the success of our endeavour during PHASE I were few. Since the beginning of January, 1944, the German Intelligence Service, at least, had been apprehensive that the opening of the Second Front was imminent. During January and February a great number of questionnaires were sent to GARBO instructing him to be on the alert and specifically enquiring for the location of formations and shipping concentrations. With the approach of D Day these questionnaires were less frequent and specific. Occasional questionnaires would be received enquiring about the notional, as well as the real, formations in the United Kingdom, from which it was possible to assess that the notional formations had been believed in by German Headquarters since most of the questionnaires which reached us had originated in Berlin as we were able to observe from the Berlin-Madrid traffic on M.S.S.

CHAPTER XXIV (B)

FORTITUDE (CONTINUED.)
PHASE II
D DAY - D + 45.
6.6.44 - 22.7.44.

21 Army Group with 1st U.S. Army and the 2nd British Army had gone overseas.

The threat to Norway was off. New American formations were being landed in the United Kingdom.

Both the Army Group in the field awnd the Army Group in England remained under the Supreme Command of SHAEF to co-ordinate the overall operation.

The notional Army Group which remained in England now threatened a second assault of even greater proportions which would be launched against the Pas de Calais. The attack was not, however, made to appear imminent for three reasons:-

(i)   The greater the postponement, the longer we would be able to retain German reserves in the Pas de Calais area.

(ii)   The enemy would be bound to realize the time required to cope with the transport problem whichs a second large scale landing would involve.

(iii) We would be expected to require the use of landing craft which were employed in the Normandy assault.

FUSAG, still under Patton's command, had grown in strength by the incorporation of formations hitherto included in the (notional) 4th British Army which moved from Scotland at intervals during June and July to take up new headquarters in Sussex. A (notional) 14th U.S. Army composed of newly arrived U.S. troops had been created and incorporated in FUSAG. Thus, for a short period, during which our armies established themselves successfully and firmly in the Cherbourg Peninsula an increased threat to the Pas de Calais area was maintained by the four Armies now represented as being in the southern half of England:-

	1st Canadian Army
	3rd U.S Army
NOTIONAL	4th British Army
NOTIONAL	14th U.S Army.

There were numerous indications of reinforcements for FUSAG which left it apparently stronger on D + 45 than it was on D Day.

Meanwhile formations from the 1st Canadian and 3rd U.S. Armies were rapidly being transferred to the battle area. A complete black out on all information about these moves was carefully and successfully maintained. The agents would have to continue to report them as still in the United Kingdom until such time as the forces in question were likely to become engaged in operations, and be identified by the enemy.

Having built up the strength of Allied Forces by the creation of notional formations, it was the role of agents during PHASE II to tell the following story:-

(a) The landing in the Cherbourg Peninsula by 21st Army Group should be considered as a one-prong thrust of a two-pronged operation.

(b) The first landing was primarily a large scale diversionary assault intended to draw German reserves to the battle area.

(c) As soon as German reserves had thus been drawn away from the Pas de Calais area, the major landing would be made there to provide the shortest road to Berlin, and, at the same time, dispose of the V weapon sites.

(d) FUSAG, assault divisions, were already fully trained and prepared for operations.

(e) Airborne forces were training for a new operation.

(f) Numerous marshalling areas had been located within the sealed areas on the east and south-east coasts.

(g) Assault craft (dummies) were assembling in eastern and south-eastern ports.

The following are some extracts from GARBO messages in support of PHASE II of FORTITUDE:-

On the evening of D Day Agent No. 3(3) communicated that whilst a state of alarm still existed in the Clyde and Glasgow area the troop transports had not yet departed neither had the troops embarked. This was hoped to maintain the threat against Norway.

GARBO reported that immediately on learning the news that the invasion had started he went to the Ministry of Information to find it in a chaotic state. All Departments, he said, had been handed copies of a special directive issued by P.W.E. in connection with the recent offensive. The official attitude to be adopted by the Ministry was that:-

(a) The offensive was a further important step in the Allied concentric attack against the fortress of Europe.

(b) It was of the utmost importance that the enemy should be kept in the dark as to our future intentions.

(c) Care must be taken to avoid any reference to further attacks and diversions.

(d) Speculation regarding alternative assault areas must be avoided.

(e) The importance of the present assault and its decisive effect on the course of the war should be clearly stated.

(A copy of the directive was printed and forwarded to the Germans.) By reading this directive in the reverse, as we had previously indicated they should, the conclusion which they were intended to draw was that there were to be one or more operations to follow which the British were trying to conceal from the enemy.

GARBO immediately pointed out to J(3) that the speeches made that morning by the Allied chiefs had made it impracticable to carry out the directive. For instance, Eisenhower, had in his speech, warned the French patriots against a premature uprising lest they should be prevented from being of maximum help to their country at the critical moment. He had said "Prepare"; "Be careful."

Prior to D Day it had been impossible for us to estimate what Press reactions would disclose to the enemy the moment the news of the landing had been released. We knew that it would be impossible to use the Press for deception since that was strictly prohibited. We anticipated that the Press would realize that the Cherbourg assault was the big, and main, attack of the opening of the Second Front and would publicise it as such, against the interests of the deception plan. We, therefore, hoped that the fore-mentioned P.W.E. directive would make the enemy believe that the Press was inspired. On the other hand, we had not anticipated that General Eisenhower and Mr. Churchill, who were to make speeches on the morning of D Day would, with knowledge of the cover plan, independently try to implement it without reference to ourselves. They clearly implied in their speeches that this was the first of a series of attacks which would be made against the fortress of Europe. Although we were given a sight of these speeches on D - 1 we were unable to have them changed. It was essential to proceed with our plan for the P.W.E. directive in view of the line which we anticipated the Press would take, and then to point out the inconsistency between the directive and the speeches, interpreting the deception touch which had been introduced into those speeches by explaining that great men and leaders of countries, are bound to tell the truth to their people even if the truth is against the interests of Security. Therefore, in reply to GARBO's observation to J(3) that the speeches had been inconsistent with the P.W.E. directive, he admitted that they had

weakened the usefulness of the directive but that he did not think
the Germans would be able to draw any definite conclusion from the
speeches. He commented that it was Eisenhower's duty to keep the
people from rising in those areas which had not yet become involved
in operations, just as it was the Ministry's duty to try to withhold
from the enemy information as to which those areas would be. He
added that the Director General had, himself, made the same
observation as GARBO, but that pending other instructions it was
their duty to endeavour to focus all attention on the present attack
to detract as much as possible from indicating future plans. The
directive was subsequently reported as having been modified and the
plan to use further similar P.W.E. directives to implement
deception had to be abandoned.

On the same day GARBO reported that he had summoned all his
agents to London for a conference. This was to prepare to be able to
put over the big deception story.

On D + 1 GARBO learnt that Agent No. 4's reports about the
embarkation of the 3rd Canadian Division had not been transmitted
until a few minutes after H Hour due to the failure on the part of
the Madrid station to be listening all night as he had requested.
Tired and exasperated he wirelessed them:-

> "I am very disgusted as, in this struggle for life and death,
> I cannot accept excuses or negligence. I cannot masticate the
> idea of endangering the service without any benefit. Were it
> not for my ideals I would abandon the work as having proved
> myself a failure......"

The Germans replied to say that it was impossible to know
whether their operator or GARBO's had been at fault. They added,
however, that they wished to stress in the clearest terms that
GARBO's work over the last few weeks had made it possible for their
command to be completely forewarned and prepared, and that his last
minute news would have had but little influence, had it arrived a
few hours earlier. They reiterated their recognition of his
excellent work and begged him to continue with them in the supreme
and decisive hours of the struggle for the future of Europe.

On D + 2 GARBO reported that the 3rd British Division had
landed in the first assault, and that the Guards Armoured Division
had left the area of Agent No. 7(4) who had learned that it was due
to go overseas on D + 3.

The first of these two items of information was true, and
indeed elements of that Division had no doubt already been
identified in the battle area by the enemy.

The second was untrue, and was passed for tactical deception purposes. To enable the American forces to establish a firmer fothold in their sector an endeavour was made to draw the German forces to the British and Canadian sectors. Thus, with wireless support, we notionally transferred the Guards Armoured Division in to the battle area more than a week before the actual disembarkation of this Division in France.

The same day GARBO sent over the most important report of his career. In this series of messages he transmitted the entire substance of Plan FORTITUDE for which the whole organization had been building up for so long. The report which was very long was ostensibly compiled from the information obtained at the conference with all his agents. GARBO requested that this information should be submitted urgently to the German High Command. The report set out, in a concentrated form, a summary of the information which we had been transmitting for the last two months. It stated that prior to initiating the Normandy assault there had been some 75 Allied Divisions in the U.K. The present activities were, in the main, carried out by forces which had recently returned from the Mediterranean, reinforced by Canadian and American troops. No FUSAG formation had taken part. A study of the information obtained from the agents showed that the following formations were still in their concentration areas in the south and south east of England without any indications that they were preparing to embark. The formations which we enumerated amounted to two Armies under FUSAG, six Corps, two Assault Divisions, five Armoured Divisions, twelve Infantry Divisions, besides contingents of Dutch and Belgian forces as well as Commandos and Rangers. All these formations and units had previously been identified and located by the GARBO network. Furthermore, we stated that over a hundred L.C.T.s (dummies) were reported as having recently assembled on the east coast and air reconnaissance was invited. GARBO concluded this report by expressing his opinion that the Normandy attack was a large scale diversionary operation for the purpose of establishing a strong bridgehead in order to draw the maximum of German reserves to the area of operations, and to retain them there in order to be able to strike a second blow with ensured success. He gave reasons why the second assault was likely to come in the Pas de Calais area.

Already the question of lifting the Diplomatic ban which had been imposed prior to D Day was being considered. It was inevitable that we would not be able to persuade the Foreign Office to maintain it for as long as we would have desired, and therefore, we decided to prepare the way for the day it was to be lifted, and to make it appear as though the motive for so doing was contrary to the true one.

On D + 3 GARBO said he had heard from his friend, J(3) that discussions were now taking place as to whether or not the

Diplomatic ban should be lifted. On the one hand it was argued that whilst the neutrals had accepted this drastic measure as a requirement of Security, pending the opening of a Second Front, to continue to impose the ban was itself an admission that other important operations were pending, on the other hand, it was argued that the ban must be kept on to ensure the security of the next operation. Thus, we made it apparent that whether it was decided to continue to impose the ban or not, either action was indicative that a second attack could be expected.

On D + 5 new marshalling areas and camps were located in the Dover area where troop concentrations were reported as continuing. This was intended to increase the threat to the Pas de Calais area.

On D + 6, in reply to a question asking for the present headquarters of General Bradley, GARBO replied to say that according to 4(3), Bradley was at present under the orders of Montgomery, now that Patton had taken over the command of FUSAG which had temporarily been held by Bradley. The headquarters of FUSAG was located as being at Ascot. A F.H.W. Situation Report prior to D Day showed that the O.K.W. was uncertain as to whether Bradley or Patton was Commander-in-Chief of FUSAG, which probably accounted for the question. Our reply was in accordance with the cover plan.

On D + 7 GARBO stole a document which he had discovered in the Ministry amonst a number of old secret papers which he had been asked to burn.

It was a "Top Secret" document - extracts of the minutes of a War Cabinet meeting of the Committee on OVERLORD preparations held on 10.5.44 at which the Director General of the Ministry of Information was listed as having been present. (The document was drafted and printed for us by the Ministry of Home Security.) The extract was headed "Railway loadings in connection with PLAN MARS."

From intelligent examination of the document the following appreciation could be drawn.

The overall Second Front operation was known under code name OVERLORD. This comprised two operation, one, NEPTUNE, the other, MARS.

The Ministry of War Transport was concerned that the balance of the transport planning for OVERLORD had been upset by the split American lines of communication due to the decision to station large numbers of U.S. troops in both the NEPTUNE and MARS areas.

In these Minutes it was implied that both the Secretary of State for War and the Minister of Production, as well as the Minister of Food, had expressed the view that the London area would be particularly effected by the fact that 60% of all the capacity of the lines would be absorbed in maintaining the flow of stores. The Minister of Information had said that the public would, if called upon to do so in the interest of operations, accept further restrictions, providing the facts could be explained to them with due regard to Security.

In other words the document implied that in May 1944, concern had been expressed at the prospects of having to maintain railway supplies for two major operations, one of which was presumably to be based on the east or south east of England. Both operations would be carried out with the assistance of U.S Forces.

Also on D + 7, to intensify the threat, we reported that the 28th U.S. Division, which we had built up as an assault Division for the Pas de Calais operation, had left the Harwich area, having finished their training.

On D + 8 Agent No. 7 located large concentrations of U.S. troops in camps in the Liverpool area. Later we were to discover that formations of the (notional) 14th U.S. Army had been concentrated in these camps after disembarkation.)

On D + 9 the departure of further forces to reinforce the Cherbourg attack was reported by agents on the south coast and the formations were identified. (This was necessary since the formations quoted were likely to be identified at any moment in the battle area.) They were, we claimed, immediately reinforced in the FUSAG area by the (notional) II British Corps and the (notional) 58th Division which we again identified, this being the first time, since they had been observed by 3 (3) to have left Scotland. In addition, the 28th U.S. Division which had been reported as leaving the Harwich area after finishing its training also turned up in south eastern area. Signposts to new camps were observed and some 70 tank landing craft (dummies) were discovered to have assembled in Dover and Folkestone harbours. GARBO interpreted the arrival of the forces from Scotland in the south eastern area of England as a significant danger.

On D + 10 the (notional) 59th U.S. Division was reported as having arrived in the Harwich area and to have taken over the camps previously occupied by the 28th U.S. Division. Thus, the strength of the U.S. Forces in Harwich was maintained. This new notional U.S. Division, it was claimed, had recently arrived from America. (It was later to be identified as one of the assault divisions of the (notional) 14th U.S. Army.)

On D + 12 GARBO gave a prerelease of the news that the Diplomatic ban was to be lifted the following day. The argument contained in the messages of D + 3 was amplified on the basis of a fight between the Foreign Office and the War Office in which the former won.

On D + 13 the 55th British Infantry Division was reported as having arrived in the south eastern area from Scotland.

On D + 14 GARBO transmitted by wireless, the copy of a letter

which purported to have been written by the Director General of the
Ministry of Information to all his staff, impressing on them the
need for maintaining utmost security in the handling of all
information relating to forthcoming operations, and pointing out
that similar reminders had been issued by all Government
Departments at the request of the Inter-Service-Security Board
etc., etc.,

On D + 16, in order to increase the threat, Agent No. 7
discovered considerable activity of forces under FUSAG in the
Gravesend area.

On D + 21 the 83rd U.S. Division was reported as having left
its south coast location. (This formation had gone overseas and was
soon to be identified by the enemy in the battle area.)

On D + 23 two brigades of the 61st Division were located in
the Dover area and the third at Ipswich, whilst further troops of
this Division were reported as being in the Newhaven area. We said
we had ascertained that they were being used as road lining troops
for the embarkation camps in these areas.

On D + 25 GARBO learnt from 4(3) that four new American
divisions had recently arrived in the U.K. to reinforce FUSAG for
the important task which it was to undertake. (These were to be
incorporated in the notional 14th U.S. Army.) He disclosed that
they were stationed in the Liverpool area where Agent No. 7 was
immediately instructed by GARBO to proceed to investigate. 4(3)
added that the war was about to enter a new and decisive phase, thus,
insinuating that following the arrival of the new U.S. Army in the
U.K. the second offensive might soon be expected to take place.

On D + 26 a further build up of troops in the Ipswich area was
reported by Agent No. 7(7).

On D + 28 the (notional) 59th U.S. Division was reported to
be an assault trained division. (This was to replace the 28th U.S.
Division in the FORTITUDE notional Order of Battle.) This division
was stated to be under the command of the (notional) 14th U.S. Army.

The build up of our forces in Normandy was proceeding
rapidly. It was important to withhold from the enemy information
which would disclose that the 1st Canadian Army and the 3rd U.S.
Army were in the battle area until approximately D + 50 by when the
enemy would probably discover this for themselves. On the other
hand, it would have been extremely suspicious had the agents in the
south and south east areas failed to observe the considerable
movement of the formations under command of these armies which we
had claimed were stationed in these areas. It was highly desirable
that the GARBO transmittor should be forced to be silent for at
least ten days. To make this possible it was decided to have GARBO
notionally arrested (in accordance with a scheme, the details of

which are set out in Chapter XXV.) The alarming news was transmitted by his Agent No. 3, then in charge of the wireless station. The Germans immediately instructed the organization to cease all activities for at least ten days until the repercussions to GARBO's arrest had been observed. GARBO was cleared of the suspicion which had caused his arrest, and was released after a few days detention. In this manner we were able to remain silent between D + 36 and D + 46 which brought this phase of the plan to a satisfactory close.

Evidence of the successful implementation of PHASE II of this vital period of the deception plan can be observed in the following material:-

(a) On 9.6.44 an urgent message was sent from Paris to K.O. Spain (in reply to what appears to have been a GARBO message transmitted to Paris) in which it is stated that the information that the 3rd English Infantry Division was in the landing area was correct and also added that the information about the bringing up of the Guards Armoured Division had been described by RUNDSTEDT as especially important and that RUNDSTEDT had requested further reports of a similar nature.

(b) On 9.6.44 a message was sent by HANSEN (Chief of the Abwehr in Berlin) to LENZ (Chief of the Abwehr in Spain) for KUHLENTHAL (GARBO's master in Madrid) expressing appreciation in the name of HIMMLER on the previous work in England (i.e. by the GARBO network.) It stated that the object of further reconnaissance must be to ascertain in good time when embarkation began and the destination of the groups of forces in south east England.

(c) On the 11.6.44 an appreciation of the GARBO information received was sent by Berlin to Madrid:-
"The report is credible. (Presumably referring to GARBO's message foretelling that the second and major assault would be made by FUSAG forces against the Pas de Calais.) The reports received in the last week from the ARABAL (GARBO) Undertaking have been confirmed almost without exception and are to be described as especially valuable. The main line of investigation in future is to be the enemy group of forces in south eastern and eastern England. It would also be especially valuable to learn in good time when the formations which are at present assembled in western Scottish ports put to sea, and what their destination is."

(d) From M.S.S. material made available to the War Room of SHAEF, which was not distributed in this Office, SHAEF, Ops. B., was able to deduce that through deception seven offensive German divisions were retained in the Pas de Calais area during the critical period of the Normandy operations, and for some time afterwards. Immediately after receipt of GARBO's messages of D + 3 the 116th Panzer Division, which had been stationed north west of Paris was ordered to move to the Somme and the 1st S.S. Panzer Division was moved from Turnhout to Ghent, i.e., both converging on the Pas de Calais. Similarly the 85th Infantry Division stationed north of the Somme which had received orders to move (presumably towards the beach-head) had its orders cancelled and was recalled.

(e) On the 6.6.44 the Japanese Ambassador, Berlin, sent a despatch to the Ministry of Foreign Affairs, Tokio, No. 548 continued by No. 551 on the 7.6.44 in which he stated (when discussing the Cherbourg assault):-

".....while these preparations had been in progress the Anglo-Americans have been carrying on operations which appear to aim at landings along the coast of the Straits as far as Dunkirk..... The forces used by the enemy in landings which he has made to date consist of three airborne and nine ordinary divisions..... These, however, constitute only the first wave and it is not yet clear whether the enemy's main offensive is to be made from here or whether he is going to attempt large scale landings elsewhere......."

(f) On the 8.7.44 the Japanese Military Attache, Berlin, sent a despatch to Tokio, serial No. 666, headed "Intelligence on the British Army (German Army Intelligence):-

".......The following British units are believed to be in Great Britain.....H.Q. of the VII Corps and the 52nd Infantry Division (in Scotland). (Writer's note:- The British VII Corps was a notional formation identified and located in Scotland by the GARBO network.)......The XX Corps and the 58th Infantry Division arrived in Kent from Scotland....."
(Writer's note:- The XX Corps is no doubt an error for the II Corps which was a notional corps which had under its command the notional 58th Division. These formations which formed part of the notional 4th Army were identified in Scotland by the GARBO network and later reported as having moved to Kent.)

(g) On the 9.6.44 the Japanese Military Attache, Berlin reported to Tokio in serial number 518, repeated to Japanese Military Attaches at Instanbul, Sofia, Madrid and Lisbon:-
"Whether landings in the Seine bay represent the chief point of the enemy's plan or whether in addition to this the main offensive, which has been kept secret, is now being prepared, is not yet clear. In view of the fact that these operations are being carried out by almost the whole strength of the American 1st Army (Normandy area) and the British 2nd Army (Seine Bay

area) which belong to the 21st Army Group which is on the south
west coast of Britain and by almost the whole strength of the
Air Force and Navy, it is thought for the time being that this
will be the only area included in their plans. But because one
separate Army Group is stationed on the south east coast of
Britain it is expected that plans will be made for this to land
in the Calais and Dunkirk areas.

(h)   On the 19.6.44 the Japanese Ambassador, Berlin, sent a
despatch to the Minister for Foreign Affairs, Tokio, No. 607,
in which he quoted information given him that morning by the
Vice-Minister of Foreign Affairs:-

"......According to investigations made by the Supreme
Command on the basis of prisoners' statements and captured
documents there were in England, in addition to the Army
Group under Montgomery, 23 divisions under the command of
General Patton ready to carry out an invasion. (Writer's
note: The reference to prisoners' statements and captured
documents was no doubt intended to conceal from the Japanese
Ambassador the fact that the information had come from
agents' reports which we know to have been the case, since
prisoners could know nothing about Patton's notional Army
Group.) This was another reason why the Germans (had
refrained?) from pouring their armies into Normandy.
Montgomery's Army Group consisted of 36 divisions and it was
thought that the original plan had been to occupy Cherbourg
and Le Havre with about 17 of these divisions and then to
advance south east down the Seine; meanwhile Patton's Army
Group would simultaneously have carried out landing
operations between Dieppe and the country lying to the east
of the port......The Germans still considered that there was
a great likelihood of Patton's Army Group landing between
Dieppe and Boulogne and were prepared for this.

(i)   On the 23.6.44 the Japanese Ambassador, Berlin, sent a
despatch to the Minister for Foreign Affairs, Tokio, No. 621,
marked "To be handled with discretion" quoting the substance
of a statement made the previous day by "Our usual source":-

".......The German High Command felt that their primary task
was to meet the main body of the enemy which still had to be
landed."

(j)   On the 24.6.44 the Japanese Ambassador, Berlin, sent a
despatch to the Minister for Foreign Affairs, Tokio, No. 626,
in which he submitted his own views of the Anglo-American
landing in the north of France:-

"......Taking a general survey of the war to date......The
Germans are in a position in which effectively to assume the

offensive it is necessary for them to call upon large numbers of troops from the rear and other areas. Moreover, in England, Patton's armies are waiting for a chance to land so that it is thought that it would be dangerous to put strong forces in Normandy.......Although the German High Command are not able to discern clearly from the Anglo-American landing in Normandy the whole of their plan they can see roughly what they are aiming at and it is now felt that there is no fear, strategically, of a surprise attack from the British and the Americans while, anticipating that the Armies under Patton now standing by will naturally land somewhere in the north of France, the German army is awaiting them, and is concentrating on the transportation of general reserves from Germany to the west with the intention of launching a general offensive after making the best possible tactical dispositions. The important point, however, is when the enemy forces in England will land and whether: (1) they will attempt a landing relatively soon in connection with the operations in Normandy (it seems that the Germans consider this very likely) or (2) the enemy will land after it has got possession of Cherbourg and has landed (reserves?) and heavy equipment and has extended his bridgehead to include the high ground round Le Havre."

(k)   On the 27.6.44 the Japanese Ambassador, Berlin, sent a despatch to the Minister for Foreign Affairs, Tokio, No. 630, on information given that day by Vice-Minister STEENGRACHT:-
      ".......The moral and political consequence of the fall of Cherbourg would be more serious than the military and he himself though it was unfortunate. ....On the other side of the picture, however, Montgomery had already poured about 30 Divisions into Normandy...... In the opinion of the German Supreme Command Patton's Army remained concentrated east and south east of Southampton. (Writer's note: This was probably intended to mean in the east and south east of England.) More than 350 large and small vessels had been got ready, and landing operations would be attempted in the near future.......The Germans, however, were determined to ambush these landing forces and smash them....."

(l)   On the 30.6.44 the Japanese Military Attache reported to Tokio in despatch No. 762, headed "Intelligence on the British Forces in the last ten days of June (German Army Intelligence.)" This contained the following information which can be attributed to GARBO:-
      "......The British VII Corps Headquarters and the 52nd Infantry Division and the British II Corps Headquarters

which were formerly stationed in Scotland have moved south
from there. (Writer's note: This was the move following the
threat by the notional 4th Army to Norway when the notional
army was brought south prior to its incorporation in
FUSAG)......According to reliable intelligence the units
which were on the south east coast and the units which were
in the county of Kent are believed to have moved to the mouth
of the Thames and to have been preparing for embarkation
(Writer's note: This probably refers to GARBO's message of D
+ 16 and others around this date.)......Investigations of
the formations which have landed in Northern France show
that there was no error in previous estimates of the
(disposition?) of troops in Britain.....The American 28th,
79th and 80th Infantry Divisions and the American 5th
Armoured Division have been identified in southern and south
eastern England......

(m)   On the 3.7.44 the Japanese Ambassador, Berlin, sent a
despatch to the Minister for Foreign Affairs, Tokio, No. 651
(?) which consisted of a report on the war situation to the
2.7.44 as told by GROTE to KAWAHARA (phonetic):-
".......In Normandy the British armies were extending their
bridgehead.......The German armies did not intend for the
present to drive the British and Americans out completely
(they were not yet using the General Army Group reserve in
the area in question) and thinking that the group of armies
under General Patton, waiting in the south of England, would
very probably attempt a landing in the Le Havre area or in
Brittany, were mainly concerned with making preparations to
surprise them."

(n)   On the 6.7.44 the Japanese Ambassador, Berlin, sent a
despatch to the Minister for Foreign Affairs, Tokio, No. 662.
"Highlights of what Vice-Minister STEENGRACHT told me
confidentially.":-
"......On the Normandy front the Anglo-American attacks
aimed at a push south by American troops from the Cotentin
Peninsula.....There were some who thought that this
opportunity should be seized to begin a general counter-
attack with part of the German forces but Marshal KLUGE who
had recently become Commander-in-Chief in the west, Vice-
Marshall RUNDSTEDT (Marshall ROMMEL is subordinate to him as
before) prudently considered that his objective would be
amply attained if he waited till the enemy attacked for the
purpose of enlarging his bridgehead......and that it was
essential to make sure what the main enemy forces in England
itself were up to. The result was that calmer thought had

prevailed. The Germans, as before, anticipated that the
enemy would next undertake landing operations in the area of
the Straits."

(o) On the 11.7.44 the Japanese Ambassador, Berlin sent a
despatch to the Japanese Minister, Sofia, Despatch No. 15:-
".....Germany appears to think that the enemy will use
Patton's forces to attempt a second landing in the area of
the Straits in the comparatively near future, and she
evidently plans to liquidate the enemy in the Normandy area
after liquidating this landing."

(p) On the 13.7.44 the Japanese Ambassador, Berlin sent a despatch
to the Minister for Foreign Affairs, Tokio, No. 693:-
"Source STEENGRACHT".......According to information in the
possession of the Germans it appears that all the forces
under Montgomery's command had been landed in Normandy but
up to the present not a single part of Patton's forces seemed
to have been landed and the German impression continues to
be that Patton's army would take part in the next landing
operations in the sector extending from a point contiguous to
the existing bridgehead up to the vicinity of Dieppe......
Of the reserves held by ROMMEL a large part of the Tiger and
Panzer forces were being kept back."

The following are extracts from O.K.W. (Fremde Herre West)
reports on Enemy Situation West:-

7.6.44 (D + 1)

".....Of the approximately 60 formations now in the south of
England it is probable that at the most 10 or 12 divisions
are at present taking part in the invasion. The main
objective may be regarded as the capture of the Cotentin
Peninsula to the south. The following are points worthy of
note:-

(a) The employment of the Air Force is limited to a narrow
area and has so far, contrary to expectations, not
included the important German headquarters in the west.

(b) Sabotage activity has been sporadic.

(c) All divisions so far identified in action have come from
the same area.

This evidence indicates that further undertakings are
planned and supports statements in this sense by Churchill
and Eisenhower. The formations which have so far appeared are
from Montgomery's 21st English Army Group which still has
over 20 formations at its disposal so that further air and
sea landing attempts appear possible in the region of the

Cotentin peninsula, possibly also against the Channel Isles
and by way of support, against the west coast of Normandy.
With 25 formations available north and south of the Thames a
further large scale undertaking in the Channel is
conceivable and may be expected to include the employment of
the strong portions of the Anglo-Saxon Air Force which have
still been held back."

8.6.44. (D + 2)

".......Great Britain. A proven Abwehr source reports that
the English Guards Armoured Division, at present in the
Worthing area will be embarked from Brighton Harbour. This
Armoured Division may therefore be expected to appear
shortly. According to a credible Abwehr message the 2 English
Army Corps, hitherto reported in the Stirling area (Scottish
Command), and the 58 English Infantry Division, stationed
west of Edinburgh, were transferred at the beginning of the
month to the Dumfries area (Solway Firth.)
At the same time the 7 English Army Corps, hitherto
assumed to be north of Dundee has been reported on the
west coast of Scotland in the Greenock area."

9.6.44. (D + 3)

"......Since the present grouping of forces, as well as
technical considerations of command, make it seem unlikely
that further forces of Montgomery will take part in any far
distant action, it is conceivable that the dividing line
between the English 21st Army Group and the American Army
Group, which is still standing by in the South East of
England, will be the same.
The fact that not one of the formations still standing by in
the south east and east of England has been identified in the
present operation strengthens the supposition that the
strong Anglo-American forces which are still available are
being held back for further plans."

10.6.44. (D + 4)

"......The arrival of the 51 English Infantry Division
(hitherto thought to be in the Cambridge area) - compare
Situation Report of the 9th June, 1944 - is not to be
regarded as an encroachment on the group of forces in
south east England since this division had already been
transferred to Montgomery's Army Group before the invasion
began. The strength of the group of forces in south east
England has therefore not been reduced.

20.6.44. (D + 14)

"......28 American Infantry Division last reported carrying out landing exercises in the Ipswich area has now returned to Kent. In the Ipswich area there is said to be a new Division which has arrived from the U.S.A., possibly the 8 American Infantry Division. This has still to be confirmed.
The intensification of resistance in Brittany which is being supported by the continuous provision of supplies and commanders by air is possibly intended to tie down German forces. There are so far no signs of further plans directed against this area apart from an air attack on a location apparatus at Brest, neither does the concentration of troops in England provide any clue in support of such a plan. On the contrary, all movements which have been recognized during the last weeks have been in a south easterly direction and the south western area has been correspondingly denuded. There are further indications from south eastern England that the formations of the First American Army Group are closing up in the direction of the south east coast. The move which has been reported but not yet confirmed of formations of the 2 British Corps (assumed to be in central England) to Kent comes within the scope of this south eastern concentration. There are as yet no documents to show the target date for operations."

23.6.44. (D + 17)

".....The portions of the English Army Group under Montgomery which are still in the south of England may, with the exception of the three Airborne Divisions already recognized there, be regarded as a reserve for future employment probably after the capture of the port of Cherbourg. Their employment in another sector of the coast is not anticipated since parts of the ten remaining Divisions already identified by number in England are most probably already being brought into the Second English Army (for 12 English Army Corps.)
The readiness for invasion of the First American Army Group (which need not be considered for any undertaking against Brittany) is emphasised by the evidence in the hands of Luftwaffe Command/Ic according to which there are recognizable indications of completed preparations for air landing and parachute operations. The reported concentration of landing craft in the harbours on the middle east coast (Harwich - Yarmouth) also deserves attention."

25.6.44. (D + 19)

"......Evidence obtained from photographic reconnaissance
tasks of formations in Montgomery's Army Group show that the
objects of this Army Group may shortly be found to lie in an
easterly direction towards Paris. The direction of the
attack again brings into relief the idea of a corresponding
and supporting attack by Patton's Army Group (First U.S. Army
Group) in the Seine - Somme area. As regards the
concentration of this group of forces it is noteworthy that
two further formations of the group of formations in Central
England (II Army Corps and 58 English Infantry Division) have
been reported in the Dover area. This concentration of forces
in the area south east of London and the intention in the
Channel area is thus given renewed emphasis."

27.6.44. (D + 21)

"......The significance of the concentration of forces in
south eastern England is continuously underlined by troop
movements recognized in this area. In this connection it must
be emphasised that the composition of the First Canadian Army
in the area London - Brighton - Dover, primarily English and
Canadian formations with their higher value (by comparison
with the Third American Army) points to an action against the
central channel area."

It should be understood that the extracts from Japanese
B.J.s, J.M.A.s, and Fremde Heer West Situation Reports have been
removed from their context. The extracts do, however, show
conclusively the favourable results of the GARBO implementation of
FORTITUDE and that his information was transmitted to the highest
Axis authorities and believed in by them.

In order that the extracts can be studied in their original
context, photostat copies of the relevant OKW documents which are
referred to in this summary are included at Appendix No. XXXIX. The
relevant B.J.s and J.M.A.s can be found in records held by the
Diplomatic Section, B.1.B.

Apart from the foregoing conclusive evidence of GARBO's
success during PHASE II of FORTITUDE; most of which was not
available to us at the time of the events, we were able to judge to
some degree the credibility which the Germans were giving to our
information from the questionnaires which we received from them at
the time, of which the following are examples:

D + 2. The Germans asked for an urgent reply as to whether
there was any news about the 28th U.S. Division recently seen by
Agent No. 7(7) in the Ipswich area. If necessary the reply, they

said, should be made by a special transmission. The significance of
this was that we had represented the 28th U.S. Division as the most
highly trained assault division under command of FUSAG, and
therefore its move to embark would have indicated a second landing.

D + 3. They pointed out to GARBO that the R.A.F. Tactical Air
Force had so far been little used in the present operation. They
asked him whether he thought it was being held in reserve to operate
on the opening of the eventual attack in another place.

D + 4. They replied that with reference to the extensive
information which he had transmitted on the 8.6.45 regarding the
concentration which still existed in the south east of England they
were interested that he should inform them with maximum urgency of
all news which he could obtain about the embarkation and destination
of these forces.

Other questionnaires to independent agents confirmed the
German belief in the notional FUSAG and in the probability that the
two independent Army Groups were intended for separate operations.

CHAPTER XXIV (C)

FORTITUDE (CONTINUED)
PHASE III.
D + 45 - D + 66
22.7.44 - 12.8.44

The information that the 1st Canadian Army and the 3rd U.S. Army had left the United Kingdom to reinforce the Cherbourg operation could no longer be safely withheld.

General Patton, who had never held a higher rank than that of Commander of the 3rd U.S. Army, was soon to become known to the enemy in this role.

Whilst it had to be admitted that the 1st Canadian Army and the 3rd U.S. Army had been transferred from FUSAG to enter into operations in France, it was stated they had been replaced by the 4th British Army (notional) and the 14th U.S. Army (notional) which had now come under command of FUSAG. Thus, after reinforcing the armies in Cherbourg, FUSAG apparently still retained the same strength as at D Day.

If the notional FUSAG was still to maintain the threat of a second attack, a new Commander-in-Chief had to be found and a satisfactory explanation made to the Germans to account for the somewhat strange change of Patton's role.

Special means were therefore used to implement the following story:-

(a) Montgomery, anxious to exploit his successful landing had requested Eisenhower to send all available forces to reinforce his Army Group at the sacrifice of postponing and reducing the scale and importance of the second operation to be undertaken by FUSAG.

(b) Patton, anxious for motives of personal prestige, strongly opposed this change of plan. Already unpopular with Eisenhower, the quarrel which ensued over this issue and Patton's insubordination in the face of his objections being over-ruled resulted in his being demoted to C-in-C of the 3rd U.S. Army which was sent to join Montgomery's armies.

(c) Eisenhower directed that the two American armies now in the field, the 1st and the 3rd, should come under the command of General Bradley in a newly constituted 12th U.S. Army Group. This brought up the issue as to who was senior of the two Army Group Commanders now appointed, Montgomery or Bradley. The transfer of Eisenhower, with SHAEF Forward Headquarters, to the battle zone resolved this issue.

NOTE:-

It should be understood that a real FUSAG was created shortly
after 21 Army Group had been formed. At the beginning of its
existence it was only a skeleton H.Q. As time passed it took
over formations which had hitherto been administered by ETOUSA.
FORTITUDE (notionally) advanced its operational status, giving it
formations which it did not possess. When the time came for FUSAG to
go overseas, it was decided to change its name to 12th USAG., so as
to leave the (notional) FUSAG free to continue its notional role.
Bradley commanded the real FUSAG from the start, and continued to
command it after it had been rechristened 12th U.S. Army Group.
Notionally 12th USAG was a new headquarters formed at the end of
June, 1944, to take command of the forces notionally released from
the notional FUSAG.

(d)   A new 9th U.S. Army had come under command of FUSAG, though
      only to remain for a brief period.
(e)   Command of FUSAG had been taken over by General McNair, who
      was a successor to Patton. When McNair was killed whilst
      visiting France, General de Witt was reported as succeeding
      him.

Thus, the FUSAG now composed of the (notional) 4th British
Army and (notional) 14th U.S. Army (supported for a short while by
the transitting 9th U.S. Army) still maintained the threat to the
Pas de Calais.

The following is a summary of the material passed by the
GARBO network in support of Phase III of FORTITUDE.

On D + 51 GARBO wrote a report which was forwarded by courier
in which he gave an account of a reconnaissance made by Agent No. 7
in the Liverpool area. This was made during the period of the
network's wireless silence from D + 36. There he located and
identified certain elements of the (notional) 14th U.S. Army with
two notional divisions under command which were later to be
identified in the Harwich/Ipswich area from which the picture was
to be drawn that after disembarking the forces of this army had
assembled in camps in the Liverpool area before proceeding to the
embarkation areas on the east coast.

On D + 54, as build up, GARBO gave the prerelease of the
breaking of diplomatic relations between Germany and Turkey which
information he had obtained from J(3).

On D + 58, GARBO, after a report from 7(2), was able to state
that the 1st Canadian Army, II Canadian Corps and 2nd Canadian
Infantry Division had all gone to Normandy. He also listed certain
formations from the 3rd U.S. Army which had previously been located in

the area covered by the agent which had gone to reinforce the battle area, in addition he reported that the XII British Corps had gone to Normandy and that it had been replaced by the (notional) II Corps. The newly arrived (notional) VII Corps, previously seen in Scotland, had now been identified in the Folkestone area. The (notional) 55th Division had also arrived in the Dover area but the (notional) 58th Division which had been stationed near Dover left for an unknown destination about the middle of July. They were soon to be received by Agent No. 7(7) in the Harwich area. The (notional) 80th Division had arrived at Canterbury and the 61st Division at Wye. Assault training exercises were reported as having taken place in his area.

On D + 61, Agent No. 7(7) identified newly arrived formations of the (notional) 14th U.S. Army in his area. The XX Corps had left and the 4th and 6th U.S. Armoured Divisions were reported as having been seen in his area a few weeks previously. (These were real formations which were soon to be identified in the battle.)

An amphibious exercise was described as having been carried out by the (notional) 59th U.S. Division on 22.7.44 in which tank landing craft had been used. This was intended to build up the 59th Division as an assault trained Division to replace the 28th U.S. Division which had previously been reported as having been transferred from FUSAG command to that of 12th U.S. Army Group in France.

With these, and other reports, the new Order of Battle was quickly built up.

All these changes established the (notional) 14th U.S. Army on the east coast and the (notional) 4th British Army in the south and south east coast of England.

To support these eye witness reports of agents, GARBO furnished the circumstantial explanations. From the point of view of the operation it was undesirable that the enemy should be told that the entire 3rd U.S. and 1st Canadian Armies had arrived in the battle area until about D + 50 by when it was considered inevitable that they would have discovered the fact for themselves. From the point of view of the security of the GARBO network we dared not continue to report formations as having been seen here at a period when it could be established by the Germans that they were in fact in the battle area.

A certain time overlap was always permissable since it was invariably reasonable to assume that an agent, whilst travelling around a rather wide area, would not always discover a departure or arrival of a division in his area until some days had elapsed. The sight of rear elements of a formation in his area might put him off his guard until he had occasion to revisit the camps in which the formation had previously been located.

The closing down of the GARBO transmitter, which we were instrumental in enforcing from D + 36 to D + 48, assisted our plans and since we were not yet operating on D + 43 when GARBO came by his information explaining all the changes which had taken place, and of the regrouping of FUSAG, it was reasonable that he should transmit his information by courier letter which we estimated would reach the enemy about D + 55. In the letter the whole story of Phase III was set out. His letter also confirmed and interpreted the reports transmitted between D + 51 and D + 58.

The source of his information was Agent No. 4(3) and the report read as follows:-

"A few days after the attack in Normandy had started General Montgomery found himself up against unexpected difficulties and asked for re-enforcements who were available to go into action immediately. The FUSAG troops being the only first line troops which were then available, he asked for certain of their formations even at the cost of delaying the plan to be undertaken by this Army Group. A few days later, General Eisenhower, in spite of the opposition of Patton, put at first the 83rd Division, and later, the Second Canadian Corps, under the orders of Montgomery. At the end of June, Montgomery was again dissatisfied, and found the situation in Normandy serious, and after having convinced Eisenhower of the necessity to strengthen the bridgehead still more, it was again decided to change the plan. This time Eisenhower promised Montgomery that if it became necessary he could make use of all the troops he required from FUSAG and that they could be incorporated with the U.S. Army already in the battle front in Normandy, in a newly formed Army Group. He made the conditions that part of the personnel of the Headquarters of FUSAG who had knowledge of the original plan should remain where they were in England so as to be able to control the operation when it was put into execution, and that in place of those who were transferred to France another staff officer would be brought from the U.S.A. direct. This new American Army Group hurriedly formed, will be known as the 12th U.S. Army Group. During this period of reorganization many staff officers anxiously started to manoeuvre for better jobs under one or other of the two Army Groups. This crisis was greatly aggravated by opposition from General Patton who is known among Americans to be a rough and brutal soldier. He opposed this plan, insisting that the troops trained for the second assault should remain under his command. This discussion was brought to an acid end

by Eisenhower, after some insubordination by Patton. He was
removed from his command of FUSAG and given instead the
command of the 3rd U.S. Army, giving over the command of the
12th U.S. Army Group to General Bradley who is Eisenhower's
"yes man" who at the same time has the experience of the
battles he had led in France. The command of FUSAG was
unfilled for a few days and was then given over to another of
Eisenhower's favourites, called McNair who has just recently
arrived from America. This reorganization was completed last
week. Meanwhile, the new FUSAG is being reorganized and is
being formed with the 9th and 14th U.S. Armies which have
arrived here during the last two months. (These are the units
which he previously told me were arriving.) He told me that
his uncle has been promoted and is now one of the chiefs of
the 14th U.S. Army, and his Division, the 48th U.S. Division,
was trained in assault before its arrival here and was
recently incorporated in FUSAG. I asked him whether the new
FUSAG was now weaker than the old. He said that it was not, as
apart from these armies, the 4th British Army was also coming
under it and would be coming down from Scotland as well as
a large contingent of English Divisions which will bring up
the total of this army to a force in excess of thirty
Divisions."

GARBO added his personal appreciation of the situation. He
reminded Madrid that the (notional) 4th British Army with the
(notional) II Corps as well as the (notional) 55th and 58th
Divisions were the forces previously located in Scotland prior to
the Normandy assault, and that since agents' reports had now
revealed that these forces were transferring to the south of England
it left only the 52nd Division in Scotland to undertake an attack
against Norway. Therefore, he logically pointed out that no threat
to Norway need be feared for the time being. He went on to say that
although there were some circles here who still believed in a direct
attack from the U.S.A. against the Bordeaux area, he personally did
not believe in this possibility.

The only danger to be faced, he said, was a landing by the
FUSAG forces in the Pas de Calais area. The added incentive to
capture the areas from which the "V" bombs were now being launched
with increasing regularity intensified the previously existent
danger of attack.

At this stage of developments the landing in the south of
France was becoming imminent. Through M.S.S. we discovered that
information had reached the enemy through which they had discovered
the general target area. An endeavour was made to try to induce them

to believe that the reports which they had received had been
inspired by the British and were therefore to be distrusted. At the
same time it presented us with an opening to suggest a prolonged
threat to the Pas de Calais area.

On D + 63 GARBO reported that he had learnt through J(3)
that an operation would take place in the Mediterranean before the
final operation from this country against the Continent would be
effected. In this connection he said that the services of the
Ministry of Information had been recruited in advance, and they had,
on this occasion, been responsible for spreading certain rumours in
the Mediterranean countries which were intended to seep back to the
enemy and cause them to suspect a false target area.

Another point with which we had to contend was the fact that
SHAEF Advanced Headquarters had now been established in France.
This was inconsistent with the launching of a further large scale
amphibious operation based on the U.K. to be undertaken by FUSAG
under the command of SHAEF. An explanation was desirable which GARBO
furnished, again attributing his information to 4(3).

On D + 66 GARBO reported that in view of Allied speculation
as to the possibility of an immediate collapse of the German armies,
the Allied Chiefs of Staff had requested Eisenhower to maintain the
closest contact with Montgomery. We therefore claimed that an
advanced section of Supreme Headquarters had been transferred to
Normandy, the main H.Q. of SHAEF continuing to operate from the
U.K. From the same source GARBO discovered that Montgomery was
functioning as Commander-in-Chief of the two Army Groups now
operating in France. At this stage it was still undesirable to
disclose that Bradley and Montgomery were equally responsible for
the command of their respective Army Groups under Eisenhower since
we wished to give the impression that Montgomery was Commander-in-
Chief of the Army Groups in France, to emphasize that Eisenhower was
the Supreme Commander, not only of the two Army Groups in France,
but also of the army groups in the U.K. whose operations he would
also be free to direct after they had entered into battle.

GARBO discovered that General de Witt had replaced General
McNair as Commander-in-Chief of FUSAG. The latter, it will be
recalled, was killed whilst visiting General Eisenhower in France.

To support the success of this phase of FORTITUDE the
following extracts from despatches from the Japanese Ambassador,
Berlin to Tokio are quoted:-

(a)   25.7.44. Despatch No. 740. Extracts from a conversation with
      Colonel GERUDAN (Japanese phonetics) who had been sent from
      the German Ministry of Defence to act as Liaison Officer to
      Foreign Minister RIBBENTROP:-

".....As enemy losses in Normandy have been unexpectedly
heavy some five divisions from Patton's army are reported to
have been placed under Montgomery's command...so that it
will be difficult for that army to undertake landing
operations in Northern France in the near future." (Writer's
Note:- It is possible that GARBO's letter of D + 43 giving
this explanation had reached the Germans by the date of this
despatch. It therefore appears likely that the Germans,
having observed the reinforcement of the bridgehead by
forces assumed to belong to FUSAG, had drawn their own
conclusions that those formations would now come under
command of 21 Army Group. They were soon to receive GARBO's
letter from which they were to learn that the 12th U.S. Army
Group had been formed in France into which these forces had
been incorporated and that FUSAG had been brought up to
strength by taking the (notional) 14th U.S. Army under its
command.

(b)   2.8.44. Despatch No. 781. Confidential information from VON
       GROTE:-
       ".....the likelihood of Patton's army landing near Le Havre
       has diminished."

An interesting and important discovery was made early in 1945
when a captured German document was brought to our notice. This was
an illustrated booklet, [1] for wide distribution to Army Commanders
in the West, in which appeared coloured engravings of the Divisional
signs of the following notional Divisions, as described or drawn by
agents in their secret communications:-

       NOTIONAL   4th British Army
                    II   "   Corps
                    VII   "   "
                    55th   "   Division
                    58th   "   "
                    5th Armoured   "
                    14th U.S. Army
                    XXXIII "   "
                    XXXVII " Corps

During Phase III the Germans, in their incoming
questionnaires, clearly indicated that they believed in the
reorganization of FUSAG in accordance with the story we had told
them.

(i)   See Appendix No. XXXII

On D + 52 they asked GARBO if he could ascertain whether the 12th U.S. Army Group recently constituted, was under the Supreme Command of Montgomery or who was the supreme chief of the two Army Groups now in Normandy.

On D + 63 they asked GARBO to make the following investigation. To ascertain how many airborne or paratroop Divisions there were actually in Great Britain. Whether the (notional) 11th U.S. Division was an airborne or infantry division and which British Armoured Divisions were still in the U.K.

On D + 66 they told GARBO that as they envisaged the possibility that he or one of his agents would get important news concerning the forthcoming operations they would, until further notice, listen every night in case he should transmit.

CHAPTER XXIV (D)

FORTITUDE (CONTINUED)
PHASE IV.
D + 66 - D + 115
12.8.44 - 30.9.44.

Two important reorganizations were reported through Special Means:-

(i) The 9th and the (notional) 14th U.S. Armies were transferred
     from FUSAG to SHAEF strategic reserve.
     Note:- The 9th U.S. Army ultimately appeared in France
            under 12th U.S. Army Group.
(ii) The 1st Allied Airborne Army (with notional formations)
     replaced the U.S. Armies in (notional) FUSAG.

Thus two things were achieved:-

(a) Two U.S. Armies were made available to threaten the
     reinforcement of whichever American Army Group in the field
     should be in need of notional reinforcements to implement
     tactical deception.
(b) The reformed (notional) FUSAG was thus constructed to be able
     to threaten an Airborne operation supported by seaborne
     troops to implement tactical deception of the British Army
     Group.

Later, the operational force in the U.K. was further reduced. From
October onwards it consisted of the (notional) 4th British Army
reinforced by a special airborne task force comprising both U.S. and
British formations.
        From this time onwards no major strategical deception was
practiced, but at the request of Army Groups, various plans were
drawn up by SHAEF (Ops. B) for Chiefs of Staff and were implemented
by special means to support tactical deception in the field.
        The questionnaires received by agents, reports on M.S.S. and
cross checks showed conclusively that the agents were still held in
high esteem and the notional formations continued to be believed in
beyond doubt. The constant threat produced by the presence in the
U.K. of these notional formations helped to unnerve the enemy during
this period when the remnants of their armies were being steadily
beaten back and destroyed by the Allied armies.
        Our objective during this phase was primarily to preserve the
cover plan and prevent the enemy from discovering that they had been
deceived.

The following is a summary of the implementation by the GARBO network of PHASE IV of FORTITUDE:-

On D + 66 GARBO reported that the 82nd and 101st U.S. Airborne Divisions had returned to the U.K. from Normandy. These two divisions, together with notional Airborne formations, were later to appear in the Order of Battle of the 1st Allied Airborne Army which we were preparing to build up to replace the 9th U.S. Army and the (notional) 14th U.S. Army in the regrouped (notional) FUSAG which was to be discovered during this phase.

In preparation to reinforce the notional 4th Army which would then be the only ground army remaining under command of (notional) FUSAG, agents identified and located certain new armoured formations not previously included in our Order of Battle. These were the 35th Armoured Brigade, the (notional) 5th Armoured Division and later the (notional) 24th Armoured Brigade. The last mentioned brigade had been used for deception in the Mediterranean as the 8th Armoured Division, and had now been reported from there as having returned to the U.K. where we were to receive it, and later, disband it. By describing the same insignia we inferred that at least one brigade of this Division had returned to the U.K.

On D + 68 agents identified airborne insignias seen in London which were those of the real formations to be incorporated in the 1st Allied Airborne Army, and they added that there were unconfirmed reports that two new British Airborne Divisions had been formed. These were the notional airborne divisions which were later to be identified and located.

Similarly a new insignia was observed on armoured columns seen moving in East Anglia. The sign was that of a blue lobster, which was later identified as the (notional) 5th Armoured Division.

On D + 70 an agent reported the presence of large numbers of 9th Army troops seen during his tour in south west England and around Bristol. He also discovered that three new U.S. Divisions were shortly to arrive to come under command of this Army. (These were real and were eventually identified.)

To create a last threat to the Pas de Calais and to prepare for the disbanding of the (notional) 14th U.S. Army an URGENT message was transmitted on D + 77 to say that the entire (notional) 59th U.S. Division (i.e. the crack assault trained division of the 14th U.S. Army) had started to leave Ipswich moving towards the south and that other formations were also preparing to leave.

On the same day we reported the transfer from Scotland to England of the 52nd Mountain Division. It will be recalled that this had previously been represented as the assault division of the (notional) 4th Army and had for several years been our mainstay in

the various phases of the threats to Norway. Now it was really
preparing to go overseas after receiving an air landing training,
and it was considered advisable to report its move from Scotland
accurately lest prisoners should later be captured.

On D + 82 GARBO wrote a long letter to summarize his
achievements to date. The following are extracts:-

"But to-day, now that the facts have proved that my judgement
has been right I only want you to understand how it is that
in spite of the superior fighting qualities of the German
soldier the Allies have been able to advance since their
landing. If you review my letters written more than a year
ago you will see the warnings which I gave you through the
information which I received from J(3) about the Allied
plan to increase their air power. I advised you then that
the Anglo-Americans were preparing for a round the clock
offensive against the fortress of Europe. I repeatedly put
you on your guard through my reports as to the enormous Air
Force which was arriving from America and landing in the port
of Glasgow, just as I told you of the disembarkation of
American bombers which were arriving.

Towards the end of last year or the beginning of this,
I communicated to you that an intensified aerial offensive
would be unleashed against Europe and on such a great scale
that the Allies in their over confidence imagined that it
would alone determine the end of the war. At the same time I
notified you that the invasion would not take place for many
months. I have believed that our High Command, confident in
these reports, was preparing to confront these facts. I had
complete confidence that Germany had an enormous reserve of
aircraft which it had been accumulating to combat the Allied
assaults at the proper strategic moment. You can imagine my
surprise when I saw that the Allies had attacked and
destroyed our coastal defences and communications almost
without opposition, making possible a landing against what
was an impregnable Atlantic Wall.

When the ingenuous pilotless aircraft came into use I
was immediately certain of the mistake which had taken place
and I could not resist explaining my sincere opinion to you
in sending you that letter in case a solution was still
possible. I considered that if instead of these thousands
of bombs which were being launched it were possible to
manufacture fighters with which to destroy the hordes of
Allied planes, the course of the war would definitely change.
The preoccupation which I feel when I think of those of our

soldiers who must be suffering punishment through these
bombardments without opposition induces me once again to
repeat my appeal, more fighters! Many more fighters! And we
must plaster these criminal planes which interfere with our
troops. I have already said that a local withdrawal of our
troops or an error of judgment cannot change the future of
the ideals for which we are fighting and we still have time
to go back to the past and if necessary we must at all costs
try to recuperate what we have lost."

"In the interview which I had with 4(3) at which, as I said,
Three was present, I tried to get from him news about the
landing in the Mediterranean. He was very excited and told us a
number of things which were so complicated that I cannot
guarantee the following reconstruction of our conversation
contains a full rendering of all that he told us, though it
should serve for your orientation until I am able to get
further details.

It seems that shortly before the Normandy campaign was
initiated there had existed a plan to bring here the 7th U.S.
Army (which is the one that has made the new landings in the
Mediterranean) in the event that the Normandy campaign should
become difficult. General Alexander warned the Chiefs of
Staff that these forces might be required by him and that it
would be a risk to move them to reinforce the Normandy
bridgehead.

Montgomery, who is notorious for his caution, refused
to open the campaign in the north of France until he had a
guarantee of immediate reinforcements should the necessity
arise. He persuaded Eisenhower, and this question was
resolved. It was then decided to ask Washington to speed up the
transfer of the 14th U.S. Army, which had been trained and
prepared for operations in the Pacific. This proposition was
accepted by Washington and the Army was sent immediately to
England in case it should have to be used. According to 4(3)
Montgomery has been much criticised by the American Generals,
a fact proved when they tried to discredit the position of
Montgomery as chief of the two Army Groups announcing in the
Press and B.B.C. that he was not chief, and having to correct
this statement on the following day. This caused much
confusion in the SHAEF Department of the M.o.I. The American
Generals had done all in their power to restrict the Normandy
operation to a tactical campaign so that they should have
reason to carry out the Pas de Calais operation as a
spectacular end to the war, bringing it about with a complete

American victory. The fact is that competition exists between the English and Americans as to which is to win the glory of the final battle but Montgomery, who has the fame of being an astute intriguer, once having initiated the Normandy operation was determined to maintain control and exploit the fame which he had achieved at Alamein. He realized that he could only do this by allowing the Americans to have the newspaper headlines for the advances which they were to make, whilst he was exploiting his fame as a tactical General. So he did all that was possible so that the weight of the German armoured armies should fall against the British and Canadians in order that the Americans should be able to advance more easily to the west and south, manoeuvring in order that this operation should develop into a large scale one and should come to be considered as the principal one, in order that he should be allowed to reinforce his front with new troops from the original FUSAG, thus delaying the second operation which they were to have carried out.

4(3) tells us that the original FUSAG attack was planned to have been put into operation approximately 40 days after the landing in Normandy but that it was delayed whilst FUSAG was reorganized and the 14th U.S. Army was incorporated in it.

4(3) who is very anti-British, is a harsh critic of Montgomery. He says that if he has been successful in the advance through France and has advanced towards Paris it is due to the reinforcements he was given in the form of the 3rd U.S. Army.

He says that Montgomery is now trying to persuade the Supreme Command to cancel the original assault which FUSAG had intended to carry out in order to obtain the 14th U.S. Army under his command in France. This would leave the 4th British Army and the newly formed Airborne Army (which 4(3) tells us is mostly American) ready to attack the Germans in the flank or rear of any strategic line they decide to defend."

By D + 82 all formations of the (notional) 14th U.S. Army had been observed preparing to move from East Anglia.

On D + 84 Airborne formations were located in the Bulford - Larkhill area. The (notional) 25th U.S. Armoured Division was identified as having come down from Norfolk. Many elements of the 9th U.S. Army were also identified.

On D + 85 GARBO transmitted by wireless the following IMPORTANT message. He said that he had learnt from 4(3) that the original plan to attack the Pas de Calais area with FUSAG forces had now been definitely cancelled. FUSAG, he learned, was again being reformed. The (notional) 14th U.S. Army and the 9th U.S. Army were now under direct command of SHAEF as SHAEF STRATEGIC RESERVE. This, GARBO pointed out explained the move of the (notional) 14th U.S Army from its location in East Anglia, where it had been situated for so long. The new strategic reserve of SHAEF would, we said, be at the disposal of the Supreme commander to reinforce the Allied armies in France should they require assistance in the advance about to be made to prevent the German armies from escaping to Germany.

The (notional) 14th U.S. Army GARBO had learned, was to be replaced in (notional) FUSAG by a new airborne army which would be identified under the name of the First Allied Airborne Army. With this rearrangement, he pointed out that FUSAG was substantially composed of airborne forces and the Army Group would, therefore, be employed in special operations and that in fact FUSAG would now become a modern version of Combined Operations, to undertake large scale Airborne operations against France, Belgium, Holland or Germany, in order to cut the enemy's lines of communications. They would also be used to occupy any areas or countries which the Germans decided to abandon hurriedly and thus, these very mobile forces would save the Armies in the field from having to make sudden dispersal of forces in the battle area at the expense of carrying out their original plans.

The whole story of the FOURTH PHASE of FORTITUDE had thus been implemented.

On the same day that this story about the regrouping of FUSAG was transmitted a further piece of Intelligence, somewhat conflicting with the above, was obtained by GARBO through the Ministry of Information. He was present at a conversation between a war press correspondent of SHAEF attached to the Ministry of Information, and J(3).

The war correspondent had said in confidence that a large scale attack by the army groups in France was now imminent. He claimed that he had recently been over in France attached to Advanced H.Q. of SHAEF where he had learnt that 21 Army Group was trying to bring influence to stop Patton advancing further with his 3rd U.S. Army. 21 Army Group was anxious that Patton should make a feint attack towards the east, retaining the bulk of his forces to turn north to attack the German flank whilst 21 Army Group, reinforced by FUSAG, should attack and occupy the Pas de Calais.

Patton was trying his utmost to influence a decision that 21 Army Group should make a feint attack against the Pas de Calais to maintain German forces there, whilst all available supplies should be put at his disposal to facilitate his making a break through into the heart of Germany.

Agent No. 3 who transmitted the message pointed out that 4(3) could have had no knowledge of this information when he made his report about the reorganization of FUSAG and had stated that the Pas de Calais operation had been abandoned.

The inference which we intended the Germans to draw from these messages was that planning was still elastic, and that in the absence of other information, it would be dangerous to make any changes in the present disposition of their troops, inclining them to the belief that since the FUSAG operation had, according to the more reliable of the two sources, been abandoned, an amphibious as well as a ground attack against the Pas de Calais was no longer to be expected. In fact, the disposition of German forces prior to Montgomery's great break through into Belgium was satisfactory and we wished to induce the Germans, if possible, to make no changes.

On D + 91 the (notional) XXXIII Corps of the (notional) 14th U.S. Army was identified by GARBO's agent in the Southampton area, substantiating our claim that this Army had now been transferred to SHAEF strategic reserve, and hinting that it might be preparing to transfer to France.

The fact that the (notional) 14th U.S. Army formations had left East Anglia at the beginning of September was also confirmed by our agent there.

On D + 94 the agent at Ipswich reported that there were indications that the (notional) 4th British Army was moving into the area previously occupied by the (notional) 14th U.S. Army, which meant that the south east would be left unoccupied. We thus prepared to be able to threaten an amphibious and airborne attack against Holland or Denmark, based on the Harwich - Ipswich area. By this time the Pas de Calais area had been by-passed by our forces in France under 21 Army Group and therefore our threat had to be focused further east.

On D + 96 the sudden changes in troop dispositions was explained by 4(3). He stated that in view of Montgomery's rapid advance into Belgium it had been decided to evacuate troops from the south eastern areas to establish shorter lines of communication for supplies which would, at the earliest possible moment, be sent through south eastern British ports. Now that the target area of the original FUSAG attack had been over run and the regrouping of the new FUSAG completed the (notional) 14th U.S. Army had moved to the Southampton area to occupy camps which had originally accommodated 21 Army Group forces prior to D Day, at the same time the old camps of the (notional) 14th U.S. formations in East Anglia were to be taken over by the (notional) 4th British Army which had moved from Kent so as to be geographically better placed for an embarkation against a more northern target than the original one, at the same

time freeing the railroads in Kent to supply the armies which had
now advanced into Belgium.

To avoid disclosing a further strengthening of U.S. Forces in
France we had been instructed to withhold information that the 9th
U.S. Army had been transferred to France. The Press was
unfortunately to release the news. To cover ourselves and conform
with policy we sent a message on D + 99 to say that the Press release
that the 9th U.S. Army was already in the field was not accurate. We
claimed that only two formations had gone overseas from this army,
which were the 94th and 95th U.S. Divisions which our agents had
located and reported as being in the Southampton area prior to
embarkation. The true facts were, we claimed that the 9th U.S. Army
H.Q. troops had been sent to France to assist command the reserves
of 12th U.S. Army Group which had reached such proportions that
another H.Q. was required.

The (notional) 14th U.S. Army was, we reported, still in the
Southampton embarkation areas, ready to reinforce either of the
U.S. Army Groups in France should they be required.

The real static formations identified in the past as well as
the notional airborne, armoured, and infantry formations created,
continued to be used after various regroupings had been effected for
tactical deception until after the crossing of the Rhine. The
numerous operational plans which were implemented by the GARBO
network after the by-passing by Allied Forces of the target area of
FORTITUDE, the Pas de Calais, are not set out in this summary.

The following is evidence in support of the successful
implementation by the GARBO network of PHASE IV of FORTITUDE:-

(a)   18.9.44. The Japanese Ambassador Berlin, reported to Tokio
      under reference No. 1021:-
      "......At present an airborne army was being formed in
      Britain (this was the first time they had made any army
      consisting solely of airborne troops which meant that they
      were holding back five or six divisions.)"

(b)   25.10.44. The Japanese Military Attache, Stockholm, reported
      to Tokio in serial No. 136 under heading: "K Intelligence":-
      ".....It appears that the organization of the First Army
      Group (FUSAG) in the north of the British Isles has recently
      been broken up. The units which formerly belonged to the Army
      Group are the American 14th Army, and the British 4th Army.
      Thus, the number of British and American divisions which now
      remain in Britain totals 11 or 12 in all."

From the incoming messages there was evidence that the
Germans were alarmed lest a new operation should be launched during
PHASE IV.

On D + 70 they signalled for information about the new Allied Airborne Army and wanted to know whether it had been created for a special important operation.

On D + 72 they asked GARBO to continue investigating the (notional) 5th Armoured Division and the 35th Armoured Brigade.

On D + 75 they sent GARBO a complimentary message to say that they were entrusted by Headquarters in Berlin with the mission of expressing their special recognition to GARBO for the results which had been achieved by him and his organization. In this connection they wished also to make reference to the information supplied since the invasion of France, which they claimed had been of the utmost value to them. They concluded by requesting GARBO to make this recognition fully known to his collaborators.

On D + 77 GARBO was asked to obtain information about forces in the Liverpool and Manchester areas, and in particular to ascertain which U.S. Division had arrived in Mersey during the past two months and those which were stationed in central England. They also asked him to continue his investigations about the two new British Airborne Divisions on which GARBO had reported the previous week.

On D + 80 they asked GARBO whether there were any British infantry divisions specially trained for use in airborne operations, how many there were, their insignias and their divisional numbers. How many gliders and how many transport planes would be available for a new important airborne operation.

On D + 84 they asked GARBO to try to ascertain whether the (notional) 8th British Armoured Division had recently arrived in England. This, it will be recalled, was the formation which the deception staff in the Mediterranean had been using and had decided to send home to be disbanded. We received it here and although we identified it by the same divisional sign as that which had been used in the Mediterranean, the letters "GO" we had described it as the 35th Armoured Brigade on the assumption that GARBO's network would only discover one brigade of this Division.

In the deception plan a great quantity of the high grade traffic had to be attributed to the American, 4(3), who, in the course of the story, we had built up as being the son of an American Colonel, and extremely well placed here. Nevertheless, it was to be wondered that the Germans would believe in the information which he passed, which at times attempted to quote conversations between Eisenhower and Patton, and was often of a category which could logically have been attributed only to a Chief of Staff. On the other hand, the message conveyed was, we hoped, a plausible one and even supposing the Germans did not believe in the information implicitly there was the hope that they would at least have been influenced by it.

On D + 85 the Germans wrote a long and complimentary letter to GARBO dealing with all his organizational problems and in it they said:-

"I can say with satisfaction that all your regular informants show that they have understood their mission . . . . outstanding in importance are the reports of your friend 4(3), who, due to the position he occupies, is the best placed for facilitating details with regard to the organization of the armies in general; about its large units, its composition, the arrival of new American divisions, plans of the high command etc., Though I imagine that in this connection you are dealing with an unconscious collaborator it is necessary to cultivate this friendship by all possible means as you yourself have pointed out. The last report of this friend of yours about the reorganization of FUSAG was excellent. Nevertheless, it is necessary to proceed with the greatest care not to arouse his suspicions through the questions which you ask him. The informants 7(2), 7(4) and 7(7) we consider to be perfect military observers and we have no further observation to make. If they continue to work as they have done up to now then we are more than satisfied."

It has been attempted in this summary to submit in the case of each phase of FORTITUDE, some evidence in support of the success achieved by this cover plan. The documents quoted represent but a very small fraction of the total evidence which exists. At the time of writing (autumn 1945) the many important documents captured in Germany during the first months of the post-war have not been given circulation, neither has the bulk of these been translated or co-ordinated.

Further evidence available to date can be summed up in the voluminous and substantially complete records of M.S.S. (ISOS and ISBA) which we have in this office on the Berlin - Madrid/Madrid - Berlin circuit which completely record all the relevant GARBO traffic as passed by Madrid to Berlin as well as the questionnaires emanating from Berlin.

There are, at the present time, in the records of SHAEF, Ops., B. Sub-Section, the original of the OKW "Invasion" files. It is possible to reconstruct the course of the GARBO information from RHSA Berlin, by teleprinter to OKW Zossen and on to the FHW to be evaluated and co-ordinated with information received from other sources. In these files are preserved the original teleprinter messages, initialled by those members of the German Supreme Command to whom they were submitted for information. On them are seen the initials of JODL and other Chiefs of Staff. Thus, it is possible to reconstruct the course of the GARBO messages to JODL's desk, having first passed through the office, and probably the hands of, HIMMLER himself.

From the photostat copies of the FHW daily situation reports which are likewise to be found at the present time in the offices of SHAEF, Ops. B it is possible to reconstruct the way in which the GARBO information was passed by the FHW of the German Supreme Command to Field Marshall RUNDSTEDT, and other commanders in chief of the Western Armies as well as the chiefs of the air force and the navy, and thus to illustrate the manner in which the GARBO reports formed the backbone of all German Intelligence appreciations on which the vital operational decisions were taken, which are so admirably summed up for us in the despatches from the Japanese Ambassador in Berlin to the Foreign Minister in Tokio which have been quoted above.

CHANNEL OF COMMUNICATIONS.

ALLIED CHIEFS	COMMANDERS IN CHIEF
OF STAFF.	WESTERN ARMIES.
:	:
:	:
:	:
:	OKW
:	(GERMAN SUPREME COMMAND)
SHAEF	FHW
OPS. B	(INTELLIGENCE APPRECIATIONS
(DECEPTION PLANNERS)	ON ENEMY ARMIES IN THE WEST)
:	:
:	:
a:	:
	GERMAN SECRET SERVICE, BERLIN
M.I.5	(RSHA)
:	:
:	:
:	:
B.I.A	K.O. SPAIN
LONDON CASE	MADRID CASE
OFFICER	OFFICER
:	:
:	:
:	:

...............GARBO...............

CHAPTER XXIV (E)

FORTITUDE (CONTINUED.)
DISPERSAL OF THE NOTIONAL FORCES.

Through various messages passed by the GARBO network after D + 120 the enemy was told that FUSAG was disbanded in October, 1944.

The 14th U.S. Army was disbanded after changing its location, first to the Southampton area and later to South Wales. Of the 14th U.S. Army troops, XXXIII Corps and the divisions under its command moved from Southampton area to South Wales, where they fulfilled a draft finding role and were ultimately disbanded. XXXVII Corps with 59th Infantry Division and 25th Armoured Division, were embarked at Southampton at the end of September, 1944, for an unknown destination.

A few months later, in January - February, 1945, the 4th British Army was disbanded. The troops were absorbed into draft finding units and into Northern Command.

The (notional) airborne divisions within the 1st Allied Airborne Army were last observed in camps in the U.K. waiting to engage in operations.

It was not without some difficulty that the Germans were finally persuaded that the dangers of amphibious and airborne operations by the notional forces created, no longer existed.

Long after FUSAG had been disbanded we were pestered by the Germans with questionnaires in which they expressed their fears that we might yet launch an attack with the (notional) 4th Army though we had already given them clear indications by that time that its formations had been dispersed. An indication of their preoccupation even as late as the 19.2.45 can be realized from the following messages:-

"We are very thankful for your prompt and detailed report about the south east coast areas. You will understand that the question of a new landing operation being undertaken from England is of the utmost importance. There are several important symptoms that this may occur although your agents have not yet discovered details. I therefore ask you to continue these investigations by all means at your disposal, especially 7(7) must control continuously and carefully the areas of Thames and Humber estuaries in view of eventual concentrations of troops, landing craft, material and so on as preparations, and troop concentrations in ports, do not begin until a very few days before embarkation. Please ask

therefore 7(7) to report as often as possible, at least once
a week even if this would be only to confirm that there has
been no change of importance, and transmit the results to us.
Note that for urgent communications and until further notice
we shall be listening here every day except Sundays."

On the 22.2.45 they sent a further message to say:-

"Special reasons which I cannot explain by message make
necessary an urgent new check up of situation at several
points of east coast. Considering the recent voyage of 7(7) I
would be obliged if you personally could make a short visit
to Hull and Grimsby areas, investigating about all kind of
military movements and concentrations of troops, material,
landing craft and other details. Result should be
transmitted to us at the earliest possible moment, and
immediately after your return by special transmission if
necessary. Newcastle and Tyne estuary could be visited by
7(2), and 7(7) should make a new trip to coastal areas south
of Grimsby such as Great Yarmouth and so on. At same time
please arrange for 7(4) to visit Southampton and Portsmouth
areas with instructions to investigate as much as possible
which units have been shipped recently in these ports and
which are going to be embarked now and in near future."

In fact it was far easier to create the threat with our
notional formations than it was to persuade the enemy that neither
the formations nor the threat any longer existed.

CHAPTER XXIV (F)

(FORTITUDE CONTINUED.)
CONCLUSIONS.

It has been asked why, in view of the successive German failures, they should not have suspected the information which had been passed to them by Special Means if, as the evidence tends to show, this information was to a large extent responsible for these failures. The reasons are probably the following:-

(i)   All the information passed through Special Means which the Germans were subsequently able to check was proved by them to have been accurate; i.e., all the divisions which operated on the Western Front were formations which had been identified by agents in the U.K. prior to the operation, and in some cases their identification could be traced back to agents' reports dating two years or more before formations were identified by the enemy in battle.

(ii)   From the above evidence there were no grounds whatever to suspect the information concerning the less numerous formations which they did not encounter in battle, but which had been reported by the agents as being in the U.K.

(iii) Assuming that the information which they received about the Allied Order of Battle had been accurate, as their evidence tended to prove, the opinion expressed by agents that the invasion would be carried out in two or more phases was not only a reasonable one but one which conformed with conclusions which had previously been reached in high German circles and by HITLER himself.

(iv)   When the two operations which had been anticipated did not materialize, the only reasonable explanation which we could put forward, and they could accept, was that circumstances had caused the plans to be changed. So successful had the first operation been, that it had been decided to exploit it. In fact, FORTITUDE was called off in August because Allied troops advancing from Normandy, over ran the target area.

(v)   To have ignored the advice of their agents, and to have sent their reserves to the Cherbourg Peninsula, might have exposed the reinforcements to heavy destruction by our incessant air onslaught, with the risk of leaving their rear exposed and the vital Pas de Calais, and their V weapon launching sites unprotected against a second and more powerful landing by the FUSAG forces.

Thus, believing in the existence of FUSAG they were "between the devil and the deep blue sea."

It is our opinion that, if the German General Staff were able to review their evidence to-day in the light of what has transpired, there is little doubt they would not alter the decisions which they then reached, providing they had no fresh evidence to cause them to suspect the existence of the First United States Army Group.

CHAPTER XXV.

THE GERMAN SECRET WEAPONS
SUMMER, 1943 - SUMMER, 1944.

During the summer and autumn of 1943 rumours were circulating about the nature of the threatened German secret weapon.

The Ministry of Home Security was particularly anxious to obtain cross checks on certain highly secret information which had been passed to them from S.I.S. sources, from which it appeared that the secret weapon would be a giant rocket with terrible destructive powers against which no effective defence measure would be practicable. To what extent the specifications about the weapon, which reached us through these sources could be relied upon, needed checking. These sources claimed that the weapon weighed between 10 - 15 tons with a range on London, travelling through the stratosphere, at supersonic speed. Fantastic as all this appeared at the time, our scientists who were consulted, would not discount the possibility of such a weapon being put into use by the enemy.

After various unproductive discussions with both S.I.S. and the Ministry of Home Security to try to discover a satisfactory method by which GARBO could provoke a reaction from the Abwehr without compromising the S.I.S. sources, we were given an opening through a publication which appeared in the daily press towards the end of September, and enabled GARBO to include the following reference to the "Rocket gun" in his letter of 6.10.43:-

> "I must now discuss another matter connected with the report of a Swedish journalist called Gunnar T. Pihl who is said recently to have returned from Berlin. This individual has published some articles, and one of them which I read in the Daily Telegraph of the 27.9.43 spoke of an enormous rocket gun which is installed on the French coast to bombard London as a reprisal and other cities which come within a radius of action of 125 miles distance. I usually consider the value of these reports very low since I always suspect that such sensational articles are published with intent to draw attention to the writer. On this occasion, wishfully hoping that it were true, I described the weapon to my wife just as it was explained in the article. The result of this was that my wife became panicky and wants at all costs to leave England. She was looking for an excuse to bring pressure on me to let her go back to Spain as she loathes this country and everything about it she finds unpleasant and tiresome.

Though late, I discovered the mistake I had made in frightening her, and promised her that if it were true I would send her to the country out of range of this weapon. I would therefore like you to tell me by radio the truth so that I can take my counter-measures in good time, since it is now difficult to find lodgings and as it is complicated to set about moving. I should, however, send my wife and the children to the country and I naturally, would go to live with them, and would come in to London regularly to attend to matters connected with the service. It has also occurred to me that I might take on the work of making daily observations (if the rocket really exists) and let you have, by radio, an exact report on the objectives hit so that you would be able to correct any possible errors of fire. The news makes me think that if it were true and we were able to make use of this weapon to liquidate all these English dogs we would produce a rude and terrible blow to our enemy for it is certainly time we brought them down from their clouds of power."

On the 18.11.43 we received the following rather unsatisfactory reply:-

"With regard to the rocket gun there is no cause to alarm yourself."

On December 15/16, 1943, quite unexpectedly, the following messages arrived which, as can be imagined caused considerable concern and excitement:-

"Circumstances dictate that you should carry out your proposition with regard to setting up your home outside the capital. This warning is strictly confidential for you and in taking the necessary measures the collaborators must on no account suspect your reasons. Should the threatened action commence, in making your preparations, leaving to your judgment their execution, you must ensure that your collaborators maintain their contact with you. You must think out the means of then establishing a service headquarters, endeavouring to set this up, if possible, wherever the principal Ministries evacuate, so that you should not lose contact with your friends and should maintain your camouflage. As soon as the first signs of the threatened action are noted, the transmittor must be removed and taken to a place of safety. Furthermore for greater security it

would be advisable that the operator should construct
quickly, as indicated by you, a second apparatus without
regard to price. This you should take charge of and hide in
a safe place, and likewise the copies of the transmitting
plan and instructions for the working of the station. If,
for the reasons given, the service should break down, ALMURA
(i.e. London station) should try to instal a transmittor
in the place decided on for the new headquarters, and if
not possible, then in some other place. The primary
consideration is that the transmittor should be situated
in a place which will facilitate the conditions for perfect
camouflage such as at present exist so as to avoid its
localization. It should not be installed in an isolated
place. Should you not be able to take the operator with you
try to get another one in his place through Seven. Should
there be a breakdown we will be here listening every day and
at the hours set out in the plan. Also of the greatest
importance is to ensure that continuous contact with the
courier is maintained in all eventualities. The situation of
the new headquarters must allow for the possibility for your
agents to make journies to visit you, and for you to be able
to travel under camouflage. With knowledge of your proved
experience I trust that you will treat these questions with
intelligence and calm. Spend whatever is necessary, and even
were it necessary in the interests of the service for some of
the agents to give up their jobs you could make good their
salary for them to work for us."

In GARBO's reply we tried to provoke an indication whether
the new weapon was likely to be put into operation in the immediate
future, we said that we intended to pack up the present set and send
it to the country for safety until the new spare set had been built
and this, we pointed out, would take several weeks. Thus, in the
meanwhile there would be no wireless service.

To provide a stand-in wireless operator (in case a genuine
misfortune should occur to our own, whose style could not easily have
been imitated) we had already built up Agent No. 4 as having trained
himself to operate a wireless set for the last several months.

To give them an opportunity to reply to our proposal that we
should temporarily close down our station we proposed that this
agent should make a trial transmission two days later, so that if he
were found to be efficient, he would take over the handling of the
wireless station in the event of the real operator meeting with an
accident. At this transmission we asked them to approve the plan for
removing the apparatus to a safe hiding place.

At the trial transmission of the new operator the part of Agent No. 4 was played by a member of the staff of M.I.5 who operated at slow tempo with his left hand to give the impression of an amateur badly in need of practice and experience.

The Germans replied the following day to say that in view of the indication that the Allies were preparing to mount an operation based on the U.K., GARBO's services and the wireless were likely to be of the greatest importance during the coming weeks and months. They suggested that if it should be necessary to transfer the wireless it would be a good plan that GARBO should, if possible, take the operator with him. They asked him only to remove the apparatus as a last resort, and if there were no other solution. Regarding Agent No.4's transmission, they said his trial had been satisfactory but that he required more practice.

These replies did not help us at all to judge the imminence of the use of the secret weapon.

On the 5.1.44 we again touched on the subject to say that in order not to interfere with the actual work of the Service, GARBO would not remove the apparatus but we asked to be given a few days notice before "reprisal" operations were started to allow time for the wireless station to be moved to safety.

On the 6.1.44 GARBO wrote to say that he had managed to find accommodation in the country for his wife and children, and that he now proposed to give up the house and stay at some pension in London. (This was in fact true. GARBO felt that having had the privilege of this warning it was his duty to send his wife and children away from London. He likewise, decided to rid himself of his house in Hendon, the address of which he had passed to the Germans. Therefore, it was advisable to inform them of these moves.)

Thus, he had taken all the measures necessary to be able to transfer his organization, should it become necessary. In a letter dated 14.2.44 the Germans approved all the measures which GARBO had taken to safeguard the continuation of the work of the organization should they commence to put the secret weapon into operation against London. They then warned him that it was unlikely they would be able to give him any further advanced information, "should we have the misfortune" they added, that the wireless should get damaged before the spare set had been completed they would continue to listen until the new apparatus was put into operation.

On the 28.2.44 we informed them that we had made the necessary arrangements for the removal of the radio. A dispute followed as to how we were to propose to the operator that he should move out of town. After all GARBO was in honour bound not to disclose the information which the Germans had confided in him; in any case the operator believed GARBO to be a Spanish republican secret agent, therefore he could not disclose his source. We proposed that GARBO should tell him that the Spanish Republican Secret Service had discovered that the Germans were preparing to use a very terrible secret weapon and had secretly warned the British Government. If put in this form, we maintained, it would be effective in getting him to move out of London with the set, completely cover up our source, and, at the same time, bind the operator to secrecy.

The Germans replied that this was not a good idea but that GARBO should instead tell the operator that German propaganda about the use of secret weapons had made him panicky and that he had decided to move out of town. They added that he should offer the operator increased pay as an inducement.

This proposal was quite unacceptable to us. How could GARBO, we said in reply, admit to the operator that he was influenced by German propaganda? On the contrary, in his role of Spanish Republican, he should ridicule all German propaganda. Embarrassed at this disclosure of their lack of foresight and cunning, the Germans decided to leave the matter to GARBO's superior discretion and judgment. How we finally induced the operator to move out of town was never disclosed. First we had to find accommodation. By showing how difficult it was to get accommodation, and thus delaying the move, we hoped we might have drawn the Germans to hint to GARBO when the danger peak was approaching, by telling him to hasten his move. Meanwhile, unable to find alternative accommodation, GARBO continued to function from his London headquarters.

On the 20.3.44 we touched on the subject again by informing them that the spare apparatus was now ready.

On the 3.4.44, in a very long letter received from the Germans, they asked GARBO whether he could arrange to facilitate the sending of a one word message over his wireless channel three or four times a week. It was of great importance that the one word message should be transmitted the same day as handed in. The plan would not be put into operation for a few weeks. The matter was one of considerable importance to them just as it was vital in making the arrangements for their man to contact the GARBO network, and to ensure that he should not discover anything about GARBO or his network. They made a poor suggestion to GARBO as to how the message could be passed to him without making contact, and asked his opinion as to whether the project was realizable.

The proposal was a very mysterious one indeed. In the first place it suggested that an agent was likely to be sent over in the course of the next few weeks; presumably he would be parachuted since there were no ordinary travel facilities to England at that time; secondly, he would come here with a series of prearranged code words. It was difficult to imagine what sort of information could be

conveyed in a single word message and why it was so vital that the
message should be transmitted the same day as it was passed to
GARBO. Although we had no idea of the significance of this message
at the time, it now seems highly probable that it was their
intention to send over an observer to report on the fall of the V
weapons. Each code word would correspond to an area of London
between two ordinates and co-ordinates which would indicate the
mean point of impact for falls on the day of the observation.
Periodical reports sent in this way would probably have enabled the
firing stations to judge the effects of their change of range.

On the 28.4.44 GARBO sent a reply agreeing to help them but
countering their proposal for making contact by suggesting that
their agent should write the code word to be transmitted, in the
telephone directory in a prearranged public telephone booth. The
code word would be inserted on the page corresponding to the day
of the month. Thus, on the 10.5.44, the tenth of the fifth month, it
would be written on page 105; on the 17.10.44, the seventeenth day
of the tenth month, it would appear on page 1710. GARBO would then
send one or other of his agents each day to look at the page
corresponding to the day of the month and take note of the code word
which appeared there. This proposal gave us the maximum security
since we would be enabled to send anyone to collect the message
without risk of compromise to GARBO and we would be enabled, by
keeping a close watch on the particular booth selected, to detect
their agent.

On the 29.4.44 the Germans approved the plan, adding the
suggestion that their man should write the code word in the
directories of several prearranged telephone booths so that GARBO's
agent could select whichever one he chose to collect the message,
without the possibility of their agent being able to identify him.
They concluded by stating that their preparations for putting this
plan into operation were behind hand at the moment and that GARBO
should take no action for the present. So far as we know the project
was abandoned by the Germans, and if we are correct in our theory
that the plan was connected with the sending of a special observer
for the V weapons, it might be presumed that it was subsequently
decided to use instead their agents already established in the
United Kingdom.

On the 12.5.44 a Most Secret Source message from Madrid to
Berlin showed that Madrid was to prepare to receive certain special
questionnaires (the nature of which was not disclosed) but Madrid
was told that they would carry the prefix "STICHLING." The replies
to these questionnaires would, Madrid was told, be of extreme
urgency and they should therefore be retransmitted to Berlin
immediately. The wireless section of Abwehr headquarters (at

Stahnsdorf) were making special arrangements to ensure that the
GARBO replies should reach Berlin from Madrid with minimum delay.

On the 13.5.44 we saw on M.S.S. Berlin/Paris that Berlin had
issued orders to Paris that they should send a courier immediately
to Arras to give the Key setting (for the cypher machine)
which would be in use by the Madrid Wireless station during the
forthcoming week. (These instructions were later renewed.) Arras
was, at that time, the seat of the main anti-invasion Abwehr
Commandos. From other unpublished M.S.S. material we were able to
reconstruct the following picture of their preparations.

Madrid, whilst being kept in the dark as to the nature of the
project involved, were to prepare to receive most immediate
questionnaires prefixed "STICHLING" for forwarding to GARBO.
GARBO's reply was to be forwarded with the same prefix to Berlin.
Berlin, on receipt of the reply, would, without re-encyphering the
messages, immediately retransmit them to Abwehr Commando H.Q.,
Arras, which station would have its cypher machine set to the same
reading as the Madrid Station so that they themselves could decypher
GARBO's replies. From this we could conclude that the STICHLING
messages were of urgent interest connected with a project of the
Abwehr Commando which was highly regarded by Berlin, the nature of
which was being kept secret from Madrid.

A special priority watch was kept on the Berlin - Madrid
M.S.S. circuit in order that we should get immediate notification
when the first STICHLING message was observed. The messages were
most carefully considered in this Office and by the J.I.C. and,
incredible as it now seems, it was never speculated by anyone that
they were to be connected with the V.1 flying bombs which were to be
used by the Germans a few weeks later, and it was not until after the
sight of the first STICHLING message that this became apparent.

The first STICHLING message was passed from Berlin to Madrid
on the 16.6.44 in a service message sent at 8.15 GMT which simply
stated:-

"Arras reports STICHLING is beginning."

Some two hours later the first questionnaire for GARBO with the prefix
STICHLING was transmitted; this was retransmitted that night to GARBO
in a rather elaborated form. They said that they had learned that the
new weapon, about which they had warned GARBO several months
previously, had been used against England since the previous night.
They stated (as we knew to be true) that Berlin had not given them any
prenotification. They told him that he should take whatever measures
he considered necessary to ensure the continuity of his most
important work without considering the expense. Should the wireless

have to close down unexpectedly to effect its removal, or for other reasons, presumably they inferred that they imagined it might get damaged, they would continue to listen for it to start up again in accordance with the transmitting timetable.

With this preamble, they arrived at the STICHLING questionnaire. GARBO was instructed to base his reports on a map of London published by "Pharus", which they said they presumed he would already possess. They asked him to inform them in which squares on the map the flying bombs were falling, giving the hours of the incidents, together with the map reading, based on the ordinates and co-ordinates of the Pharus map, for example, between 15.00 hours and 16.00 hours there were four incidents in square K.10. No further information was required.

It seems that Madrid was probably annoyed with Berlin on account of the rather off hand way in which they had been treated, and for having put them in a rather embarrassing position vis-a-vis GARBO in having to spring this rather unpleasant mission on him this way, for they concluded their message by saying:-

> "The foregoing is only intended for your guidance knowing
> that it will be almost impossible for you to obtain these
> details...your primary objective is not to endanger or take
> risks with the rest of the Service which continues to be of
> primordial importance."

Possibly they were cautious of attaching too much importance to this questionnaire when retransmitting it to GARBO lest he should have interpreted their failure to give him prenotification of their intentions to employ this weapon as a demonstration of their lack of confidence in him.

Their message crossed with one from GARBO in which he told them, somewhat sarcastically, that if instead of learning of the use of this weapon from the enemy he had been told about it in advance by them, he would already have left London. He asked whether these bombardments were going to continue, as if so, he would make arrangements to move somewhere nearer London so that the work of the organization should not be seriously disrupted.

Madrid replied that they had received the explanation from Headquarters that they had been unable to give advanced warning of the use of the secret weapon since they, themselves, had not been notified due to an order issued by the High Command that only those persons directly concerned with the operation should be informed. So far as moving the service out of London was concerned, they said that GARBO had already had their approval to take all the measures he considered necessary. This was also true, for we know that it was not until the 16.6.44 that the Madrid wireless station acknowledged receipt of a special emergency cypher for the STICHLING material.

The following day Berlin asked Madrid the language in which they communicated with GARBO and on the 19.6.44 they sent Madrid an urgent message to say that Arras was enquiring whether the first STICHLING message had been forwarded on to GARBO as the matter was very urgent.

The desirability of GARBO reporting on the incidents caused by this new weapon were considered. In the absence of a plan we were instructed to stall as long as possible, and so on the 18.6.44 GARBO sent a lengthy message from which they were intended to conclude that the weapon was so far ineffective and uncontrollable in range and that the enemy and, even neutral, propaganda which had already started to grossly exaggerate the effects of this weapon were quite untrue. He said:-

"......I am proud that you have been able to prove the fantastic reprisal weapon, the creation of German genius. Although I have not personally seen the apparatus in flight, from what I have heard said it must be an object of marvel and when the present trials have finished, and when the scale on which it is used is increased, I am certain that you will manage to terrify this very pusillanimous people who will never admit they are beaten. I am also proud that my services may be of use in obtaining this objective. Although I have not got the plan of London which you suggest, I shall send the Widow to buy one to-morrow......The work will nevertheless be difficult as according to rumours current in the Ministry of Information the area effected is so extensive that it embraces a semi-circle from Harwich to Portsmouth, circling London to the north and west, but nevertheless I repeat, we will do all in our power to assist in the work which my agents, like myself, will find pleasure in realizing."

The message was also intended to infer that their range was too long. In fact it was too short. If we could induce them to shorten their range, the missiles would eventually fall in the sea, whilst, by discovering the truth, and lengthening their range the mean point of impact would get nearer to the centre of London. This first idea to deceive the enemy was later developed to form the basis of a constructive plan for reporting. Meanwhile we were asked to refrain from reporting any individual incident.

We were somewhat fortunate in that the Pharus map, which we had been instructed to use in our reporting, was a German publication which had been out of print in England since 1908.

From the examination of earlier questionnaires and a copy of the map which we eventually discovered to exist in the British Museum Library, it became apparent that the German Intelligence Services in Berlin had used this, now entirely out of date, map as their basis for all references to London.

On the 20.6.44 GARBO reported that the Pharus map was unobtainable and asked whether he could not instead use the Stanford Map of London. In order to further cry down the efficiency of the V.1 he added that the Ministry of Information had issued a directive which implied that the lifting of the Diplomatic ban had to some degree been inspired by a desire to facilitate neutral diplomats to be able to report the truth about the effects of the V weapon, and thus, discredit the very exaggerated German propaganda reports.

On the 22.6.44 Madrid informed Berlin of GARBO's expressions on the effectiveness of the V weapon so far, and made it clear that they had not passed on this information to Arras, but were only passing them the reports of actual hits.

On the 22.6.44 Madrid asked for the Stanford Map readings for three specified points, stating that with this information in their possession GARBO could report the Stanford readings in the same way as he had been instructed to use the Pharus.

On the same day we sent a report on a few incidents without mentioning the times. We disclosed some objectives hit in the West End which we could assume would already be familiar to neutral diplomats who were now commencing to travel again between London and their capitals where news such as we had given would presumably reach German ears.

This, GARBO followed up with the following long, and strictly personal letter addressed to KUHLENTHAL:-

"STRICTLY PERSONAL FOR CARLOS. Dear Friend and Comrade, In writing this letter I do so in order to address my Chief as the head of the organization which I represent here being absolutely sure that this letter will be received by you as a statement of opinion between two friends who share the same ideals and are fighting for the same end.

My work is not that of a propagandist and still less is it my intention to sustain false opinions, programmes or intentions of Ministries which are removed from our vital work of military information. My work and duty is to inform my chief secretly, which is yourself, as to the truth about what I see in the very camp of the enemy, even if the truth is harsh or unsatisfactory, as in the present case. Having satisfied my conscience about the truth it is for you to decide whether or not to transmit to Berlin this class of report.

As both you and I proudly belong to the German Secret
Service we do not require propaganda or empty words to
maintain our morale. We are too level headed to allow our
spirits to be weakened by adverse incidents or to allow our
hopes to be smashed. This only happens to pusillanimus people
who gradually adjust their views alternatively as they are
influenced by optimism or pessimism. For me, individual
incidents in this hard war have been nothing more than
evolutionary scenes in a gigantic development of a grandiose
act. The war continues, and within it the daily events, the
official communiques, the temporary battles, are only
episodes of the day, of the week, or of a month, but the
magnitude of the great undertaking carries on and at least
for me the temporary adverse episodes have no significance
whatsoever. Always remember the saying that "He who laughs
last laughs best." I do not know why it is that I have the
feeling that you share this opinion with me and therefore I
address this letter of a strictly personal character to you
so that nobody in the Madrid office can read it or interpret
the contents in the wrong way. For the same reason I have
kept from all my agents any knowledge as to the contents or
the reason of the present letter. This is, therefore, I
repeat, a matter between you and me, leaving it to your
judgment as to whether you should show it to our chief
in Berlin or any other personality who shares our views
because we must always avoid any possibility of there being
differences of opinion amongst our Ministries. In talking
to you in this way I feel that I must clarify this paragraph
and I wish to point out that I refer to our Ministries of
Propaganda and War, the synthesis of the present letter. The
theme involved is the new secret weapon.

Now that a few days have passed during which it has
been used I ask myself "What is the use of this new arm? Has
it a military aim? No! Its effect is nil. Is it then intended
for propaganda? Possibly, yes!" I do not challenge that in
this respect it had at the beginning flattering success. In
considering these two questions I must give priority to the
one of the greatest importance. I do not wish to deny or try
to belittle the importance of an arm as strong as that of
propaganda but when one comes to analyse these two questions
the thing which immediately comes to my mind, as I imagine it
does to yours, is the tangible and net conclusion. This is,
that we must win the war with fighting weapons. The other
weapon, which is that of propaganda, has its limitations and
its very name would not make a complete phrase or commonsense

if the subject for its oration did not exist. The best
propaganda are deeds and these only take place in the field
of battle. In talking in this way it is only in the fear that
in order to justify one thing we have sacrificed the other.
I do not know what the production is, neither have I
the least idea technically of the labour involved in the
production of the device to which I allude, but if it is
being produced at the partial sacrifice of the production
of battle weapons, the mistake which we will have suffered
is serious and the consequences fatal to the outcome of our
undertaking. I speak thus, because it is my duty to inform
you of what is taking place, and as is natural, no one is in a
better position than I am to speak the truth, so that if it is
in accordance with what you are wanting to know you will be
able to find a solution before it is too late, and before we
have to lament the past.

The new arm has passed through two completely opposed
phases. The first lasted for three or four days, and was
surprisingly successful, if not destructive, it was at least
destructive to morale. The second phase is the present one.
This is what I am commenting on and can be summed up in a
simple phase "We are wasting our time." To continue I will
explain my use of this phrase.

When I was first told about this weapon and its
existence was confirmed by you (I am referring to several
months ago) I had hoped to see my ambitions realized in the
destruction of this useless town which surrounds me. Though
the employment of this weapon was delayed I had not the
slightest doubt that its effect would one day be felt when
once it had been perfected, and thus I had the key to what I
had imagined was going to materialize and be put into
effect. Days passed and at last it arrived and the effect
which it produced, as I say above, if it was not altogether
destructive, was at least a bloody weapon against the
morale of these people, because the fear of the unknown is
sufficient to break down the highest spirit. I must, however,
deal with facts and not with arguments, and you will remember
that I then sent you a message in which I made clear my
illusions about the future employment of this weapon,
then conceiving the first episode as being a trial. Without,
therefore, paying much attention to the decomposition
which this might bring about on the phlegmatic English, I
awaited the second phase which I thought would be the vital
one which I expected to bring about, if not the total
destruction, at least a partial destruction, which would

have counterbalanced the work of genius which had been put
into this and would have out-weighed the energy and material
expended in its fabrication. Days have passed and to-day I
can sum up what has happened as follows.

This weapon is not only ineffective from a military
point of view but also from the point of view of propaganda.
Analysing these two points and putting my arguments crudely I
have the following to say. First, the morale of the public
was for a moment brought down to the point of this weapon
taking first place to the battle front as a theme of
conversation. The new arm is now being discussed in quite a
different strain and what is happening is not only that the
situation has quietened down but the device is now being
ridiculed both by words and insinuations about it effects.
What has happened to produce this change? It is that measures
have been taken not only to counterbalance its effectiveness
but to destroy its usefulness. Even now though a state of
precautions alertness still exists in case one of these
weapons should fall on London, the public in spite of hearing
the sirens, do not go to the shelters nor do they interrupt
their daily work. The traffic in the streets continues
normally and the activity in the city remains unchanged. The
public has absorbed the counter-propaganda which is that
they give out for their own benefit what said in German
sources, such as, London is burning; London is evacuating;
the railway communications have been stopped; the
Metropolitan system has been suspended; Big Ben has been
destroyed; etc. etc., This, as is only natural, is checkable
by the ordinary citizen with ease and as they can see with
their own eyes that none of it is true they calm themselves
in the knowledge that his arm is created to terrorize them.
The result is unproductive from our propaganda point of view,
not only so far as this country is concerned, but also for
the neutrals, who, as soon as they received their reports
from their representatives in London, will be face with the
truth. This may not be the case in districts outside the
capital where quite a number have fallen but this is not what
we were aiming to achieve, since these weapons may destroy,
ten, fifty, a hundred, a thousand houses in a city where
buildings are to be found in hundreds of thousands, but they
do not destroy the capital of its industry or the importance
centre of national communications which would make the
manufacture of such an arm worth while.

Second: If, in order to put this weapon into operation
forces have to be taken away from military industries the

consideration is still less pardonable, as this does not add in the very least to the strategic aims of the war which we are following. I have not the slightest idea of the time or the material which is taken up in the fabrication of this weapon neither can I make comparisons as to how many bombers or fighters might have been produced in their stead, nor their proportionate value. This is a matter for technicians whose intelligence and good will take care of these interests for the German nation, and know the respective importance of each of these weapons and where vital energies can best be used, not only for the continuation of the war, but also for final victory. Naturally they cannot analyse this conception because they are not in the least aware of the effects of this new weapon, and therefore I am going to give you some facts.

If one goes about the streets of London one sees the scars of the period of destruction which occurred during the years 1940 - 1941. The effects of what is taking place now are no more than light editions which do not add to the whole a further one ten thousandth part of the destruction of the city, though of course the periods covered are very unequal. If we study the amount of explosives then used and the number of casualties suffered through our action, and we compare this with the present expensive construction of the new arm we can then decide on a basis of effort value which of these has been most effective.

The following important detail which I learnt from J(2) should be taken into account, which is that only 17% of the bombs fell in "Greater London." 22% in other urban towns were either destroyed by the defences or fell in open country due to lack of precision. As I have never liked to embark on a problem without at the same time finding its solution, and as I am not a technician I can only make the suggestion that the two following questions should be dealt with.

Firstly, the speed of the weapon, and secondly its precision. If we can remedy the first in such a way that the Fighters and the antiaircraft of the enemy should be unable to cope with the apparatus and the second point can be dealt with, then we will have been successful in our aims. Possibly the second matter is one in which I can help you, and if through my reports you are able to improve your aim it would be most satisfactory. But before this can be of any use our scientists who created this wonder must find a way of protecting it and this can only be done if the speed can be increased.

My conclusion therefore is the following:-

Until a way of improving it can be found its effectiveness is nil, and therefore all the efforts which had been spent on it have been wasted and they should be employed in the manufacture of war weapons which may have more disastrous effects on our enemy. I do not know whether you are now working on its improvement or whether there may be in production others which are better. Since I remember that when we were dealing with this we had always referred to it as the rocket weapon, which seems to me to have nothing to do with what is now being used.

I base all I have said on what I have seen as I know nothing about what may come. The present trials have shown me that the High Command does not have absolute confidence in me or my service to advise me in advance as to what is taking place. I say this not because I am annoyed at not being told in advance the date that this was to be used but because I feel some bitterness at not having been shown the recognition of my loyalty by my superiors by their having strictly kept this information from me. This is a matter which does not really effect the case as I know that I have fulfilled my part in obtaining the military information, having given it most scrupulous care and my conscience rewards me for these small annoyances which, when all is taken into consideration, merely means that I have been relieved of further responsibilities. I end this letter, my dear chief, in the same strain as I started it, giving you a strictly impartial opinion as you requested in your message. I speak to you as a comrade, as if we were equals and frank as always, I speak my mind. Another person who did not know me as you do without the proof of the conduct of the work which I have achieved might think this letter disillusioning and demoralizing. On you, or on me, it can only produce a vigorous reaction and call for urgent and necessary counter-measures. This can bring perfection in our work, which after all we share by mutual ideals and sincere wishes.

I am now going to confess to you something which, being opposed to flattery, I have never before expressed, but which I now feel obliged to say, which is that I have always had a very strong feeling of respect and admiration for your advice which you have offered me in all moments of danger. It has been advice full of good sense and calmly expressed, and in it I have found a value which I can never overlook. This is perhaps why I could never cheat you with false hope, but feel

that I must be frank and open up my heart to you and unload
the truth which in the long run is never malignant. I have
been a severe critic of our faults, just as I have praised
our victorious achievements. The latter one can fulfil with
pleasure but too much of this can create a state which can
become dangerous. The former are bitter to administer, but by
talking freely about them we awaken our commonsense and
strengthen our decision to continue to look for a solution
which will lead us on a better path towards the objective we
wish to reach. These things can only be dealt with between
men of spirit and tenacity, and by people who follow a
doctrine, by fighting men and bold combatants. This
unfolding of confidences can only be made between comrades.
One could not say to an English lord what one may say to a
National Socialist Comrade. The former would consider
himself ridiculous if he had to accept an observation from a
subordinate. We accept, within the discipline of hierarchy,
the advice of the subordinates. Thus, the great Germany has
become what it is. Thus, it has been able to deposit such
great confidence in the man who governs it, knowing that he
is not a democratic despot but a man of low birth who has only
followed an ideal. The Fatherland! Humanity! Justice and
Comradeship!

On approaching the completion of the third year of my
stay here I now, more than ever, feel pride in my work, and
desire to prove myself worthy of all the evidence of
friendship which you have expressed to me. I feel more than
ever a sensation of hatred, more than death, for our enemy,
and an ever increasing irresistable urge to destroy his
entire existence. The arrogance of this rabble can only be
conceived when you live among them.

Receive a cordial embrace from your comrade and
servant,

JUAN. "

A further long delay in sending concrete reports on the bomb
incidents was achieved, after an exchange of messages between the
22.6.44 and the end of the month.

The Stanford map, we informed them, had no ordinates or
co-ordinates. Therefore, GARBO decided to go to the British Museum
and copy the position of the ordinates and co-ordinates, on the
Pharus map, and place them in the same positions on the Stanford
map. This he did in duplicate, sending one copy to Madrid and
retaining the other for his own use. We knew that it would be several
weeks before the map could reach Arras, and meanwhile we could

satisfy their impatience by sending some isolated reports citing a few incidents.

By the end of June there had been a further development, which resulted in both sides adopting the use of the Baedeker map and we started to quote readings from this guide to locate incidents.

It was about this time that the Third U.S. Army and the First Canadian Army were starting to move to the battle area and we were accordingly instructed by SHAEF to reduce all military reporting to a minimum, although we were at the same time requested to endeavour to maintain the threat to the Pas de Calais. This period, prior to the reorganization of the notional FUSAG, coincided with the period of our having to evade the issue of reporting on the effects of the flying bomb, and in the absence of a policy for the latter topic, the position of the GARBO case became especially precarious, since we had been particularly requested by Berlin to give specific details about the new weapon as well as about the movements of any of the formations which, according to GARBO's agents, were under command of FUSAG.

It became apparent that some drastic action had to be taken if we were to avoid subjecting the GARBO network to suspicion. It was then that it was decided to put into operation a plan to close down the GARBO channel of communications for a period long enough to enable the above-mentioned formations to reach the battle area without the necessity for the GARBO network to give advance notification of their departure, and at the same time to dissuade the Germans from taking any further risks in using their important network of military observers for such relatively unimportant activities as the reporting on the results of the new weapon. The essence of the plan was that GARBO should be arrested whilst personally investigating a V bomb incident.

On the 30.6.44, just as the plan was about to be put into operation we received a message from Madrid in which they directed that information on troop movements was to be GARBO's principal mission, and that he should only devote the energies of his organization to the collecting of information about V bomb damage, if, and when, circumstances permitted.

To be able, therefore, to put our plan into operation we had to take the initiative, and this we did by sending a GARBO message the following day in which he stressed that in spite of their opinion that the reporting on the V bomb incidents was a matter of secondary importance, he felt it was essential to get precise information on this subject, as alternatively they would be wasting their energy since, as we pointed out, they were still far from attaining the success for which they were striving. GARBO expressed his opinion that he considered this matter so vital that he proposed undertaking the investigations personally since he was dissatisfied with the results produced by his agents to date who, he emphasized, seemed frightened to ask the necessary questions by which one could obtain the desired information. This message was followed by a long report on bomb damage which he had collected that day in which he gave the precise time of incidents (though inaccurate) and details such as the number of people killed or injured, as well as the damage to property. The following day a similar long report on bomb damage was transmitted and attributed to GARBO's personal observation. It was already obvious from these few reports that GARBO was taking personal risks even if the results which he was obtaining were infinitely better than his agents had produced.

On the 4.7.44 there was no transmission. The following night Agent No. 3 transmitted some military information received from sub-agents on the east coast to which he added the news that GARBO had not made an appearance the previous day nor at their regular morning meeting that day. He expressed surprise at GARBO's silence and feared that he might have been hurt by one of their bombs. To try to ascertain what had occurred he proposed sending the Widow of Agent No. 2 to enquire from GARBO's wife.

On the 6.7.44 the result of the Widow's investigations were transmitted. Mrs. GARBO had had no news from her husband whom she had imagined was in London with Agent No. 3. This fact preoccupied GARBO's Deputy, who commented that it seemed unlikely that GARBO had met with an accident since his wife would surely have been notified. He asked the Germans for their advice and what he should do with Mrs. GARBO, whom he said was in a terrible state and had threatened to make enquiries from the police, this he thought might prove disastrous since it was always possible the explanation of GARBO's silence would turn out to be that he had gone off on some new track or clue, which had taken him to a prohibited area from where he was unable to communicate.

A day later the mystery of GARBO's disappearance was clarified, for the Widow brought Agent No. 3 the alarming news that the police had called on Mrs. GARBO to collect GARBO's Spanish Republican documentation (with which the Germans had previously supplied him) and all that was known so far was that GARBO had been arrested for reasons unknown. Agent No. 3 proposed that in view of the critical situation he should break off all contact with the other agents. The message crossed with a long series of messages which were received the same night, in reply to Agent No. 3's first warning of GARBO's disappearance. The Germans said that everything must be done to prevent Mrs. GARBO from making any enquiries about her husband, and after dealing with various possibilities as to what

might have happened to GARBO they concluded that in the worst
events, by which they meant that had GARBO been arrested in
connection with his activities with the result that it become
impossible to save the rest of the service, GARBO's Deputy, Agent
No. 3, should take immediate measures to safeguard the rest of the
organization and see that no evidence to compromise them should fall
into the hands of the British police. They then went on to deal with
the disposal of the funds and the steps which should be taken to
assist Mrs. GARBO and the children. They ended up their messages
with a word of flattery for GARBO's Deputy by saying:-

> "I know that should these events occur you are dealing with a
> very hard and difficult task and I rely on your skill and
> your intelligence of which (GARBO) has so often informed me.
> You know that in case of doubt or questions that may arise we
> are here to advise you. Let us hope sincerely that everything
> turns out to have been only a fright and that by the time
> these messages reach you (GARBO) will have appeared in
> perfect health."

The following day they sent a message to say that in the event
of GARBO not being released from detention they wished to appoint
Agent No. 3 to take over the control of the organization, they
requested him to endeavour to do all in his power to save at least part
of it. They told him that he should temporarily leave London and close
down the wireless station for a period to be decided by him. They
promised to be listening every day until communications were re-
established at a time when Agent No. 3 thought safe.

This development gave us precisely the break which we had
tried to engineer and had so badly needed. To avoid any possibility
that they might suspect that GARBO, through his arrest, had been
broken or converted to double cross, we decided not to keep up the
scare for longer than necessary. Therefore, on the 12.7.44 Agent No.
3 transmitted the surprising news that GARBO had already been
released. The Widow, who brought the news, had been unable to obtain
from her Chief any information as to the cause of his detention,
though through her, he had instructed his Deputy to return
immediately to Glasgow to await further orders. He was ordered to
give the wireless operator ten days holiday after having notified
the Germans that they were to collect a letter from a Lisbon cover
address to which GARBO would be writing by courier in which he would
give them details of what had transpired.

The letter referred to above was dated the 14.7.44 and
explained in detail the circumstances of GARBO's detention. Briefly
what had happened was that he had aroused the suspicion of a plain

clothes policeman whilst investigating the damage caused by a bomb which had fallen in Bethnal Green. Whilst being taken to the police station he had swallowed a piece of paper on which were some incriminating notes. Though he was observed doing this, and thus had intensified the suspicions of the police, during the period of his interrogation he had consistently denied that the incident had ever occurred. After several days detention he was able to prove to the satisfaction of the police authorities that he was in fact a Republican refugee, producing as evidence the false documentation which the Germans had forged for him nearly two years previously. Furthermore his good friend, J(3) of the Ministry of Information, on being informed by the police of GARBO's detention, had taken immediate action to try to clear him for he had never doubted his loyalty to this country. So angry was he that GARBO should have been "unjustly" treated that he persuaded him to write to the Under-Secretary of State at the Home Office to complain of his unlawful detention, for it appeared, on examination, that GARBO had been detained under an emergency Defence Regulation D.R. 18D which only entitled a Divisional Superintendent of Police to detain a suspect for 48 hours for interrogation. GARBO had been detained longer than the period provided for by the Regulation.

GARBO's appeal brought about his release, for a few days later a letter from the Home Secretary was received in which he apologized to GARBO for the inconvenience caused by the mistaken and excessive zeal of the Police in the exercise of their duty. The letter from the Home Secretary as well as the order under which GARBO had been detained (both forgeries which were produced by this Office)* were enclosed with GARBO's letter to the Germans in evidence of the frightening events which had occurred. From this evidence it was intended that the Germans should continue to rely on GARBO with the same confidence as in the past.

On the 29.7.44, following messages of congratulations on GARBO's liberation, they informed him "With great happiness and satisfaction" that they were able to advise him that the Fuehrer had conceded him the Iron Cross for his extraordinary merits. They pointed out that this decoration was, without exception, only granted to first line combatants for which reason they all joined in congratulating him. GARBO's reply was characteristic, he said:-

> "I cannot at this moment, when emotion overcomes me, express in words my thanks for the decoration conceded by our Fuehrer, to whom humbly and with every respect, I express my gratitude for the high distinction which he has bestowed on

* See Appendix No. XLII.

me, for which I feel my self unworthy, since I have never
done more than that which I have considered to be the
fulfilment of my duty. Further more, I must state that this
prize has been won, not only by me, but also by Carlos and the
other comrades, who, through their advice and directives,
have made possible my work here and so, the congratulations
are mutual. My desire is to fight with greater ardour to be
worthy of this medal which has only been conceded to those
heroes, my companions in honour, who fight on the
battlefront."

We know from Most Secret Sources that discussions were
subsequently held in Berlin as to whether or not GARBO should be
used again for reporting on the V weapon, and it was decided that, in
view of the exceptional value of the GARBO network to the Service
Intelligence Departments, and the narrow escape which GARBO had
personally experienced, that all his energies should, in future, be
concentrated on military reporting.

In spite of this we did, at a later date, use GARBO in
connection with an operational plan to misinform the Germans as to
the true mean point of impact of the V2 incidents in order to induce
them to shorten their range.

CHAPTER XXVI.

THE BUENAGA INCIDENT.
GARBO GOES INTO HIDING.

By August, 1944, some degree of political rift within Germany was becoming apparent. There was already an increasing tendency amongst people who had been members of, or connected with, the German Secret Service, to seek refuge with the Allies in exchange for information, and the threat of compromise to the GARBO organization was steadily increasing. Already several people had indicated to our representatives in Lisbon and Madrid, the existence of the GARBO organization, though to date no one had given us sufficient concrete information to enable us to identify the agents operating. In particular a Spaniard, Roberto BUENAGA, had given us information about German espionage activities from which it became apparent that he was at least aware of the existence of the GARBO network.

Had he not come forward with this information there was always the danger that one of the members of the Madrid Stelle might at some time decide to give us information about GARBO in exchange for preferential treatment. Such an approach would either have forced us to effect the notional arrest of GARBO and dispense with the services of his organization or take the risk that our failure to arrest him would indicate to our informant that GARBO had, in fact, been working for us. What was worse, was the possibility that in a case of uncertainty we would find it necessary to take the decision to effect his notional arrest, whilst subsequent developments might prove that the course adopted had not, in fact, been necessary.

At this juncture we were gravely threatened with the danger that the Germans might discover the operational deception passed over by the GARBO network, in addition to the loss of the GARBO organization.

It was therefore decided that if we could get GARBO out of the picture and hand over the entire organization to his Deputy, Agent No. 3, the case could never be blown since we knew that the Germans themselves were unaware of the identity of any of GARBO's agents, and therefore there was no one who could possibly denounce them to us.

BUENAGA had already promised to give us the full name of the chief German agent in England whom, he maintained, was communicating with Spain by wireless. Though we were convinced he was referring to GARBO we could not afford, either in the interest of GARBO's security, or in the interests of Security generally, to refuse to accept the information. Since, however, BUENAGA was demanding a monetary consideration in exchange for the information we had an opportunity to delay whilst his offer of information was ostensibly being considered by London. An appointment was made for a meeting with BUENAGA at which it was decided we would allow him to give us all the information in his possession, including GARBO's name, if in fact, he were able to do so. A few days prior to the meeting GARBO sent the following message:-

> "Through the friend of the courier who told him about
> the betrayal of the Lisbon addresses which resulted in
> Censorship discovering my letters, I have to-day learnt that
> an individual called BUENAGA, who has worked in our service,
> has betrayed us after having discovered our work. For this
> reason immediately I have despatched these messages I shall go
> into hiding because I believe that in this way I shall be able
> to save the rest of the service. I am writing a detailed letter
> with all the facts which please collect personally. Suspend
> all correspondence and the sending of money to the bank after
> the 15th of this month.......Let Three know immediately
> whether the wireless is endangered due to BUENAGA having
> knowledge of the frequencies on which we work."

On the same day GARBO wrote a long letter in which he made it appear that the courier had a contact in Lisbon who probably worked in Embassy circles and knew the S.I.S. contact who was in touch with BUENAGA from whom he had learnt all the details of his interviews with BUENAGA. The courier's contact apparently worked with the courier in his Black Market dealings and was using his Embassy position as cover. Exactly how the news of BUENAGA's betrayal reached the courier was never made too clear for our own convenience, but for our own security all the information, which we received from BUENAGA and passed back to the Germans via GARBO, was strictly in accordance with BUENAGA's statements.

GARBO explained in his letter that by going into hiding before he was denounced, having had the good fortune of being warned in advance of BUENAGA's intentions, he hoped to be able to save the service which he would leave in the charge of Agent No. 3. He explained that he was going to a safe hideout in south Wales which had been previously furnished by Agent No. 7 to Agent No. 4 when he had been forced to take refuge during the summer. GARBO had warned his wife that if he were denounced, in accordance with BUENAGA's threat, she would undoubtedly be interrogated by the British police and he instructed her exactly as to how she was to behave. He arranged all financial matters before departing and told the

Germans that the courier would facilitate a new address to
substitute the address at the bank to which they had been writing
since 1941, lest BUENAGA should also have knowledge of this address
and betray it. In fact a safe address in Lisbon was supplied by
S.I.S. Lisbon, this was passed to the Germans who subsequently used
it for sending all GARBO mail.

In reply to GARBO's wireless message the Germans said that
BUENAGA had no idea of GARBO's identity, neither was he aware of any
of GARBO's secrets.

A few days later BUENAGA in fact gave us GARBO's full and
correct name as well as that of GARBO's wife and her address in
Spain. This information we passed back to the Germans through GARBO
and they had to admit that they had been very much taken in by
BUENAGA, and they heartily approved the prompt and intelligent
action which GARBO had taken in the circumstances.

From this time until the end of the war with Germany, the GARBO
organization was conducted by the notional Agent No. 3. But GARBO was
not allowed to die out of the picture. One of the sub-agents
maintained a courier service between GARBO in his hideout and Agent
No. 3 at his headquarters in London. Agent No. 3, through the Widow,
maintained contact with Mrs. GARBO, from whom he learnt of the police
enquiries which were being made to locate GARBO. GARBO, through a sub-
agent, maintained contact with the courier and thus, from his
hideout, he was able to forward secret letters by courier, reporting
on the new developments in the negotiations with BUENAGA, and
whenever necessary he could, with a twenty-four hour delay, send
wireless messages via Agent No. 3 in London. Thus, when we wished to
attach special importance to an operational wireless message we would
arrange a meeting between Agent No. 3 and GARBO, in his hideout, so
that they could together discuss and interpret the various reports
received from their sub-agents before formulating a joint report.

The Germans went into the question of BUENAGA's betrayal in
very considerable detail. They were completely mystified as to how
the information passed by BUENAGA to an S.I.S. representative
should reach GARBO and yet they had concrete evidence that it in
fact did so. On one occasion they expressed their doubt as to the
plausibility of the whole of the courier set up, not in the sense
that they doubted the veracity of GARBO, but rather with a view to
protecting themselves in GARBO's estimation. They said they
considered it improbable that a member of the British Secret
Service, sworn to secrecy, should betray confidential information
of this nature to the courier's contact. GARBO had reported that the
leakage had reached the courier through a person whose identity the
courier was concealing, and throughout the correspondence GARBO had
referred to him as "A". He referred to BUENAGA as "B". The following

is an extract of GARBO's reply to the hint from the Germans as to the incredibility of the leakage:-

"Another question which you bring up in your letter is that you want to know how it is possible that the statements of B. reach A. and that the latter should pass on the information to the courier and the courier to me. In the first place many of the confusing details which we cannot explain may well be due to the number of persons through whom this has to pass before it reaches our hand and it may result that by the time it reaches us the story has been somewhat mutilated or added to. I don't know who A. is, to tell the truth, and in spite of what the courier has told me, I am still in some doubt as to the true identity of this man. Is he Portuguese? Is he English? Is he a contact? Is he a real English agent? Be he what he may this is not the moment to discuss him, when I am lacking knowledge of the antecedents of the person in whom we are interested.

What I do not find so incomprehensible as you do is that this individual should be disposed to perform against the interests of his duties. Here we have an elastic point for discussion. I have never believed in the oaths and promises which are made with regard to the secrecy and discretion which are the requisites of certain work. I do not believe in the word of all men, nor in the sentiments they express unless they are supported above all by a high concept of honour. In all existing organizations, in spite of the fact that a great number of the people of whom they are composed are patriots, who would allow themselves to be killed before they would betray the secrets with which they are entrusted, there are also others who, due to the necessity of having to recruit collaborators, are made up of different nationalities, desirous of co-operating for an ideal or for self-interest. There are even nationals of the country for which they are working who have extremely individualist instincts who above all things wish to see their own ambitions realized.

This war, as all others, has shown us many cases of betrayal induced by an ambition for power or possessions. You should, for example, reflect for a moment on the cases of those unfortunate nations who, through fear and cowardice, abandoned us during the most difficult moments of the war. What happened to Rumania? Bulgaria? Hungary? Finland? Etc., In all these countries there were men in position of power who had given their word of honour to fight closely by the side of their German ally. They had all committed themselves to defend the same ideal. In spite of this what happened? These same men who held high posts who should, through their hierarchy and position as leaders, have given an example, instead handed themselves over through insidious cowardice to the enemy. Even worse, they now fight against those who were once their Allies and friends. What have you to say about the responsibility and oaths of the men who have done this? Leaving aside these cases which may to some extent be attributed to cowardice, what have you to say with regard to the treacherous attempts which have been made against the lives of Mussolini and Hitler? There is no doubt that all the men concerned had sworn allegiance. They held responsible and high political or military posts, and in spite of this they assisted the enemy. They made contact with the enemy and finally played their cards openly with the enemy. If these men, who by reason of their standing, should have honour and dignity, descend to such things what do you expect of men like B. or contacts or agents like A. or individuals such as the courier and an unlimited plague of little people whom experience has shown as every day exist, and are motivated only by the caprices of the golden god."

In a series of letters from GARBO he made it apparent that he suspected all his troubles had been due to some indiscretions on the part of FEDERICO who had obviously confided in BUENAGA more than he should have done. Whilst FEDERICO's name was never mentioned as the person considered to have been responsible for GARBO's misery in hiding it was made abundantly clear by inference that FEDERICO was the man he suspected. At the same time to protect FEDERICO, GARBO said that he realized that whatever indiscretions he had made had not been intentional and that were CARLOS to take any disciplinary measures against him in this connection GARBO would take exception to such action.

At our instigation the Germans wrote an en clair letter to BUENAGA warning him that information had reached them to the effect that he had been associating unwisely with members of the opposite camp and that although they were reluctant to believe this of anyone who had for so long been a friend of theirs, they wished to warn him that should he continue to maintain this association it was likely that measures would be taken against him by another organization with which they were connected, thus inferring that he would be dealt with by the Gestapo.

The letter was brought to our notice by BUENAGA and thus we were able to check that the Germans were in fact acting in accordance with our recommendation.

Having allowed sufficient time to elapse for the British

police to have unsuccessfully made a search for GARBO, we then took
the action which the Germans might have assumed we would have taken
had GARBO been a real German agent.

Our Embassy in Madrid registered a Diplomatic protest at the
Spanish Ministry of Foreign Affairs, bringing to their notice the
fact that information had reached us through an ex-member of the
German Secret Service, now in Lisbon, disclosing the activities of
a German spy ring operating in this country, controlled by German
agents in Madrid. In particular we had been informed that these
hostile activities had been directed by Federico KNAPPE, an agent
whose expulsion from Spain we had previously ineffectively
requested, together with other Germans, whose particulars we had
supplied to the Spanish Ministry of Foreign Affairs. We pointed out
that failure to take action on the part of the Spanish authorities
to expel this German agent from Madrid had made possible the
continued activities of an agent operating in the U.K. whose present
whereabouts was only known to KNAPPE. We therefore requested the
Spanish authorities to take steps to expel KNAPPE forthwith from
Spain. We suggested that since the continued activities of the agent
in the U.K. had been due to the failure of the Spanish authorities to
take earlier action against KNAPPE, we should now be compensated by
being given facilities to interrogate him prior to his expulsion, in
order that we might request him to disclose the whereabouts of the
individual whom we were now seeking.

We had no doubt at the time that the Germans would be given
immediate warning of this Diplomatic protest. We did not envisage
the likelihood of the Spanish authorities handing us KNAPPE for
interrogation but we nevertheless thought that the action taken
would induce the Germans to believe that we had so far been unable to
locate GARBO.

To give further verisimilitude to our story GARBO frequently
reported on interviews between his wife and the British Police at
which she had been questioned about her husband's whereabouts and
past activities.

GARBO wrote a series of letters which he sent by courier to the
Germans asking them to mail them in order of their advance dating from
various regions of Spain. These letters were written by hand by GARBO
and addressed to his wife in England. From their context it was made
to appear as though GARBO had escaped from England to Spain and was
wandering about the country, repentant for what he had done during the
war which had lead to his enforced separation from his wife and
family. He made it appear as though he did not intend to engage in any
further hostile activities against the Allies and that his only
thought now was to be united with his family. The letters though
written in his own hand were signed with various names as if it were

his intention to evade British Censorship. They were mailed by the
Germans in accordance with GARBO's instructions, and shortly after
the arrival of the first letter from Spain GARBO reported that his
wife had again been interrogated as to the identity of the writer of
the letter. She had pretended, he said, that the letter was from one
of her cousins in Spain. After the arrival of further letters we made
it appear as if British Censorship, having intercepted the letters,
had arranged, through the Security Service, for a comparison to be
made between the hand writing of the author of the letters from Spain
and that of GARBO, using for comparison of GARBO's hand writing
certain documents which had been recovered from the Ministry of
Information whilst he had been working there. Having conclusively
proved to their satisfaction that the author of the letters coming
from Spain was no other than GARBO himself, Mrs. GARBO was again
interrogated by the British authorities. Thus, GARBO's plan was
beginning to materialize. The British had drawn the conclusion from
these letters that GARBO had escaped from England, therefore, in
accordance with GARBO's instructions Mrs. GARBO allowed herself to be
broken when further interrogated on the evidence of the comparative
hand writing which they produced before her. She admitted that the
letters were from her husband and that he must therefore, by means
unknown to her, have escaped from England to Spain.

Meanwhile, dissatisfied with their failure to make progress
in their investigations the British police informed Mrs. GARBO that
she was considered to be an undesirable alien and that she would
therefore be deported from this country. GARBO, on hearing this
news, and worried lest her deportation should arouse the notice of
the Spanish Security authorities and eventually disturb the Germans
in Spain, told his wife to approach the British authorities and
explain to them that a Deportation Order against her and the
children would result in forever prejudicing the children in the
light of both the Spanish and British authorities for an offence for
which they were far too young to be responsible. This logic appealed
to the British sense of justice and Mrs. GARBO was told that,
providing she proceeded to take steps to return to Spain of her own
free will, no action would be taken against her or the children.
Thus, on the 1.5.45, assisted by this Department, Mrs. GARBO and the
children returned to Madrid by air.

We were influenced, in our decision to allow Mrs. GARBO to
return to Spain, by the fact that the domestic situation in the
GARBO household had become extremely complicated. Mrs. GARBO was
unable to find satisfactory living accommodation for herself and
the children due to the most difficult domestic servant situation
existing at that time. She was for long periods without a servant,
having to look after the two children and do the house work. This she

was incapable of doing satisfactorily, partly due to the fact that she was then under orders from her doctor not to work on account of an illness from which she was then suffering.

In spite of this we were somewhat reluctant to allow her to return to Spain lest she should take it into her head to contact the Germans. This we considered her capable of doing, not in order to endanger her husband's work but because she might be unable to resist the temptation of such an adventure. To safeguard against this possibility, having notified the Germans through GARBO's letters that she was returning, we wrote to them at the time of her departure to warn them that Mrs. GARBO felt very hostile towards them since she considered them responsible for having broken up her family life. GARBO went on to say that it was, in his own opinion, certain that the British had insisted on Mrs. GARBO's return to Spain, believing that her presence there would attract GARBO to her side. By watching her therefore, they hoped to track down GARBO. The Germans, he pointed out, must therefore at all costs, avoid contact with her, since not only would this contact compromise them but it would also prove that Mrs. GARBO had been lying when she had said she had no knowledge of her husband's German contacts or activities on their behalf. The Germans did not make any attempt to contact her, neither did she attempt to get in touch with them.

BUENAGA continued to make occasional contact with our representative in Lisbon until after the cessation of hostilities when he pointed out to our representative that he could not comprehend why it was that he had taken no steps to reward him for the valuable information which he had given us about GARBO and which he knew to be true. Our representative was somewhat worried lest our failure to recognize the merits of his information should lead BUENAGA to suspect that we had already been aware of GARBO's activities and hence that we had been controlling them.

To safeguard against this predicament BUENAGA was told that the British authorities had taken a poor view of his information since it seemed too much of a coincidence to them that GARBO had so successfully managed to go into hiding somewhere beyond their reach just twenty-four hours before BUENAGA had parted with his name. They therefore believed that BUENAGA, having knowledge of the fact that GARBO was about to escape and had already safely removed himself from the reach of the British authorities, had given out the information which purported to be helpful, and which he had hitherto withheld knowing that by the time it would reach us it would be too out of date to be of any value to us.

This was a view point which BUENAGA must, in all conscience, have known to be mistaken, but was one which he was reluctantly forced to accept as final.

CHAPTER XXVII.

THE ESCAPE OF AGENT NO. 4 TO CANADA.
THE CANADIAN WIRELESS STATION.
GARBO'S PLANS FOR ESCAPE FROM ENGLAND.
THE END OF THE WAR IN EUROPE.

To remain in hiding indefinitely was, as GARBO pointed out in many of his letters, unthinkable. His hideout in south Wales was a remote farm where he lived with an old Welsh couple, a Belgian deserter and a half witted relative of the owners. There was no electricity or sanitation, the food was bad, the weather terrible. GARBO was almost unable to understand his hosts since their accent was broad. In any case they mostly conversed in Welsh and altogether the situation was undermining his morale. For a considerable period in hiding GARBO was ill.

Agent No. 4 who had hidden there between June and October 1944, had found the experience so demoralizing that he had resorted to escape to Canada even with the perils that involved. Fortunately, through the good offices of the seaman agent, No. 7, he had successfully made his escape to Canada in the role of a seaman. GARBO began to scheme a similar escape for himself, in his correspondence he had told in detail the story of Agent No. 4's escape.

Whilst he had been in hiding Agent No. 4 had occupied his time practicing morse. He had, it will be recalled, already studied wireless procedure with GARBO's operator and it became apparent that if he could succeed in escaping to Canada he could there serve Agent No. 5 as a wireless operator. When the plans for his escape had been worked out, the operator was instructed to modify both the wireless set which he was using as well as the duplicate set which he had previously built, in case the former should have been destroyed by enemy action, and to make them both capable of working to the Western Hemisphere. He was told that the Spanish Republicans in Mexico were anxious to maintain contact with Madrid and with London, and that as soon as he had adapted the sets to be able to transmit over these distances the spare set would be sent out to Mexico City by the Mexican Diplomatic Bag. On the strength of this story the operator modified the sets accordingly and the spare set was rebuilt so that it could easily be dismantled in order to make less bulky packages for sending to Mexico by Bag.

To arrange the transport of both the agent, and later, the wireless set, Agent No. 7 returned to the Merchant Navy, signing on one of the fast ships on the route from Canada to Britain. Having well established himself on this line, and having made friends with the Purser, he managed to supply Agent No. 4 with the documentation of a seaman which he acquired. There was a great shortage of seamen at the time and it was not therefore difficult to manage to sign on his friend, Agent No. 4, as a steward, particularly as this agent had previously had experience as a waiter.

On arrival in Canada Agent No. 4 deserted and, in accordance with pre-arranged plans, he made contact with Agent No. 5 there, who managed to find accommodation for him and taught him the tricks by which he would be able to avoid the vigilance of the Canadian Police. Agent No. 7 transported, and smuggled ashore, the wireless set which was delivered in various consignments to Agent No. 5. It was reassembled by Agent No. 4 who prepared to make contact with England, and, later, Madrid.

A transmitting plan was first furnished by the London operator so that practice trials could be made, later a very comprehensive plan, and cyphers similar to the one in use by the GARBO network, were supplied to Canada via GARBO for this new station which had been prepared by the Germans.

All these arrangements took several months. Eventually we were ready to start the trial transmissions on the 15.1.45.

To conform with our statement that the operator had increased the output of his wireless set, and to ensure making good contact, we acquired, through the War Office, an American Army Corps Signal set which, according to the experts, should have been capable of making contact anywhere in the world. Though it had an output of 500 watts we made it appear to the Germans as if the output of our set was no more than 70-100 watts. Thus, when transmitting to Madrid, we would only use a fraction of our maximum volume, whilst we had available a considerable reserve power for making contact with Canada.

In Canada we operated a 350 watt set which again was considered more than adequate for our requirements. Prior to starting the trial transmissions we sent a copy of our trial plan to the Germans so that they should be able to monitor our inter-network service. We told them that after we had successfully established contact they should endeavour to do likewise. It transpired that due to extremely unfavourable atmospheric conditions which existed over the period of the trials, contact between London and Canada was never successfully established. The Germans, however, who were monitoring our attempts to make contact, decided one day to intervene. Without warning Canada or ourselves, realizing that Canada was not hearing us, and able to hear Canada calling us, they decided as an experiment to call from Madrid using our call sign.

Canada, though unable to hear us managed to hear Madrid, though in our opinion their station was less powerful than our own.

Thus it was that Canada, without realizing the fact, established contact with the Germans and received their first message without, at first, knowing its origin. This was on the 16.1.45, and from then until the cessation of hostilities with Germany contact was maintained twice weekly between Canada and Madrid. The Germans would frequently inform us of their negotiations with our Canadian branch network, and retransmit messages from Agent No. 5 to his brother, our Deputy Chief, Agent No. 3.

All these developments had proceeded so successfully that it was not unnatural that GARBO should have felt inclined to try to use the same channels for his own escape. In his case, however, the problem was greater. Firstly, he was a foreigner, and secondly, it was to be assumed that the British authorities would be watching for him at every port of exit. To disguise himself he grew a beard, but even this, without other facilities, would not ensure his safe escape. For a period of several months GARBO discussed the possibilities of his escape. If he could manage to get to Canada he knew that he would there be helped by Agent No. 5 who would no doubt find some way of getting him to Venezuela, the agent's native country where he had numerous friends who would, no doubt, facilitate GARBO with new documentation. GARBO expressed this thought, and other ideas for escape in his lengthy correspondence whilst in hiding.

Through a friend of Agent No. 7, a captain of a freighter, he proposed that he might escape to Cuba. This captain, like all GARBO's associates, was engaged in illegal traffic, and he specialized in smuggling Cuban tobacco. This was not a very dangerous matter for him, since he had, in Havana, a Cuban mistress whose brother was a Customs Officer, and thus the trio managed affairs at the Cuban end, whilst through friends in the British Customs the smuggled merchandize was safely landed in England. For a monetary consideration this smuggler said he could quite easily land GARBO in Cuba. The brother of his mistress there would arrange to stamp his documentation to make it appear as though he had landed on the Island at a date to coincide with the arrival there of a ship from Spain.

Another plan which GARBO proposed was that he should adopt the identity of his Agent No. 4 who, before leaving for Canada, had left his documentation with GARBO. After the long interval which had transpired since this agent had deserted from the N.A.A.F.I. GARBO thought there would be no risk were he to adopt this man's identity, furthermore, he suggested that once established as a Gibraltarian he might well make his was to Gibraltar, and thence to Spain.

Another plan was that GARBO should escape to France and there, facilitated by the American, No. 4(3), make his way to Spain over the Franco-Spanish frontier. He would proceed through France in an American uniform which he said he would be able to obtain. To carry out this, or the Cuban plan, GARBO would require the Germans to supply him with false Spanish documentation in an assumed name so that he could circulate when he had reached the south of France (or Cuba.) He also requested that they should send him some used clothing made in Spain and other effects so that when once he took on his new identity there would be no trace of his having come from England. He said that he knew how to cross the Franco-Spanish frontier but he would require them to make arrangements to receive him on his arrival in Cataluña and to guarantee that they would facilitate his entry into Spain and arrange for him to have the necessary Spanish documentation to circulate when once in Spain without risk of getting himself involved with the Spanish Police authorities.

All these projects were examined here and satisfactory cover plans were worked out for each of them. We left it very much to the Germans to decide which course GARBO should adopt. They showed preference for the Cuban plan or the escape through France. In particular they liked the former and they guaranteed to pave the way for GARBO with the Spanish authorities. They also undertook to supply him, through the courier, with the necessary personal clothing which he had requested, and notified GARBO that they were arranging to supply him with a set of documents which had belonged to a Spanish Republican refugee in France whose background they promised to supply so that GARBO should have a perfect cover story. In fact the war came to a close before the documentation was completed and, during the last days before the Germans surrendered, they had to admit their inability to see GARBO through his difficulties.

When the end of the war was imminent, and we foresaw the possibility of communications suddenly ceasing, we tried to prepare the way for this break. Our main object was to get GARBO quickly to Madrid to make contact with his German masters as it was thought that he alone would be able to ascertain whether or not the Germans were proposing to carry on any form of underground organization in the post war.

Through S.I.S. representatives in Madrid we had already received notification that Federico KNAPPE had been put under town arrest by the Spanish authorities and sent to join other Germans in Caldos near Barcelona. KUHLENTHAL, who had similarly been listed for detention had, through his influence in Spanish official circles, managed to get a permit to reside in Avila.

Whilst we were anxious to make our preparations we felt that it would be out of character for a fanatical fascist such as GARBO was represented to be, to suggest the possibility of the Germans having to surrender. It would seem that they too were somewhat embarrassed to approach the subject to GARBO. Therefore we decided on the 1.5.45 to take the initiative. The following are extracts

from a series of messages which were exchanged between the 1.5.45
and the night of the 8.5.45, the night of celebration of victory in
Europe. The following extract is from a message from GARBO to Madrid
sent on the evening of the 1.5.45:-

> "Your last messages which arrived after the recent Anglo-
> American-Bolshevik onslaught leave me very preoccupied, and I
> appeal to you for the closest co-operation in our planning at
> these critical moments when I envisage that it will be more
> than ever essential that our secret organizations all over
> the world should function with the maximum efficiency
> in order to be able to serve our Chief and leaders who guide
> us in our cause and who alone can save us in the present
> crisis and carry us forward to the victory of our aspirations
> which will undoubtedly come about due to the confusion
> of our enemies during the next phase of events. I have
> given detailed consideration to the possibility of such
> disagreements and I have no doubt that you also have made plans
> in order to deal with any eventuality........I am convinced
> that, providing we take the necessary steps in order to
> organize ourselves adequately and efficiently at the present
> time, we will be able to maintain contact with Three and Five
> after (my) departure, and thereby control a network, the
> benefits of which may be of incalculable value in the future."

This curiously enough crossed with a message from the Germans
to GARBO which was very similar in tone:-

> "For (GARBO). The rapid course of events and the confusion
> reigning all over the world makes it impossible to see
> ahead with clarity the future developments of the general
> situation or to take decisions in this connection. We thank
> you with all our heart for the offer from (GARBO) and Three
> for their continued future collaboration, understanding and
> fully appreciating the motives which animate this. On the
> other hand you will understand that in a situation which does
> not allow one to look ahead it is our greatest wish and duty
> as colleagues to arrange matters in such a way......so
> as to ensure generally for your safety and that of the
> collaborators, giving them an opportunity to return to their
> private activities. We therefore submit the following to you
> for your consideration. The documentation for the planned
> journey of (GARBO) has been definitely promised to us for
> the end of this week. As soon as this is in our possession,
> and if circumstances permit, it will be sent to you through

the usual channel. If, in spite of all our efforts this should not arrive in time to be able to be sent on to you we trust that the post war situation will give (GARBO) greater facilities for him to be able to make the necessary escape from his hideout. The remittance which is en route, together with the funds you already have over there are for the purpose of helping all the collaborators, including 7(3) and Five, to be able to return to their normal work, resolve the situation during this period, and above all, to facilitate the solution of the problem of (GARBO). The distribution must be left to the discretion of (GARBO). In order to leave open the possibility to be able to make contact, should circumstances make this necessary, with Three or with (GARBO), should he manage to remain on there, you should let us have by message, the name, surname and address, where we could send a plain postcard which would be sent from a man, FERNANDO GOMEZ, and would communicate to the addressee.......his intention to travel to that country on a given date. On this date Almura should start up contact in accordance with the yearly plan which is in your possession. We leave to the judgment of (GARBO) or Three to make similar arrangements with the network of Five. We do not think it is necessary for us to reiterate in these bitter hours our profound sentiments of gratitude and appreciation. We firmly hope that Providence will inspire the leaders and people responsible for the future in order that we may avoid at the last moment a definite chaos which would envelop Europe, in defence of whose ideals we have struggled together. We will be listening daily from to-morrow so that Three can communicate his approval of our suggestions and send the above mentioned address as soon as he has consulted with (GARBO). Before definitely suspending the present contacts with Almura we await our instructions in this connection. Very cordial regards from us all. End."

On the 2.5.45 Agent No. 3 acknowledged the message of the previous night in the following form:-

"Am leaving on afternoon train to take messages to (GARBO) hoping to get back for to-morrow's transmission."

The seriousness of the news made GARBO decide to take a risk and come to London to be together with his colleagues at the last critical hour. So presumably after an evening's hard work encyphering he managed to send off the following messages on the 3.5.45:-

"In view of the urgency of the situation I have returned to
London where I am sheltering in the house of Three. I shall
endeavour to maintain daily contact by radio. I will not go
into explanations but I am in a safe place. The address to
which you can send the postcard in the future is […] I
wish you to destroy all documentation and papers of the
organization and those relating to me and likewise
my photograph. You should only retain this address and the
present transmitting plan for making contact in the future.
Everything here will be destroyed with the exception of the
transmitting plan and the address in Madrid or any other town
or foreign country which I hope you will supply me with so
that I can in due course make contact with you. The financial
question has been satisfactorily resolved and a substantial
sum in sterling has been set aside and is at the disposal of
Three for future work. It is my desire that you should allot
a sum in pesetas in Spain for my future and a certain amount
in escudos in Portugal to be able to facilitate my movements
abroad should this become necessary. This sum should be
deposited at an address which you can let me have later on. I
wish to know your situation in order to be able to help you.
If you find yourself in any danger let me know since I have
several plans which might be adapted according to the present
state of your safety in Spain. Do not hesitate in confiding
your difficulties fully in me. I only regret not being at
your side to be able to give you real help..............I
have absolute confidence in spite of the present crisis which
is very hard, that our struggle will not terminate with the
present phase and that we are entering into what is
developing into a world civil war which will result in the
disintergration of our enemies."

Foreseeinq the necessity of getting GARBO to Spain quickly we
amplified his message the following night:-

"Please let me have definite confirmation as to whether (my)
documentation will be forthcoming at the end of this week or
the beginning of the coming week. As if the contrary is the
case I would have to study other possibilities such as the
journey to Cuba or attempting to set out as a seaman using
the documentation of 7(2) for some port on the Spanish coast.
Should it become impossible to get (my) documentation here I
would be grateful if you will let me know what difficulties
are to be anticipated on disembarking as a deserter in a
Spanish port, the subject concerned not being an Englishman

but a Spaniard who has used a documentation stolen from an Englishman, that is to say, the documentation of 7(2). It should also be taken into account that he has a pro-Franco background and fought in the war of Spanish liberation and would be able to produce documents to confirm this, for example his military book. I have learnt to-day that my family left by plane for Spain at the beginning of this week without incident."

The following is a message from GARBO of the 5.5.45:-

"I am astonished that you do not reply to my messages. I repeat the urgency of immediately obtaining an address for the future in order not to completely lose contact. I hope that the abovementioned address will be in my possession before I receive orders to suspend the present transmissions."

Message from Madrid of the 6.5.45:-

"For (GARBO). Grateful for your latest messages and especially your offers of unconditional collaboration. The heroic death of our Fuhrer clearly points the course which must be followed. All future work and efforts, should they be carried out, must be directed exclusively against the danger which is threatened by a coalition with the East. Only a close union of all the sane peoples of Europe and America can counteract this tremendous danger against which all other questions become unimportant. You will understand that in view of the very rapid evolution of the situation during the past week it has become completely impossible for us to be able to tell you now whether we will later on be able to dedicate ourselves to the work, the basis of which is indicated above. Should we do so we hope that we will be able to count on your proven friendship and enormous experience in service matters. We therefore fully approve your plan to return to Spain where, when once you have arrived, the plan for a new organization directed from here can be dealt with. Having suspended all work your side we cannot judge whether Three can be more useful to you where he is or whether you would prefer to give him some other task. The decision is left to you to arrange with him and to take the necessary measures. We consider that the network of Five should be disolved and would ask you to issue the instructions and at the same time to resolve the financial situation for these

friends so far as circumstances permit. From here they will
only receive a message to suspend work and to await news from
you. You will understand that in view of the impossibility
of our definitely working out any details for the future
work so far as we are concerned at the present moment, it
is difficult to suggest a system for you to make possible
contact with a person of our confidence who may later be
selected. In spite of this you will to-morrow receive a
message with details of a method through which you should
periodically attempt to establish contact. We consider
that it would also be advisable that you should let us know
the name of some good friend of yours in Spain through whom
the person of our confidence would be able to find you. Our
person will be called Fernando GOMEZ which is the name of the
sender of the postcard. With regard to funds, there is a
further sum of 50,000 pesetas which has been reserved for you
and we would be pleased if you would let us know if you wish
this amount to be sent to Lugo in the usual way since we have
no possibility of being able to put it aside in any other
safe place. With regard to the escudos this will have to be
dealt with if the hoped for contact is made. The delay of the
documentation is due to our difficulty with contacts. We are
very much upset about this, we hope, nevertheless, to be able
to arrange to remit it. In spite of this it is advisable that
you should study other possible ways of effecting (your
escape) which we imagine will become less difficult due to
the termination of hostilities. For reasons expressed in a
previous message it is difficult for us to be able to give
you details regarding the control of ports and this would
require most careful study on the spot. We consider that in
order to desert as a member of the crew or a stowaway on the
ship (you) would have to avoid passing through any control
and to escape the authorities. As it not (you) would be
detained until (you) were able to prove (your) identity and
this would probably create a difficulty for reasons which you
yourself have suggested. Please ask Almura to listen for us
to-morrow when we will send you the abovementioned details.
Cordial regards."

Message from GARBO on the 7.5.45:-

"With regard to funds. You may send them as previously, that
is to say, to Lugo. I am very grateful. I will reply to your
messages to-morrow. I hope you will be listening."

Message from Madrid on the 7.5.45:-

"The details mentioned in yesterday's messages will be sent
to-morrow since for technical reasons it is impossible to
communicate this to-day. Please be listening to-morrow.
Regards."

Message from GARBO on the 8.5.45:-

"With regard to the address of a friend of mine in Spain. It
is altogether impossible to let you have a safe address from
here. It is nearly four years since I have corresponded with
my friends due to my arrival here on a secret mission. Also
it is possible that those people whom I consider could be
used as contacts for our future meeting may have changed
their addresses. I consider that as soon as I am in Spain and
in possession of the address which you should let me have
that I will, once over there, be able to give you an address
from where you will be able to learn my movements. I could
also use your address for making contact verbally or by
letter when I could, at the same time, give you the address
which you have asked for. I understand the present situation
and the lack of guidance due to the unexpected end of the
military struggle. News of the death of our dear Chief shocks
our profound faith in the destiny which awaits our poor
Europe, but his deeds and the story of his sacrifice to save
the world from the danger of anarchy which threatens us will
last for ever in the hearts of all men of goodwill. His
memory, as you say, will guide us on our course and to-day
more than ever I affirm my confidence in my beliefs and I am
certain that the day will arrive in the not too distant
future when the noble struggle will be revived which was
started by him to save us from a period of chaotic barbarism
which is now approaching."

Message from Madrid on the 8.5.45:-

"For (GARBO). To make contact with the person employed in
Madrid we ask you to frequent the Cafe Bar la Moderna, 141,
Calle Alcala, every Monday between 20 hours and 20.30 hours,
starting on June 4th. You should be seated at the end of the
Cafe and be carrying the newspaper "London News." A person
will meet you there one Monday who will say that he has come
on behalf of Fernando GOMEZ. For security reasons this person
has no knowledge whatever about this affair and we therefore

ask you not to put any questions to him but you may hand him a letter for Don FERNANDO with your address. If you do not receive any further advice you should carry on with this procedure. We repeat that we cannot be certain whether we will really manage to reorganize the service directed against the East later on, nor do we know what is likely to be the eventual date on which the person employed will make contact with you in Madrid."

CHAPTER XXVIII.

GARBO'S ESCAPE FROM ENGLAND VIA
CUBA AND VENEZUELA TO SPAIN.
GARBO'S POST WAR REUNION WITH FEDERICO KNAPPE
AND CARLOS KUHLENTHAL IN SPAIN.

After the cessation of hostilities with Germany every effort was
made to hasten GARBO's arrival in Madrid. We then envisaged that
steps would be taken by the Allied authorities to force the hand of
the Spanish Government to deport those Germans who had operated
in Spain against this country, and we were then mistakenly under
the impression that it was a race against time to get GARBO to
Spain before his contacts there would have been forced to leave.

The war now over, we had to give first consideration to
GARBO's personal security if we were to ask him to engage in any
further activities of investigation on our behalf. He quite rightly
felt that it would be unsafe for him to circulate in Spain unless
with valid Spanish documentation. This meant that he would have to
enter Spain legally in his own name with his own passport. On the
other hand it was essential that there should be nothing in Spanish
police records to prove that he had come from England, for there was
the risk that the Germans were still maintaining their liaison with
the Spanish Security authorities. From the German point of view
it was essential that they should believe GARBO had left England
clandestinely since he was supposed to be a wanted man here. On the
other hand it was not advisable that the Spaniards should gain this
impression of GARBO. In other words the passport on which GARBO left
England, which necessarily would have to bear the British Exit
Permit stamp, could not be used by GARBO to enter Spain. This
presented enormous difficulties. Strange as it may seem we now
embarked on what transpired to be perhaps the most complicated and
difficult problem of the entire GARBO case.

To state the facts briefly the matter was resolved in the
following way.

GARBO in fact travelled by air to the U.S.A. where he applied
to the various Latin and South American countries for visas to visit
their countries. He passed as a student of art who had been at the
London University, who was now proceeding to Latin-American to
study the influence of Spanish architecture on Latin-American
architecture. In collaboration with the Acting Director of the
Courtauld Institute of Art of the University of London we supplied
him with letters of recommendation to each of the Consulates of the
Central and South American States in Washington. These were to serve

him purely as cover to enter the Latin-American countries. Without
adequate cover, or officially facilitated, there would have been
little or no chance for a Spaniard to have obtained a visa to enter
such countries as Cuba, and without official backing he would
certainly not, at the time, have managed to get either a U.S.
Transit Visa or travel facilities.

Before he left the U.K. he obtained, through an introduction
here, a visa for Bolivia which he was to use as a long stop should
the plan which he was to carry out fail to materialize in Cuba or
Venezuela, the two countries where he was first to attempt to put
his plan into operation.

Eventually he succeeded in reaching Cuba on his own passport
having, after considerable difficulty, managed to obtain from the
Cuban Consulate in New York a Cuban Transit Visa. Once there, he
attempted to obtain a permit to take up residence. In possession of
this permit he would have been entitled to apply for a new Spanish
passport, issued in Cuba, so that he would have then been able to
proceed to Spain on a new travel document which would have shown
no signs of his ever having been in England. Thus, he could have
adapted his cover story to the Germans in accordance with the escape
story which he had previously outlined to them; i.e., that he had
been smuggled into Cuba by the captain engaged in illegal tobacco
trafficking.

In fact the Cubans in Habana were not willing to give him a
Resident's Visa and so he proceeded to Venezuela. There the
authorities were more accommodating and they immediately acceded to
his request to take up permanent residence. Once this had been
arranged the manoeuvres to obtain a new Spanish passport issued in
Venezuela were relatively simple.

In possession of this new document GARBO proceeded to Spain
on a Spanish Trans-Atlantic liner, arriving in Barcelona on the
9.8.45 where he was landed by the Spanish authorities without
incident.

Since GARBO had reached Spain from Venezuela his cover story
for the Germans had to be modified and adapted to the original escape
plan which was that he had taken the same escape route as his Agent No.
4. In brief outline his story was that he had worked his passage to
Canada, facilitated by his Agent No. 7. There he had deserted his ship
and made contact with Agent No. 5. This agent, a Venezuelan, had lent
him his documentation on which he had proceeded clandestinely to
Venezuela as if a Venezuelan subject returning home. Once there he had
contacted the Spanish Consulate to whom he had applied for a new
passport, maintaining that he had lost his old one. As evidence that
he had originally possessed a Spanish passport he furnished the
Consul with the particulars of the passport which had been previously

issued to him in London. This the Consul could check by sending a
telegram to London. Through his other Spanish documentation which he
had carried with him, such as his Military Carnet, he was able to
identify himself. The rest of his story substantially conformed to
the truth.

GARBO proceeded forthwith to Madrid where he was met by his
Case Officer who had previously travelled with him to South America
but had returned from there to Madrid via London. A plan of action
was decided upon and GARBO, after unsuccessfully attempting to make
contact at the Cafe in accordance with the rendez-vous given on the
8th May proceeded to Caldas in Cataluña to force a meeting with
Federico KNAPPE.

During the period that GARBO had been travelling in America
we ascertained through Mrs. GARBO that a payment of 35,000 pesetas
had been made to GARBO's banking account in Spain. This payment,
though anonymous, had quite obviously been made by the Germans,
and this in itself was an incentive to continue our investigations.
It indicated that the Germans had been taking an interest in
GARBO at least a month after the cessation of hostilities in
Europe.

The fact that a number of Germans had been put under house
arrest in Caldas was fairly common knowledge throughout Spain;
whereas the fact that KUHLENTHAL had taken refuge in Avila was not
generally known. Furthermore, GARBO could not enquire for
KUHLENTHAL since he had never been given his proper name. GARBO had
always known him under the alias "DON CARLOS."

GARBO, on his arrival there, made enquiries from the local
residents for the address of FEDERICO which he obtained without
difficulty.

On arrival at FEDERICO's house GARBO found that he was out
and so he waited at the door until he returned. FEDERICO appeared to
be very overcome by GARBO's surprise visit and he was very
perturbed. He told GARBO that he could not invite him into his house
since he was not permitted by the Spanish police to have any
visitors at his home without their prior approval. He therefore
suggested that GARBO should follow him to some nearby woods where
they could talk.

FEDERICO explained that he was in a desperate plight and
was living in fear of being forced, through Allied pressure on the
Spanish Government, to be repatriated to Germany. He said that he
had been singled out amongst the hostile Germans in Spain due to the
fact that a protest had been made by the British Government to the
Spanish Ministry of Foreign Affairs following on the BUENAGA
denunciation. He said that he was quite at a loss to understand why
BUENAGA had behaved so treacherously, particularly in view of the

fact that he had hitherto proved himself to be perfectly loyal in his work for the Germans.

FEDERICO admitted that he had completely lost touch with the case during the last few months on account of his expulsion from Madrid, and that this had caused him much regret since he had always taken keen personal interest in GARBO's activities and in particular he had been responsible for arranging the wireless timetables. Up to the time of his expulsion from Madrid he admitted that he had never been absent from their wireless station on any transmitting night. He said that he was no longer in contact with his colleagues, neither was he aware of their plans, and he recommended that GARBO should proceed to Avila where he would find CARLOS at an address which he disclosed to GARBO. He said that it was not his intention to allow himself to be forced to return to Germany, and rather than accept this fate he would go into hiding in Spain.

GARBO warned him of the discomforts of living the life of a fugitive from justice, based on his own experiences. He gave FEDERICO a descriptive account of the mental suffering which he had experienced during his period of hiding in south Wales and told him that had it not been that he had had, through his colleagues, an assurance that he would ultimately escape, the experience, if prolonged without hope, would have become unbearable and driven him insane. FEDERICO asked GARBO whether he could not, with his ingenuity, think out some means of escape for himself and for KUHLENTHAL whom he known had the same intentions of going into hiding. GARBO said he would discuss the matter with KUHLENTHAL and see what he could do.

The meeting lasted little more than an hour for FEDERICO was in a highly nervous state and afraid lest he should be discovered together with GARBO.

From there GARBO proceeded to Avila. He called at the address which had been given him by FEDERICO where he was met by Mrs. KUHLENTHAL who broke the news to her husband of their unexpected visitor. KUHLENTHAL was overcome by emotion when he welcomed GARBO to his sitting room. He told him how he had visualized this reunion and marvelled at GARBO's ability to overcome the apparently impossible obstacles which must have been in his way.

During the conversation which followed, which lasted for more than three hours, KUHLENTHAL made it abundantly clear, not only that he still believed in the genuineness of GARBO but that he looked upon him as a superman.

GARBO briefly outlined the story of his escape from England, his travels in America and his arrival in Spain. He expressed his willingness to continue to operate for them should they have any plans for the future. KUHLENTHAL explained that the Germans in Spain were, through circumstances, bound to accept their national defeat and were forced to abandon their hopes of rendering their country further service. He then went on to give GARBO an account of his life history. He told him how he had been forced to abandon his commercial career in Germany due to the fact that one of his grandparents had been of Jewish origin. He said that he had come to Spain during the Spanish Civil War and that having good connections in that country his services had been used during the European war. He told GARBO that if ever he had opportunity to serve Germany in a similar capacity in the future he would not hesitate to do so. So far as GARBO was concerned he said that he regarded him as a colleague and a brother with whom he would always wish to share whatever good fortune might come his way in the future.

He said how much he regretted not being able to hand GARBO the Iron Cross which he had been awarded. Due to certain reorganizations which had taken place in Berlin the award had not come through. He had done everything possible to try to influence his chiefs in Berlin to deliver the promised decoration. He explained that after the medal had been recommended and approved, and subsequent to the reorganization in Berlin, the question was reviewed and a decision reached that only a German national could be eligible for this particular military decoration. They had therefore proposed that GARBO should, instead, be given the Blue Division medal which KUHLENTHAL had, in GARBO's name, turned down. To force the issue the matter had been taken up by several representatives in Berlin who had finally brought the affair of GARBO's activities to the notice of Hitler.

Shortly before the German collapse Hitler, KUHLENTHAL told GARBO, had personally ordered that the medal should be granted in GARBO's case. Unfortunately the certificate in evidence of this had not reached Madrid prior to the German collapse on account of the difficulty of communications between Germany and Spain during the latter months of the war.

Discussing the GARBO network, KUHLENTHAL made a number of most interesting comments. For instance, he asked GARBO whether Agent No. 3 had tired of them towards the end. He said that he had been compelled to forward repeated questionnaires to check up on the possibility of a further landing being made based on Great Britain during the last phases of the war. In spite of the assurances received from Agent No. 3 that no such preparations existed, Berlin insisted on frequent re-checks. Time proved, KUHLENTHAL pointed out, that Agent No. 3 had been correct in his denial of this possibility. Towards the end KUHLENTHAL felt that Agent No. 3 had, in his messages, expressed himself as if he were

slightly irritated by their questionnaires, but GARBO assured him
that no such feeling had existed.

In their exchange of confidences GARBO asked KUHLENTHAL
whether he had not, at times, considered him a little crazy on
account of the sometimes superfluous contents of his long letters.
KUHLENTHAL replied that on the contrary those letters had in
themselves been evidence to him of GARBO's good faith and honesty.
He said that they had considered his letters to express the normal
psychological reactions of any conscientous person forced to
operate alone, in the most difficult circumstances, in the camp
of the enemy. It was natural that anyone in these circumstances
should have felt an urge to express their personal feelings to the
only parties in whom they could confide and to have an outlet in this
way for discussing with a colleague the many problems with which one
was bound to be faced in organizing and directing a large network
such as GARBO had maintained.

He said that the news of GARBO's arrest whilst investigating
the V bomb incident came as such a shock and was so dramatic that it
created amongst them the feeling of great despondency and grief for
GARBO.

After further praising GARBO for his successes and valuable
work KUHLENTHAL admitted his own personal preoccupation lest he
might be forced by the Allies to return to Germany. He, like
FEDERICO, said he would sooner go into hiding. He asked GARBO
whether he could make any helpful suggestion to save him from
deportation and to help him to escape should he go into hiding in
Spain. GARBO said that this would need consideration but that he had
no doubt he would eventually be able to rescue him should he decide
to take this course.

In the first place GARBO instructed KUHLENTHAL to
communicate his place of concealment to Mrs. GARBO's address at
Lugo. He would then have to remain patiently in his hideout until
GARBO could evolve a plan to facilitate his escape. He told him that
one day he would probably receive a communication or a call from one
of his network and whoever it might be, whether Agent No. 3 or Agent
No. 7, he could be assured that the agent would come with a cleverly
worked out plan drafted by GARBO, and that he should simply obey the
agent's instructions to the letter if he wished to save himself.
This KUHLENTHAL promised to do.

The question of the agents' finances was discussed.
KUHLENTHAL said that towards the end he had stepped up the payments
to GARBO in order to build up a reserve. He asked what GARBO had done
with this reserve, to which he replied that he had distributed it
amongst the network, retaining a small amount for himself. The
agents, he assured KUHLENTHAL, would not suffer hardship since none

of them had come under suspicion and they were all men who could revert to their peacetime occupations and earn a reasonable living. If, and when, their services were required again GARBO had no hesitation in believing that they could be counted on.

GARBO acknowledged the 35,000 pesetas which had recently been made to his bank in Spain and KUHLENTHAL told him that the amount agreed with the German paymaster prior to his flight from Madrid was to have been 70,000. He promised to make enquiries through Madrid to ascertain why the balance of 35,000 pesetas had not been paid and to see that the money reached him.

This payment was subsequently made to Mrs. GARBO in Madrid through an anonymous agent of the Germans who delivered the money in cash.

KUHLENTHAL enquired into GARBO's future plans. GARBO said that with the realization that he could not be of further service to the Germans in Spain he would decide to leave Spain as quickly as possible. He added that he had the feeling that he was being watched for by British agents and that sooner or later he would get caught if he remained on in Spain. He said that he therefore proposed to depart for Portugal and thence he would probably make his way to South America.

The interview terminated when KUHLENTHAL asked him how he proposed to get from Spain to Portugal, to which GARBO replied "clandestinely."

GARBO returned to London by air via Lisbon to report on his meeting with the Germans. This brought his war time engagement for our office to a close.

The problem of his future was a matter which received the attention of this Office and the Case Officer was authorized to assist him as much as possible in obtaining agencies for British firms so that he might be able to return with them to Venezuela where he proposed to take up residence until the Franco regime in Spain had been superseded.

Though, as from the time of his departure from England, his connection with this Office was considered to have terminated GARBO expressed his desire to renew the association at any future date should an occasion ever arise in which his services could be used.

CONCLUSIONS.

On the frailest of evidence, it has frequently been claimed that the enemy's Secret Service, corrupt and dishonest, has been guilty of permitting suspect cases to continue to operate, protecting the doubtful integrity of their agents, in the interests of their own prestige and personal comforts.

All the evidence contained in the present summary proves beyond doubt that this was not the case so far as the GARBO network was concerned. Had there been grounds for suspicion in the minds of GARBO's spy masters, these would soon have been dispelled by the appreciations made by the O.K.W. on the information provided by GARBO.

The Case Officer of a straight agent is bound, once he has reasonably satisfied himself as to the bona fides of his agent, to accept, in the absence of other Intelligence sources, a favourable appreciation of the Service Departments by which the agent's reports are vetted, as conclusive evidence of the genuineness of the source.

If the case of a controlled double agent is handled, in time of war, with infinite care for detail and is assisted by good planning, protected by maximum security, facilitated by the Service Departments, carefully co-ordinated with parallel or similar activities and presented to the opposition with courage, initiative, and imagination, it is, in our opinion, impossible for the opponents to discover that the agent thus operated, is controlled and that they are therefore being deceived.

In considering the GARBO case from its counter-espionage and Security aspects it would seem right to conclude that a deception plan (or a constructive plan for reporting) is as essential to the success of a double agent's work as is a double agent to deception. Similarly, stringent Security measures are as vital to the efficiency of a double agent as is the double agent to Security. Thus, provided with the special channel of double agents, Security is as much a requirement of deception as is a constructive and long term deception policy a requirement of Security.

On the evidence of the present case, if a claim were made by our Operational Intelligence Service that a particular agent had, whilst not under control, facilitated valuable Intelligence and they offered in evidence of their claim, appreciations by our Service Departments in support of the reliability of his work, and those appreciations went so far as to state that the agent's information about the enemy had been proved by them to have been accurate, checkable and of the utmost importance to our war effort we would be entitled to challenge the value of such an appreciation on the grounds that the German Supreme Command had similarly assessed the completely false and deceptive reports which we had passed over the channel of the GARBO network during a period of several years.

We can therefore state from our experience in this case that, given the circumstances set out above, it may be impossible, even after a careful analysis of the traffic in relation to the events, to prove conclusively that an agent had been under control.

Although it cannot be pretended from the evidence in this summary that it would be impossible to operate an agent in carefully controlled enemy territory in time of war, which is to say in territory where the population is mainly hostile, and where the Security Service of the enemy is able to operate efficiently; there are ample grounds to show that the benefits to be gained by so doing are likely to be heavily outweighed by the incalculable damage which can be done by the undetected double agent.

Thus, it can be concluded that the straight long term agent is, in time of war, a potentially dangerous weapon, the effects of which cannot be detected or calculated by the belligerent on whose behalf the penetration is undertaken, just as the controlled double agent is potentially an equally valuable weapon in the hands of the belligerent whom the agent was recruited to penetrate. For example, had the enemy refrained from sending any agents to the U.K. during the period of hostilities, we would have been immeasurably worse off and their own position greatly strengthened.

The contents of this report should therefore be kept a carefully guarded secret, as, were our future enemy ever to discover the experiences which we have gained from this case, they might be induced to refrain from attempting to use long term penetration agents in time of war and thus rob us of one of the weapons which has proved so vital to the success of our operations during World War No. 2.

                                                    T. Harris.

21.11.45

APPENDIX I.

A CHART OF THE NOTIONAL CHARACTERS OF THE GARBO NETWORK.

The following diagram is intended to show the "GARBO NETWORK" as built up by February, 1944, in preparation for the deception role which this source was to plan in connection with OVERLORD.

Later in 1945, after the arrest of "J" @ GARBO the organization continued to operate along the same lines although J(2), J(3), J(4) and J(5) were no longer operative. Furthermore "J" was substituted by Agent No. 3 who was thus promoted from Deputy Chief to Acting Chief of the Organization.

A summary description of each of the notional characters will be found at Appendices Nos. II-XXVIII.

It will be noted that in the story reference is omitted to those members of the organization who did not play a material part in the case.

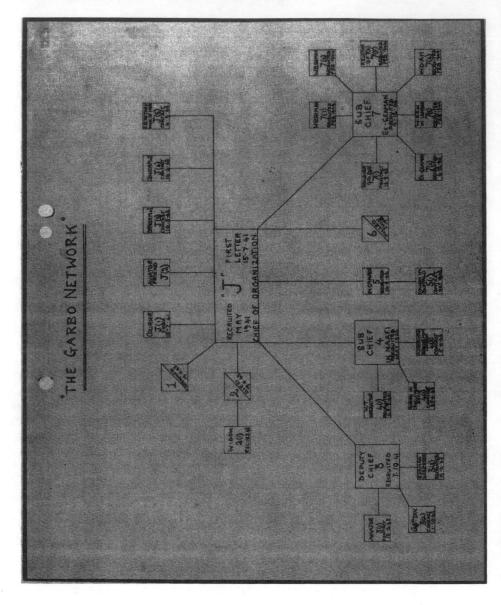

APPENDIX II.

J(1) @ THE COURIER.

NAME: Not mentioned.
NATIONALITY: Presumably British.
OCCUPATION: Employed as an official of one of the airline
                   companies running a service between U.K. and Portugal.
                   (Note:- From the regularity of the service it would
                   appear more likely on analysis that the actual
                   carriers of the letters were members of the K.L.M.
                   rather than B.O.A.C.)
ADDRESS: Not mentioned.
RECRUITED: Prior to 15.7.41.

From the early information about this character, it would have
appeared that he was a rather accommodating individual who, taking
advantage of his position in a Trans-Continental Air Line Company
was prepared to facilitate the sending of correspondence to
Portugal without passing through Censorship, pretending he thought
he could justify his conscience by the knowledge that the writers
were political refugees, whilst increasing his income by so doing.

Though he was never definitely identified with SMITH JONES,
the person who received the incoming correspondence for GARBO (and
presumably the other characters in England whom the courier was
facilitating) the Germans nevertheless frequently referred to him
as "THE COURIER SMITH".

It was not advisable that the Germans should believe that the
courier carried the correspondence to and from Portugal personally
lest they requested that he should be put in contact with them.
Therefore we took pains to impress on them that though he did at one
time make the journey as a member of the planes's crew, he later made
use of various friends of his who were members of the crew to co-
operate in this and other business of smuggling.

It is a fact that the crews of planes became notorious
through the Press for engaging in smuggling and though these
activities were mostly confined to the smuggling of watches
purchased in Portugal for sale in England, it was reasonable that
the Germans should imagine that they engaged in other traffic.

As time went on the courier developed into a very sinister
character who, it became apparent, was trafficking in the sale in
Portugal of Bank of England notes, the proceeds of robberies in the
U.K., which were exchanged in Lisbon for other Bank of England notes
which, when brought into circulation in the U.K., were no longer
traceable to the robberies.

It subsequently became apparent that in order to engage in this very dangerous business the courier made use of a number of rather well placed British subjects in Portugal, one of whom at least was in direct contact with a person either employed by, or used as, an outside agent by S.I.S.

By means which were never disclosed, the courier came to discover that one of the cover addresses to which GARBO had been writing in Lisbon was a German cover address which had become the subject of investigations by the British in Lisbon.

With this valuable information in his possession, and realizing that GARBO was therefore a German agent and not a refugee, he decided to blackmail him. We informed the Germans of this situation. They reacted to it as if it had been news of good fortune rather than bad and promptly authorized GARBO to pay the courier the sum of £2,000 which he was demanding for his silence, pointing out to GARBO that when once he had accepted this blackmail money he would be entirely in GARBO's power.

Though the courier could never be induced to supply the Germans with military information against this country he did, in the interests of his self-protection, produce valuable counter-espionage information for GARBO which enabled him to escape the vigilance of the British Security Service when, towards the last stages of the case, the Germans were made to realize that the British had become aware of his activities and identity.

APPENDIX III.

J(2) @ GARBO'S AVIATOR FRIEND.

NAME: Not mentioned.
NATIONALITY: British.
OCCUPATION: Officer in the R.A.F.
ADDRESS: British Overseas Club, London, and Bentley Priory,
                   Headquarters of Fighter Command.
RECRUITED: Operated as an unconscious informant from 12.4.42.

The first piece of genuine information supplied by GARBO after his
arrival in the U.K. which was a report on the rocket batteries in
Hyde Park was attributed to this contact. He was quoted as a source
at infrequent intervals throughout the case and was primarily
instrumental in serving as a build up for GARBO.

APPENDIX IV.

J(3) @ GARBO'S FRIEND AT THE MINISTRY OF INFORMATION.

NAME: Not mentioned. (By a careful examination of the traffic and check on the movements of W.B. McCANN, Head of the Spanish Section of the Ministry of Information, whilst in Spain, the Germans would have been bound to draw the conclusion that J(3) and McCANN were identical.)

NATIONALITY: British

OCCUPATION: A high ranking official in the Spanish Department of the Ministry of Information.

ADDRESS: Not mentioned. (Address in Madrid given as Palace Hotel.)

RECRUITED: Was first mentioned as being in contact with GARBO on the 16.5.42.

This character has certainly been the most important of all GARBO's contacts. He was represented as having been increasingly indiscreet as his confidence and liking for GARBO grew. GARBO firstly worked as a part-time employee in the Ministry on J(3)'s recommendation and a great deal of important deception material which was passed over shortly after D Day was attributed to this source. McCANN was told in confidence about GARBO's activities and informed that one of the notional characters in the GARBO case had been built up around him.

APPENDIX V.

J(4) @ CENSOR AT THE
MINISTRY OF INFORMATION.

NAME: Not mentioned.
NATIONALITY: British.
OCCUPATION: Employed at the Ministry of Information.
ADDRESS: Not mentioned.
RECRUITED: Was first mentioned as a contact of GARBO on the
                    10.4.43.

This character was created primarily with the object of building him up as a source for deception material.

It was planned that this source should eventually provide GARBO with "STOP" and "RELEASE" notices issued to Press Censors. Thus, by indicating a complete Press "STOP" on all mention of a certain area the enemy would be expected to deduce that the area indicated was likely to be a target area for operations.

To implement this plan the Germans were told that the Censor had introduced himself to GARBO in the Ministry, and after they had become acquainted, he disclosed to GARBO that he was extremely Left Wing and had been passing certain secret information to the British Communist Party. It happened that at this time the Press had raised the question of certain secret information having been passed to Mr. Shinwell by someone, unidentified, imployed by the Ministry of Information, and questions were raised in the House. The Censor, therefore, assumed the role of the source of these leakages to Shinwell and told GARBO that he was now lying low since the question had been given so much publicity. He offered to assist the Spanish "Reds" in a similar capacity if GARBO would act as his cut out.

Although the character was built up on these lines it was not found necessary to use him in any serious role to implement the cover story for OVERLORD so that after March, 1944, the Censor was allowed to fade out of the picture.

APPENDIX VI.

J(5) @ THE SECRETARY
AT THE MINISTRY OF WAR.

NAME: Not mentioned
NATIONALITY: British
OCCUPATION: Secretary in the Secretariat of the "Ministry of
                  War." A more precise definition of the nature of her
                  work was never given.
ADDRESS: Not given.
RECRUITED: This contact was first referred to on the 4.9.43.

This character was mainly created as build up for GARBO and it was proposed that she should have played an important role in the final deception story. We built her up by passing over rather high grade general information attributed to her indiscretions.

Domestically, she was represented as having falled in love with GARBO.

GARBO was authorized by the Germans to spend money on her as lavishly as he wished in the hope that he could extract more valuable information from her. She supplied GARBO with information about the Moscow Conference in 1943, attributing the source of her information to a colleague who had attended the Conference as secretary to the Chief of the British Military Mission.

She was given as the source for a certain amount of high grade chicken food about the movements of important British Service Chiefs. She was used to implement PLAN BODYGUARD.

In the spring of 1944 the Germans were very much on edge and apprehensive as to the possibility of an imminent attack and J(5) was used until early May to reassure them that there was no possibility of an immediate invasion. Although at that date this information should have served her as a good build up, it did not in fact do so as the Germans, in reply, warned GARBO that he should not place too much confidence in her word as it was common practice in Government offices to mislead the subordinate personnel lest they should, through knowledge of the true facts, cause a leakage through indiscretion.

She was, however, used again immediately after D Day to support the build up of the notional FUSAG by confirming that there were 75 Divisions in the U.K. prior to the Normandy landing, whereas there were in fact less than 50.

This character was then allowed to fade out of the scene on the assumption that GARBO did not think it prudent to continue to forward her information in view of the warning which he received from the Germans.

APPENDIX VII.

AGENT NO. 1.

NAME: CARVALHO.
NATIONALITY: Portuguese.
OCCUPATION: Commercial traveller.
ADDRESS: Newport, Mon.
RECRUITED: Prior to 17.8.41.

This character was the first to be created by GARBO whilst he was still in Portugal. Though he lived in Newport the majority of his reports were on the counties of Devon and Cornwall. He was allowed to remain, throughout his career, a rather colourless individual who worked regularly but without great zeal, presumably picking up information, mostly about airfields and military camps, which he came by in the course of his commercial travels.

He was eventually given secret ink and a cover address in Lisbon to which he corresponded direct, receiving his questionnaires and replies through GARBO. The writing was done by a member of this Office.

In view of the fact that there was no one in the Office to whom we could delegate the work of writing who had fluent Portuguese it was decided to make him write in French. The Germans were given the excuse that although a Portuguese, he had fluent French. Since there were a lot of Belgians and Frenchmen in the area where he was living we said that to write in French would serve him as perfect cover should one of his letters be detected by the British Censor, since they would undoubtedly look for the author amongst these nationals, and be unlikely to suspect a Portuguese.

It was decided to give this agent an opportunity to go to Northern Ireland with commercial cover in place of another agent who it had originally been intended to send there. He was one of the principal sources used in support of Operation STARKEY, during which period he covered the area of Southampton.

We realized that though he was required on that operation his presence in south west England would be undesirable during Operation OVERLORD as he would see too much in this part of England. It was, therefore, decided to have one of his letters supposedly discovered in Censorship during the time of Operation STARKEY with the result that several Belgians were detained in the Southampton area and all non residents including the agent, ordered to leave.

Though the agent himself was not discovered the incident greatly shook his confidence and when GARBO accordingly came to realize that his morale was seriously shaken he decided a few months later to pay him off and allow him to resign from the service.

APPENDIX VIII.

AGENT NO. 2

NAME: William Maximilian GERBERS
NATIONALITY: British (of German-Swiss descent.)
OCCUPATION: Not mentioned.
ADDRESS: Bootle, Liverpool.
RECRUITED: Prior to 17.8.41.

This agent, one of GARBO's creations during the period he was working in Lisbon was perhaps one of the most colourful characters of the organization, though he came to an untimely end. Not only was he responsible for the Malta convoy report but for numerous other Naval reports of rather high grade which were forwarded after GARBO's arrival in the U.K. He worked well until the preparations for Operation TORCH had commenced, when it was realized by the Admiralty that his presence in Liverpool was most undesirable. The agent was therefore reported as having fallen ill and about to have an operation for what appeared to be cancer. Three months went by during which time the agent was paid, though due to his illness he was unable to contribute any information.

On visiting Liverpool during November, 1942, GARBO discovered that the agent had died on the 19.11.42 and an obituary notice, which was inserted at our request in the Liverpool Daily Post, was forwarded to the Germans in evidence.

APPENDIX IX.

AGENT NO. 2(1) @ THE WIDOW.

NAME: Mrs. William Maximilian GERBERS.
NATIONALITY: British
OCCUPATION: Housewife
ADDRESS: Bootle, Liverpool.
RECRUITED: Prior to the 10.4.43.

Following on the death of her husband Agent No. 2 she found herself in a very difficult financial situation and stated her willingness to do anything to help GARBO in return for employment. GARBO, realizing that she was not well suited to engage in espionage decided, nevertheless, not to abandon the loyal wife of an ex-collaborator and that it would be wise to employ her to look after his household, as, by having a woman of complete confidence about the house, there would be less danger of his activities being discovered. One or two low grade reports were sent over as attributed to her, but they were so bad that GARBO decided to suppress any further reports she might submit to him.

She did, however, serve a very useful role in the organization. When the volume of wireless traffic became great she assisted GARBO with the encyphering of messages, and later she was used as a cut out for contact between the agents, and finally as a contact between GARBO and Mrs. GARBO, and GARBO and Agent No. 3, and between Agent No. 3 and the operator after GARBO had gone into hiding.

APPENDIX X.

AGENT NO. 3.

NAME: Not mentioned. (His letters to the Germans were
                    signed PEDRO.)
NATIONALITY: Venezuelan.
OCCUPATION: Of independent means.
ADDRESS: Glasgow.
RECRUITED: Prior to the 7.10.41.

This was the third and last of the agents recruited by GARBO whilst
he was operating in Lisbon. He was represented as having been
educated in the University of Glasgow and was still in the U.K. at
the outbreak of war. Though his exact means of livelihood were never
disclosed, the impression was given that he was a man of means,
whose family had properties in Venezuela, one near Comuna and
another in Caracas.

From the outset GARBO showed a preference for this agent and,
being the oldest survivor of the network, after disposing of Agents
Nos. 1 and 2 it was natural that he should have finally gained the
rank of Deputy Chief of the GARBO network.

He was the first to be given secret ink to write direct to the
Germans who furnished him with a cover address in Lisbon for this
purpose. The letters were written in this Office. They were written
in English, a language which the Germans were told he knew as well as
his native Spanish, if not better, since he had been absent from
Venezuela for many years. His traffic was, on the whole, higher
grade than that of any other agent during the first two years of the
history of the network.

After GARBO's first arrest in 1944 the entire organization
was directed by this agent and the Germans came to regard him as an
able substitute for the Chief of the organization. The purpose of
handing over the organization to this agent, and removing the
control from GARBO, was primarily with a view to being able to
run the organization entirely through this Office without the
personality of GARBO entering into it, and this was achieved. Thus,
during the last months of the running of the case, this Office was
in direct communication with the German Intelligence Service,
utilizing only officers of this Department to communicate in
English on a wireless transmitting set which was installed within
our Office building.

APPENDIX XI.

3(1) @ THE N.C.O. IN THE R.A.F.

NAME: Not mentioned.
NATIONALITY: British.
OCCUPATION: N.C.O. in the R.A.F.
ADDRESS: Glasgow.
RECRUITED: First mentioned as a contact of Agent No. 3 on 23.2.43.

This man was represented as drunkard and a gambler with whom Agent No. 3 made contact, believing him to have been capable of parting with confidential information for a monetary consideration.

We did acquire through this Source an aircraft recognition manual which helped considerably in building up the case. We also used this character as a means of demonstrating to the Germans the complete integrity of GARBO and his Agent No. 3. When the opportunity first arose to acquire this book GARBO decided that he should consult the Germans before parting with cash and ascertain from them the approximate sum which this information might be worth. He was authorized to pay up to £100 for it. However, when it came to discussing the price with 3(1), Agent No. 3 discovered that this man, contrary to his expectations, was very small minded so far as financial matters were concerned, and thus he succeeded in getting the book for the small sum of £3.

Through this incident the Germans were able to appreciate that GARBO and his Agent No. 3 were honest to the extent that though they had been authorized to pay £100 for the book they did not take advantage of the fact that they were able to purchase it for so small a sum as £3 with which the Germans were charged.

This character was allowed to fade out of the picture in September, 1944.

APPENDIX XII.

3 (2) @ THE LIEUTENANT IN THE 49TH DIVISION.

NAME:	Not mentioned.
NATIONALITY:	British.
OCCUPATION:	Lieutenant in the 49th British Infantry Division.
ADDRESS:	Not mentioned.
RECRUITED:	First mentioned as being in contact with Agent No. 3 on the 1.10.43.

Agent No. 3 made contact with this rather talkative Lieutenant on a train journey from Glasgow to London. In the first place the contact was used to confirm and explain certain reports which Agent No. 3 had made on his own observations in the Troon area where a Brigade of the 49th Division was represented as undergoing assault training.

In support of TINDALL I we implied, through this source, that the 49th Division which had been trained in mountain warfare would be an assault Division in an attack against Norway. Thus, when the preparations for Operation TORCH were well advanced this contact was reported as returning to Scotland to join his Division. A great number of troops employed in the TORCH Operation did in fact leave from the Clyde and when it was later ascertained that the 49th Division had not embarked we were able to maintain the threat to Norway instead of, perhaps, exposing it as a cover plan for the TORCH Operation.

This source played a very small role henceforth. He was active as late as September, 1944, when, after the 49th Division had entered operations in France, and been identified by the Germans, we had an occasion to make contact with him again through Agent No. 3 when, this officer, now promoted in rank, told the agent of all his adventures overseas, and the routing of his Division through France. This was passed back to the Germans, who, having taken prisoners, were in a position to prove the accuracy of the information.

APPENDIX XIII.

AGENT NO. 3(3)

NAME: Not mentioned.
NATIONALITY: Greek.
OCCUPATION: Seaman.
ADDRESS: Glasgow.
RECRUITED: Prior to the 19.12.43.

When building up the network to implement FORTITUDE (NORTH) and
FORTITUDE (SOUTH), though these cover plans for Operation OVERLORD
had not then been developed in detail, it was realized that at least
two GARBO agents would have to operate in Scotland, one on the west
coast, the other on the east coast.

Agent No. 5, who had at one time worked with Agent No. 3 in
Scotland, had left for Canada a few months earlier in order to build
up a sub-organization for GARBO there. Therefore this new character
was created to substitute Agent No. 5.

He was a Greek merchant seaman who had been working in the
s.s. BRISTOL CITY at the time she was torpedoed by the Germans in
May, 1941. This experience caused him to decide to desert from the
Merchant Navy, and prior to his recruitment as our agent he had, for
nearly two years, been living on his wits and on small sums of money
which he would occasionally borrow from his friends, amongst whom
was our Agent No. 3.

The problem of recruiting him, however, was a difficult one,
since he was a man of strong Communist sympathies. Apart from this
he was ideally suited. Therefore it was decided to recruit him by
deceptive means. Agent No. 3 approached him as if he himself, were a
secret agent of the Russians, and stated that as the Russians were
unable to get information from the Anglo-Americans, about the
Second Front, they had found it necessary, in the interests of their
own operations, to try to discover as much as possible about British
plans by secret means. He was promised good pay and at the same time
given the assurance that he would be assisting the Inter-Allied
cause. After accepting, he was warned that any indiscretion might
lead to complications between the British and the Russian
Governments, and that if he were indiscreet the Russians would have
no hesitation in liquidating him.

During the first few months of his activities he stayed close
to Agent No. 3. They made joint reports. Thus, we were able to cut
down the volume of information passed over until we were due to
implement FORTITUDE (NORTH). They parted company and 3(3) was moved
over to the east coast of Scotland.

His usefulness to us came to an end shortly after D Day and so we allowed the standard of his reporting to deteriorate until, in November 1944, when he asked Agent No. 3 if he might be allowed to resign. GARBO had already commented on the very poor grade of his reports by this time and expressed a desire to be rid of him. It was, therefore, much to GARBO's relief that the suggestion to resign came from the agent.

Greece had by then been liberated, and the agent decided that he wanted to return to his native land, even if to do so meant handing himself over to the British authorities as a deserter and paying the penalty for this. After being further threatened by Agent No. 3 as to the consequences if he were indiscreet about his work for the "Russians" he was told that he might carry out his plan, and he was given the sum of £100 as a final pay off.

His punishment for desertion was a fine and a few weeks imprisonment after which he was given employment on a coaster prior to signing on a ship going to the Mediterranean where he again proposed to desert on touching at the first port of call of his native country.

APPENDIX XIV.

AGENT NO. 4.

NAME: Alias, FRED.
NATIONALITY: Gibraltarian.
OCCUPATION: Waiter.
ADDRESS: Soho. Later, Whitelands Hotel, (Gibraltarian Centre)
                   Putney. Until burnt out by enemy action.
RECRUITED: Prior to 27.5.42.

On the 27.5.42 GARBO reported that after having cultivated this man for a long time and having satisfied himself as to his loyalty, he had decided to recruit him as an agent.

The primary objective in this recruitment was to ascertain from the Germans the area of England which they were most interested to cover. It was also taken into consideration that the Germans had instructed GARBO to build up a network, and as seven months had passed since he had last recruited an agent personally it was considered that a new recruitment was in fact overdue.

After operating for three months on the east coast Agent No. 4 presented GARBO with the opportunity of acquiring a wireless transmitter which he had discovered was for sale in the Black Market in Soho. GARBO used the agent as a cut-out for making the purchases of the radios as well as for recruiting the operator.

In December, 1942, GARBO decided that this agent might most usefully be employed in a West End London hotel where he would be likely to pick up gossip. With these plans in mind the agent went to the Ministry of Labour where, to his great disappointment, and in spite of his qualifications as a waiter, he was directed to take work in a quarry, on the assumption that all Gibraltarians ought naturally to be good at tunnelling. He was directed to take employment with Highways Construction on work which he at first believed would be connected with the construction of underground factories. In fact he was sent to work in the Chislehurst Caves where vast tunnelling operations had commenced to convert the caves into a huge arms depot. It was later to be discovered that the caves were connected to the London Underground railway system by a miniature electric railway and thus the depot was enabled to supply ammunition to the various airfields defending London.

Agent No. 4, through his friends in the hotel business, provided GARBO with an assortment of writing paper with the headings of the leading West End hotels which provided excellent camouflage for those of GARBO's secret letters which were sent by air mail.

He also served as contact with the wireless operator and from March, 1943, he himself practiced under the supervision of the operator so that he might later be qualified to substitute the regular operator in the event of his ever falling ill.

Reports on the development of the underground occupied a great bulk of the GARBO traffic between January and September of 1943. By this time we were beginning to feel that the German reactions to the story about the Chislehurst Caves were none too good and it appeared a little dangerous to push this story further with the knowledge that we might have to maintain it for another year if we were to be able to make use of it for deception purposes in connection with the Second Front. It was, therefore, decided to remove the agent from his employment in the caves. This was done by his making friends with someone in the canteen there through whom he eventually obtained employment in the N.A.A.F.I. This gave him greater freedom of movement for a while, and more time to spend in his haunts in Soho. For several months he was posted by the N.A.A.F.I. from one place to another from where he sent in military reports until April, 1944, by when the role he was to play in the implementation of FORTITUDE (SOUTH) had been settled. He was then requested by the N.A.A.F.I. to sign a Military Security Certificate so that he might be posted to one of their canteens within a sealed area. Thus, he was situated in one of the most important concentration areas in the Southampton district. There he was allowed to collect very important information until he finally discovered the secret of D Day which, by breaking camp, he managed to get to GARBO, who transmitted it to the enemy just too late for it to be of any use to them.

Having deserted from a sealed area at such a time the agent was inevitably in danger, but he managed to escape arrest by taking refuge in a safe hideout in the south of Wales which was provided for him by another member of the organization.

Later, having furnished himself with false seaman's papers, he managed to sign on as a steward on a ship which he deserted on its arrival in Canada. There he was protected by Agent No. 5 who was already well established in Montreal.

By this time Agent No. 4 had become proficient as a wireless operator and he was therefore given charge of the wireless station for the Canadian network which had meanwhile been developed.

APPENDIX XV.

4(1) @ THE OPERATOR

NAME: Not mentioned.
NATIONALITY: British.
OCCUPATION: A wireless mechanic employed by the EKCO factory.
ADDRESS: London.
RECRUITED: Prior to the 28.8.42.

It was through 4(1) that Agent No. 4 heard of the transmitting
apparatus which was for sale. Being himself of strong Left Wing
sympathies he quickly jumped at the proposition put to him by Agent
No. 4 to work secretly for what he believed to be the Spanish
Republican exiles in this country, and thus facilitate them
to be able to maintain rapid and clandestine contact with their
underground movement in Spain. He was to be well paid with a minimum
salary of £6 per week even when he did not transmit. During the long
period over which he was operating he was never given grounds to
suspect that he was working other than for the Spanish refugees, in
spite of the fact that there was always a marked activity in the work
at the time of every operation. The reason for the burst of activity
was explained to him by GARBO who made it appear as though it was
always the hope of the Spanish refugees to bring the underground
movement to revolt to coincide with an Allied success. Though the
story was not very convincing the operator never appeared to be
inquisitive. During the periods of great activity he would earn
upwards of £100 a month, and it became more and more apparent that he
was working for this liberal award rather than for any true desire
to help the unfortunate Spanish refugees. The messages were always
handed to him encyphered and he was never aware of their contents.
He was responsible for building the set which was later used by
Agent No.5's network in Canada. He was told that it was to be used by
the Spaniards in Mexico who also wished to establish wireless
contact with London and Madrid.
        Another inducement for him to work with enthusiasm was the
fact that all the equipment which had been paid for by GARBO was
promised to him as a gift on the termination of his services.
        To avoid arousing the suspicions of the operator when, after
VE Day, communications with Spain suddenly broke down, he was told
that the Spanish underground movement, stimulated by the total defeat
of the Germans, had come out into the open too soon with the result
that their leaders and their wireless station had been discovered by
the Falangist Police, thus bringing their activities to an end.

APPENDIX XVI.

4(2) @ THE GUARD IN THE CHISLEHURST CAVES.

NAME:	Not mentioned.
NATIONALITY:	British.
OCCUPATION:	Guard in the Chislehurst Caves.
ADDRESS:	Not mentioned.
RECRUITED:	First reported as a contact of Agent No. 4 on the 25.4.43.

The guard in the Chislehurst Caves was responsible for prohibiting the entrance of all unauthorized persons into the depots of the caves. Thus, he served as a source of information for Agent No. 4 about the activities within the caves, without putting Agent No. 4 in the position of having to give too much first hand information which might have been the case had he been allowed access to all the underground workings. The information about the caves was intentionally always kept rather vague in the absence of a concrete plan, and thus this contact served a useful purpose.

After Agent No. 4 left his employment at Chislehurst, contact with the guard was not maintained regularly, and in September, 1944, GARBO informed the Germans that they could consider this contact as no longer operative.

APPENDIX XVII.

4(3) @ THE AMERICAN N.C.O. IN SERVICE OF SUPPLIES.

NAME: Not mentioned.
NATIONALITY: U.S. Citizen.
OCCUPATION: U.S. Army Service of Supply.
ADDRESS: COMZ Headquarters, London.
RECRUITED: First reported as a contact of Agent No. 4 on 5.11.43.

This character was created purely to assist in reporting on U.S. formations in the U.K. in connection with the deception plan.

He was first represented as having met Agent No. 4 (the Gibraltarian) in Soho, and believing him to be a Spaniard he got into conversation with him about the Spanish Civil War, showing that his sympathies had been with Franco. He took advantage of the friendship which thus sprung up to practice Spanish with Agent No. 4. He showed himself to be extremely anti-British and a great boaster who took delight in demonstrating how well he was informed about the formation of the U.S. Army and their operational plans.

In December, 1943, he had occasion, in conversation with Agent No. 4, to mention the return of landing craft from the Mediterranean theatre of war. This information was based on a Most Secret Source message on information received through German observers operating at Algeciras. The information was accurate but there was no harm in it being repeated through GARBO channels since it was already out of date and known to the Germans. In passing on this information, GARBO suggested that they should check with Berlin to ascertain whether it was accurate or not and let him know, as, on their reply, he would be able to estimate the potential future usefulness of this new collaborator. The Germans, as was anticipated, replied that the information was entirely accurate, and that the contact should therefore be developed. This gave him a very good start. From then on he reported mostly on the build up of American forces in the U.K. in accordance with the cover plan for OVERLORD.

Nearly all the material relating to the formation of the First U.S. Army Group (FUSAG) was attributed to this agent, and he was given as the source when reporting on the outcome of most secret disputes which we alleged were taking place between Eisenhower, Montgomery, Patton and Bradley; all of which had it been true would not have been likely to have been known to a person of this calibre. The Germans, however, never hesitated for a moment in believing it all.

This source was of especial importance in implementing the deception plan during the post D Day period and his services were maintained until the cessation of hostilities.

APPENDIX XVIII.

AGENT NO. 5
(THE BROTHER OF AGENT 3.)

NAME: Not mentioned.
NATIONALITY: Venezuelan.
OCCUPATION: Of independent means. Later employed as a commercial
                   traveller in Toronto.
ADDRESS: Glasgow and, later, Toronto.
RECRUITED: Prior to 14.6.42.

He was first mentioned by GARBO during the period when GARBO was
working in Lisbon. He was brought on to the scene in connection with
a provocation by GARBO to ascertain whether the Germans were
refuelling their submarines in the Caribbean. He then offered the
services of this individual to set up a refuelling base near his
parents' property in Venezuela. The offer was turned down. He was
later used as bait to draw the Germans to disclose whether they were
interested to have an agent in Northern Ireland. Finally he was
recruited in June, 1942, as an active member of the GARBO network.

       At that time the Germans were very interested in the Isle of
Wight. It would, in fact, have been difficult, if not impossible, to
have got an agent in there but we decided to satisfy their request to
send Agent No. 5 to investigate activities there. To make it appear
plausible that he should have been able to enter the Island, we
depicted this agent as an adventurous young man prepared to take any
risks for his masters. We set out in great detail the story of his
adventurous clandestine entry to the Island and the perilous
experiences he had there.

       Though the story told was similar to that which one might
read in any spy novel the Germans liked it, believed it to be true,
and thus he rose in their estimation.

       Having completed this dangerous mission, and toured the
south coast of England and Wales the agent, a restless character,
decided that he wanted a change.

       With the help of Agent No. 7 he eventually smuggled himself
out of England to Canada, having received instructions from GARBO to
endeavour to set up a sub-organization there. This he successfully
did, and, by August 1943, he was already communicating in secret
writing to a cover address in Lisbon provided by the Germans for
this purpose. To avoid Censorship the letters were sent from Canada
to a cover address in Scotland provided by Agent No. 3 on the
assumption that there was no testing for secret writing in

correspondence between these two countries. The letters were then handed by Agent No. 3 to GARBO who forwarded them to Lisbon by his courier service. After the arrival of Agent No. 4 a wireless station was established in Montreal. Communications from Montreal by wireless to Madrid were started up in February, 1945. Though trials were made to establish contact between Montreal and London the results were never successful.

In addition to Agent No. 5's correspondence with the Germans, all organizational matters were dealt with in direct correspondence between GARBO and the agent. GARBO would send a monthly report summarizing their correspondence, and occasionally extracts of the original letters received from him by GARBO would be forwarded to the Germans to add colour.

The ink used by the agent for his correspondence with the Germans was [...] ink, for which GARBO did not have the developer. Therefore, the long process of forwarding the letters to Lisbon, instead of developing them here and transmitting their contents by wireless, was necessary. GARBO was, of course, in possession of the developer for the inferior ink used for the service intercommunications in which Agent No. 5 used to correspond with him.

APPENDIX XIX.

AGENT NO. 5(1)
(THE COUSIN OF AGENT NO. 5.)

NAME: @ CON.
NATIONALITY: Not mentioned.
OCCUPATION: Commercial traveller.
ADDRESS: Buffalo, U.S.A.
RECRUITED: Prior to 5.1.45.

Shortly after the arrival of Agent No. 5 in Montreal he met his cousin who, though residing in Buffalo, used to travel frequently to Canada.

In the first place Agent No. 5 used to extract information from him, and in January, 1945, he got his cousin to hand him, periodically, espionage reports, knowing that the information he was supplying would be passed to the Germans. These reports, which were very extensive, were forwarded via GARBO to the Germans where they were well received, and in spite of the mass of detail and unimportant information which they contained (much of which had already appeared in the Press in a different form) it was nevertheless seen to pass from Madrid to Berlin on M.S.S. in its entirety.

It was envisaged at the time of recruiting this agent, to increase the network of Agent No. 5, that the Canadian organization might have continued to operate against the Japanese after the collapse of Germany. The sudden German collapse made this impossible.

APPENDIX XX.

AGENT NO. 6.

NAME: DICK
NATIONALITY: South African.
OCCUPATION: Independent means. He had contacts in the Ministry of Information and other Government Departments.
ADDRESS: London and, later, Algeirs.
RECRUITED: Prior to the 10.8.42.

Agent No. 6 was violently anti-Communist and worked for the Germans for ideological reasons. GARBO had promised him an important post in the New World Order after the war. This agent was the person responsible for introducing GARBO to J(3). He was a first-class linguist, intelligent and capable. From the time of his recruitment the Germans were told that he did not like living in England and proposed to take advantage of the first available opportunity to get abroad. He had been GARBO's intermediary in PLAN DREAM, and before he left the U.K. he made the necessary arrangements for GARBO to be able to continue to carry out these final transactions through a friend of his who performed in his role.

In October, 1942, GARBO wrote to say that he was studying a plan of the greatest importance for this agent. It later materialized, for Agent No. 6 managed to get himself recruited to go to North Africa a few days prior to OPERATION TORCH. He was taken on by the War Office on the strength of his linguistic abilities.

When his recruitment and departure from the U.K. materialized very rapidly and unexpectedly, there was just time for GARBO to instruct him in secret writing and supply him with the necessary inks so that he was able to maintain contact with GARBO through a cover address in London, and send him military and naval reports as soon as he was established in the Mediterranean.

GARBO, who had no developer for the ink which he had supplied for these communications, had to forward the original letters to one of his cover addresses in Lisbon, and thus the Germans had the satisfaction of handling material which, to all appearances, had passed through the Censorship of Algiers.

Though there was frequently a delay of up to six weeks between the date of the letter and the time of its arrival in German hands, they were nevertheless delighted with their new agent. During the period of his build up it was possible to pass the Germans very accurate information which served them no useful purpose as it was already very out of date by the time it reached them.

An attempt was made to get the Germans to send GARBO the developer for [...] ink which he was using so that the contents could be transmitted to them by wireless from London. This was not forthcoming, probably due to the fact that the development of [...] is somewhat complicated and they were afraid that GARBO might have been unable to develop the letters successfully.

When the case of this agent had started to develop well, a real misfortune occurred. The person in this Office who had been acting as scribe for this notional agent, met with an air crash whilst returning from leave in Scotland and was killed. It was considered inadvisable to take the risk of imitating his handwriting and so it was decided that the case would have to be brought to an untimely end.

GARBO reported that the agent had been killed in an accident in Algiers, having learnt the news from the agent's mistress in London. Through her GARBO was also able to discover that none of his espionage material had been discovered after his death. Thus, there was no risk of any developments as a result of this incident which might reflect on the security of GARBO or the rest of his organization.

APPENDIX XXI.

AGENT NO. 7.

NAME: @ STANLEY
NATIONALITY: Welsh
OCCUPATION: Seaman
ADDRESS: Swansea.
RECRUITED: Prior to the 24.12.42.

During the period when we were first considering breaking down the airman courier system of communication, the alternative of using a seaman courier was considered. It was envisaged that a seaman courier in the organization would permit bulkier objects to be sent out than would be possible by air.

Another consideration at the time was that after Agent No. 6 had left for North Africa, his letters, which would bear the Field Censor's stamp of North Africa could not very well be sent on by the airman courier without arousing his suspicion. Therefore Agent No. 7, a seaman, was recruited and it was to transpire that he would have numerous friends in the Merchant Navy who, for a monetary payment, would be prepared to do a little smuggling of correspondence and parcels at his request. He was introduced to the GARBO network by Agent No. 4 who guaranteed his loyalty. From the very beginning GARBO pointed out that no one could be better placed to assist the work of his organization than a member of the Merchant Navy. He then prophesied that this agent would facilitate the growth of the network. His prophecy was fulfilled a year later.

The recruitment of a seaman agent was at first frowned upon by the Admiralty because it was feared that the Germans would ask him a number of embarrassing questions about convoy routing and composition. We therefore emphasized to the Germans from the beginning that on account of his long association with the sea, the agent had stipulated that he would not give information about the movements of ships which might lead directly to the death of his fellow seamen. He nevertheless gave a considerable amount of information about convoy protection which the Admiralty considered might be misleading to the enemy.

With time it became obvious that the agent's primary consideration in helping the GARBO network was a monetary one. At the same time he was a Welsh Nationalist and as such, anti-British. He pestered GARBO a good deal for money, but in return gave him good service, and in particular, supplied him with numerous seamen couriers operating in ships which put in at south Wales and Portuguese ports. The agent was an ill man, suffering from a defect of the spine which had developed after an accident, and towards the middle of 1943 he was invalided out of the Merchant Navy.

Between then and December, 1943, he operated mainly as a military reporter and in December that year he brought to GARBO's notice an organization known as the BROTHERS IN THE ARYAN WORLD ORDER. This was composed of a number of fanatical Welsh Nationalists who had long ago abandoned the too moderate Welsh Nationalist Party. From this "Order" no less than six operative agents were recruited who played an important role in implementing the cover plan for OVERLORD.

Agent No. 7 thus became head of one of GARBO's sub-organizations until July, 1944, when, shaken by the arrest of Agent No. 7(5), a member of his network, he decided to return to the Merchant Navy. This did not result in his breaking with the network for he offered to continue to serve GARBO to the best of his ability in his new employment.

He was responsible for hiding Agent No. 4 after the latter had exposed himself to the danger of arrest. He later succeeded in smuggling this same agent to Canada.

He found a safe hideout for GARBO in south Wales after his activities had brought him to the notice of the British authorities. Finally he operated as courier on the North Atlantic route, facilitating the clandestine communications exchanged between the GARBO network in the U.K. and his Canadian network.

APPENDIX XXII.

7(1) @ SOLDIER IN THE 9TH ARMOURED DIVISION.

NAME: Not mentioned.
NATIONALITY: British
OCCUPATION: Soldier in the 9th Armoured Division.
ADDRESS: Not mentioned.
RECRUITED: Prior to the 16.9.43.

The 9th Armoured Division, frequently referred to in the traffic as
the Panda Division (since its insignia was that of a panda) was
built up as a first line formation by the GARBO organization at the
time of Operation STARKEY. The Germans took a lively interest in the
activities of this Division. The association of the words PANDA and
PANZER seemed to register in German minds. They were prepared to
accept this Division as a likely assault division for the Second
Front.

        In the absence of a directive we built up the potential of
the 9th Armoured Division until January, 1944, after which period it
was allowed to fade out since the plans then revealed that it was not
amongst those Divisions which were to be used in the Order of Battle
of FORTITUDE (SOUTH). In fact it never operated in France and was
disbanded.

APPENDIX XXIII.

AGENT NO. 7(2)

NAME: DAVID

NATIONALITY: Welsh

OCCUPATION: Retired seaman. Ex-Welsh Nationalist.

ADDRESS: Swansea.

RECRUITED: Prior to the 6.12.43.

He was introduced to the GARBO organization by Agent No. 7 as
a seaman who had left the sea seven years previously. He was a
fanatical Welshman who had left the Welsh Nationalist Party to form
the "BROTHERS IN THE ARYAN WORLD ORDER."

This agent started to report in January, 1944, and was given
the important area of Dover and district to cover during the period
of build up for the FORTITUDE (SOUTH) deception. He continued to
operate from there until August, 1944. He then travelled around the
country for GARBO to obtain military reports and continued to be an
important source until VE Day.

APPENDIX XXIV.

AGENT NO. 7(3)

NAME: THERESA JARDINE.

NATIONALITY: English.

OCCUPATION: Secretary to the "BROTHERS IN THE ARYAN WORLD
                 ORDER." From January, 1944, Leading WREN (Writer)
                 W.R.N.S.

ADDRESS: From August, 1944:- C/O D.I.C.A. Headquarters,
                 S.E.A.C., Ceylon.

RECRUITED: Prior to the 6.12.43.

To explain her strange association with the BROTHERS IN THE ARYAN
WORLD ORDER she was represented as the mistress of an Indian (Agent
No. 7(4)), a member of this Brotherhood.

No sooner had she been recruited than she found herself
conscripted into the W.R.N.S. and on account of her predilection for
Indians she did all in her power to ensure that she would be posted
to India. She was first sent to a W.R.N.S. Office in London and later
to a training school at Mill Hill, and finally to the W.R.N.S. camp
near Newbury where she studied Hindustani, which she had already
learnt from her Indian lover, and was trained in secretarial work.
This training covered the period from January - July, 1944 when,
during a period of embarkation leave in London she was trained by
Agent No. 7 in secret writing and given a cover address in the U.K.
to which she was instructed to send her reports from Ceylon, where
she was about to proceed.

Her first letter from Ceylon was forwarded by GARBO to his
Lisbon cover address in September, 1944. She continued to write
until early in 1945, when she met with a car accident. It was then
considered necessary to bring her activities to an end, since a
close similarity in her reports and those of other agents,
controlled from Ceylon, had been noticed by the enemy and aroused
slight suspicion. The speedy termination of hostilities did not
give us an opportunity to bring her case to a tidy close.

APPENDIX XXV.

AGENT NO. 7(4)

NAME: "RAGS"
NATIONALITY: Indian
OCCUPATION: Poet
ADDRESS: Swansea
RECRUITED: Prior to the 6.12.44.

This individual had joined the Brothers in the Aryan World Order to uphold his fanatical belief in the superiority of the Aryan race.

Since his occupation was that of a poet he was presumably able to win the affections of his English mistress, 7(3).

He was recruited together with the other members of this Brotherhood, and in February, 1944, he was established in the Brighton area to operate as an observer for the GARBO organization. He continued to send in a stream of high grade military reports until April, 1945, when he confessed that he had tired of his association with the Welshmen to which he had been attracted mostly on account of their association with 7(3). On her instructions £500 which had accrued to her for services rendered were entrusted to him to hold for her until they were able to meet again.

APPENDIX XXVI.

AGENT NO. 7(5)

NAME: Not mentioned.
NATIONALITY: Welsh
OCCUPATION: Employee of a commercial firm in Swansea.
ADDRESS: Swansea.
RECRUITED: Prior to 6.12.43.

Though he was a member of the BROTHERS IN THE ARYAN WORLD ORDER, and a relative of 7(2), it became apparent that he was either less intelligent, or less fanatical, than the other members of this Brotherhood. This came to notice when he failed to establish himself in the Exeter - Plymouth area where he had been instructed to proceed as an observer. In fact it was undesirable that he should have been successful since the cover plan did not provide for reporting from this area, though it would have looked suspicious had no attempt been made to cover it. 7(5) did get as far as Taunton from where he produced reports, and in May, 1944, he entered the prohibited area around Exeter in spite of the continual police check-ups on documentation. He was, however, arrested a few days prior to D Day. He was only sentenced to one month's imprisonment for the offence of having entered a restricted area without permission. The true nature of his mission there was not discovered or suspected.

On his release he returned to his family in Swansea but his narrow escape had completely demoralized him; he had lost his nerve and he became useless as an agent. He was given a pension from September, 1944, until March, 1945, when he was finally paid off.

APPENDIX XXVII.

AGENT NO. 7(6).

NAME: Not mentioned.
NATIONALITY: Welsh
OCCUPATION: Employed in an office in Swansea.
ADDRESS: Swansea.
RECRUITED: Prior to 6.12.43.

This agent, though recruited on the strength of his association with the BROTHERS IN THE ARYAN WORLD ORDER, turned out to be a very low grade spy. Though he accepted his mission he did not want to leave his employment in Swansea to travel. Since an observer was needed in South Wales (which area the Germans had asked us to cover) his offer of services to operate from Swansea was promptly accepted. In fact it was inconsistent with the cover plan for OVERLORD that we should pass reports on military activities in south Wales and therefore it was admirably suitable that this agent should not only be working part-time, but also that he should turn out to be a low grade reporter.

GARBO first pointed out the low category of his reports in March, 1944. He was used in a rather half-hearted way to implement PLAN IRONSIDE, a threat to the Bordeaux coast. When the operation did not materialize the information passed did not tend to discredit the GARBO organization since the Germans had been forewarned that this agent was not a high grade reporter.

In January, 1945, the agent was put on half pay and in March we finally terminated with his services.

APPENDIX XXVIII.

AGENT NO. 7(7)

NAME: Not mentioned
NATIONALITY: Welsh
OCCUPATION: Treasurer of the BROTHERS IN THE ARYAN WORLD ORDER.
ADDRESS: Swansea.
RECRUITED: Prior to the 6.12.43.

As the Treasurer of the Brotherhood it was recommended that he should be given an important allocation in the GARBO network, and therefore he was situated in the Harwich area which GARBO believed would become one of the most important areas at the time of the opening of the Second Front.

He established himself in residence in the Ipswich - Harwich area prior to the imposition of the coastal ban, and his first report which GARBO received in April, 1944, was one of ten pages of secret writing which, though unsubstantial in part, tended to show the importance of this area which had for some while been relatively neglected by the GARBO network. The details contained in this report not only showed the thoroughness of the agent but also introduced a style which would permit the inclusion of apparently minor, though significant details in subsequent reports.

He continued to report from this area in considerable detail, in particular on the notional 14th U.S. Army which he, in due course, located in this area. Later he extended the area of his control further north so as to cover Northern Command.

He was one of the agents who continued to operate until VE Day.

APPENDIX XXIX.

MRS. GARBO

In contrast with her husband Mrs. GARBO was a hysterical, spoilt and selfish woman. She was, nevertheless, intelligent and astute and probably entered into her husband's work because it was dangerous and exciting. When, in April 1942, GARBO came to this country to be interrogated, both he and his wife were assured by S.I.S. that he would only be absent from Lisbon for three to four weeks. It was on this understanding that Mrs. GARBO agreed he should leave her. After we had satisfied ourselves as to his genuineness it was decided that his case could only be run satisfactorily by his remaining here, and that this would not be safe unless his wife came over to join him. When she was told to leave for England she put up strong opposition and it was not without difficulty that she was convinced to come here.

Her journey to this country was the first she had ever made outside the Peninsula. On her arrival, domestic household complications immediately set in and it was only after several months of domestic upheaval that we managed to find her a house where she could run her home without interference from this Office. At the time this move was made, GARBO assured me that we would no longer be put to worry over their household domestic difficulties, and this undertaking was fulfilled to the best of his ability.

Mrs. GARBO at first found it difficult to adapt herself to the English way of living, neither had she been able to learn the language. GARBO very carefully supervised her contacts and took every possible precaution to avoid her mixing with Spaniards, or any other aliens here, through whom there might have been the slightest possibility of the Germans being able to check up on their activities. All these causes intensified the already acute homesickness from which Mrs. GARBO had been suffering ever since her arrival here. Her desire to return to her country, and in particular to see her mother, had driven her to behave at times as if she were unbalanced. For many months she begged me to make arrangements for her to return to her home town, even for a week.

She is a highly emotional and neurotic woman and therefore we never definitely disillusioned her in her hopes that she might be allowed to see her mother before the termination of the war, neither did we, on the other hand, give her any reason to believe that we would accede to her request. As her state worsened she became more desperate, and in order to impress us that we should pay attention to her request, she threatened that she would leave her husband. As

this did not produce the desired effect she threatened to take
action which would spoil the work and leave her free to return.

The following account of a crisis created by Mrs. GARBO is
recorded in detail because it is characteristic of many tense
moments which existed from time to time in the GARBO domestic set
up.

Mrs. GARBO and her husband become friendly with a Spanish
family in London, Mr. and Mrs. GUERRA, with whom they had
occasionally dined. The GUERRAs invited the GARBOs to attend a
dinner at the Spanish Club at which all the Spanish Embassy
personnel were to be present. Mrs. GARBO was very keen to go but
GARBO refused to allow her to do so, explaining that it might
endanger his work if he were known to be in contact with members of
the Spanish Embassy, particularly as he had told the Germans that he
was now out of these circles. He explained to her that it was always
possible that someone in the Spanish Embassy might be in touch with
the Germans and that any contact with the Embassy would therefore be
most dangerous.

Apart from her disappointment at this decision, it gave her
the idea that if her husband were anxious for her to keep away from
the Embassy a threat to visit the Embassy would frighten us into
paying attention to her request. It appears that the husband and
wife quarrelled rather violently over this, and later Mrs. GARBO
threatened him that she was going to tell us that she intended
calling at the Embassy to disclose the work he was doing for us.
The row happened on the evening of the 21.6.43. After this threat
he left the house to telephone from a public call box to warn us that
if his wife should telephone and be offensive in any way we should
ignore her remarks as she was in a highly excited frame of mind.

That evening Mrs. GARBO telephoned the Case Officer and
said:-

> "I am telling you for the last time that if at this time
> to-morrow you haven't got me my papers all ready for me to
> leave the country immediately - because I don't want to live
> five minutes longer with my husband - I will go to the
> Spanish Embassy. As you can suppose going to the Spanish
> Embassy may cost me my life - you understand, it will cost me
> my life - so telling you that I am telling you everything
> ....As I haven't got any further with threats even if
> they kill me I am going to the Spanish Embassy. I know very
> well what to do and say to annoy you and my husband I
> shall have the satisfaction that I have spoilt everything.
> Do you understand? I don't want to live another day in
> England."

Whilst we were not unaccustomed to such outbreaks the present crisis seemed particularly serious.

GARBO was rather embarrassed when told that evening of what had transpired, though he clearly expressed his view that he, personally, was convinced that she would not carry out her threat. It, nevertheless, seemed clear that he was somewhat hesitant to take full responsibility for her actions, being aware that she was in a desperate state.

We discussed the matter at some length and he recommended that in order to tide matters over we should telephone his wife the following morning, after receiving his signal that he was no longer in the house, to say that we would give her the answer to her question at 7 o'clock that evening, and that meanwhile she should give her husband the message that the Head of Section wished to interview him in town as soon as possible.

We further agreed with GARBO that a watch should be kept on the Spanish Embassy and that should she approach it we would detain her.

The following morning Mrs. GARBO was called by telephone in accordance with the plan arranged with GARBO the previous night.

That afternoon we met GARBO who, having given the whole matter his careful consideration, put forward a rather drastic plan, which was subsequently put into operation.

He took full responsibility for all possible reactions which his plan might produce on his wife, and expressed confidence that, providing it was properly carried out it would produce a good effect on her. It was agreed, before putting the plan into operation, that we should enter into it on the understanding that it would be directed by GARBO, and that if the reactions were not as we had anticipated, we would be prepared to modify it in accordance with any special request which GARBO might make. The plan was as follows:-

GARBO wrote a short note to his wife to tell her that he had been detained, and requesting her to hand to the bearer his toilet requirements and pajamas.

Shortly after 6 p.m. the note was delivered to Mrs. GARBO by C.I.D. officers. After an hysterical outburst she refused to accede to her husband's request for clothing.

Meanwhile, her first reaction had been, as he had hoped, to telephone the Case Officer.

She was in tears when she got through and pleaded that her husband had always been loyal to this country and would willingly sacrifice his life for our cause. It was therefore inconceivable that he should have been arrested.

This gave us the opening we had anticipated to be able to tell her our story.

We explained that when we had met GARBO that afternoon and he had been taken before the chief, the latter had expressed his absolute willingness to give Mrs. GARBO her papers to return to Spain, but had said that he wished GARBO and the children to return there with her. Before doing so, however, he instructed GARBO to write a letter making some excuse to the Germans for discontinuing his work. GARBO, at this stage, she was told, became offensive to our chief, stating that they had made a contract with him which he intended to see should not be broken. Even if they had approved that she should return to Spain they could not force him also to do so. Rather than write the letter they requested, he would first go to prison. He asked the reasons for their request for the letter. They replied that they needed it to protect their interest against a betrayal by his wife in Spain such as she had threatened here. Mrs. GARBO was told that when the word "betrayal" was mentioned by the chief, GARBO completely lost his temper and had behaved so violently that his immediate arrest had been necessary on disciplinary grounds.

Mrs. GARBO replied to this by saying she thought that her husband had behaved just as she would have expected him to do. She said that after the sacrifices he had made, and her knowledge that his whole life was wrapped up in his work, she could well understand that he would rather go to prison than sign the letter we had asked for. She said also that she was convinced he had behaved in this way to avoid the blame for all that had happened falling on her. The conversation ended.

Having reflected for a little while, Mrs. GARBO telephoned again, this time in a more offensive mood, threatening to leave the house with the two children and make a disappearance. A little later our wireless operator telephoned to say that Mrs. GARBO had telephoned him, apparently in a desperate state, asking him to come round within half an hour.

He arrived at her house a little after eight to find her sitting in the kitchen with all the gas taps turned on. For some time after his arrival she was incoherent.

She again attempted suicide later that evening. There was a 90% chance that she was play acting. There existed a 10% chance of an accident. To avoid any risk of an accident arrangements were made for someone to stay the night at her house.

The next day, at her request, she was interviewed. She pleaded that it was she who had been at fault and that if her husband could be pardoned she promised she would never again interfere with his work, or behave badly, or ask to return to Spain. She signed a statement to this effect.

By this time she was extremely nervous and had been weeping incessantly for hours on end, and though she was left with the feeling that the matter was serious, the interview had given her hope that a solution to her troubles would soon be found. She was told that she would be allowed to see her husband in detention that afternoon, and that a car would call for her at 4 o'clock.

Under escort she was taken to Kew Bridge, and at 4.30 transferred to the closed van of Camp 020. Blindfolded she was taken to the camp. Her husband was brought to her dressed in Camp 020 clothing and unshaven. He first of all asked her to tell him on her word of honour whether or not she had been to the Embassy. She swore that not only had she not been there, but that she had never intended going, and only used this threat to force us to pay more serious attention to her request. She promised him that if only he were released from prison, she would help him in every way to continue with his work with even greater zeal than before. She would never ask again to go back to Spain and leave him here. She said she thought he had been quite right in refusing to allow us to break our contract with him. She told him how she had been interviewed that morning and of her signing a confession, taking all the blame on herself. She said she was optimistic that something would soon be done for him, and therefore she had decided not to bring him the parcel of clothes which she had prepared. She was hopeful that he would not be detained very long. He told her that he was coming up before a tribunal the following morning and that since she had not been to the Embassy he had a plan which he thought would convince his judges that she had never intended going there.

She left Camp 020 more composed, but still weeping.

The following morning she was told she would be interviewed by a chief of the Service at the Hotel Victoria, Northumberland Avenue.

At that interview she was told in brief that her husband had been before the tribunal that morning which had recommended that he should be allowed to continue the work. She was warned against a repetition of her recent behaviour. She returned home very chastened to await her husband's arrival. He returned to his home that evening.

This episode was not without interest in assessing the qualities of GARBO and his wife. We learnt that she had never intended to carry out her threats, and even had she crossed the threshold of the Spanish Embassy she would never have discussed there anything to do with her husband's work. She had only made the threat in order to cause us to pay greater attention to her request. This confirms that the conclusion which GARBO had drawn before putting the plan into operation had been correct. It gave us further evidence of the implicit confidence which GARBO placed in us, for him to have allowed us to put into operation a plan which, had it

failed, would have ruined for ever his matrimonial life. It
showed us the degree to which he was prepared to co-operate in
order to ensure that his work should continue uninterrupted. The
extraordinary ingenuity with which he conceived and carried through
this plan saved a situation which might otherwise have been
intolerable.

To convince Mrs. GARBO of the genuineness of the manoeuvre
GARBO presented her with a document which purported to be a copy of
the statement he was supposed to have submitted to the Tribunal
prior to his release. The statement is set out in full as an
excellent example of GARBO's inimitable style.

It should be added that Mrs. GARBO gave us no parallel
trouble thereafter.

A STATEMENT BY GARBO TO HIS TRIBUNAL MADE AFTER HIS NOTIONAL ARREST BY THE BRITISH SECRET SERVICE.

Mr. President of the Tribunal and Members:
        I should be indeed discourteous if I failed in
my duty of bearing well in mind the words of counsel and
advice which Your Excellency was good enough to say to me. I
do not wish to minimise the seriousness of my offence nor
to win approval by means of humbug or by daring deceit.
My conscience has always disliked the difficulties and
imbroglios which are the pestilential result of angry
excuses and argumentative battles, for there is no greater
calamity nor more contagious plague than is to be found in
trouble makers who love discussions of motives, and the more
they stir them around the deeper they become involved. But on
finding myself here, and recognizing my offence, the result
of my violent temperament, I nevertheless wish to give the
reasons for my actions and for the resulting consequences.
        I hold myself responsible for all my actions and for
those unhappily performed by my wife, although in the latter
there may be no cause for taking so draconian and severe a
step. There are two accusations against her and both of them
I wish to refute, as although the words were spoken, the
facts condemn the former, and one should always take into
account from whom and from where they came, as well as the
motives existing for saying them. It is certainly true that
my wife made threats, but the threats did not come from an
exactly powerful source. What harm can there be in her if the
powerful, who are above meanness, and conscious of their
generosity and strength, are not afraid, and cannot feel the
effects concealed in the words? What would it matter, for

instance, if Great Britain were to learn of the audacity of
an unknown person who, with no power and no strength,
threatened to take possession of the Island? Because
although the comparison is not relatively adequate, it can
nevertheless be applied to the situation where a poor woman,
defenceless and without weapons - because any she may use
would be turned against her - takes any action or makes any
threats. The accusation against her would result, first of
all, in disaster for her family in Spain, and above all in
the responsibility which would attach to her husband and
family living in the injured country. Further, the threat is
immediately justified if it is followed by acts. I found, by
means of questions, that she did not go to the Spanish
Embassy; nor did the watcher placed by you see any sign of
her prowling in the neighbourhood. My wife declares that she
did not go and never had any intention of going, and is so
certain of this, and I presume will still be so in the
future, that I am prepared to sign a document making myself
responsible for all her future actions which are directly or
indirectly related to the services I am voluntarily
performing in this country.

The second word, which I think is what upset my
equanimity, is that used by my chiefs when, intending to
annul the agreement made by both sides a year ago, they
accused me of violating the document signed - the word,
treachery.

Your Excellencies cannot fully realize the strength
of the feeling of indignation which rose in my breast when I
- who have battled arduously, who have put real love into the
work, which because it is the product of my labours, the
child of my industry, the fruit of my toil, seems good to me
and I love it well, indeed, I worship it - heard fall from the
lips of friends and collaborators words which sound harshly
in one's ears and strike through the heart.

I was blinded, I confess that I lost my reason and
said words which, because of the high standing of those to
whom they were addressed and because it was not gentlemanly
to pronounce them, I ought to have swallowed. But I was
enraged when I saw so great a labour destroyed in a few
seconds, though I realized I should avoid such madness and
preserve what had been achieved, for though work over which
one knows one has a mastery is pleasant, it is much more
estimable to preserve such work with one's constancy and
ability. This is the excuse which I put forward for my
behaviour. At that moment the consequences of my action did

not matter to me, it did not matter to me that I should lose in one second the laudable reputation acquired through what I had achieved, for glory meanly attained does not endure and soon passes. My aspirations are larger, I regard as mere words all the praises which may come my way before the final outcome. My resolve is success; my desire is victory. Until then I will not relax my efforts and will battle, as I have done in the past, against all those who try to obstruct me in my path which lies in the direction of the salvation of Humanity.

I invoke the support of my toil and hardships, of all my vicissitudes and all my past sufferings and perils, in order to obtain the pardon of those whom involuntarily I offended. My mind is at rest; I know that I am appealing to a chivalrous Tribunal and I trust in their decision. May the Lord deliver us when power is coupled with ill-will; fortunately this country, innocent of artifice and subterfuge, controls with scrupulous legality the common weal of her people and of those who collaborate with them.

APPENDIX XXX.

FINANCIAL ARRANGEMENTS.

All monies paid to GARBO by the Germans were handed to this office
for retention, and to be dealt with in accordance with the financial
agreement which was made with GARBO on his arrival. This agreement,
which provided for him to receive 25% of all incoming monies, was
drafted by us and submitted to him in English, which language he was
unable to understand at all at the time of making the agreement. It
also provided for the payment of a salary of £100 per month during
the period that he was working for us. When we submitted the
agreement to him for his approval and signature we started to
translate it for him, but he interrupted, saying that there was no
need to do this since he was unaware of the cost of living in this
country, or to appreciate what might be considered a generous
proposal or otherwise. He said that since any secret agreement with
a British Government Department must by necessity be a gentleman's
agreement and because he believed that any proposal we made him
would be a proper one, he was prepared to sign without knowing the
contents. After signing, and exchanging agreements, we handed him
his copy whereupon he gave it back to his Case Officer, saying that
he neither had the facilities for keeping a confidential document of
this nature, nor did he wish to retain it. He has never asked to see
it since that time, nor referred to it again.

In addition to his salaries and earnings GARBO was promised a
bonus of £500 on the termination of his services and free travel for
himself and his family to Spain or Latin-America at his choice.

The agreement was, however, periodically modified in his
favour in recognition of his good services which turned out to be
far above our expectations. Additional bonuses to be paid to him at
the end of the war with Germany were granted from time to time.
Between 1942 and the cessation of hostilities the special bonuses
approved amounted to £10,000. The Case Officer was authorized to
disclose these bonuses to him as, and when, he though fit, and in
general principle he was told of his having been granted a bonus of,
say, £1,000 at intervals when it was thought that the knowledge
would help his morale, alternatively, after a successful operation.

All monies received from the Germans were taken over by this
Office, out of which the entire expenses of the GARBO case were
paid.

GARBO used to receive his payments from the Germans by two
methods. In the early part of the case, and towards the end, he was
paid in U.S. dollar bills, or Portuguese escudos, which were

enclosed in letters and brought to the U.K. by GARBO's notional
courier. That is to say, the Germans would mail the money to an
address in Lisbon given to them by GARBO. The S.T.S. representative
in Lisbon would collect the money there and send it to London. GARBO
would acknowledge receipt as if the money had been brought over by
his courier.

The other method of getting payment from the Germans was by
the operation known as PLAN DREAM. The essence of this plan was that
the Germans paid pesetas to GARBO's nominee in Spain. The recipient
in Spain would authorize his nominee in London, who was in
possession of sterling funds, to pay the equivalent to GARBO in
London. In all these transactions the Germans used to buy sterling
in pesetas at two and a half times the official rate of exchange. In
spite of these transactions being so costly they nevertheless
parted in this way with two and a quarter million pesetas for which
we received over £13,000 in this country.

Between May, 1942 and April, 1945 the Germans paid GARBO more
than £31,000 for the expenses of running his notional organization.
GARBO was finally allowed by this Office to retain in earnings and
bonuses the sum of £17,554. 4. 11 out of this amount.

GARBO appeared to be satisfied with this remuneration
although, so far as financial arrangements were concerned, it was
difficult ever to judge GARBO's attitude towards our proposals and
in this connection he was never forthcoming with suggestions. It was
certainly as obvious to him as it was to us, that not only did we
have his extraordinary services gratis but we made a considerable
financial "profit" in addition.

APPENDIX XXXI.

METHOD OF CHARGING EXPENSES.

Throughout the entire case GARBO was represented as meticulous in all matters concerning the financial running of his organization, as he was in other matters. During the period he was operating in Portugal he had no idea of the cost of living in this country. He had been told by the Germans that the dollar had an equivalent value of 10/- in England in spite of the fact that the current exchange was approximately $4 to the £1. Since he was paid in dollars he used, during the early running of the case, to render his monthly accounts in that currency. When PLAN DREAM was introduced, and he received payments in sterling, he was bound to keep a sterling account. When, later the Germans reverted to making him payments in dollars he continued to keep his accounts in sterling, crediting the dollar payments at the rate of $4 to the £1.

His first accounts were calculated on the basis of payments of two dollars per day pay to himself and each of his agents, in addition to personal expenses incurred whilst travelling. The hire of his typewriter, English lessons, purchase of stationary and entertainment of contacts were debited as extras. All expenses were kept extremely low. In fact, it is questionable whether he could ever have lived, or got agents to work for him, for the small sums which they were being paid.

He used to give each agent a bonus of £10 for each piece of special information of value they provided. Later he reduced this to a bonus of £10 per month on the grounds that all the information was good, and only one piece of special merit could be considered worthy of bonus each month. He would never accept bonuses himself, and his total entertaining charges would never amount to more than £1 or £2 each month.

On his arrival in the U.K. GARBO was informed that his expenses were, in our opinion, too low and we tended thereafter to increase them. After the arrival of his wife in the U.K. in June, 1942, he wrote to say he would need $200 or £50 per month to cover the expenses for himself, his wife, and child. This amount included his salary. The courier, who used to charge a dollar a letter, became more costly and although the expenses gradually started to rise this could never be attributed to extravagance on the part of GARBO, but rather to the rise in the cost of living, and above all the greater activity of the network and the increase in its membership.

For the purposes of our records we used to keep an expense account, the summary of which was sent to the Germans on the first of each month, showing the balance of money in hand.

By June, 1944, GARBO was charging the Germans the still moderate sum of £50 per month salary as chief of the organization, in addition to a family allowance of £40 a month. The agents received amounts varying from £24 - £38 per month for their work in addition to travelling expenses. The wireless operator was paid at the standard rate of £3 per transmission.

The courier, after receiving the £2,000 for which he blackmailed GARBO, was put on a working basis of £50 a month.

Agent No. 7(3) received two amounts for her services in Ceylon. She was paid £300 on joining the organization, and a subsequent sum of £500 was passed to her several months later.

Agent No. 5 was advanced a lump sum periodically against which he would render a detailed statement of his expenses to GARBO.

An example of GARBO's expense account, and one of Agent No. 5's expense accounts are set out as follows:-

GARBO

June 30th, 1944	Family	£90.0.0.
	Widow	20.0.0.
	Agent No. 7(3)	30.0.0.
	" " " travel	5.0.0.
	" " " on leaving for India	300.0.0.
	Agent No. 4	38.0.0.
	" " " extra while hiding	30.0.0.
	" " " travel	10.0.0.
	Agent No. 7(5)	24.0.0.
	" " " salary	30.0.0.
	" " " travel	5.0.0.
	" " " extra while detained	50.0.0.
	Agent No. 3	50.0.0.
	Agent No. 3(3)	25.0.0.
	" " " travel	10.0.0.
	Agent No. 7	38.0.0.
	" " " travel	15.0.0.
	Agent No. 7(2)	30.0.0.
	" " " travel	15.0.0.
	Agent No. 7(4)	30.0.0.
	" " " travel	5.0.0.
	Agent No. 7(6)	30.0.0.
	Agent No. 7(7)	30.0.0.
	" " " travel	10.0.0.
	Operator	120.0.0.
	Extras	30.0.0.
	Total	£1,070.0.0.
	Payment to courier (4,500 escudos)	450.0.0.
	Sent to Agent No. 5 ($2,000 received)	500.0.0.
	BALANCE	£4,750.0.0.
	BALANCE AT 1.6.44.	£6,770.0.0.

AGENT NO.5.

January - April, 1945.

Five's salary for December	$250
Four's salary for December	192
Seven's salary for December	192
Five's salary for January	250
Four's salary for January	192
Seven's salary for January	192
Five's salary for February	250
Four's salary for February	192
Seven's salary for February	192
Rent of Four's house and premium for February, March and April.	640
General travelling and entertaining expenses	87
Expenses re radio	26
Man to shovel snow at Four's house. (he could not do it himself as he is supposed to be sick)	9
BALANCE	474
	$3,138

APPENDIX XXXII.

THE WIRELESS STATIONS.
(LONDON AND CANADA.)

The first suggestion made by GARBO to the effect that he had an opportunity of establishing wireless communication was made in July, 1942. After evolving a satisfactory cover plan to justify the installation of a wireless station, and having satisfied the Germans, instructions together with a transmitting plan and cyphers were eventually forwarded to GARBO in January, 1943. Wireless communications were established in March that year without great difficulty. Contact was made direct to Madrid and during the entire period of operation the control did not leave the hands of the Madrid Stelle. The apparatus used this end was a German made portable set of 100 watts which had been seized from a German agent in transit to South America. The operator was a member of this Office, a self-taught amateur. The apparatus was installed at a house belonging to this Office in Hendon. During the time of the flying bombs it was moved out to Beaconsfield and subsequently it was restored to London.

The location of the apparatus was given to the Germans and changes of its location were notified in case they should detect it through a D.F. check.

In January, 1945 the 100 watt apparatus was substituted by a 500 watt Army signal set which was technically adjusted to prevent detection by means of Radio "Fingerprinting." The increased power was explained to the Germans by saying that the operator, who was reputed to be a first class technician had added a power amplifying unit to the existing apparatus. The more powerful new set was actually operated from this Office building, suitable aerial masts having been erected.

By this time Agent No. 5, who had already established his organization in Canada, had also established a wireless station. An amateur Canadian operator was used there. In the eyes of the Germans the operator was GARBO's Agent No. 4 whom they believed to have been trained in wireless over a long period by GARBO's London operator. The apparatus used was, in German eyes, a transmitter which had been constructed by the London operator and smuggled into Canada by Agent No. 4 when he left England for that country to become operator for Agent No. 5's network.

In fact the apparatus used in Canada was a 350 watt set built and modified to suit, by the amateur operator used there. It was intended that we should have established three way communications,

ie., London - Montreal, Montreal - Madrid, and Madrid - London.
The London - Montreal link was never properly established due to
unusually adverse atmospheric conditions which existed during the
period of trials.

Though it was always intended to keep transmissions down to a
minimum, there were frequent occasions when we were on the air, in
communication with Madrid, for periods in excess of two hours. The
Germans would occasionally worry that we would be detected but the
fact that we transmitted 1,320 messages of an average of 70 groups
and received 447 messages of similar length, without detection,
never aroused their suspicion.

It is true to say that over a considerable period of this
time we were using British military procedure, which had been
supplied to us by the Germans, which proved to be difficult to
detect. Whilst we were using the ordinary amateur procedure our
apparatus was detected and reported as suspect, by listeners not
only in this country, but as far afield as Scotland, Canada and
Gibraltar. I think that from this experience it can safely be
stated, that had GARBO been a genuine spy, operating as the Germans
believed him to be, he would certainly have been detected.

It should also be noted that although it took some six weeks
to pick up the GARBO transmitter after he changed from amateur
procedure to British military procedure, his transmitter was
eventually picked up and the apparatus located. This was done
without giving any information to assist the R.S.S. personnel
responsible for the detection.

The encyphering and decyphering of all wireless messages,
which at times amounted to more than twenty messages exchanged per
day, were handled by GARBO and the operator.

Apart for occasional short periods when transmissions
between London and Madrid were held up due to unusually bad
atmospheric conditions, a continuous flow of traffic was maintained
until the night of V.E. day. The following day the Germans closed
down their transmitting station in Madrid. Their communications
with Germany had already broken down some days previously.

APPENDIX XXXIII.

CYPHERS AND TRANSMITTING PLANS.

On the 25.12.42 and 22.1.43 GARBO was supplied with the following cypher and decypher tables:-

A.

	TABLE I.						TABLE II				
	1	2	3	4	5		1	2	3	4	5
A	G	E	A	Q	D	A	U	J	A	L	H
B	H	F	Z	R	E	B	V	K	D	K	I
C	I	G	Y	S	G	C	W	L	F	M	J
D	J	H	B	Z	F	D	X	M	H	O	A
E	K	I	X	U	I	E	Y	A	J	N	B
F	L	J	C	V	H	F	Z	B	K	P	D
G	M	R	W	W	J	G	A	C	N	R	C
H	N	L	D	X	A	H	B	D	O	Q	F
I	O	M	V	Y	B	I	C	E	R	P	E
J	P	A	E	Z	C	J	D	F	S	S	G
K	Q	B	F	B	K	K	E	G	U	V	K
L	R	C	U	A	O	L	F	H	W	U	M
M	S	D	T	C	L	M	G	I	X	W	N
N	T	N	G	E	M	N	H	N	Z	Y	O
O	U	O	H	D	N	O	I	O	Y	X	L
P	V	P	S	F	P	P	J	P	V	Z	P
Q	W	Q	R	H	R	Q	K	Q	T	A	R
R	X	R	I	G	Q	R	L	R	Q	B	Q
S	Y	S	J	J	T	S	M	S	P	C	T
T	Z	T	Q	I	S	T	N	T	M	D	S
U	A	Z	K	L	V	U	O	V	L	E	V
V	B	U	P	K	U	V	P	W	I	F	U
W	C	V	L	M	Z	W	Q	X	G	G	Z
X	D	W	M	O	X	X	R	Y	E	H	X
Y	E	X	O	N	Y	Y	S	Z	C	I	Y
Z	F	Y	N	P	W	Z	T	U	R	J	W
	ENCYPHER						DECYPHER				

The instructions for working the cypher were as follows:-

TO ENCYPHER

Example of a message which has to be encyphered:

"EL DOS DE NOVIEMBRE SALIO CONVOY COMPUESTO DE.... "

<u>1st operation</u>: The message must be divided into groups of five consecutive letters:-

"ELDOS DENOV IEMBR ESALI OCONV OYCOM PUEST ODE...."

<u>2nd operation</u>: Each letter in the group corresponds to one of the numbers, 1,2,3,4 or 5 to be found on the Table I, and on the Table are indicated alphabetically the corresponding letters to be found in the corresponding space to the number of each letter. The letters now must be substituted for those composing the group.

<u>Example</u>: The first group cited above "ELDOS" with the help of the Table I we find the following letters "KCBDT" and in this way we obtain the group "KCBDT". This must be done with the rest of the groups which gives us the following cypher message: "KCBDT JIGDU OITRQ KSSAB UGHEU UXYDL VZXJS".

TO DECYPHER
Messages received should be decyphered at Table II. The operation is the reverse as the cypher messages will be composed of five letter groups.

<u>Important</u>: If when encyphering a message in setting it up in five letter groups there should not be sufficient letters to finish a group the group should be completed by filling the vacant spaces with the letter X. The message must always be made up of complete groups of five letters.

<u>B.</u>
On the 17.7.43 GARBO was instructed to use the above cyphers for part-encoding his letters in the CODEX system.

<u>C.</u>
On the 19.4.43 GARBO was instructed to double encypher on the above table for greater security.

<u>D.</u>
On the 7.5.43 GARBO was instructed to change his cypher and prepare to use a camouflage plan for wireless transmission. His London station would, in accordance with this plan, appear to be a military station and thus he would avoid detection.

   The instructions which he was then given are set out here in full.

<u>NOTE</u>: On the 14.2.44 this plan was further elabourated and call signs to cover the entire year 1944, were supplied in addition to an assortment of frequencies to correspond with certain fixed hours of

transmissions incorporated in the plan. A new cypher table based on the same system, but composed on a different code phrase was substituted.

TRANSMISSION ALMURA - CENTRO.

NOTE: ALMURA = OUTSTATION i.e. LONDON
              CENTRO = HOME STATION i.e. SPAIN

On the basis of the experiences and results obtained to date in the transmissions held between ALMURA - CENTRO, different forms, characteristics and rules have been studied for the elaboration of a new plan for future transmissions, which, when once it has been studied, confirmed and proved, will be put into operation.

Meanwhile and until all pending matters have been clarified to the satisfaction of both parties transmissions will continue to operate in accordance with the attached plan ANNEX NO. 1. in which you will find the dates, hours, call signs and frequencies fixed for the transmission for the coming months.

Instructions for putting the transmissions into operation in accordance with the plan ALMURA - CENTRO:- ANNEX NO.I.

The basic principal for transmissions between ALMURA - CENTRO is brevity!

On the fixed dates according to custom CENTRO will start the transmissions calling for 2 - 3 minutes with its call sign, followed by "K" to which ALMURA should answer. The latter will reply with its call sign several times keeping on the look out, for CENTRO will interrupt immediately it has been picked up. ALMURA should immediately state whether it has any message to transmit and proceed immediately to transmit, without delay and without asking whether everything is all right as we here will ask for any incomplete groups at the end of the message should there be need. CENTRO will then transmit its messages. When both parties have sent out their messages the transmission must quickly be brought to an end without doing as we have done up to the present, which is to say, giving out cyphered groups such as ZUI: CDE: GHJ: etc., for the next transmission as the method for dealing with this is all explained in the plan.

Special transmissions not provided for in the plan should be announced in cyphered messages in which should be fixed the date, hour and exact frequencies. The call signs for this purpose are set out at the foot of Plan ANNEX NO. 1 according to the day to which they correspond.

It is essential that ALMURA should check his watch daily with GMT so as to be punctual for transmissions. The cyphered messages should never exceed 40 - 50 five letter groups. In no circumstances should telegraphic abbreviations be transmitted or special signs be given to announce that there are storms, local disturbances etc., etc., in the region of ALMURA, or if for any reason the transmission has to be suspended, as for example, on account of an air raid or even that ALMURA notices in its vicinity some plane flying slowly which might be a localising (D.F.ing) aeroplane. The transmission should then be broken off immediately. Contact will again be made on the corresponding day according to the plan. It is imperative that you should let ALMURA know all these points with full instructions so that the service should be perfect and so that at the same time instructions should be carried out to the letter by him.

As soon as this plan and instructions are in your possession and have been studied carefully by you and ALMURA you should forward a cyphered telegram to CENTRO, the password of which is as follows:-

"PABLITO WILL BE TRAVELLING NORTH ON........."

The date should be selected from the Plan Annex No. 1, which is to say, the date you select must be the date on which this new plan will come into operation.

PLAN ALMURA – CENTRO, 1943/44.

ANNEX NO. 1.

JUNE

GMT:	2	4	7	10	16	17	21	23	25	28	30
	21.30	20.45	21.15	22.00	21.45	20.30	22.00	21.15	20.45	21.00	22.00
ALMURA 6.900	GRF	GSA	GDZ	GHJ	GIO	GPO	GGK	GRE	GDI	GJE	GGI
CENTRO 6.600	CVP	NQB	BLD	PMV	ZVF	XGD	SQF	YAM	PST	BAS	RLN

JULY

GMT:	1	2	5	7	13	15	16	19	23	28	30
	21.15	22.00	21.00	21.30	20.30	22.00	21.00	21.30	20.30	21.00	22.00
ALMURA 6.900	GLK	GFR	GHU	GTZ	GWQ	GNI	GIO	GFF	GRE	GJE	GGI
CENTRO 6.600	RSI	CVP	TLZ	BLD	MSR	IDT	ZVF	AKI	YAM	BAS	RLN

AUG.

GMT:	3	5	6	11	13	17	18	23	27	31
	20.30	21.30	21.00	20.45	22.00	21.15	20.30	22.00	20.30	21.15
ALMURA 6.900	GDE	GHU	GJI	GCV	GWQ	GPO	GZZ	GRE	GFD	GCX
CENTRO 6.600	HBS	TLZ	EFV	ASE	MSR	XGD	FHQ	YAM	FPE	VOX

SEPT.

GMT:	2	3	6	8	14	16	20	23	24	29
	20.45	22.00	21.00	21.30	22.00	20.30	21.30	21.00	20.30	22.00
ALMURA 6.900	GFR	GDE	GJI	GKE	GZH	GIO	GSS	GRE	GGV	GNN
CENTRO 6.600	CVP	HBS	EFV	ACX	EPC	ZVF	MEP	YAM	OTC	MLG

OCT.

GMT:	1	5	7	11	15	19	21	25	27	29
	20.45	21.15	20.30	22.00	20.45	21.45	22.00	20.45	21.30	21.00
ALMURA 6.900	GLK	GHU	GTZ	GCV	GNI	GFF	GGX	GBI	GFD	GNN
CENTRO 6.600	RSI	TLZ	BLD	ASE	IDT	AKI	SQF	PST	FPE	MLG

NOV.

GMT:	2	4	8	11	15	18	23	25
	21.30	20.45	21.15	22.00	21.45	20.30	21.15	20.45
ALMURA 6.900	GFR	GSA	GKE	GCV	GIO	GZZ	GRE	GBI
CENTRO 6.600	CVP	NQB	ACX	ASE	ZVF	FBQ	YAM	PST

DEC.

GMT:	1	2	6	7	13	15	16	20	23	28	30
	21.15	22.00	21.00	21.30	20.30	22.00	21.00	21.30	20.30	21.00	22.00
ALMURA 6.900	GLK	GFR	GJI	GTZ	GWQ	GNI	GIO	GSS	GRE	GJE	GGI
CENTRO 6.600	RSI	CVP	EFV	BLD	MSR	IDT	ZVF	MEP	YAM	GAS	RLN

JAN.

GMT:	3	5	11	13	17	18	25	27	31
	20.30	21.30	20.45	22.00	21.15	20.30	22.00	20.30	21.15
ALMURA 6.900	GDE	GHU	GCV	GWQ	GPO	GZZ	GBI	GFD	GFX
CENTRO 6.600	HBS	TLZ	ASE	MSR	XGD	FVQ	PST	FPE	VOX

FEB.

GMT:	2 20.45	3 22.00	8 21.30	14 22.00	16 20.30	21 21.30	23 21.00	24 20.30
ALMURA 6.900	GFR	GDE	GKE	GZH	GIO	GGK	GRE	GGV
CENTRO 6.600	CVP	HBS	ACX	EPC	ZVF	SQF	YAM	OTC

CALL SIGNS.

DAY	1	2	3	4	5	6	7	8	9	10
ALMURA	GLK	GFR	GDE	GSA	GHU	GJI	GTZ	GKE	GXY	GHJ
CENTRO	RSI	CVP	HBS	NQB	TLZ	EFV	BLD	ACX	FKO	PMV

DAY	11	12	13	14	15	16	17	18	19	20
ALMURA	GCV	GXC	GWQ	GZH	GNI	GIO	GPO	GZZ	GFF	GSS
CENTRO	ASE	CKD	MSR	EPC	IDT	ZVF	XGD	FVQ	AKI	MEP

DAY	21	22	23	24	25	26	27	28	29	30	31
ALMURA	GGK	GIK	GRE	GGV	GBI	GLM	GFD	GJE	GNN	GGI	GCX
CENTRO	SQF	CUS	YAM	OTC	PST	SCK	FPE	VAS	MLG	RLN	VOX

SPECIAL EXPERIMENTAL TRANSMISSIONS ALMURA - CENTRO.

For the perfection and completion of the NEW COVER PLAN projected, it is essential that several special experimental transmissions should be made between ALMURA and CENTRO on three selected days which are not included in the plan details of which you will find below and on these occasions you will make trials to contact on fixed frequencies.

These days, hours and fixed frequencies are:-

Special experimental transmissions for the 9th June, 1943:

GMT:	20.30	21.00
ALMURA:	GXY	GXY
KCS:	7.070	6.900
CENTRO:	FSI	FSI
KCS:	6.750	6.750

Special experimental transmissions for the 15th June, 1943:

GMT:	21.00	21.30
ALMURA:	GNI	GNI
KCS:	6.800	6.840
CENTRO:	FNT	FNT
KCS:	7.030	6.500

Special experimental transmissions for the 28th June, 1943:

GMT:	20.45	21.15	21.45
ALMURA:	GJE	GJE	GJE
KCS:	6.650	6.730	6.600
CENTRO:	RAG	RAG	RAG
KCS:	6.450	6.850	6.750

Each pair of frequencies should be given a heading as follows:-

AAA	BBB	CCC	DDD	EEE	FFF	GGG
7.070	6.900	6.800	6.840	6.650	6.730	6.600
6.750	6.600	7.030	6.500	6.450	6.850	6.750

As you will appreciate these trails are intended specially to experiment making contact with the new frequencies which will serve later if the result is positive to substitute the frequencies used to date.

During these special transmissions only one short exchange will be made between ALMURA and CENTRO just sufficient to be certain that the frequencies are valid for future transmissions. In this case ALMURA should mark on the dial of his receiver the exact spot where he receives CENTRO so as to be able to pick it up again later with greater ease. To initiate these special transmissions CENTRO will call at the indicated time for 10 minutes consecutively so that ALMURA can get his position clearly. Each partial transmission should be interrupted with a simple OK. The result of the experiments obtained by ALMURA you should communicate to us by letter.

NEW CODE: ALMURA - CENTRO.

As announced we send you herewith a description and instructions for the use of a new code ALMURA - CENTRO. We must tell you that this code is not complicated but that it must be carefully studied to be able to be used and the cyphering or decyphering of the messages with the same must be carried out meticulously to avoid confusion and difficulties.

You should therefore study at your leisure this new method, making various trials until you are completely experienced. As soon as you are ready to use it you should send us in the cypher which you have been using up to the present a password telegram to the CENTRO as follows:-

"I am grateful for the kind wishes which you sent me."

From then on you can encypher your messages with the new system and we in the old code will send you a cyphered message of confirmation as follows:-

"There is no reason to thank us. It was a duty between friends."

From then on we will encypher our messages in the same new code. I repeat there is no hurry to make use of the new code until you have thoroughly studied it.

Refrain from sending cyphered messages such as you have transmitted to date on several occasions such as "Without news." "Without anything to report." And suchlike.

Refrain also from signing your telegrams with your name or any other name.

CYPHER.

```
                                   1
                               U V W X Y
                            ┌───────────┐
                          N │ L A C O N │ L
                          G │ F I Z E G │ F
CODE PLAN            4    H │ B R T D H │ B    2
                          S │ J M P Q S │ J
                          Y │ U V W X Y │ U
                            └───────────┘
                               L A C O N
                                   3
```

1a. Example of a message to be encyphered on the 15th of April:

"Las operaciones siguen siendo llevadas a cabo con tada normalidad obteniendose exitos locales en algunos sectores."

The message is then divided into groups of five letters:

1 2 3 4 5	1 2 3 4 5	1 2 3 4 5	1 2 3 4 5	1 2 3 4 5
L A S O P	E R A C I	O N E S S	I G U E N	S I E N D
O L L E V	A D A S A	C A B O C	O N T O D	A N O R M
A L I D A	D O B T E	N I E N D	O S E E X	I T O S L
O C A L E	S E N A L	G U N O S	S E C T O	R E S X X

1b. Using the code plan these groups should be encyphered letter by letter and group by group. The letters to be converted will be found within the rectangle of the code plan and are substituted in the following way: You proceed by substituting each letter in order of its position in the group working in a clockwise direction. The first letter (L) is substituted by (U) which is to be found above it. The second letter (A) is substituted by (C) which is to be found at the right of it. The third letter (S) is substituted by (Y) which is to be found below it and the fourth letter (O) is substituted by (C) which is found to the left of it. The fifth letter (P) remains unchanged.
The result is

L=U;	A=C;	S=Y;	O=C;	P=P;	1st Group
E=O;	R=T;	A=I;	C=A;	I=I.	2nd Group

If the letter K appears in the text to be encyphered which does not appear in the code plan this letter should not be encyphered but remains as it is within the group without changing the correlative order of the five letter group.

The transposed message then appears as follows:-

```
U C Y C P O T I A I X L D Q S A F L Z N H Z D O D X A F Z V
V H I C A W C I C C X L P C D V L E B M V A R T A E N J R E
Y Z D O D X J D Z X A D E Q L X O C N E H F G L L N V G C S
H G Z R O I G Y W X
```

2a. We now apply a number code which is composed of 31 correlative numbers but arranged in the following order:-

16 1 7 23 19 12 14 2 20 31 3 8 21 9 17 13 24 6 15 10 27 22 25 11 28 4 29 26 30 5 18

The converted message obtained through the operation at 1b is now applied to the number code table as set out below in such a way as to start below the number corresponding with the date on which the message is to be transmitted. The first day of the month would start below the number 1, the second day below the number 2 and the third below the number 3 etc., etc., So that for example on the 15th of April one would commence below the <u>number 15</u>:

```
16  1 7  23 19 12 14  2 20 31  3  8 21  9 17 13 24  6 15 10 27 22 25 11 28 4 29 26 30  5  18
                              U  C  Y  C  P  O  T  I  A  I  X  L  D
Q  S  A  F  L  Z  N  H  Z  D  O  D  X  A  F  Z  V  V  H  I  C  A  W  C  I  C  C  X  L  P  C
D  V  L  E  B  M  V  A  R  T  A  E  N  J  R  E  Y  Z  D  O  D  X  J  D  Z  X  A  D  E  Q  L
X  O  C  N  E  H  F  G  L  L  N  V  G  C  S  H  G  Z  R  O  I  G  Y  W  X
```

3a. You then get your result by reading from top to bottom, that is to say reading down the columns under the numbers in consecutive order:

> First Column: (1) - SVO
> 2nd Column: (2)   HAC
> 3rd Column: (3) - OAN

etc., etc., so that by grouping them together consecutively you get the complete composition:

3b.

```
S V O H A G O A N I C X L P Q V Z Z A L C D E V A J C C I O O O C D
W Z M H Z E H N V F U H D R Q D X F R S D C L L B E Z R L X N G C A
X G F E N V Y G P W J Y I X D Y C D I T I Z X A C A X L E D T L
```

4a. You then again transcribe your result horizontally from left to right on the same number table but this time starting under the number of the month which is to say in the case of the example given, under No. 4 to correspond with the month of April.

NOTE:- For January you would start under No.1, for February under No.2, for March under No.3, for April under No.4, for May under No. 5, and for June under No.6 etc., etc.,

```
16  1  7   23 19 12 14  2 20 31  3  8 21  9 17 13  24  6 15 10 27 22 25 11 28  4 29 26 30  5 18
                                                          S  V  O  H  A  G
 O  A  N  I  C  X  L  P  Q  V  Z  Z  A  L  C  D  E  V  A  J  C  C  I  O  O  O  C  D  W  Z  M
 H  Z  E  H  N  V  F  U  H  D  R  Q  D  X  F  R  S  D  C  L  L  B  E  Z  R  L  X  N  G  C  A
 X  G  F  E  N  V  Y  G  P  W  J  Y  I  X  D  Y  C  D  I  T  I  Z  X  A  C  A  X  L  E  D  T
 L
```

4b. You then again read off your result column by column from top to bottom following the numbers of the columns consecutively just as you did in paragraph 3a. commencing with column 1.

```
        1st Column:  (1) - AZG
        2nd Column:  (2) - PUG
        3rd Column:  (3) - ZRJ
```

etc., etc., which when grouped together consecutively produces the complete composition:

```
        A Z G P U G Z R J S O L A A Z C D V D D N E F Z Q Y L X X J
        L T O Z A X V V D R Y L F Y A C I O H X L C F D G M A T E N
        N Q H P A D I C B Z I H E E S C I E X O D N L C L I O R C V
        C X X H W G E V D W
```

4c. You next divide this composition of letters into five letter groups thus obtaining the final encyphered message ready for transmission as follows:-

```
AZGPU  GZRJS  CLAAZ  CDVDD  NEFZQ  YLXXJ  LTOZA  XVVDR  YLFYA
CICHX  LCFDG  MATCN  NQHPA  DICBZ  IHEES  CIEXO  ONLCL  IORCV
CXXHW  GEVDW
```

DECYPHER.
1a. Example of a message to be decyphered which has been received on the 15th April:

```
AZGPU  GZRJS  CLAAZ  CDVDD  NEFZQ  YLXXJ  LTOZA  XVVDR  YLFYA
CICHX  LCFDG  MATCH  NQHPA  DICBZ  IHEES  CIEXO  INLCL  IORCV
CXXHW  GEVDW
```

1b. You first calculate the number of letters in the message to be decyphered. In the present example it is composed of 100 letters. You apply the number code preferably using squared paper (in order to facilitate the operation which is explained hereafter) and you first look for, as a starting point, the number corresponding to the month which in this case is four (April). In the first line of squares on your number code you cross off the squares up to the square below the number four always working from left to right. From No. 4 onwards you continue to count the squares line by line up to the number of squares corresponding with the number of letters in the message which in this example is 100 squares which brings you, in the example set out below, to the first square in the fifth line:-

16 1 7 25 19 12 14 2 20 31 3 8 21 9 17 13 24 6 15 10 27 22 25 11 28 **4** 29 26 30 5 18

You then mark off the remaining thirty squares of the fifth line. To further facilitate the operation you can outline the hundred squares which will be used as indicated above.

1c. The message to be decyphered is then written in within the outlined space into the blank squares on the number code into the columns starting with No.1 then into columns 2,3,4,etc., always working from top to bottom within the outlined contours as for example:-

       1st Column:(1) - AZG (There are only three squares available)
       2nd Column:(2) - PUG ("   "   "   "   "   ")
       3rd Column:(3) - ZRJ ("   "   "   "   "   ")

Continuing thus from column to column until all the squares within the outlined space are filled.

16 1 7 23 19 12 14 2 20 31 3 8 21 9 17 13 24 6 15 10 27 22 25 11 28 4 29 26 30 5 18

/ S V O H A G
O A N I C X L P Q V Z Z A L C D E V A J C C I O O O C D W Z M
H Z E H N V F U H D R Q D X F R S D C L L I B E Z R L X N G C A
X G F E N V Y G P W J Y I X D Y C D I T I Z X A C A X L E D T
L /

2a. You then again use another squared sheet set out under the number code just as in paragraph 1b covering over all the squares on the

first line up to the one corresponding to the date which in the
present example is 15 (15th April.) You then again count out 100
spaces starting from this space (or as many spaces as there are
letters in the message) marking them again with an outline and marking
off the rest of the squares in the last lines which will not be used.

16 1 7 23 19 12 14 2 20 31 3 8 21 9 17 13 24 6 15 30 27 22 25 11 28 4 29 26 30 5 18

2b. Within the 100 squares which are outlined you then write in
again in columns according to the number code from top to bottom
commencing with column 1 and following on to columns 2,3 and 4 etc.,
the result of the letters you obtained in paragraph 1c, line by line
and commencing with SVOHAGOANI etc., etc., in such a way that when
the columns are filled the result will be:

      1st Column: (1) - SVO (There are only three squares available)
      2nd Column: (2) - HAG ("   "   "   "   "   ")
      3rd Column: (3) - OAN ("   "   "   "   "   ")

Passing thus from column to column until the columns are filled
within the outlined squares.

16 1 7 23 19 12 14 2 20 31 3 8 21 9 17 13 24 6 15 10 27 22 25 11 28 4 29 26 30 5 18
/ U C Y C P O T I A I X L D
Q S A F L Z N H Z D O D X A F Z V V H I C A W C I C C X L P C
D V L E B M V A R T A E N J R E Y Z D O D X J D Z X A D E Q L
X O C N E H F G L L N V G C S H G Z R O I G Y W X / / / / / /

3a. The composition of letters thus obtained is transposed line by
line and then divided into five letter groups:

1 2 3 4 5	1 2 3 4 5	1 2 3 4 5	1 2 3 4 5	1 2 3 4 5
U C Y C P	O T I A I	X L D Q S	A F L Z N	H Z D O D
X A F Z V	V H I C A	W C I C C	X L P C D	V L E B M
V A R T A	E N J R E	Y Z D O D	X J D Z X	A D E Q L
X O C N E	H F G L L	N V G C S	H G Z R O	I G Y W X

3b. With the help of the code plan which is now numbered in the
reverse the groups obtained above are decyphered, that is to say
letter by letter. The letters to convert are looked for within the
rectangle of the code plan and are then substituted in the following
way:-

You proceed to substitute correlatively each letter according to its place number in the group in a clockwise direction. The first letter "U" is substituted for "L" which is found below; the second letter "C" for the "A"; the third "Y" for the "S" and the fourth "C" for the "O"; the fifth "P" remains "P".

The result obtained is

U=L;	C=A;	Y=S;	C=O;	P=P
O=E;	T=R;	I=A;	A=C;	I=I
etc., etc.,				

Thus we obtain the completed decyphered groups:

LASOP ERACI ONESS IGUEN SIEND OLLED ADASA CABOC ONTOD
ANORM ALIBA DOBTE NIEND OSEEX ITOSL OCALE SENAL GUNOS
SECTO REAXX

which is:

"Las operaciones siguen siendo llevadas a cabo con toda normalidad obteniendose exitos locales en algunos sectores."

3

U V W X Y

		L
N	L A C O N	L
G	F I Z E G	F
CODE PLAN 2 H	B R T D H	B 4
S	J M P Q S	J
Y	U V W X Y	U

L A C O N

1

PROJECT FOR A NEW COVER PLAN ALMURA - CENTRO.

The object of this cover plan for transmitting is to achieve the effect that the enemy listening centres on picking up the transmission of ALMURA will believe that they are listening to an English station due to the fact that all its characteristics will be the same, i.e., its call signs, frequencies adopted, contact signals, method of carrying out the transmission etc., etc., and they will not be able to discover easily that ALMURA is in contact with CENTRO.

Attached is sent a transmitting plan which will eventually be used and the only thing that is missing are the details of the corresponding frequencies for each day of transmission which will be notified to ALMURA as soon as the special experimental transmissions have been carried out from which one will learn which are the most suitable.

Therefore the attached plan is sent so that ALMURA can go ahead studying the instructions in advance so that as soon as the frequencies have been decided it will only be necessary to communicate which frequencies have been chosen.

So that this cover plan should give the result hoped for it is imperative that ALMURA should follow out the instructions to the letter just as they are set out below and that in no circumstances should ALMURA, during a transmission, made any alteration either in the working out of the transmission or in contact signs which would create immediately irregularities and bring suspicion on the service and facilitate the enemy to discover you.

You should note that CENTRO will continue to carry out its transmissions in the same way as it has been doing up to the present, which is to say, that it should work in the customary way basing itself on the new system for transmitting from ALMURA.

PLAN FOR TRANSMITTING.
The timetable and call signs for either party is to be that set out on the detailed plan attached. The frequencies will be communicated, as mentioned above, later when the experimental transmissions have been carried out. You should take into account that every ten or twelve days you will re-use the frequencies employed up to the present which is to say ALMURA 6.900 KCS. and CENTRO 6.600 KCS. So that in this way we can always guarantee contact if for some reason there should be a breakdown in making contact on the other frequencies which there is no reason to suppose will happen.

I again repeat that the abbreviations ZUI, CDE, etc., are permanently prohibited. Also take note that any request for special transmissions should be made in a cyphered message.

METHOD FOR TRANSMITTING.
At the hours agreed on the plan for starting transmissions CENTRO will be the one first to call during the first five minutes at the end of which ALMURA will start up sending VE VE VE, continuing with its call signs which should be given several times (10-15 times) finishing its period of calling with VE VE AR. ALMURA should not call for more than two minutes. Even though CENTRO should interrupt ALMURA's call signs it is imperative that the latter should end its period of calling always with VE VE AR. The English tuning in sign is not a "V" but "VE".

Therefore the result will be that in order to make contact:
ALMURA: VE VE VE, Call signs VE VE AR.

As soon as ALMURA has finished the prescribed period for
calling CENTRO will repeat its call signs a few times, continuing
with "K" just as it has done up to the present, whereupon ALMURA will
commence straight away if it should have a message to transmit but
in accordance with the following rules:

1st:	Call sign (only once).
2nd:	Z (Password meaning that there is a message).
3rd:	GR - (The number of groups of which the message is composed and not the number of letters as has been given up to the present.)
4th:	Three letters, for example, BWC (this is at your discretion, it is not necessary always to give this.)
5th:	Separation - . . . -; this signifies that a cyphered message follows.
6th:	Number of the message. This number also at your discretion but it should never correspond with the true number of the message which will not be transmitted.
7th:	Date of the message, for example: 27 (Only the number of the day and not the month.)
8th:	To assist the camouflage still more it is necessary to add to the true cyphered message an invented group both at the beginning and at the end of it (a total of two groups) which should be composed so as to be able to be pronounced, such as "LARUM" "NOTAR" "BEREB" "BERUM" "NORAB" "NURAB" " SERUM" "CASAR" etc., (in contrast to the ordinary groups of the cyphered text such as XLDVH SNJIO RYEDM AWTGX which cannot be pronounced.) The invented group at the beginning and end of each message must be identical.

RESUME: Example of a cyphered message of four groups:

"LARUM LDNOG NSEVI KBPYE GVUSH LARUM"

Example for the transmission of a cyphered message to be sent
by ALMURA under date of the 27th May:

ALMURA:	VE VE VE JGD JGD JGD VE AR
CENTRO:	Will reply in the usual way!
ALMURA:	JGD Z 6 BWC-121 27 LARUM LDNOG NSEVI KBPYE GVUSH LARUM AR

The messages must be cyphered in five letter groups as has been done up to date. If CENTRO has a message to transmit to ALMURA this will be announced in the usual way with the International sign QIC and when ALMURA replies with "K" CENTRO will start to send the message.

ALMURA shall only use the following agreed signs (abbreviations):

X 626	= Send more VE VE VE for tuning in.
X 236	= Not receiving your signs clearly the receiving wave is bad check up your transmitter.
X 261	= Increase your power.
X 279	= How are you receiving me? (When CENTRO asks the question QSA ALMURA should answer R1, R2, R3, etc., etc., according to the reception d 1-9)
Q	= Wait
RPT AA GR	= Repeat everything onwards from........
RPT WB GR	= Repeat the group before........
RPT AB GR	= Repeat the group after.......
X 613	= Reduce slightly the number of KCS. (i.e. instead of 6.600 reduce to 6.592)
X 617	= Increase slightly the number of KCS. (for example instead of 6.600 increase to 6.605)
X 257	= I have nothing to transmit.

These "X" groups should be repeated several times (2 or 3) i.e. X 626, X 626, X 626 but they should be avoided as much as possible.

Other contact signs, abbreviations, etc., will remain definitely prohibited for ALMURA.

During the transmissions of the call signs or of a cyphered message from CENTRO, ALMURA must not interrupt but must wait until CENTRO finishes transmitting and it is for this reason that we have given the different "RPT" groups so that when it has ended ALMURA can ask for the parts of the message which has not been well understood.

In conclusion the method or system of corresponding between ALMURA and CENTRO which has been used in the first Plan on the system "BK" is definitely prohibited during the period of time during which the camouflage plan is in use.

Our proposal is to employ alternatively during the transmissions from one month to another both the old plan for transmitting (that which has been used to date) and the camouflage plan which has been described above.

For this reason it is imperative that you study carefully

point by point the instructions which you will have to hand on later
to ALMURA making him understand categorically that he must follow
the rules for the service to the letter without any excuse as if this
is not done the object we are looking for in this system will be
defeated.

IMPORTANT:
We hope that you will be able to guard completely and
conscientiously all this material which we confide in you and
prevent it at any time ever falling into the hands of the enemy. You
should only confide in ALMURA those things which are absolutely
necessary for the carrying out of the service.

PLAN OF CAMOUFLAGE: ALMURA – CENTRO, 1943/44.

JULY

GMT:	1 21.15	2 22.00	5 21.00	7 21.30	13 20.30	15 22.00	16 21.00	19 21.30	23 20.30	28 21.00	30 22.00
ALMURA	SMK	UHI	KNO	WTJ	IVQ	FNT	DIO	DRF	MAC	TJI	FKN
KCS:											
CENTRO	KBI	CFT	SBJ	NLO	FSA	PRT	EVK	POA	BXI	RAG	HLM
KCS:											

AUG.:

GMT:	3 20.30	5 21.30	11 20.45	13 22.00	17 21.15	18 20.30	23 22.00	27 20.30	31 21.15
ALMURA	BFC	IHN	ACV	KAQ	TOP	JZA	DZK	RFN	WCX
KCS:									
CENTRO	CXY	SBA	AHK	ASF	LVT	KWE	KXQ	FOZ	SAW
KCS:									

SEPT.

GMT:	2 20.45	3 22.00	6 21.00	8 21.30.	14 22.00	16 20.30	20 21.30	23 21.00	24 20.30	29 22.00
ALMURA	LOR	SBH	YKI	EMF	PAZ	CUN	WST	FRI	MTZ	WIO
KCS:										
CENTRO	FSI	CXD	BGA	JCV	PPO	RAB	JOP	SHA	KUZ	HTK
KCS:										

OCT.

GMT:	1 20.45	5 21.15	7 20.30	11 22.00	15 20.45	19 21.45	21 22.00	25 21.30	27 21.00
ALMURA	DWK	JDU	HFA	SVR	AIE	LGF	KSE	SCI	JGD
KCS:									
CENTRO	KIJ	SVP	LSP	KHL	TOP	OQA	FPA	PXT	FQZ
KCS:									

NOV.

	2	4	8	11	16	18	23	25	28	30
GMT:	21.30	20.45	21.15	22.00	21.45	20.30	21.15	20.45	21.00	22.00
ALMURA	EMG	NTA	RSZ	BIK	PJO	LPU	ATE	MCI	TUJ	FKM
KCS:										
CENTRO	FSI	JHP	KNO	LMO	HAZ	BGT	SHN	PET	RAG	HLM
KCS:										

DEC.

	1	2	6	7	13	15	16	20	23
GMT:	21.15	22.00	21.00	21.30	20.30	22.00	21.00	21.30	20.30
ALMURA	SMK	UHI	KNO	WTJ	IVC	FNT	DIO	DHF	MAC
KCS:									
CENTRO	KBI	CFT	BBJ	NLO	FSA	PRT	UVK	POA	BXI
KCS:									

JAN.

	3	5	11	13	17	18	25	27	31
GMT:	20.30	21.30	20.45	22.00	21.15	20.30	22.00	20.30	21.15
ALMURA	BFC	IHN	ACV	KAQ	TOE	JZA	BZK	RFN	WCX
KCS:									
CENTRO	CXY	SBA	AHK	ASF	LVI	KWE	KXQ	FOZ	SAW
KCS:									

FEB.

	2	3	8	14	16	21	23	24
GMT:	20.45	22.00	21.30	22.00	20.50	21.30	21.00	20.30
ALMURA	LOR	SBA	EMF	PAZ	CUM	WST	FRI	NTZ
KCS:								
CENTRO	FSI	CXD	JCV	TPO	RAB	JOP	SHA	KUZ
KCS:								

CALL SIGNS.

Call signs for ALMURA – CENTRO detailed below which total 31 have been worked out to be used in the special transmissions and can be adapted for the different days of each month since the call signs set out in the camouflaged plan do not correspond to the days of each month and are not the same.

DAY	1	2	3	4	5	6	7	8	9	10
ALMURA	SKE	VFC	LDT	QEO	HSA	VKU	HSG	XFN	KZJ	TPF
CENTRO	FDA	ESL	ASH	RCO	IHO	ERM	TIU	PDS	BSC	FVS

DAY	11	12	13	14	15	16	17	18	19	20
ALMURA	JIL	HNB	SZG	EWR	FXI	LCG	XFE	OSS	UKB	APQ
CENTRO	LXP	MEL	RMN	CVA	TEY	BVS	DIS	LZF	VGK	EHX

DAY	21	22	23	24	25	26	27	28	29	30	31
ALMURA	TDL	CTZ	TFE	KDX	EGF	GKC	NVF	USL	AVP	NSJ	PZY
CENTRO	KWT	KPG	LXE	DWR	HNL	KGJ	YFG	LFG	DQS	MOZ	VEP

FREQUENCIES.
The frequencies omitted in the camouflaged plan will be decided as
soon as the special experimental transmissions have taken place and
will be communicated to ALMURA by cyphered message giving the
following headings, for example, AAA CCC GGG etc., corresponding to
the pairs of frequencies to be used on the predetermined days.

E.
On the 21.8.44 the military transmitting plan was cancelled and the
following new instructions and cyphers substituted.
        A new cypher table based on the previous system but on a new
code phrase was provided. This was given the code name "CLARION."

NEW INSTRUCTIONS FOR ALMURA.
From the 15th September, 1944, Almura shall give up using the signs
at present in use which are embodied in the camouflage plan, which
is to say, all indication that makes it appear that it is an English
military wireless set in operation as was provided for in this plan.
Thus the following signs and passwords are annulled:-

        X 626 - X 236 - X 261 - X 279 - X 613
        X 617 - X 307 - X 257 - Q

        We will again return to the normal transmissions as were at
first carried out. Almura will again work on the basis of the radio
amateur system, which is to say, that all transmissions should be
carried out using the Q groups "Q CODE". Just as Centro has been
using in their transmissions to date.
        The only exception which continues in operation is that part
of the preamble of the messages to be transmitted by Almura, for
example, the message transmitted to date:-

ALMURA: JCD JGD Z GR 6 BWC 121 27 LARUM LDNOG
           NSEVI BKPYE G. USH LARUM AR

Will in future be transmitted as follows:-

ALMURA: GR 6 27 LARUM LDNOG NSEVI BKPYE G. USH LARUM AR

i.e. the number of groups - date - camouflage group x message -
camouflage group - AR.
        The composition of the actual message remains unchanged,
that is to say the first and last phantasy groups should be the same
and in accordance with custom they should be groups which are so
composed as to be pronounceable.

The change of frequencies will be carried out as to date, that is to say, either party will only give the correct code sign to indicate the frequency to which the other side is to change. I.E.,

        NUT
                    = Code to indicate the desired frequency.
        KET

It is unconditionally prohibited to request a wait giving an indication of the length of time, as for example:

        QRX 20 minutes QRX 30 minutes or QRX 45 minutes.

To do this, should Almura or Centro desire to split up the transmission of several messages into two separate transmissions during the same night, the second transmission will take place two hours after starting the first, as a password, and to mislead the enemy as to when the second transmission will take place, Almura or Centro must close down at the end of the first transmission giving the code sign:-

        "QRX?"

For example: "QRX TMN" which means "We will make contact again two hours after the time of having started the present transmission."

For the second transmission on the same night both will use corresponding frequencies.......and as call signs those corresponding to two months earlier. For example, in August use June call signs and in September those for July.

DENOMINATION OF PLANS AND CODES.

To simplify the determination of the use of codes and plans already in your possession and plans and codes which will in future be sent to you, it is necessary, in order to avoid confusion in the transmission or application, to give each plan and code a separate name.

PLAN ALMURA/CENTRO, 1944.

This plan is to operate when Almura/Centro only work on fixed and obligatory days which are marked on the plan with the thick black lines.

This is called PLAN CHAVES.

PLAN ALMURA/CENTRO, 1944.

When this plan is used Centro will be listening every day in case Almura should have anything urgent to transmit in the way that it is being used at the present time, it shall be called:

PLAN CASINO.

PLAN ALMURA/CENTRO, 1944.

Emergency plan for special and urgent transmissions in connection with which Centro would be permanently listening nearly all hours of the day and night, which is to say the plan given on the 2nd May. This is called:

PLAN CUBAS.

The code which is in your possession i.e., the table for primary encyphering and for last decyphering which will remain in operation up to the 14th September, 1944, is called:

CODE BRAVE.

The new code which is enclosed in this letter i.e., the table for primary encyphering and for the last decyphering and the plans of the code which is to come into operation after the 15th September, 1944, is called:

CODE CLARION.

The dates previously mentioned have been fixed in advance on the calculation that the present letter will have arrived in your possession by that date.

Should it become necessary through any unforeseen eventuality to take the security measure of stopping Almura from transmitting over a period (Centro will transmit their messages normally for you on the fixed dates in accordance with PLAN CHAVES and will repeat each message twice and when you again make contact you will send a message confirming the number of messages received on each date.)

F.

On the 3.10.44 a provisional transmitting plan for use by Agent No.5 in Canada was forwarded to GARBO. A cypher based on the system used in D. above, but on a different code phrase was supplied.

<u>G</u>.
On the 4.2.45 the final transmitting plan for permanent use was
completed and forwarded to GARBO for sending on to Agent No. 5. The
plan which is set out below was to be used with the cypher referred
to in para. F. above.

INSTRUCTIONS FOR THE USE OF THE PLAN COMETA - CENTRO.

This plan is composed of parts I and II. Part I contains the data for
the days 1-15, and Part II for the days 16-31 of each month of the
year. The hours are marked: V - W - Y - Z. The frequencies for COMETA
are marked with A - B - C - D, with the auxiliary frequency F.

The frequencies for CENTRO are marked with E - G - H - K, with
the auxiliary frequency L. The hours and frequencies for both
stations are set out at the foot of the Plan.

The denominations of the frequencies vary each month. The
details for carrying out a change of frequency during a transmission
are set out in the columns at the side.

The auxiliary frequencies are only given in order that each
station should have one more frequency available if need should
arise.

In order to change frequencies it is compulsory to use the
call sign for the previous day.

It has been decided <u>only to establish one fixed contact per
week</u>. Between these fixed days an optional date has been arranged
when CENTRO will be listening in order to receive COMETA should he
have anything urgent to communicate.

The <u>fixed days</u> are those whose call signs have been outlined
and which are written in capital letters:- KLM. On these days it is
compulsory for both stations to try to make contact.

The <u>optional days</u> are those whose call signs have also been
outlined but which are written in small letters:- klm. During these
optional days CENTRO will be listening in case COMETA should have
anything important to transmit. If on the fixed days it is not
possible to establish communication, or if this should not be
completed due to atmospheric conditions or for any other reason, it
will automatically be compulsory for both parties to listen on the
following day at the hour and frequencies fixed in the plan. The
same applies to the optional days, if on one of these a message
should be started which it is impossible to finish.

If one of the stations requests the other to give an extraordinary transmission on the following day all he must do is to give
the group:- QRX NEXT without indicating the time and frequencies as
these will be given in the corresponding plan for the following day.

Any hint at a future contact is absolutely forbidden as
everything for this is set out in detail in the plan.

Any other hint at a future contact is absolutely forbidden as, should this be necessary, everything is arranged in the plan.

An extraordinary contact for a future date can only be requested by message.

COMETA's station should only be used for transmitting urgent messages of a military nature, that is to say, the exchange of messages will be reduced as much as possible.

Needless to say the period of calling between one station and another at the beginning of a contact should be reduced to a maximum of FIVE MINUTES, since the trials have shown that it is sufficient to call for less time.

MODEL FOR THE DEVELOPMENT OF THE TRANSMISSIONS.
It is essential that COMETA should classify more accurately the strength of reception ("scale used to express strength of signals".)

QSA 1 = Hardly perceptible
QSA 2 = Weak
QSA 3 = Fairly good
QSA 4 = Good
QSA 5 = Very good

Abbreviations most commonly used for our contacts:-

CHART FOR COMETA:

QRA	=	What is the name of your station?
		The name of my station is..........
QRI	=	Is my note good?
		Your note varies.
QRJ	=	Do you receive me badly? Are my signals weak?
		I cannot receive you. Your signals are too weak.
QRK	–	What is the readability of my signals (1-5)?
		The readability of your signals is (1-5)
QRL	=	Are you busy?
		I am busy (or, I am busy with........)
QRN	=	Are you troubled by atmospherics?
		I am troubled by atmospherics.
QRQ	=	Shall I send faster?
		Send faster.
QRS	=	Shall I send more slowly?
		Send more slowly.
QRV	=	Are you ready?
		I am ready.
QRO	=	Shall I increase power?

		Increase power.
QSB	=	Does the strength of my signals vary?
		The strength of your signals varies.
QSD	=	Is my keying correct? Are my signals distinct?
		Your keying is incorrect; your signals are bad.
QSL	=	Can you give me acknowledgment of receipt?
		I give you acknowledgment of receipt.
QSO	=	Can you communicate with.........direct.
		I can communicate with.........
QSW	=	Will you send on............KCS.
		I am going to send on............KCS.
QSU	=	Shall I send.......KCS (or reply on......KCS)
QSZ	=	Shall I send each word or group twice?
		Send each word or group twice.
QSY	=	Shall I change to transmission without changing the type of wave?
		Change to transmission without changing type of wave.
QTA	=	Shall I cancel telegram No........as if it had not been sent?
		Cancel telegram No..........as if it had not been sent.
QTR	=	What is the exact time?
		The exact time is......

TABLE I

DAY:	1	2	3	4	5	6	7	8	9	10	11	12	13	14	15
HOUR:	V	W	Y	Z	W	Y	Z	V	Y	Z	V	W	Z	V	W

COMETA:

KCS:	D	C	B	A	C	B	A	D	B	A	D	C	A	D	C
MONTHS:															
1-7	drv	BNT	kgf	uzr	hje	los	was	iht	shr	lbx	FCV	mnw	igq	pje	tfn
2-8	TED	cur	jml	bon	vhs	zqc	gpz	koi	FHM	nhv	iqg	lsk	rew	bmg	SCJ
3-9	uif	gpj	hrt	nvo	kch	LYZ	pgl	fod	tre	sni	rgb	cws	pug	JFD	mrt
4-10	izn	hrf	rmq	IET	tvk	wbs	ptk	yzl	mvh	GQE	lse	dtf	isn	gqe	piz
5-11	hyt	kuc	vqd	atf	xbh	nfl	YDM	nax	fib	cks	urq	gqz	prh	ozf	MSL
6-12	auf	lod	xnb	ltd	rzs	FUV	jzb	ocu	jxt	vsr	rxh	bmf	CEY	itq	dwc

CENTRO:

KCS:	K	H	G	E	H	G	E	K	G	E	K	H	E	K	H
MONTHS:															
1-7	aex	UFH	dmt	xby	rsa	spg	koz	elr	bzg	tvq	DYK	vcl	iqr	bnf	zhw
2-8	NBJ	hns	zfe	hrv	udε	ple	cag	xsm	RCE	zay	shi	cvr	fay	gtn	HDU
3-9	vby	zmx	ybh	kcu	tnε	DET	msq	par	nrf	kdq	nxh	uvp	wjh	SGE	yxf
4-10	fhl	ozc	mbe	CRH	isg	slk	fjp	dbt	mqr	RUE	hwx	vyz	nrk	dqv	pws
5-11	ket	cgb	fhv	gwf	hsγ	ukl	BSZ	tke	lar	nyk	msh	lbs	zwh	rnu	PEQ
6-12	lva	tek	frs	dlk	ghε	DGP	cwb	pim	sfq	ben	cqr	zje	VHU	wky	yqn

Reference columns (COMETA):

MONTHS	A	B	C	D	F
1-7	sho	cwf	jrk	btn	PEV
2-8	npu	dem	afi	sgy	HTC
3-9	kir	bto	vxc	nqw	UZJ
4-10	mye	ghs	ckp	lfi	ZNB
5-11	igs	ekv	trb	phy	BPZ
6-12	bfu	nrd	lsh	two	MGE

Reference columns (CENTRO):

MONTHS	E	G	H	K	L
1-7	ewn	pkl	ghs	drw	TIU
2-8	cqo	yad	tzb	xde	NFW
3-9	atr	zkv	gjm	ben	NSP
4-10	fia	uyk	rbh	lzn	VEG
5-11	afu	ilt	naz	hex	MDR
6-12	wcz	yhg	sml	rda	FCN

TABLE I CONTINUED.

HOUR	COMETA	CENTRO
V = 20.40 GMT	A = 9.300 KCS	E = 9.120 KCS
W = 21.20 GMT	B = 10.900 KCS	G = 10.400 KCS
Y = 22.05 GMT	C = 11.900 KCS	H = 11.300 KCS
Z = 22.45 GMT	D = 13.800 KCS	K = 12.300 KCS
	AUXILIARY FREQUENCY F = 8.490 KCS	AUXILIARY FREQUENCY L = 8.720 KCS

TABLE II

DAY / HOUR schedule:

	16	17	18	19	20	21	22	23	24	25	26	27	28	29	30	31
DAY:	16	17	18	19	20	21	22	23	24	25	26	27	28	29	30	31
HOUR:	Y	V	W	Y	Z	W	Y	Z	V	Y	Z	V	W	Y	Z	W

COMETA:

	16	17	18	19	20	21	22	23	24	25	26	27	28	29	30	31	A	B	C	D	F
KCS:	B	D	C	B	A	C	B	A	D	B	A	D	C	D	A	C					
MONTHS:																					
1-7	kst	RBM	tch	lio	saw	ncu	slh	tyh	akr	nbv	UFE	lhs	zhc	jsq	lkh	sfn	sho	cwf	jrk	btn	PEV
2-8	lhd	ujn	mdr	gsj	NSY	lig	wsx	poi	nge	bfs	ysd	hgv	DCK	lzr	bvj	rsb	npu	dem	afi	sgy	HTC
3-9	anv	krn	ltb	HMR	fmc	hqm	rbp	uct	msg	bvn	fjt	SLF	yci	twx	zrj	avd	kir	bpo	bxc	nqw	UZJ
4-10	nyt	ksq	ulp	fjw	VHZ	hto	bga	nec	pyb	SNU	gsl	khz	wgz	byj	GDQ	ugb	mye	ghs	ckp	lfi	ZNB
5-11	ayc	lfb	tei	jos	frg	unk	dsh	CDT	hjw	gxt	ram	cqf	snc	KVR	pgq	ztc	igs	ckv	trb	dhy	BPZ
6-12	vtl	eds	rqf	nug	lvh	spi	ZNB	dwk	thl	bsm	YRC	xtn	weo	kgp	fyu	bfs	bfu	nrd	lsh	twc	MGE

CENTRO:

	16	17	18	19	20	21	22	23	24	25	26	27	28	29	30	31	E	G	H	K	L
KCS:	G	K	H	G	E	H	G	E	K	G	E	K	H	G	E	H					
MONTHS:																					
1-7	mkc	YQS	vhu	cgt	zbs	lmr	ibg	fps	yka	wnx	BWM	gat	sxb	htl	wdk	psi	ewn	pkl	ghs	grw	TIU
2-8	tav	ked	dts	rqf	ZVC	ung	vkh	psi	whf	htg	sxm	gab	RMY	cew	kpx	fyu	cqo	yad	pzb	xde	NFW
3-9	mvi	lag	brm	CYL	fhq	jus	dhp	twt	bxs	rmw	nqc	KGN	fku	bpr	cti	zhg	atr	zkv	gjm	bon	HPS
4-10	fuk	gpj	wdi	khs	MTI	nbr	ckq	pfu	smt	LDG	lth	znq	vgf	atk	TLS	dun	fia	uyk	rbh	lzn	VEJ
5-11	tis	dgn	ukl	vfj	fid	wxh	khb	NIV	gst	rmq	xau	yfr	nit	dle	cls	zhr	sfu	ilt	naz	hcx	NVR
6-12	vcg	zqe	nib	sfu	fxm	ket	YCQ	rbo	gpw	biv	WNH	flu	tiq	lvr	tym	gsj	wez	yhg	sml	rda	FCN

TABLE II CONTINUED.

HOUR	COMETA	CENTRO
V = 20.40 GMT	A = 9.300 KCS	E = 9.120 KCS
W = 21.20 GMT	B = 10.900 KCS	G = 10.400 KCS
Y = 22.05 GMT	C = 11.900 KCS	H = 11.300 KCS
Z = 22.45 GMT	D = 13.800 KCS	K = 12.300 KCS

AUXILIARY FREQUENCY F = 8.490 KCS

AUXILIARY FREQUENCY L = 8.720 KCS

APPENDIX XXXIV.

SECURITY MEASURES AND HANDLING.

In spite of the great confidence and trust which we gained in GARBO as time went on, routine security checks were maintained during the entire period of his working for us. These were ultimately limited to a H.O.W. and the supervision of his secret writing.

Telephone Check and H.O.W. were imposed and, in addition, he was escorted during the first few weeks of his stay here by an F.S.P. sergeant in plain clothes. His escort was introduced to him as a companion and he was provided with funds to take GARBO about and entertain him. He resided at the same house as GARBO and they took their meals together.

During the first days GARBO was in England his escort offered to take him around to see the bomb damage, anti-aircraft defence system, etc., GARBO refused to go, and avoided any other opportunity of obtaining information about this country's war effort until the decision had been reached that he was to remain here for the duration of the war.

Immediately on his arrival here GARBO handed us over a supply of the paper and envelopes which he had been accustomed to use whilst operating on his own in Portugal, a complete record of all outgoing and incoming letters exchanged with the Germans, as well as his secret writing material.

During the entire running of the case the secret ink was never left alone with him, nor would he ever accept the charge of any documents.

Secret writing was always executed by GARBO in the presence of a member of this Office. The washing of letters and the writing of cover texts, as well as the sealing of the envelopes and mailing, were always witnessed by an officer. In spite of the fact that the actual writing of the letters was supervised, periodical checks were made in order to ensure that no special control sign had been inserted unobserved by the supervising officer. This was done by creating some excuse for having to rewrite the letter after it had been finished, making available the cancelled letter for development and examination.

In the early days officers in contact with GARBO used aliases but, for convenience, these were soon dropped. GARBO not only knew the identity of various members of the Office but frequently visited the Case Officer at his home. Towards the later phases of the case the work was conducted on the basis of GARBO and the case Officer being fellow officers, employed by the same organization.

GARBO was never given any passes to Government Offices, neither did he ever enter this Office. Meetings between GARBO and members of SHAEF or Service Departments were usually conducted at the home of the Case Officer. As the volume of work increased it was found impracticable to draft and write the letters and do our planning at GARBO's house and an office was taken in Jermyn Street which was made available for his use. An extension telephone was supplied there from this Office so that confidential conversations on a direct line could be carried on with this Office, SHAEF, and the other Service Departments.

GARBO, of his own volition, never wrote even to his family in Spain without submitting the letter to the Case Officer for censorship and mailing.

All private letters which he received from abroad were, at his suggestion, sent to an address which we provided for him, which gave added facilities for censorship.

All incoming secret ink letters were developed by the Case Officer in his presence. Letters in duff were transcribed for him.

GARBO was never allowed to gain the impression that an organization existed for the running of special agents. He did, however, in the course of time, get to know our method of approving traffic. The bulk of traffic was such that it was frequently necessary to telephone approving authorities in his presence for approval of last minute alterations before transmission.

During the period of his deception work he came to realize that this was conducted by SHAEF and he was allowed to meet members of SHAEF Ops. B., with whom plans were frequently worked out in his presence. He was entrusted with information about the Order of Battle and was told which divisions and formations were notional and which were real so long as this information reflected on his work. He was not, however, given any secret information which was not directly relevant to his work.

It became necessary to disclose to him the cover plan for OVERLORD in considerable detail but the real operation was not divulged, though by implication he must have been able to discover its nature. Planning of traffic had to be worked out some time in advance so that it could be considered and co-ordinated, and thus he frequently had advance warning of our plans.

In view of the very personal style and characteristic eccentricities which the Germans had come to associate with GARBO it was necessary to consult him on his traffic well in advance of D Day so that approval could be obtained for the modifications and alterations which he would invariably insist on making to conform with his style. One can, therefore, say that GARBO was aware of the date of Y Day several weeks in advance.

The exact Department for which he was working was never disclosed to him and he was satisfied to know that he was working for the "British Secret Service." Only at the time of his departure from the U. K. did he learn to connect this service with M. I. 5 through Press, and other announcements.

It was necessary at times to boost up his morale and the best method was found to be to introduce him to a senior member of the Office who would assure him that he was rendering a great service to the war effort. He was given three interviews by the Director General at intervals of several months and it gave him the greatest satisfaction to know that his work had received notice at so high a level.

GARBO came to regard his Case Officer as a personal friend in whom he eventually confided his most intimate and personal affairs.

APPENDIX XXXV.

COVER ADDRESSES.

The following is a list of cover addresses which were given to GARBO between July, 1941 and May, 1945:-

1.   Manuel Rodriguez IGLESIAS,
        91, Lista 4,
        Madrid.

2.   Manuel Rodriguez IGLESIAS,
        51, Ayala,
        Madrid.

3.   Senora Araceli GONZALEZ,
        Viriato 73 - 2 Dr.
        Madrid.

4.   German DOMINGUEZ,
        Apartado 1099,
        Madrid.

5.   Don Rafael Morales (Abogado)
        Calle Genoa 15,
        Madrid.

6.   Lucio Crespo GARCIA,
        Farmacia,
        Gral. Pardinas 20,
        Madrid

7.   Sra. Da. Concepcion FERNANDEZ,
        e/c "La Rosa de Oro"
        Plaza de Callao 1,
        Madrid.

8.   Sra. Doña e de OLIVEIRA,
        Rua Castello Branco Saraiva 64,
        Porta 12,
        Lisbon.

9. Pedro ALVAREZ,
    Francisco Silvela 15,
    Madrid.

10. Juan GONZALEZ,
    San Bernado 120,
    Madrid.

11. Petras GARCIA,
    San Bernado 120,
    Madrid.

12. Sra. Doña Maria do ceu PEREIRA,
    Rua Coelho da Rocha, No. 82 - 1° da,
    Lisbon.

13. Antonio de SOUZA LOPEZ,
    Rua Castillo 31,
    Lisbon.

14. Sr. Joaquim F. VIEIRA,
    Rua Alves Correira 47,
    Lisbon.

15. Sra. Gina M. DAMIAO,
    Rua Basilio Telez 15, R-Ch,
    Lisbon. (A Palhava)

16. Jose Dias de SILVA,
    Rua Antonio Pereira Carrilho, No. 1 - loja,
    Lisbon.

17. Mlle. Odette da CONCEICAO,
    Rua Teofilo Braga No. 59, loja,
    Lisbon.

18. Manuel CORTEZ,
    Rua Santo Amaro 23 r/ch E°,
    Lisbon.

19. Jose Dos Santos,
    Rua Castelo Branca Saraiva,
    90 r/ch ESQU,
    Lisbon.

20.   Senora Doña PAZ TRUJILLANO,
        Calle Principe 13,
        Madrid.

21.   Sra. Maria ESTRELLA,
        Rua Jose Falcao 22/1°,
        Lisbon.

22.   Sra. Clementina MARQUES,
        Rua Castelo Branca Saraiva 64,
        Porta 10,
        Lisbon.

23.   Jose P. CAL,
        Rua das Taipas 67-71,
        Lisbon.

24.   Jorge NUNES,
        Rua Santa Marta 72, 3rd Floor Dto,
        Lisbon.

25.   Excmo. Señor CARLOS DE MELLO,
        Praca do Comercio, No. 7, 5th Floor,
        Lisbon.

26.   Excmo. Sr. Rui HUMBERTO DE OLIVEIRA,
        Rua Carlos Mardel No. 110 - 3° E,
        Lisbon.

27.   Excmo. Sr. Miguel SEMEDO,
        Rua Ponta Delgada No. 44 - cave,
        Lisbon.

28.   JIMENEZ SALINAS Y CIA.,
        Caixa Postal 399,
        Lisbon.

29.   Señor Cosmo GUILHERME,
        Rua Boa Vista 56 r/c,
        (Alges), Lisbon.

APPENDIX XXXVI.

SECRET INKS.

A.

GARBO was instructed by the Germans in Madrid in the use of this ink in 1941. They then told him that it was their highest grade ink and could not be detected. We know the same ink was given to other high grade agents at that time. The ink was supplied to him in the form of small impregnated cotton wool pellets which he was told he could conceal in his ears for the purpose of passing through the British controls. Large supplies of this ink were subsequently forwarded to GARBO at intervals. They were forwarded by courier and the pellets were usually concealed in the cotton wool packing of Panflavinia pastilles or similar packages. In all, sufficient pellets were sent to make up several litres of secret ink. This ink was made up in various strengths and given to Agents Nos. 1, 3, 5, 6, 7 and 7(3), who all corresponded direct to German cover addresses in this ink.

GARBO, in his original instructions was told to write with an orange stick, the end of which, to protect the surface of the paper, was to be wrapped in a thin layer of cotton wool. He kept to this tedious procedure until the middle of 1942 when he took to writing with a quill pen which did not appear to scratch the paper. Later the quill pen was substituted for celluloid nibs which greatly facilitated the writing and speeded up the process.

The Germans never remarked that they had noticed these changes, though from the miniature size of the writing finally achieved by GARBO it must have been apparent to them that the letters could not have been written with an orange stick.

Agents Nos. 1, 3, 5 and 7 likewise used a celluloid nib and used to wash the letters and press them before writing the cover text.

Agents Nos. 6 and 7(3) used ordinary steel Waverley nibs and did not wash the letters after writing. Both these agents were supposed to be writing from Service Headquarters abroad and, as their letters only had to pass military Censorship, it was implied that secret ink tests were not made and the additional protection to the secret writing which washing would have given was therefore unnecessary. No mention was ever made to the Germans that these agents did not wash their letters, and presumably they took the decision not to do so on their own initiative, realizing that they were more likely to be discovered had they gone to the elaborate processes of washing and then pressing the letters for twenty-four hours which this entailed.

The secret ink applied to the backs of letters lightly written with a steel nib leaves no trace of secret writing which is visible to the naked eye. The Germans in Madrid did not appear to have been aware that these letters were not washed. At least they made no reference to their having discovered this fact, and on the contrary, always remarked how well the letters had developed.

Although GARBO was given instructions to select a semi-matt, rather thick, paper for writing in this ink, experience showed that almost any type of paper could be used. GARBO, who himself wrote several hundred letters during the period he was operative, used every class of hotel paper. All were found to be satisfactory.

Agent No. 7(3) used thick watermarked foolscap Stationery Office paper.

GARBO did not have the developer for [...] ink, neither were they prepared to supply it to him.

From the number of secret letters which were allowed to evade Censorship in spite of striping, the Germans were led to assume that the British Censorship did not test for this ink. It was not until the autumn of 1943 that Censorship applied the [...] developer, from the visible markings of which the Germans came to realize that we were looking for secret letters in [...] A number of GARBO letters were thus intercepted, and from that time all secret letters were sent by courier only, abandoning the ordinary air mail service.

B.

During GARBO's period of uncontrolled work in Lisbon, and after he had recruited the first of his notional agents it occurred to him that it would be advisable to provoke the Germans into disclosing their method of secret inter-communication between agents, assuming that the information conveyed did not have to pass through high grade Censorship. On the pretext that he considered it unsafe for his agents to communicate with him in writing, en clair, GARBO asked the Germans to provide him with a safe method for sending internal communications within the network. The Germans supplied him with some pills which they sent by courier concealed in a tin of throat pastilles. They instructed GARBO to disolve the tablets in gin, vodka or whisky, and after writing with the solution formed, the screed should be put into a bath of similar alcohol. The alcohol for bathing the screed could subsequently be drunk without harm. GARBO pretended that he used this method over a long period, though in fact experiments with this ink proved that it was a clumsy and poor process.

After GARBO's arrival in England and his realization of the scarcity of alcoholic drinks in the U. K. he decided to ask for a substitute, complaining that the method was impracticable for use by the agent of low, or medium calibre.

C. THE BOY SCOUT METHOD.

This was the procedure which they instructed him to use to substitute the [...] The process for writing was to moisten a sheet of writing paper which was then pressed out on to a sheet of glass or similar hard surface. A second piece of paper was placed on top of the moist piece and the message written on the uppermost sheet with a hard pointed pencil. The pressure caused thereby on the moist undersheet caused a sort of water mark script to be made which was invisible to the naked eye when the paper had been pressed and dried. The cover text was then added to the dried sheet of paper, which when subsequently immersed in water would bring out the water mark impression caused at the time of writing.

GARBO complained that he thought this method too elementary, and therefore unsafe to use.

D. WAX METHOD.

As the case progressed we had to represent that a very considerable correspondence was maintained between GARBO and his numerous agents and in particular with his network in Canada. To have written in [...] would have been impracticable. The Boy Scout Method was found, on experimenting, to be most unreliable since its success depended mainly on the class of paper used. Some papers would take no impression at all, therefore it was decided to inform the Germans that, without their permission, GARBO had on his own initiative, adopted for some time past a procedure which he had learnt during his school days. This method was that of using a wax surface paper in the same way as a carbon is used, either for pencil, ink or typewriting. As explained to the Germans rolls of waxed paper for cooking and other purposes were obtainable from Woolworths and this proved to be perfectly adequate for writing in the wax process. The deposit of wax which formed the secret writing was invisible to the naked eye and could be developed by applying finely ground graphite or red lead to the secret screed.

In evidence of our claim letters from Agent No. 5 in Canada to GARBO in London were frequently forwarded by courier to the Germans. These were invariably typewritten in the wax method on the packing paper of a parcel and forwarded after development, on the assumption that GARBO would have first wanted to ascertain the contents which were normally intended for him. Though this is perhaps one of the most elementary methods of secret writing, the Germans maintained that they had not known about it until it was brought to their notice by GARBO.

APPENDIX XXXVII.

SYMBOLS FOR THE GARBO NETWORK
MOST SECRET SOURCES.

During the entire running of the case it was controlled in Madrid
by Karl KUHLENTHAL whose code name on M.S.S. was FELIPE, and later
substituted by FUNDADOR. GARBO, in all his communications with
Madrid used symbols to distinguish the origin of his reports. The
Germans in their secret communications used symbols for the members
of the GARBO network as shown in the following comparative table:-

SYMBOLS USED IN OUR COMMUNICATIONS WITH MADRID	SYMBOLS USED BY THE GERMANS IN MADRID IN THEIR COMMUNICATIONS WITH HEADQUARTERS IN BERLIN
J NETWORK	ARABAL UNDERTAKING.
J	V-MANN 319 SP of STELLE FELIPE @ V-MANN ALARIC of ARABAL UNDERTAKING.
J (3)	V-MANN AMEROS.
J (5)	V-MANN AMY.
AGENT NO. 1	V-MANN 371 SP via V-MANN 319 of STELLE FELIPE
AGENT NO. 2	V-MANN 372 SP via V-MANN 319 of STELLE FELIPE.
AGENT NO. 3's SUB-ORGANIZATION	BENEDICT NETWORK of ARABAL UNDERTAKING.
AGENT NO. 3	V-MANN 373 SP of STELLE FELIPE @ V-MANN BENEDICT.
AGENT NO. 3(3)	V-MANN BEN of BENEDICT NETWORK OF ARABAL UNDERATKING.
AGENT NO. 4	V-MANN 377 SP via V-MANN 319 SP of STELLE FELIPE @ V-MANN CAMILLUS of ARABAL UNDERTAKING
AGENT NO. 4(3)	V-MANN CASTOR of CAMILLUS NETWORK.
AGENT NO. 5's SUB-ORGANIZATION	AHORN NETWORK of ARABAL UNDERTAKING.
AGENT NO. 5	V-MANN 374 SP of ARABAL @ LEADER OF AHORN NETWORK of ARABAL UNDERTAKING.
AGENT NO. 5(1) @ CON	V-MANN PRESCOT of ARABAL - AHORN NETWORK.
AGENT NO. 6	V-MANN 365 SP of STELLE FELIPE

AGENT NO. 7's SUB-ORGANIZATION	DAGOBERT NETWORK of ARABAL UNDERTAKING.
AGENT NO. 7	V-MANN 1245 SP via V-MANN 319 of STELLE FELIPE @ V-MANN DAGOBERT of ARABAL UNDERTAKING.
AGENT NO. 7(2)	V-MANN DONNY OF DAGOBERT NETWORK.
AGENT NO. 7(3)	V JAVELIN of ARABAL UNDERTAKING.
AGENT NO. 7(4)	V-MANN DICK of DAGOBERT NETWORK.
AGENT NO. 7(5)	V-MANN DRAKE of DAGOBERT NETWORK.
AGENT NO. 7(6)	V-MANN DROMMOND of DAGOBERT NETWORK.
AGENT NO. 7(7)	V-MANN DORRICK of DAGOBERT NETWORK.

Reports were always compiled either by GARBO or by Agent No. 3 and forwarded in Spanish or English. They were given three categories:-

A = Information obtained through personal observation.
B = Information obtained through third party or indiscretion.
C = Information obtained through rumour or public opinion.

Thus a GARBO report transmitted in the following form:-

3(3A) GLASGOW. Many vehicles etc., etc.,

would be re-transmitted from Madrid to Berlin:-

Undertaking ARABAL via FELIPE. V-MANN BEN of NETWORK BENEDICT reports from Glasgow result of personal observation. Many vehicles etc., etc.,

APPENDIX XXXVIII.

FORTITUDE ORDER OF BATTLE.
GENERAL ORGANIZATION.

NOTE:-
All formations and units are NOTIONAL or DISBANDED except where
underlined.

FIRST (US) ARMY GROUP.

NINTH (US) ARMY.

FOURTEENTH (US) ARMY.

FOURTH (Br.) ARMY.

XXXIII (US) CORPS.

11th (US) INFANTRY DIVISION.

21st (US) AIRBORNE DIVISION.

II (Br.) CORPS.

35th (Br.) TANK BRIGADE.

2nd (Br.) AIRBORNE DIVISION.

61st (Br.) INFANTRY DIVISION.

5th (Br.) ARMOURED DIVISION.

90th (Br.) INFANTRY DIVISION.

77th (Br.) INFANTRY DIVISION.

48th (US) INFANTRY DIVISION.

25th (US) ARMOURED DIVISION.

XXXVII (US) CORPS.

17th (US) INFANTRY DIVISION.

59th (US) INFANTRY DIVISION.

9th (US) AIRBORNE DIVISION.

55th (US) INFANTRY DIVISION.

55th (Br.) INFANTRY DIVISION.

58th (Br.) INFANTRY DIVISION.

VII (Br.) CORPS.

80th (Br.) INFANTRY DIVISION.

48th (Br.) INFANTRY DIVISION.

76th (Br.) INFANTRY DIVISION.

9th (Br.) ARMOURED DIVISION.

NOTE:-
Insignias of notional formations were described in agents' eye
witness reports.

All formations were broken down to regiments, brigades,
battalions and companies, enabling agents to report the
identification of small units of troops belonging to Ordnance,
Medical, Q.M., Signals, Engineers, etc., giving their unit number
as well as their imaginary locations.

APPENDIX XXXIX.

O.K.W. INTELLIGENCE SUMMARY.

67 1019

OBERKOMMANDO DES HEERES
Gen St d H / Abt Fremde Heere West/Ia

9.4.1944

[Nur zur persönlichen Unterrichtung!
Weitergabe verboten!]

Geheim

Lagebericht West Nr. 1230

I. Italien:
  a) Feindtätigkeit:
    An Landungs- und Südfront geringe feindl. Spähtrupptätigkeit und vereinzelte Artl.-Feuerüberfälle.
    1.) **Landungsfront:**
      In der Nacht zum 9.4. stärkeres feindl. Artl.-Feuer, am 9.4. Artl.-Feuerüberfälle mit Schwerpunkt auf Arden. Rege feindl. Luftaufklärung in gesamten Abschnitt, ein schwerer Jaboangriff auf Littoria.
    2.) **Südabschnitt:**
      Am späten Abend des 8.4. O des Garigliano-Abschnitts starker feindl. Kfz.-Verkehr auf den Straßen zur Front. Auf Cassino lag weiterhin starker Nebelbeschuß. Über gesamten Abschnitt rege feindl. Luftaufklärung.
    3.) **Mittelabschnitt:**
      Keine Kampftätigkeit.
    4.) **Nordabschnitt:**
      O Orsogna verlor der Feind bei eigenen Spähtruppunternehmen Gefangene. Im nördl. Küstenabschnitt scheiterten 2 feindl. Stoßtruppunternehmen.
  b) Truppenfeststellungen:
    Durch Gefangene wurde 2.Inf.Brig. der 1.engl.I.D. 3 km O Campo di Carne bestätigt und I.R. 133 der 34.amerik.I.D. nach noch unsicheren Angaben 7 Pte.Rotto erstmalig im Landekopf festgestellt. Nach Gefangenenaussagen soll die 2.engl. Fallsch.Jg.Brig., die bisher O Pennapiedimente eingesetzt war, seit 14 Tagen aus der Front zurückgezogen worden sein.

II. Balkan:
  Kroatien:
    Zunehmende Verkehrssabotage und Bedrohung eigener Nachschubwege mit Schwerpunkt Bosnien – Dalmatien.
  Feindl. Lufttätigkeit:
    Normale Aufklärung. Bombenangriffe auf Stadt und Hafen Rhodos und Korfu.

III. Seelage:
    Während der Nacht zum 9.4. wurden 4 Landungsboote mit Kurs Anzio beobachtet; außerdem wurden mehrere Schiffsgruppen unbekannter Zahl geortet. Am Vormittag des 9.4. lagen in Hafen und auf der Reede Anzio 3 Transporter, 6 LST, 12 kl. Landungsboote und 2 Zerstörer.
    Die Aufklärung im Adriatischen Meer zwischen Rimini und Cap Gargano erbrachte bei lückenloser Einsichtnahme weder am 8.4. noch am 9.4. vormittags wesentliche Ergebnisse. Im Seeraum um Bari wurden am 8.4. nachmittags 3 kl. Kriegsfahrzeuge und 25–30 Segler erfaßt.

– 2 –

67 1020

- 2 -

An Ausgang des Golfs von Tarent wurde am 8.4. nachmittags ein auf
SW-Kurs laufender einzelner Transporter gesichtet.
NO Alboran wurde am 8.4. vormittags ein ostlaufendes Geleit mit
15 Frachtern beobachtet.
An 9.4. mittags liefen nach einer vorläufigen Meldung 77 Frachter
unter Geleitschutz von Atlantik in das Mittelmeer ein.

Lageberichtverteiler

Bemerkung: Skizze "Feindlage Italien"
          wurde am 9.4. nicht ausge-   I.A.
          geben.

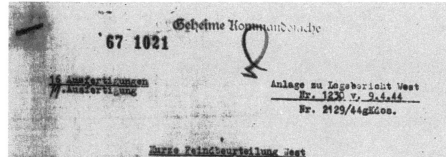

67 1021

Geheime Kommandosache

15 Ausfertigungen
17.Ausfertigung

Anlage zu Lagebericht West
Nr. 1230 v. 9.4.44
Nr. 2129/44gKdos.

Kurze Feindbeurteilung West
(Nur für begrenzten Verteilerkreis)

Englandbereich.

Das Bild der rasch vorgetriebenen Absprungbereitschaft hält auf allen Gebieten an; parallel laufen zahlreiche Ankündigungen in Truppenansprachen und offiziellen Verlautbarungen nahe bevorstehender Großkämpfe.

Im Rahmen der mehrwöchigen Truppenverschiebungen in Großausmaß ist es zu einer außerordentlichen Verdichtung der bereitgestellten Kräfte in Südengland, in etwas aufgelockertem Umfange auch in Ostengland gekommen. Dieser Vorgang wird durch die Feststellung von drei neuen Divisionen (2 amerik. in Ostengland, 1 engl. in Südengland) in diesen Räumen unterstrichen. Das Auftreten dieser bisher im Verbleib unbekannt in Großbritannien geführten Verbände in den Bereitstellungsräumen bestätigt die Erwartung, daß auch die übrigen 8 - 10 im Verbleib unbekannt geführten Divisionen sich in diesen Räumen befinden. Von Bedeutung erscheint, daß die stärkste erkennbare Konzentration sich in Südostengland (Küstenabschnitt Ramsgate - Portsmouth) abzeichnet. Die Luftlande-Verbände sind hierbei nicht in Betracht gezogen, da ihr derzeitiger Konzentrationsbereich keinen ausreichenden Aufschluß über ihre mutmaßliche Einsatzrichtung gibt.

Das erkannte Vorschieben höherer Luftwaffenführungs-Stäbe in den Schwerpunktbereich der Küste weist in gleicher Richtung. Ebenso ist die Gleichschaltung des Funkverkehrs zwischen den brit. und amerik. Nahkampfverbänden als Steigerung der Absprungbereitschaft zu werten.

Weitere Anzeichen in diesem Sinne sind die Einschränkung des militärischen Funkverkehrs in England, die laufende Steigerung des Agenten- und Sabotageeinsatzes in Frankreich und die gesteigerte Luftwaffentätigkeit im Westen, die z.T. als Aufklärung des Eisenbahnverkehrs nach Nordwestdeutschland hinein gewertet ird und im Zusammenhange mit vermutlich erkannten deutschen Abtransporten stehen kann.

- 2 -

923

67 1022

- 2 -

Da auch die Wetterlage z.Zt. Landungen zuläßt, rundet sich das
Gesamtbild im bisherigen Sinne dahin ab, daß der Absprung zum Groß-
angriff jeder Zeit erfolgen kann. Der stark beeinflußte Zeitpunkt
des Absprunges bleibt weiterhin, trotz zahlloser Gerüchte, ohne konkrete Unterlagen.

Mittelmeerbereich.

Den Feindverbänden im westl. Mittelmeerbereich sind in der letz-
ten Woche personelle und materielle Verstärkungen in 3-Geleiten zuge-
flossen. Auch der Bestand an Landungsschiffsraum hat eine geringe Zu-
nahme erfahren. Danach ist die Durchführbarkeit neuer Unternehmungen
im westl. Mittelmeerbereich als gegeben anzusehen; ihr Ausmaß wird
in erster Linie durch den Schiffsraum begrenzt sein.

Als Vorbereitung einer neuen Planung ist deutlich erkennbare Luft-
waffenverstärkung auf Korsika zu werten, dessen Belegung jetzt ins-
gesamt mindestens 1200 Flugzeuge umfaßt. Auch zeichnet sich die Be-
reitstellung eines bisher an der ital. Front gebundenen Nahkampf-
Korps für neue Zwecke ab.

Für die Zielsetzung haben sich gegenüber den bisherigen Mut-
maßungen konkrete neue Anhaltepunkte nicht ergeben.

Im ostwärtigen Mittelmeerbereich unterstreichen mehrere Fest-
stellungen das stark begrenzte Ausmaß der Balkanplanungen. In dieser
Richtung weist das erneut bestätigte Fehlen größerer Truppenkörper
in Gegend Brindisi und Tarent. Ferner die Beobachtung, daß die feindl.
Führung anscheinend auf dem Wege des Funkspieles Truppenverstärkungen
und -bewegungen im ägyptisch-libyschen Bereich betont vorzutäuschen
sucht.

1 Anlage.

`67 1023`

Anlage zu Kurzer Feindbeurteilung West
vom 9.4.44 Nr. 2123/44 g.Kdos.

1.) Untenstehend wird die Ausführung eines oft bewährten V-Mannes
mit einem Bekannten im brit. Informationsministerium wiedergegeben (Zeitpunkt Ende Februar).

"Vor 2 Tagen hatte ich erneut Gelegenheit, mich ausführlich
mit meiner Verbindung aus dem Informationsministerium zu unter-
halten. Indem ich auf die Bemerkung meines Gewährsmannes in Bezug
auf einen möglichen Rückzug der Deutschen aus Frankreich zurück-
kam und ihm meine Zweifel in dieser Hinsicht zum Ausdruck brach-
te, erklärte er, daß man in maßgeblichen engl. Kreisen eben an-
ders darüber denke. Wenn die Deutschen zwischen zwei Übeln zu
wählen haben, fuhr er fort, so werden sie vorziehen, daß die
Alliierten es sein sollen, die mit der Besetzung Berlins auch
die Friedensbedingungen diktieren werden. Aus diesem Grunde werden sich die Deutschen gezwungen sehen, für den Fall, daß der
russische Vormarsch im augenblicklichen Tempo anhält und wenn
sie überhaupt verhindern wollen, daß diese die deutschen Gren-
zen überschreiten, Truppen aus dem Westen abzuziehen, um die Ost-
front zu verstärken, und dann wird der Moment gekommen sein, wo
wir ohne Schwierigkeiten landen können."

2.) Untenstehend werden Berichtsauszüge, von Augenzeugen gemacht,
die engl. Truppenbewegungen im März in England beobachteten,
wiedergegeben.

a) "Am 9.3.1944 fuhr der Beobachter in einem Pkw. von Manchester
nach Carlisle (Grafschaft Cumberland). Auf der Straße zwischen
Kendall und Appleby begegnete er langen Kolonnen mit amerik.
Material (Panzer, gepanzerte Fahrzeuge, Lkw., Pkw. usw.),
die in südl. Richtung fuhren und kurz vor Kendall in die
Straße, die nach Leeds führt, einbogen. Zwischen den beiden
Orten Kendall und Appleby nahm diese Transportbewegung so stark
zu, daß es zu Marschstockungen und erheblichen Störungen führ-
te. Dadurch wurde der Beobachter als Privatfahrer gezwungen,
von der Fahrbahn herunter zu fahren und auf dem Feld neben der
Straße 3 Stunden zu warten, bis er seine Fahrt wieder fortsetzen konnte. Gegen Abend hielten die Kolonnen an und biwa-
kierten abseits der Straße auf freiem Feld. Nach Angaben des

- 2 -

- 2 -   67 1024

Beobachters sollen sich u.a. 720 Panzerkampfwagen verschie-
denster Typen in der Kolonne befunden haben. Besonders auffällig war dabei ein dem Beobachter bisher unbekannter Typ,
dessen hervorstechendes Merkmal 3 Kanonen im Turm gewesen
sein sollen. Dieser Panzerkampfwagen ist angeblich der schwer-
ste und größte Panzer, den der Beobachter bisher in Großbritannien gesehen hat. In seiner Gesamtbeurteilung betont der
Beobachter, daß es sich bei diesen Kolonnen mit größter Wahr-
scheinlichkeit um Nachschub-, Material- und Transportkolonnen
gehandelt hat, jedoch nicht um Truppenbewegungen. Auf seiner
Rückfahrt von Carlisle, über die Einzelheiten nicht genannt
werden, hatte der Verkehr nachgelassen. Es befanden sich jedoch an vielen Stellen große Parkplätze motorisierter Fahrzeu
abseits der Straße auf den Feldern."

b) " Ein zweiter Beobachter fuhr etwa um den 10. März durch den
Raum von Halifax (Grafschaft York) und beobachtete dort eine
beträchtliche Zusammenziehung nordamerik. Truppen in Black-
bourne, Keighley und Bradford. Nach Auffassung des Beobachters
hatten diese Truppen eine Marschpause eingelegt und befanden
sich anscheinend auf dem Marsch in den Ostteil der Grafschaft
York. Besonders auffällig war der starke Anteil von gepan-
zerten Fahrzeugen, die den Stern der Vereinigten Staaten tru-
gen. Die Überwachung des Straßenverkehrs durch Angehörige
der Heimatverteidigung war besonders scharf. Der betreffende
Beobachter wurde sogar selbst einmal festgenommen und erst
nach Erbringung sicherer Ausweise wieder freigelassen. So
durfte er seine Fahrt nach Lancaster fortsetzen, allerdings
mit der Beschränkung, sich nicht länger als 40 Stunden dort
aufzuhalten."

c) "Ein dritter Beobachter stellte Mitte März starke nordamerik.
Truppenzusammenziehungen im Raum Gateshead (S Newcastle) und
Carlisle fest. Dabei konnte er feststellen, daß beträchtliche
Teile dieser Truppen um die Meldezeit sich in der Verlegung
in die Grafschaft York befanden. Auch ihm fiel bei seinen
Fahrten die starke Überwachung der Landstraßen und Eisenbahnen
besonders auf."

APPENDIX XL.

LOCATION MAP OF THE ALLIED ORDER OF BATTLE.

FORMATION IN THE U. K. ON D - 30 OF OVERLORD AS REPRESENTED BY FORTITUDE. (THE SITUATION AS WE WISHED IT TO APPEAR TO THE ENEMY.)

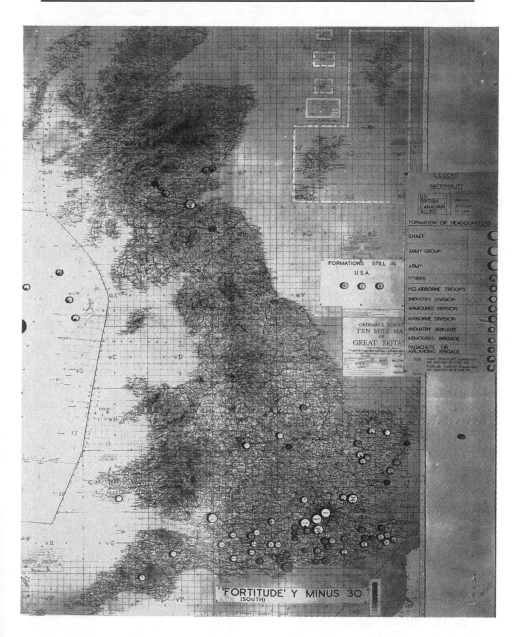

GERMAN MAP OF THE LOCATION OF ALLIED FORCES IN THE U.K. AT D - 24. (THE GERMAN APPRECIATION WHICH DEMONSTRATES THE INFLUENCE OF FORTITUDE.)

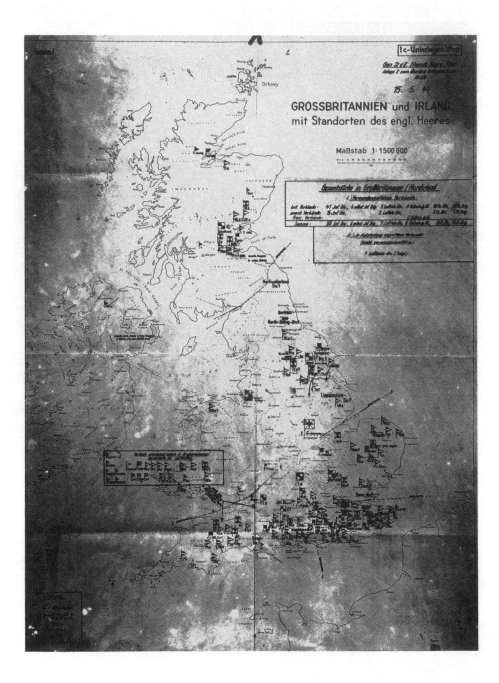

LOCATION OF THE TRUE ALLIED ORDER OF BATTLE. FORMATIONS IN THE U.K. SHOWN IN THEIR REAL LOCATION AS AT D - 30 OF OVERLORD. (THE REAL SITUATION WHICH WAS CONCEALED FROM THE ENEMY.)

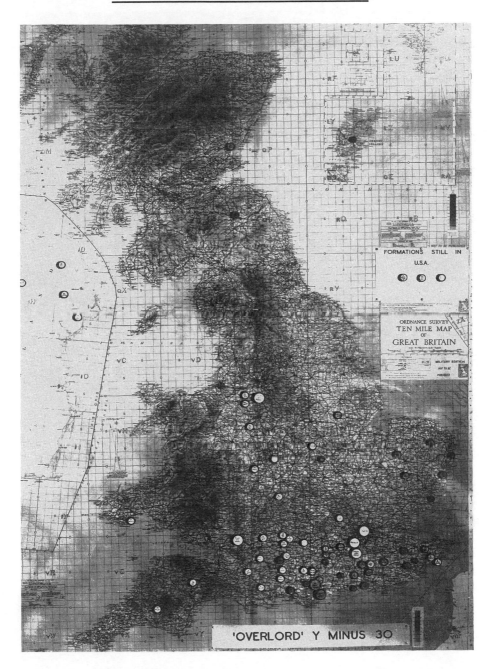

APPENDIX XLI.

GERMAN PUBLICATION ON THE INSIGNIAS USED BY BRITISH FORMATIONS.

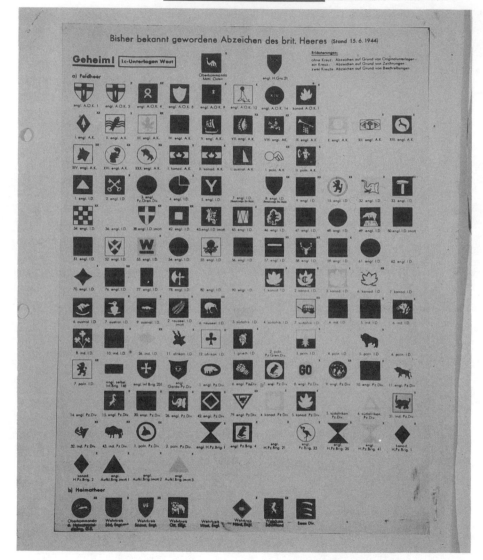

APPENDIX XLII.

DETENTION ORDER UNDER DEFENCE REGULATION 18D
LETTER OF APOLOGY FROM HOME SECRETARY TO GARBO.

D.R. Form 18d.

EMERGENCY POWERS (DEFENCE) ACTS 1939 & 1940.

THE DEFENCE (GENERAL) REGULATIONS 1939.

WHEREAS (Name)   Juan P. Garcia

(Address)   Amerden Priory,
Taplow, Bucks.

was found at   Old Ford Road, E.3., in the neighbourhood of
Driffield Road,

on   July 4th, 1944, at about 2.10 p.m.

and upon being questioned by a constable acting in the course of his duty

failed to satisfy the said constable

*Strike out
and initial
words not
applicable
(if any)

* xxxxxxxxxxxxxxxxxx as to the purposes for
NLR   which he was in the place in which he was found

AND WHEREAS the said   Juan P. Garcia   was brought

to   Bow   Police Station and detained, there being ground to

suspect that the said   Juan P. Garcia   was at the time and place

aforesaid about to act in a manner prejudicial to the public safety or the

defence of the realm,

AND WHEREAS I am satisfied that the necessary enquiries cannot be

completed within forty-eight hours from the time of his said detention

NOW THEREFORE by virtue of the power vested in me by

†See over   Regulation 18D of the Defence (General) Regulations, 1939,† I hereby

authorise the further detention of the said   Juan P. Garcia

for a period not exceeding seven days.

Date: July 6th, 1944

Signed: N.L. RICHARDS.
Ch lago. for Supt.

Chief Officer of Police "H" Division.

Metropolitan   Police Force.

15000/40/W.P.S.

DEFENCE REGULATION 18D.

1.   If any person upon being questioned by a constable or by a member of His Majesty's forces acting in the course of his duty as such fails to satisfy the constable or member of His Majesty forces as to his identity or as to the purposes for which he is in the place where he is found, the constable or member of His Majesty's forces may, if he has reasonable ground to suspect that that person is about to act in any manner prejudicial to the public safety or the defence of the realm, arrest him without warrant and may detain him pending enquiries.

2.   No person shall be detained under the powers of detention conferred by this Regulation for a period exceeding twenty-four hours except with the authority of an officer of police of a rank not lower than that of inspector or, subject as hereinafter provided, for a period exceeding forty-eight hours in all :

   Provided that if such an officer of police as aforesaid is satisfied that the necessary inquiries cannot be completed within the period of forty-eight hours, a chief officer of police may authorise the further detention of the person detained for an additional period not exceeding seven days but shall, on giving any such authorisation, forthwith report the circumstances to the Secretary of State.

3.   Any person detained under the powers conferred by this Regulation shall be deemed to be in lawful custody and may be detained in any prison or in any police station or other similar place authorised by the Secretary of State.

4.   The Secretary of State may give directions :—

   (a) for authorising or requiring chief officers of police to make reports required to be made by virtue of paragraph 2 of this Regulation to a Regional Commissioner instead of to the Secretary of State ;

   (b) for providing that persons detained under the powers conferred by this Regulation may be detained in places authorised by Regional Commissioners.

5.   Paragraph 4 of this Regulation shall not extend to Northern Ireland.

Any communication on the subject of this letter should be addressed to—

THE UNDER SECRETARY OF STATE,
HOME OFFICE,
LONDON, S.W.1.

and the following number quoted:—

P. 17829.

HOME OFFICE,
WHITEHALL.

10th July 1944.

Sir,

I am directed to acknowledge the receipt of your letter dated 7th July, 1944.

The Secretary of State has caused inquiries to be made into the incident to which you refer and is satisfied that your conduct on the afternoon of the fourth instant at Old Ford Road was of such a nature that you have only yourself to blame for your arrest. The detective officer concerned was doing no less than his duty in detaining for the purpose of inquiries an alien who appeared to him to be a visitor in the district and to display an undue inquisitiveness into the extent and circumstances of damage caused by enemy action. In making the arrest this officer was acting fully within the powers conferred upon him as a police constable by the Defence Regulations.

In view of the explanation of your conduct and of your presence in the Bethnal Green area which you made to the police shortly after your arrival at Bow Police Station, it is regretted that steps were not immediately taken to verify your story with the Ministry of Information. On receipt of your letter this Department at once made inquiries of the Ministry of Information as a result of which the Secretary of State directed your immediate release. Further inquiries are being pursued into this aspect of the matter.

Senor Juan Pujol-Garcia,
Amerden Priory,
Taplow,
Bucks.

/OVER

It has been brought to the notice of the Secretary of State that the police officer who executed the Order authorising your detention beyond the usual statutory period of 48 hours was a Chief Inspector who was at the time deputising for the Superintendent of the Division. This department does not support the view that a Chief Inspector of Police or indeed any police officer other than the Commissioner of Police or a Chief Constable is entitled under the Defence Regulations to make such an Order and the Secretary of State is satisfied that in purporting so to do the Chief Inspector acted in excess of his authority.

I am accordingly instructed to tender to you the sincere apologies of the Secretary of State for the inconvenience caused to you by the mistaken and excessive zeal of the police in the exercise of their duties and to inform you that the incident is being referred to the Commissioner of Police of the Metropolis to consider whether disciplinary action should not be taken against the officers concerned or against any of them.

I am, Sir,

Your obedient servant,

Index